# A Commentary on Jean-Paul Sartre's *Critique of Dialectical Reason*

Volume 1, *Theory of Practical Ensembles*

# A Commentary on Jean-Paul Sartre's *Critique of Dialectical Reason*

## Volume 1, *Theory of Practical Ensembles*

## Joseph S. Catalano

The University of Chicago Press
Chicago and London

JOSEPH S. CATALANO, professor of philosophy at Kean College of New Jersey, is the author of *A Commentary on Jean-Paul Sartre's "Being and Nothingness."*

The University of Chicago Press, Chicago 60637
The University of Chicago Press, Ltd., London

© *1986 by The University of Chicago*
*All rights reserved. Published 1986*
*Printed and bound by CPI Group (UK) Ltd, Croydon, CR0 4YY*

95 94 93 92 91 90 89 88 87 86    5 4 3 2 1

*Library of Congress Cataloging-in-Publication Data*
Catalano, Joseph S.
    A commentary on Jean-Paul Sartre's Critique of
dialectical reason, volume 1, Theory of practical
ensembles.

    Bibliography: p.
    Includes index.
    1. Sartre, Jean-Paul, 1905–1980.   Critique de la
raison dialectique.   1. Théorie des ensembles pratiques.
2. Dialectic.   3. Philosophy, Marxist.
4. Existentialism.   I. Title.
B2430.S33C7297   1986          194          86-11323
ISBN 978-0-226-09700-8 (hbk)
ISBN 978-0-226-09701-5 (pbk)

For my parents
and
for the members of the group-in-fusion,
St. John's University, 1966

# Contents

# Acknowledgments

Without grants from the National Endowment for the Humanities (grant no. FB 21958-80) and the Research Committee of Kean College, the writing of this work would have been more arduous and its completion much slower.

Thomas R. Flynn and Ronald Aronson read the manuscript carefully; I am grateful for their suggestions, but of course they are not responsible for the book's shortcomings. Roland Houde made helpful editorial suggestions, and Laurent Lamy did a preliminary index. Juliann Lundell Lipson did a wonderful job of editing the final draft of the manuscript; in addition, she put the index into its finished form, enabling it to be used also as a glossary. Edith Jaskoll patiently typed numerous preliminary versions of the manuscript.

Finally, there was indirect but equally important aid: Calvin O. Schrag and William L. McBride have always encouraged my research. And Ruben Abel unwittingly introduced me to the philosophy of Jean-Paul Sartre when he offered the striking members of St. John's University (my dedication refers to this strike, which occasioned the formation of the United Federation of College Teachers) the opportunity for adjunct work at the New School of Social Research. I accepted his offer to teach a course in existentialism.

# Prefatory Remarks

Sartre's two most important philosophic works are *Being and Nothingness* and the *Critique of Dialectical Reason.* In the latter, Sartre presents the historical dimension lacking in his earlier existential classic. Both works are difficult, not because Sartre wished to be esoteric but because of his conviction that philosophic methodology should arise from the subject matter itself, which, for Sartre, was always the human reality in its concrete situation. Despite the *Critique's* formidable complexity, Sartre had in mind a wide readership: students of philosophy, political science, and sociology—indeed, everyone who was willing to work toward that time in which we would consciously direct the course of our history.

The scope of the *Critique,* at first, offends our Anglo-Saxon modesty. Does it not attempt too much? Perhaps. On the other hand, the *Critique* challenges the philosophic stance of pluralism and questions the apparent modesty of the pluralist, whose boundaries frequently mask self-imposed borders. Sartre here espouses a distinctive monism, one that arises not from a traditional a priori perspective on reason or reality but rather from a recognition of the way institutions, pressure groups, and social and economic relations tie each of us to every other.

Although the *Critique* rejects the philosophic perspective of pluralism, it does not provide in its place a foundationalism. Sociology and anthropology, for example, are not lesser studies waiting for philosophy to fix their scope or provide their conceptual basis. Indeed, Sartre uses the findings and reports of specialists in these fields. Nevertheless, he unveils the presuppositions in disciplines that pretend to be philosophically neutral, and he reveals the human relations behind the quest for knowledge for its own sake. Research is not a mirror of reality, but a practical attitude toward people.

In the *Critique,* Sartre naturally steers a middle course between a view of philosophy as a foundational enterprise and a view that dilutes philosophy by extending it into every discipline when that discipline "acts philosophically." There is nothing wrong with studying how things loosely hang together, except that things may not hang together loosely. We may indeed be heading toward that day in which philosophy will disappear as a special discipline, a day when there will be no more Philosophy but only "philosophy."[1] For Sartre, that day has not yet arrived, and one merely adds to the mystification of the present by proclaiming too early the demise of philosophy as a special discipline.

Sartre, however, agrees that there is no perennial Philosophy. One distinctive function of philosophy is to provide the people of a historical period with an understanding of themselves, an understanding that is different, for example, from that enabled by literature. Good philosophy, like good literature, puts everything into question. Literature, however, has style, a cultivated ambiguity that speaks to us on several levels. But the bond of reader to writer, in a world where so many are illiterate and undernourished, is an unspoken elitism that literature cannot directly address without becoming didactic. Philosophy also works within ambiguity, but it struggles to say something clear about the human condition.[2] The *Critique* aims at unveiling the mystifications within human relations, so that, at least from one perspective, we can see ourselves in a univocal light. In such a philosophy, the issue of its own elitism is substantive, and the status of the investigator becomes an integral part of the investigation.

Just as pluralism and foundationalism are seen as philosophic extremes, Western capitalism and Soviet socialism are seen as cultural extremes. The success of capitalism's mystification calls for an unmasking of its socioeconomic system's ideal of nonrepressive and nonoppressive exploitation. One might call it a "soft alienation," except that its long-term goal is to alter the general population into well-fed sheep, while retaining for the elite an exciting pluralism in culture and politics. The tragedy of Soviet socialism, for its part, demands a questioning of the roots of socialism to see how this large-scale failure could have been possible. A mystified exploitation has become essential to Western capitalism; brute oppression and repression have become

1. See Richard Rorty, *Consequences of Pragmatism* (Minneapolis: University of Minnesota Press, 1982), xiv–xv. Rorty's general thesis is that, following Plato and Kant, philosophy is Philosophy only if it is foundational. In *Philosophy and the Mirror of Nature* (Princeton, N.J.: Princeton University Press, 1979), Rorty presented a more sustained view of his thesis. In general, I am in sympathy with Rorty's critique of philosophy as a foundational discipline. Nevertheless, the two extremes of philosophy and Philosophy point to the middle road that Sartre's philosophy has always transversed. Rorty, for his part, has always been ambivalent in his view of Sartre. In the concluding two chapters of *Philosophy and the Mirror of Nature*, he seems sympathetic to Sartre and appears to leave the door opened to philosophy as an "edifying discipline" with a nevertheless distinctive function. In the introduction to the *Consequences*, he appears to dilute Sartre's philosophy to a "philosophy of the will" and he does not show a familiarity with Sartre's philosophy after *Being and Nothingness*.

2. See Sartre's "The Purposes of Writing," in *Between Existentialism and Marxism*, trans. John Mathews (New York: Pantheon Books, 1974), 9–32.

the results of a Soviet socialism gone astray. Indirectly, the goal of the *Critique* is to point to the pitfalls that a true socialism must avoid.

Of course, the scope of Sartre's methodology is a substantive claim. A philosophic methodology is like the Midas touch: everything it handles becomes a philosophic issue, including the methodology itself. Sartre here views a dialectical method as more likely than an analytic one to provide a critical perspective, because the dialectic continually accepts that "the question, the questioner, and the questioned" cannot be separated. The dialectic, however, is not an intellectual tool that one first prepares and sharpens before proceeding to reason dialectically. One reasons dialectically only if a content is being developed in a way that also reveals the dialectician at work. The size and complexity of the *Critique* arise, therefore, from the enterprise itself.

Nevertheless, Sartre admitted that in some places the *Critique* is poorly written.[3] But this first volume is a finished book, and Sartre allowed it to be published as such during his lifetime. At various times, Sartre gave different reasons for never completing the second volume: he did not know enough history, the work on Flaubert was difficult, his eyesight was failing, and, finally—the most Sartrean answer of all—he "just didn't do it."[4] He also never finished the work on Flaubert, but as many commentators have remarked, the distinguishing feature of Sartre's work may be its open-endedness, its character as an enterprise "to be completed." Sartre did write a substantial part of the second volume of the *Critique,* which was published posthumously by Gallimard in 1985. Ronald Aronson had access to that manuscript prior to its publication. Aronson's own study, *Sartre's Second Critique: An Explication and Commentary,* will be published by the University of Chicago Press in 1986.

The original French edition of the *Critique,* with its lengthy paragraphs and few major subdivisions, is forbidding. The English translation and the revised French edition make the *Critique* appear more like a book, with proper paragraphing, major divisions, and chapters. I feel more sanguine about shortening the paragraphs than about altering the division. Here, the delicate issue of methodology arises, not in the sense of a list of criteria distinct from the content but in the sense of the way language is used and bespeaks its own relation to reality. The *Critique,* as a book, is itself dialectical; it does not avoid the issue of the relation of writer and reader to its words, on the one hand, nor that of the relation of the entire ensemble to the historical world the book attempts to signify, on the other hand.

---

3. See Paul A. Schilpp, ed., *The Philosophy of Jean-Paul Sartre* (La Salle, Ill.: Open Court Publishing Co., 1981), 11; Simone de Beauvoir, *Force of Circumstance,* trans. Richard Howard (Harmondsworth, England: Penguin Books, 1968), 397.

4. See Sartre's *Life/Situations,* trans. Paul Auster and Lydia David (New York: Pantheon Books, 1977), 129–30; Schilpp, *Sartre,* 27.

At times, the divisions in the English translation impose a foreign methodology onto Sartre's dialectical effort. Since this commentary is written, however, with an English speaking audience in mind, it refers to the English translation, but I have also indicated the major divisions of the original French edition (1960) and the revised critical French edition (1985). Wherever the editor of the English edition has added to the French editions either a section number or title, I have put the added material in parentheses. For example, the division, 1. (Dialectical Monism) indicates both that there is some division in the French texts, not necessarily indicated by a number, but that the title has been provided by the English editor. I should note that, for simplicity, I have not attempted to reflect the numerous divisions given by the editor of the revised French edition. At times, these parallel those in the English edition, except that chapter divisions are not given, and thus book II, in particular, does not appear as fractured. I have also called attention to questionable translations of key French terms.

Sartre's goal of attracting a wide readership led him to make a special effort to write the *Critique* so that it could be read by those unfamiliar with his earlier philosophy, as expressed mainly in *Being and Nothingness*. The *Critique* is not an "occasional" work, as were *The Communists and Peace* and *The Ghost of Stalin*. It can be viably interpreted within the limits of its own internal discourse. In this respect, the reader may profitably begin this commentary from the exposition of Sartre's own introduction.

In a work as complex as the *Critique*, it is difficult to provide introductory remarks that will be useful for every reader. My own perspective has been to emphasize the philosophic aspects of this dialectical work. To be specific, I have always viewed Sartre primarily as a philosopher of being, in his own unique sense of this term. Consequently, some of my observations, both here and in the chapter on background, may be more intelligible or may seem more obviously significant after a reading of my entire exposition of Sartre's work. The ambiguous status of an introduction to a dialectical work is noted by Sartre himself in his own *Search for a Method*, which precedes the *Critique* in the French edition and is examined in the following chapter.

The *Critique* is indeed a difficult book to understand, but this is not the only reason it has not been widely discussed. The *Critique* lacked the favorable milieu in which *Being and Nothingness* was published. When the book appeared in 1960, the mainstream of French intellectual life had shifted away from a dialogue with Marx into a celebration of structuralism. "Repeating the success of existentialism in the Post-War years, the wave of structuralism splashed loudly on Paris in the early 1960s." [5] But the *Critique* was not com-

5. Mark Poster, *Existential Marxism in Postwar France: From Sartre to Althusser* (Princeton, N.J.: Princeton University Press, 1975), 306. See also Perry Anderson, *In the Tracts of Historical*

pletely bypassed. Lévi-Strauss questioned Sartre's distinction between analytic and dialectical reason.[6] Raymond Aron, who had introduced Sartre to
phenomenology and helped him plan his trip to the French Institute in Berlin,
where Sartre studied Husserl and Heidegger on his own, continued what Aron
called his "one-sided dialogue" with Sartre.[7] Merleau-Ponty had apparently
heard parts of the *Critique* in lecture form, but his early death in 1961 brought
to a close a lifetime of fruitful dialogue.[8]

Sartre's remarks were not always an aid in interpreting his *Critique*. He
freely answered questions about his own works, and it is always important to
recall the context of these interviews. Nevertheless, it seems that Sartre did
change his mind about the relation of the *Critique* to the thought of Marx. In
the *Search for a Method* (*Question de méthode*), Sartre was ambiguous about
the relation of existentialism to Marxism; but toward the end of his life, in an
interview given for the Schilpp volume dedicated to his philosophy, Sartre
claimed that the *Critique* is "non-Marxist." [9] But, of course, Sartre could very
well be wrong in his judgment about his own work.

---

*Materialism* (Chicago: University of Chicago Press, 1984), 36–38; Arthur Hirsh, *The French
New Left: An Intellectual History from Sartre to Gorz* (Boston: South End Press, 1981); and
George Lichtheim, *Marxism in Modern France* (New York: Columbia University Press, 1966).
Poster gives some of the early reviews of the *Critique* (265–66, n. 4). In general, I follow Poster
in my description of the cultural background for the writing of the *Critique*. His remarks are
consistent with Sartre's own numerous interviews and Simone de Beauvoir's autobiographical
writings as well as other secondary sources. Aside from differences in scope and emphasis, these
books differ from each other in their substantive examination of Sartre's own philosophy. Lichtheim, for example, relies almost exclusively on Merleau-Ponty's view of Sartre's philosophy.

6. Claude Lévi-Strauss, *The Savage Mind* (Chicago: University of Chicago Press, 1966),
245–69.

7. Aron asked, "Was I right or wrong to prolong this dialogue and to suggest my own view by
way of an indirect route of the *Critique* of Sartre?" (*History and the Dialectic of Violence*, trans.
Barry Cooper [Oxford: Basil Blackwell Publishing, 1975]), xiv. See also Aron's *Marxism and the
Existentialists*, trans. Helen Weaver, Robert Addis, and John Weightman (New York: Harper &
Row, 1969). Aron's reservation is well taken. Despite the nuances of his interpretation, he constantly returns to his own pluralistic perspective without facing Sartre's critique of pluralism, with
its implicit correspondence theory of truth. Concerning Aron, Sartre remarks: "I read his last
book, where he argues against the *Critique of Dialectical Reason*. He poses problems and questions that he has a right to pose from his point of view but which don't concern me at all."
(*Life/Situations*, 56–57). See book I, chapter 3, notes 1 and 3. For a further analysis of Aron's
interpretation of Sartre, see Thomas R. Flynn, *Sartre and Marxist Existentialism* (Chicago: University of Chicago Press, 1984), 175–204, passim.

8. See Kenneth A. Thompson, *Sartre: Life and Work* (New York: Facts on File, 1984), 125–
33. This year-by-year account of Sartre's life and works is very readable and appears accurate.

9. When reminded that he had defined the *Critique* as a work "opposed to the Communists
and yet endeavoring to be Marxist," Sartre commented: "Opposed to the Communists, certainly.
But Marxist is a word that I used a bit lightly then. Today, I think in certain areas, the *Critique* is
close to Marxism, but it is *not* a Marxist work." When asked what elements of Marxism he retained, Sartre replied, "The notion of surplus value, the notion of class—all that reworked how-

In one of the first expositions of the *Critique* in English, in 1964, R. D. Laing and D. G. Cooper noted the relation of the *Critique* to the thought of Marx but did not see the need to label Sartre's work.[10] And in an incisive article in 1966, André Gorz placed crucial notions of the *Critique*, such as that of the group, within the Marxist tradition, while also emphasizing the distinctiveness of Sartre's approach to the dialectic.[11] In the first booklength study of the *Critique* in English, Wilfrid Desan referred merely to "Sartre's Marxism."[12] Nuances have been added by other commentators: William McBride and Mark Poster refer to Sartre's stance in the *Critique* as a form of Neo-Marxism or existentialist Marxism; Thomas Flynn reverses the emphasis and sees it as a form of Marxist existentialism.[13] There is general recognition today that Sartre could never take seriously any form of economic determinism, and, as we will see, he does not regard the dialectic itself as deterministic.

The problem, therefore, of wedding existentialism to Marxism centers for some, like Pietro Chiodi, primarily around the viability of Sartre's notion of alienation and for others, like Ronald Aronson, around the problem of the status of the "collective we" and the reality of social entities.[14]

Other commentators have correctly noted that how one interprets the *Critique* depends to a great extent on how one interprets *Being and Nothingness* itself. James F. Sheridan notes, for example, that Mary Warnock's view of the *Critique* as a radical conversion results from an interpretation of *Being and Nothingness* that emphasizes its literary character.[15] In like manner, Fredric

ever (Schilpp, *Sartre*, 20). For the reference to Sartre's *Question de méthode*, see "Background" chapter, note 3.

10. R. D. Laing and D. G. Cooper, *Reason and Violence* with a foreword by Jean-Paul Sartre (London: Tavistock, 1964). This is an excellent, if cryptic, introduction to Sartre's *Search for a Method, Saint Genet: Actor and Martyr*, and the *Critique*. For a study of Laing's use of Sartrean concepts, see Gila J. Hayım, *The Existential Sociology of Jean-Paul Sartre* (Amherst: University of Massachusetts Press, 1980), 98–102.

11. André Gorz, "Sartre and Marx," *New Left Review* 37 (1966): 29–53. Gorz correctly draws attention to the significance of Sartre's rejection of a unified dialectic and, unlike such critics as Chiodi and Aron, he very early perceived the viability of Sartre's notion of alienation.

12. Wilfrid Desan, *The Marxism of Jean-Paul Sartre* (Garden City, N.Y.: Doubleday & Co., Anchor Books, 1965) and *The Tragic Finale* (New York: Harper Torchbooks, 1944).

13. William L. McBride, *The Philosophy of Marx* (New York: St. Martin's Press, 1977), 154. Also, particularly for his examination of Sartre's notion of totalization, see McBride's *Fundamental Change in Law and Society: Hart and Sartre on Revolution* (The Hague: Mouton Publishers, 1970), 176–86. See also Poster, *Sartre's Marxism* (Cambridge: Cambridge University Press, 1982), 15; Flynn, *Sartre and Marxist Existentialism*. Flynn claims, "We must admit that Sartre's Marxism is adjectival to his existentialism" (xiii).

14. Pietro Chiodi, *Sartre and Marxism*, trans. Kate Soper (Atlantic Highlands, N.J.: Humanities Press, 1976), 79–101; Ronald Aronson, *Jean-Paul Sartre* (London: New Left Books, 1980), 243–73.

15. James F. Sheridan, *Sartre: The Radical Conversion* (Athens, Ohio: Ohio University Press, 1973), 1–11, passim. See also Mary Warnock, *The Philosophy of Jean-Paul Sartre* (London: Hutchinson Publishing Group, 1965).

Jameson remarks that, after the publication of the *Critique, Being and Nothingness* itself now appears different; Jameson's implication is that the label "existentialist" as applied to Sartre can no longer mean the same thing.[16] I consider this perspective crucial; in the final analysis, it is impossible to separate one's view of the *Critique*'s relation to Marx from one's view of Sartre's earlier works.

Perhaps, because of this, some critics sidestep the issue of how to label the *Critique*, considering it basically a development of Sartre's thought. Some, like George Kline, maintain that the *Critique* is almost a complete repudiation of Sartre's former existentialist stance.[17] Others, like Marjorie Grene, claim that the *Critique* can fundamentally be translated into the categories of *Being and Nothingness*. And still others, like Hazel Barnes, Joseph Fell, and Peter Caws, see at least a shift in emphasis when comparing Sartre's earlier and later thought.[18]

My main concern is the text itself, which has not yet entered the mainstream of our philosophic tradition. My use of the word "commentary" in the title indicates that my purpose is to introduce the reader to the details of the *Critique*'s main arguments. This perspective has required a compromise: in order to develop critically themes that I see as central to Sartre's general presentation, such as his unique dialectical nominalism, I have had to collapse other aspects of his thought into the form of a mere summary. Furthermore, in order not to distract from my efforts to elucidate Sartre's own very complex argumentation, I will consider the basic contributions and objections of other critics mainly in footnotes.

16. Fredric Jameson, *Marxism and Form* (Princeton, N.J.: Princeton University Press, 1971), 208–9.

17. George L. Kline, "The Existentialist Rediscovery of Hegel and Marx," in *Phenomenology and Existentialism*, ed. Edward N. Lee and Maurice Mandelbaum (Baltimore: Johns Hopkins University Press, 1967), 137.

18. Marjorie Grene, *Sartre* (New York: New Viewpoints, 1973), 227–62, 270, passim. Grene's claim is based mainly on her criticism of Sartre's view of the "practical organism." She misses, however, the radicalness of Sartre's analysis of the correspondence theory of truth, with its implied transcendent perspective that places the human organism as a step in an evolutionary hierarchy. See also Hazel E. Barnes, *Sartre* (New York: J. B. Lippincott, 1973) 105, 135; Barnes, *Sartre and Flaubert* (Chicago, University of Chicago Press, 1981), 105–6, 248–49; Joseph P. Fell, *Heidegger and Sartre: An Essay on Being and Place* (New York: Columbia University Press, 1979); and Peter Caws, *Sartre* (London: Routledge & Kegan Paul, 1979), 2. Fell's study correctly emphasizes the early influence of Heidegger and Husserl in regard to Sartre's view of the thoroughly relational aspect of consciousness. Although, unfortunately, Fell appeals to *Nausea* for substantiating his interpretation of Sartre's view on language, he correctly recognizes that the Cartesianism in *Being and Nothingness* is more apparent than real. On the broader issue of the relation between Heidegger and Sartre, Fell thinks that "the truth to which Heidegger refers is prior to the truth to which Sartre refers" (400). On the contrary, it is true both that Sartre has been profoundly influenced by Heidegger *and* that their philosophies are incommensurate. Sartre has indeed understood the later Heidegger, but Sartre has rejected Heidegger's claim that we are mere participants in the epoch-making event of being (see Fell, 400–19). Caws' book is, in general, a well-balanced overall view of Sartre's thought, the best that we have to date.

Since my main concern is Sartre's text, I shall leave to others more qualified the task of judging how close Sartre's efforts are to the work of Marx and revisionist Marxists. I will, however, consider Sartre's own remarks about his relationship to Marx as he discusses this within the text itself. In this respect, I will mention in advance that Sartre frequently notes that he considers his own work to be on a different level from that of Marx. Nevertheless, it is also clear that just as *Being and Nothingness* could not have been written without the influence of Husserl and Heidegger, so too the *Critique* could not have been written without Sartre's decision to take seriously the Marxist's problem of the relation of theory to practice.[19] Because considerable time has elapsed between the publication of the *Critique* and the writing of this commentary, I have sidestepped a complex problem by referring to "traditional Marxists" where Sartre speaks of "contemporary Marxists" and where it is also not clear that Sartre is referring to his own understanding of Marxism in 1960.

The task of interpreting the *Critique* also indirectly raises the broader issue of the relation of Sartre's philosophic works to the corpus of his writings. It is easy to see Sartre as a *littérateur*, a grand essayist who turned his pen now here, now there, writing plays, novels, articles, and works that defy classification, such as his studies on Genet and Flaubert. This view partly fits the picture. After the publication of *Being and Nothingness*, Sartre never isolated himself from the world. He lived in Paris and participated in its changing cultural and political life. He wrote in response to situations. This does not mean that his writings were all "occasional." On the contrary, he was aware of the different ways a writer tailors language to fit not merely different topics but also diverse literary genres. He wore many hats as a writer, and, in this respect, Kierkegaard is his only rival.

It is tempting to conflate Sartre the writer and Sartre the philosopher. The supposition of many critics is that Sartre the existentialist found it appropriate to write more concrete expositions of his philosophy in literary form.[20] Again, there may be a complex level—relating the total man to his works—

19. The link between the *Critique*'s notion of the group-in-fusion and the aborted 1968 demonstration in Paris has been noted by several authors. See Kenneth A. Thompson, *Sartre*, 129.

20. See Iris Murdoch, *Sartre, Romantic Rationalist* (New Haven, Conn.: Yale University Press, 1953). Murdoch perceptively notes that Roquentin is not Sartre and continues, "Sartre, as we shall see, going beyond the situation of Roquentin and beyond his solution, wants to connect in a great equation literature, meaning, truth, and democracy" (36). Even if this is true, it does not follow that this enterprise is that of Sartre's philosophy. Marjorie Grene, on the contrary, views Sartre's language as primarily autobiographic-philosophic. After noting Sartre's own remark, "I write so many languages," she continues by commenting, "Both the manner and matter of his philosophy are just what one would expect of the author and subject of *Les Mots*" (*Sartre*, 21). But *Les mots* or *The Words* (New York: George Braziller, 1964), Sartre's grand farewell to literature, is a work of irony; his "autobiography" is a story of a mature man conscious that his narrated childhood is not the same as his lived childhood.

on which this claim may be true. But the task of elucidating this relation would require care and effort. Simple facts would have to be noted: Sartre always wanted to be a "writer," even before he wanted to be a philosopher; he claimed that he never wanted to do the same thing in his literary and philosophic works; and indeed the "philosophies" expressed in the literary works are not univocally translatable into the "philosophy" expressed in the philosophic works. This last claim is too extensive to be established here, but I would like to make one point about Sartre's view of language.

When Sartre examines language in *Being and Nothingness* and here in the *Critique*, it is clear that it is for him an aspect of the total way we exist within the world. Words are not mere labels applied to concepts or things. Sartre does speak of a nominalism, particularly in the *Critique*, but it is a unique nominalism, one that works within a language already binding people and things. In the novel *Nausea*, however, Sartre describes Roquentin as gradually awakening to the realization that what we call a "thing," for example, a "tree," involves a technological conception of the roots as "pumps." This realization does not fit, for Roquentin, the massive reality he is experiencing.[21] This intuition crystallizes his earlier gradual feeling of separation from the world in its normal, harmless appearance. Can we abstract a philosophy or philosophies from this? Of course. Can we suggest that perhaps Sartre was influenced by his reading of Husserl and by his living alone in Berlin? Indeed. Can we also inquire whether the presence of the Nazis may have affected his perception, despite his conviction, at that time, that one does not write about political matters in novels? This may also be true. Assuming *Nausea* to be a good novel, we can find in it many questions not only about itself but about our relation to it. The one thing we cannot do, however, is to map unequivocally Roquentin's experience with language onto the expositions of language in either *Being and Nothingness* or the *Critique*.

It is indeed possible to do the converse, namely, to map the philosophic expositions onto the literary descriptions. Although this is never very interesting, it can be pedagogically useful to interpret a literary work as a concrete expression of a philosophic view.[22] This requires that one first understand the philosophic position within the limits of its own discourse. For example, given an understanding of the internal relation between seeing and color, as described in the difficult and overlooked section "Transcendence" in *Being and Nothingness,* and of the way language is an aspect of our existence for others, as elucidated, for example, in the sections entitled "The Concrete Re-

---

21. Sartre, *Nausea,* trans. Lloyd Alexander (New York: New Directions, 1959), 126–35. Sartre's original title for this work was *Melancholia;* see Axel Madsen, *Hearts and Minds* (New York: William Morrow & Co., 1977), 44.

22. I used this approach to *Nausea* in my own work, *Commentary on Jean-Paul Sartre's "Being and Nothingness"* (Chicago: University of Chicago Press, 1980), iv–xiv, 3–4 (hereafter cited in notes as *Commentary BN*).

lations with Others" and "My Fellowman," one can then interpret *Nausea* as the expression of the way language and reality can be altered when a life is lived in isolation amid others. Even this simplistic approach is dangerous; it too lazily projects nontechnical meanings of "abstract" and "concrete" onto both Sartre's philosophic methodology and the relation of his philosophic works to his literary ones. For Sartre, the concrete is never an instance of a universal the way an isosceles triangle is a member of the class of triangles; the concrete restructures the abstract the way a possessing love that destroys another reconstitutes love, even where love in the abstract is conceived as a positive reciprocal bond. Thus, given the usual acceptance of the relation of the abstract to the concrete, I do not think that one will reveal anything interesting in approaching Sartre's literature merely as a concrete expression of his philosophy. The proper way would be first to examine each genre separately; then one could raise the question of the "thought" of Jean-Paul Sartre.

It is important to "bracket" the image of Sartre, the writer, when trying to understand his philosophy. We should admit the possibility that he may have worked harder than most, and, of course, that he started young and had the fortune of a relatively long life. Let us also grant that, as a writer, he yielded, now and then, to the temptation of being literary in his philosophic works; of writing that fine sentence that just had to be written. The classic example is the shocking last line of the final chapter of *Being and Nothingness,* the philosophically vacuous claim "Man is a useless passion" ( *"L'homme est une passion inutile"*). Such sentences should not mislead us. There are no crucial sentences in the expository writing of Sartre's philosophy. There are sentences that are important because they bring into focus a long discussion and carry it forward. But no sentence or paragraph can summarize a philosophic view; a certain degree of commitment and effort is needed. Sartre's two major philosophic works, *Being and Nothingness* and the *Critique I,* are *books;* their sections are not a string of essays whose only unity is their mapping onto the system of numbers. The descriptions of bad faith or scarcity, for example, cannot be separated from the book as a whole. These books require readers sensitive to the organized unity of a book as a synthetic whole. It is the book that gives meaning to the sentence, and it is the book that elucidates how it is to be read. Philosophically, this implies not only that methodology substantively contributes to philosophic content but also, reciprocally, that methodology is continually being altered by the developing content. Sartre is well aware that philosophy implies a healthy circularity in which methodology and content mutually justify each other. As we will see, Sartre's principles are heuristic; they are parameters or webbings that require a rethinking, at each level, of the concrete in relation to its former abstract state.

Although the *Critique* was written to be read independently of Sartre's earlier philosophy, it may be useful to sketch the origin of his existentialist views. I also wish to lay the background for supporting my claim that the *Critique* expresses an evolution of his thought, rather than either a break in it or a mere updating. This claim will also be elaborated throughout the commentary, where Sartre's own remarks make a reflection on his earlier philosophy appropriate.

In the 1930s, Raymond Aron mentioned to Sartre that Husserl had developed an approach to philosophy called "phenomenology," which allowed one to philosophize about a cocktail. Sartre, it is said, became flushed with emotion. He left for Berlin and read Husserl's *Ideas*.[23] What he learned influenced him for the rest of his life. While never adopting the techniques of Husserl's method, Sartre adopted two general aspects of Husserl's thought. The first was that philosophy must stop concerning itself with theoretical debates about the existence of things and accept the world in all its qualitative richness. Philosophically, the splashing reds of a sunset, for example, must not be conceived in a Cartesian fashion; they are not merely waves or other quantitative displacements of matter that first interact with a complex machine called the human body and then are interpreted by the mind as colors. Every quality is measurable, but no quality is reducible to its quantitative aspects.

For Husserl, each phenomenon, such as the red of a rose, has its own appropriate essential structure. But these structures are not viewed as floating, as it were, in a timeless space. All essences, for Husserl, are relational, and the relation is primarily to the human consciousness.

The relation, however, between the subject and object, or more accurately, between the noesis and noema, is not immediately given in all its clarity. The object is crusted with historical residues, and the subject is colored by personal background and private opinions. What Husserl calls his "reduction" is a logical knife that alternately peels away the cultural aspects of the object and the subject's individual relations to it. The goal is to reveal a pure object, whose essential structure is guaranteed by its relation to a pure subjectivity, a transcendental ego.[24] The tie of subjectivity to objectivity is one of Husserl's major insights, and it is that second aspect of his thought that Sartre accepted. This relation is a bond uniting consciousness to its object, a bond that Husserl called "intentionality." By this term, Husserl meant that the primary movement of consciousness is not to turn in on itself but to go out toward an object other than itself.

23. Apparently, Sartre had discovered Husserl on his own in Emmanuel Levinas's book *La theorie de l'intuition dans la phénoménologie de Husserl* (Paris: F. Alcan, 1930). What is clear is that Aron had studied in the French Institute in Berlin the previous year, had read Husserl, and had encouraged Sartre to do the same.

24. Edmund Husserl, *Cartesian Meditations,* trans. Dorian Cairns (The Hague: Martinus Nijhoff Publishers, 1969), 25–42.

Husserl's insistence that consciousness spontaneously discovers a qualitatively rich world was just what Sartre needed to develop a philosophy that was not just "toward" the concrete but *of* the concrete.[25] Sartre, however, did not accept the whole phenomenological package. His own suspicion of the privileged status of the interior life led him indeed to accept the intentionality of consciousness with its tie to the world.[26] He broke from Husserl, however, in two crucial respects: he rejected the need for a special method that was aimed at unveiling a pure phenomenon in relation to a transcendental ego, and he also denied that the question of the empirical existence of things could be bracketed in order to describe their structures.[27]

In a very general way, this split from Husserl was consistent with Heidegger's earlier development in *Being and Time*, which Sartre had also read.[28] Heidegger had studied with Husserl, and he had also accepted his mentor's general program of describing essences as relational. But he saw this task as consistent with an effort to elucidate the way history may have constituted structures to be essential. In particular, Heidegger called into question not only the Cartesian model of a mechanical universe but also the Aristotelian conception of a natural gradation of reality, from minerals to plants, animals, and finally humans. In *Being and Time*, Heidegger described the human reality as "*Dasein*," a "there-being," whose internal relation to reality is the origin of our Aristotelian and scientific conceptions. In this context, the term

25. Sartre, *Search for a Method*, trans. Hazel E. Barnes (New York: Alfred A. Knopf, 1963), 19. See also Arthur C. Danto, *Jean-Paul Sartre* (New York: Viking Press, 1975), 45.

26. "Peter's emotion is no more *certain* for Peter than for Paul." (Sartre, *The Transcendence of the Ego*, trans. Forrest Williams and Robert Kirkpatrick [New York: Noonday Press, 1957], 94–95.) Sartre never wavers from questioning the privileged status of the so-called interior life with its reflections, although he modifies and enlarges his view. In his early work, where his emphasis is to show that the "I" or ego is the "product" that exists in the world, he calls spontaneous consciousness "impersonal" or "nonpersonal." In his ontology, he more accurately refers to the prereflective cogito as "prepersonal." See his *Being and Nothingness*, trans. Hazel E. Barnes (New York: Philosophical Library, 1956), 103 (hereafter cited in notes as *BN*). In the *Critique*, Sartre usually speaks of praxis rather than consciousness, and in his study of Flaubert, the notion of praxis is further developed into that of "lived experience": "In my present book on Flaubert, I have replaced my earlier notion of consciousness (although I still use the word a lot) with what I call *le vécu*—lived experience" (*Between Existentialism and Marxism*, 39). It would be a mistake, however, to equate Sartre's notion of *le vécu* with Husserl's notion of lived experience. Sartre's notion is adumbrated in *Being and Nothingness*: "My body is co-extensive with the world and spread across all things, and at the same time it is condensed into this single point which all things indicate and which I am without being able to know it" (*BN*, 318).

27. See "Background" chapter, note 27.

28. This is not to imply that Sartre's *Transcendence of the Ego* represents the more radical break from Husserl found either in Heidegger's *Being and Time* (trans. John McQuarrie and Edward Robinson [New York: Harper & Row, 1962]) or in Sartre's *Being and Nothingness*. In both these works, the subject-object relation is consequent upon a more primary relation of the human reality to being. See also part 2 of Sartre's introduction, note 5.

"relation" has the same basic meaning for Sartre as it does for Heidegger. That is, an internal relation is one that defines the relata, or things related. For example, a hat has an internal relation to a head. Since this relation is in only one direction—a head is not defined in relation to a hat—Sartre will call such relations "univocal." In English, the more appropriate term is "unilateral." If the relation defines in both directions, it is a reciprocal relation. For example, a human heart is a heart only because it is part of a human body, and a human body is defined only in relation to a human heart.

For Heidegger, as for Sartre, the human reality is not merely added to a natural world. For Heidegger, *Dasein* is in place in such a way that both *Dasein* and place come to be through each other. That is, through *Dasein*, a world exists as something that is "in place," and, reciprocally, through a world-in-place, there exists the being *Dasein*.[29] In *Being and Time*, Heidegger also exhibited time to be an "internal relation." He distinguished three types of time: psychological time, which is our daily awareness of time passing slowly or quickly; objective time, which can be measured, as by clocks; and ontological time, the very structure of *Dasein* in its relation to being, which Heidegger described as a "temporal spread," an "*ekstasis.*" The *ekstasis* was the origin of both psychological and objective time.[30] Later, Heidegger was to reject this aspect of his thought as still too traditionally metaphysical and human. In *On Time and Being,* he claimed that the human reality was open to a time and being that was greater than that of *Dasein.*[31]

Sartre embraced Heidegger's program of describing a world that was both thoroughly human and "objectively there" in a way that Heidegger himself never fully understood. Sartre had found his key to a philosophy of the concrete. In *Being and Nothingness,* he set about elucidating how the qualitative richness of the world resulted from the internal relation of the human reality to being, or, in the language of *Being and Nothingness,* of the for-itself to the in-itself, where we can think of the in-itself as "matter" as long as we do not conceive of matter scientifically. Consequently, for example, consciousness has a mode of knowing called "sight" because there are colors, and, reciprocally, colors exist in the world only because of sight.[32]

There are similarities between *Being and Nothingness* and *Being and Time.* The distinctive being of the human reality is, for Sartre, its internal negation and, as with time in Heidegger's view, negation may be conceived in three ways: there is the psychological negation expressed by the word "not," as

29. See Fell's excellent discussion of this aspect of Heidegger's thought in *Heidegger and Sartre,* 91–145, passim.

30. This threefold division of time is a simplistic summary of division two in *Being and Time.*

31. Heidegger, *On Time and Being,* trans. Joan Stambaugh (New York: Harper & Row, 1972), 55–73. See also book I, chapter 3, note 11.

32. "The senses are contemporaneous with objects" (*BN,* 318).

when we form a negative judgment; there are objective negations in the world, such as the phenomenon of missing a fourth person at bridge; and there is the "nihilation" that is the very reality of the human being and the source of the other two negations.[33] Nevertheless, the general direction of Sartre's thought differs radically from that of Heidegger. For Sartre, nihilation is both our primary freedom and that by which and through which "things" are distinguished and have meaning. Meanings enter things through the very reality of the human existence and not from a projection of meaning onto being. There could thus be no appeal to a meaning within reality that was greater than human. In the *Critique,* Sartre will admit that during any one historical period there is indeed a greater-than-human meaning, but he will insist that this itself has been produced by past human activity.

Not only *Being and Nothingness* but also the *Critique* can be read more fruitfully if the general background of Husserl and Heidegger is kept in mind. On the positive side, Sartre remains a phenomenologist to the extent that he accepts the totality of the world as *there* to be described. Sartre is never attempting to deduce the existence of things or human relations. He always proceeds from the abstract to the concrete, but the concrete is already on the horizon awaiting critical examination. For example, in *Being and Nothingness,* the examination of the "look" (*le regard*) does not establish the existence of others, which is accepted by experience; it rather describes the way we are internally related to each other.[34] And, here in the *Critique,* the description of the way a third person is a means for integrating others into groups does not prove the existence of groups or collectives but elucidates how the social order occurs through human relations. The descriptions, which are first abstract, operate always in the presence of the concrete, which is also the goal of the discussion.

Although the *Critique* can be read independently of *Being and Nothingness,* there is a close methodological connection between these two works. The nominalism functioning in Sartre's ontology sheds light on the dialectical nominalism of his social philosophy. Classical nominalism implies that only terms or "names" or things are universal. Words, such as "humanity," "country," "society," "animal," and "tree," are merely convenient linguistic tools for speaking about things as if they had something in common. Sartre's nominalism shares in this view to the extent that he admits to the existence only of individual entities. Nevertheless, Sartre claims that there *is* a basis for univer-

33. *BN,* 3-45; *Commentary BN,* 51-91. It is true that in emotional states, such as anger, the individual projects personal and "magical" meanings onto the world, but for Sartre these meanings do not intrinsically alter the world. See Sartre's *Sketch for a Theory of the Emotions,* trans. Philip Mairret (London: Methuen & Co., 1962), 90-91.

34. *BN,* 252-302; *Commentary BN,* 159-68. See also "Background" chapter, 31-35.

sal judgments, but what is common to things is not an Aristotelian nature that is empirically one and fundamentally many. In his ontology, the objective unity of the world and the basis for universal terms arise from the presence of the human reality in matter. Terms such as "for-itself," "in-itself," "consciousness," and "world" are thoroughly relational. The relation is aimed at the total concrete, which in Sartre's ontology is the way the presence of the human reality alters matter into a world. The total concrete is a complex of relations, originating from the human organism within matter, and the nominalism of *Being and Nothingness* is aimed at elucidating how the abstract state of a phenomenon becomes restructured at each stage of the investigation.

Even in the most abstract stages, the term "in-itself" (*en soi*) never indicates a Parmenidean one or a Kantian noumenon, and the term "for-itself" (*pour soi*) never means a consciousness devoid of a body. These terms always point to a matter already altered into a world by the presence of human existence. On each level of the discussion, the term "for-itself" draws attention to the humanized aspect of a phenomenon, what freedom does to matter, whereas the term "in-itself" highlights the material aspect. For example, the red of a red rose is an in-itself: in relation to sight, it is the red it is and no other. On the other hand, without the presence of consciousness as sight in the world, there would be no red rose in the world. The world, for Sartre, is already matter differentiated through the organic presence of the conscious human body. Thus, in relation to a theoretically possible but de facto nonexistent state of matter as a pure in-itself, the red of a rose would be a for-itself. On a more concrete level, the hand of a person asleep, for example, is an in-itself, in contrast to the hand that cooks, writes, or greets another, as these are for-itselfs. And, in a phenomenon such as bad faith, a hand can be used to take advantage of both aspects. One may "hold hands" pretending that only the other's hand is active.[35] In *Being and Nothingness,* Sartre's nominalism restructures the abstract at each new concrete stage of the investigation, so that elements that previously seemed inessential are now seen to be both novel and essential. The goal, again, is both to describe a matter that has become a world only through the de facto presence of an organic consciousness and to reveal that only through a world is consciousness a human organism.

In the *Critique*, Sartre's nominalism is complicated because the total concrete that is always present and waiting to be critically examined is not merely the world of nature but also the world of history. We are now confronted with the complex interaction between individual freedoms, which does *not* mean

---

35. *BN*, 55–56. See also my two articles, "On the Possibility of Good Faith," *Man and World* 13 (1980): 207–28; "Good and Bad Faith: Weak and Strong Notions," *Review of Existential Psychology and Psychiatry* 17 (1984): 79–90. Robert V. Stone, in an article "Sartre on Bad Faith and Authenticity" contained in Schilpp's *Sartre* (245–56), also distinguishes bad faith as self-imposed from the bad-faith structures in the social order.

freedoms in isolation, and the numerous ways freedoms have become frozen in culture. Sartre here tells us that this interaction can be pictured as a spiral, originating from our organic existence in its immediate environment and including in its ever-widening circles all other lives. This image of spiral existence is fleshed out by means of a nominalism that is now also dialectical. There is thus a constant give-and-take between the abstract that is being explained and the concrete that is awaiting critical examination. For example, the early section on biological needs, such as our need for food, is already modified by the possibility of class struggle. From the beginning, our need for food is a need satisfied through wages.

Sartre's notion of spiral existence, and it is a notion insofar as it is effectively worked out through the *Critique*, is the basis for my constant emphasis on the distinction between the local and historical contexts of our lives. Here again we encounter Sartre's nominalism. Terms such as "other" and "object" are not universal classes in which the more concrete is merely an instance. At each level of the discussion, novel elements are introduced in such a way that these notions do not share a univocal, general characteristic. For example, a picture on my wall may represent for me in paint something that I would have liked to say about the world myself. On this personal level, the picture as object implies no alienation. But if, unknown to me, the artist has become famous, my now valuable painting may represent for me an exchange value for other goods. It has become an "object" in a different sense, and this alteration has come to the picture and to my relation to it through changes in the art market that were beyond my control. I may indeed be happy to own a valuable painting, but the fact remains that alienation has entered into my relation with this object. From day to day, its value may go up or down; it is no longer a simple objectification of my view of the world. And if a friend, another person whose "otherness" I enjoy, should become interested in buying my painting, his otherness may now become alienating. He now enters the world of those competing others, each of whom wants my picture as a possible hedge against inflation.[36] On a local level, I may be able to eliminate this alienation. I may give the painting to my friend. But my action does not touch the alienation inherent in an art market whose values are determined through the buying and selling of art as investment.

In the *Critique*, one therefore has to be sensitive to the way words are used on each level of discussion. In regard to a term such as "other" (*autre*), Sartre, in the French, indicates these nuances by sometimes speaking of the other as "other," sometimes capitalizing "Other" or "*The* Others," and some-

36. I have varied feminine and masculine examples, and I have made an effort to avoid the term "man" where it signifies humanity. Given Sartre's complex terminology, there were times however, where "he" and "man" seemed to make for easier reading.

times using the noun *altérité*, which he created and which can be translated simply as "otherness," but which the English edition renders as "alterity." [37] I have stayed with the more awkward English term, because the context in which it is used is always that in which a specific kind of alienation is introduced into otherness, namely, the distinctive separation and union we encounter insofar as we are members of a collective. For the same reason, I have retained the translation of *le statut* as "statute." Many critics have observed that this term could be rendered more appropriately by the English "status." But "status" does not seem to bring out either the relation between the individual and the group or the symbiotic relation of the entire ensemble to the complex of institutions and documents. The real issue, however, is not the translation of one term but the understanding of how Sartre uses language to express his philosophy. Here the English translation is more than adequate, and even those who have read only the French are not immune from completely misunderstanding Sartre's enterprise.

These introductory remarks about Sartre's use of language are merely tentative. Strictly speaking, it can be misleading to suggest that his nominalism is a modified version of classical nominalism. The very use of the word "term" already implies that words are mere signs of concepts or things. But we shall see that, for Sartre, language is an aspect of our total conscious organic being.

My view of a close methodological tie between *Being and Nothingness* and the *Critique* is consistent with Sartre's rejection of a unified dialectic that could apply to both history and nature. Sartre limits the dialectic to history, and, for many critics, this view seems to imply an unbridgeable gap between nature and history. Sartre's rejection of a unified dialectic is again a substantive issue that will be discussed as we proceed. Here I wish merely to sketch the general context within which his position should be understood.

Neither in his ontology nor in his social philosophy does Sartre deny that we have ties to nature that are apparent to us on a commonsense level. The problem centers on our ability to elucidate these ties. Sartre's position turns on a distinction that is implied in his entire philosophic approach, but never explicated. This is the fundamental distinction between describing the world from the perspective of the human organism "down" to animals, trees, and other material entities, and describing it from the perspective of some elementary matter "up" to the human organism. The first perspective, from the human organism downward, is the phenomenological view within which the nominalism of both *Being and Nothingness* and the *Critique* unfold. The second perspective, from some possible elementary matter upward, is, in *Being and Nothingness*, the perspective of metaphysics as opposed to ontology and, in the *Critique*, the uncritical acceptance of a unified dialectic. The position

37. See Caws, *Sartre*, 167.

of science would seem to use both perspectives, but, in the final analysis, science aims at understanding and controlling the world for human purposes.

It is important to emphasize, however, that Sartre never denies that we are bound to nature. For example, every child who has a dog for a pet knows, on a commonsense level, that the animal has awareness. The problem arises when we use terms like "animal intelligence" to explain this awareness, for such a term conflates the two orders of knowing and implies a universality in our understanding of intelligence that has not been established. We may indeed claim that common sense is the basis for our philosophic knowledge, but this claim is not justified by common sense.

Sartre does not explicate his reasons for denying the validity of a unified dialectic in relation to the Neo-Aristotelian tradition. Nevertheless, this tradition has taught us that causal connections within a nature devoid of human existence can be validated only by a leap to a transcendent mind. The Hegelian and Marxist dialectic does not eliminate this requirement, even as it reinterprets this static Neo-Aristotelian schema as a movement of Spirit or Matter.[38] To the extent that Marx was concerned only with history and praxis, it is doubtful that he was interested in a unified dialectic that embraced nature, knowledge, and praxis. On the other hand, if Marx merely turned the Hegelian dialectic on its head, then Marx also put the Absolute in matter. Traditional Marxists may think that the dialectic of itself guarantees the felicitous union of nature and humanity. Their view, however, presupposes a Neo-Aristotelian perspective in which the human mind mirrors nature and sees itself mirroring nature in another mind as mirror.

No method is perfect, and Sartre's attempt to wed a phenomenological perspective to a nominalism does produce tensions. Critics have correctly noted that, in *Being and Nothingness,* the chapter entitled "Concrete Relations with Others" seems at times to be more a task of logic than an exercise in phenomenological descriptions of an ontology. And here in the first volume of the *Critique,* Sartre's dialectical approach forces him to accept the possibility that we are living within a unified historical experience without first critically examining this experience. Nevertheless, the *Critique* does reveal the symbiotic relations within a regional sense of history.

38. Klaus Hartmann observes, "Sartre himself mistakes transcendental philosophy as a position imposing its alleged laws from outside" ("Sartre's Theory of *Ensembles,*" in Schilpp, *Sartre,* 655 n. 7). In a crude sense of the term "outside," Hartmann is correct; a transcendental perspective does not require a commitment to another mind as a distinct entity. Nevertheless, a transcendental perspective does imply that there is within human reason a relation to a broader Reason. Sartre indeed admits, both in *Being and Nothingness* and in the *Critique,* that the individual as an individual discovers "laws" in nature, and an "objective mind" within a historical period. But the former arises from the insertion of organic consciousness within the fabric of matter, and the latter from praxis.

# Background: *Search for a Method*

The French edition of the *Critique* is introduced by an occasional work, *Question de méthode*. In the preface, Sartre explains the publishing history of the smaller work and its relation to the *Critique*. Originally, this relatively short piece was written for a Polish magazine that requested Sartre to discuss the situation of existentialism in 1957.[1] Although reluctant to write about existentialism as though it were a closed enterprise, Sartre nevertheless accepted, because, as he says in the preface, he saw an opportunity "to explain to a country with a Marxist's culture, the present contradictions in its philosophy." Later the work was revised for a French audience, and its title changed from *Existentialisme et Marxisme* to the present *Question de méthode*. In this form, it was included as an introduction to the *Critique de la raison dialectique*.[2]

The appearance of the English translations paralleled the original separate publications of the two works: the *Question de méthode* was translated first by Hazel Barnes, and the work appeared in America under the title *Search for a Method* and in England under the title *Problem of Method*.[3] Afterward, the *Critique of Dialectical Reason* appeared in English translated by Alan Sheridan-Smith, who did not include the earlier translation of the shorter work, *Question de méthode*.[4]

1. Sartre, "Marksizm i Egzystencjalizm," trans. Jerzy Lisowski. *Twórczość*, Instytut Prasy "Czytelnik," Warszawa, April 1955, no. 4, 33–79.

2. Sartre, *Critique de la raison dialectique (précédé de Question de méthode)*, Tome I, Theorie des ensembles pratiques (Paris: Gallimard, 1960); rev. ed., revised by Arlette Elkaïm Sartre (Paris: Gallimard, 1985).

3. Sartre, *Search for a Method*, trans. Hazel E. Barnes (New York: Alfred A. Knopf, 1963). *Problem of Method*, trans. Hazel E. Barnes (London: Methuen & Co., 1964).

4. Sartre, *Critique of Dialectical Reason, vol. I, Theory of Practical Ensembles*, trans. Alan Sheridan-Smith (London: New Left Books, 1976). References to the French editions of the *Question de méthode* and the *Critique* will be indicated simply by "F" for the original edition and "NF" for the new (with page number). The American edition of the English translation of *Question de méthode* will be referred to as *Method* (with page number). References to the English translation of the *Critique* will be indicated simply by "E" (with page number).

In relation to the *Critique*, the *Method* is both an introduction and a summary. Logically, it is the larger work that establishes the claims of the smaller. Sartre nevertheless agrees that the *Method* should be placed first, not only because it is shorter and simpler, but also because "in the dialectical method the chronological order is the most important."[5] But much of that is discussed in the *Method*, and what will be said about it in this background chapter will be clarified only as the details of the *Critique*'s main argument are examined.

The three major divisions of this background chapter follow Sartre's divisions in the *Method;* the subdivisions are here my own but are not here put in parentheses. Although I have tried to at least touch upon all the major issues examined in the *Method*, I consider my introductory remarks an occasion not so much to comment on the text but to discuss the relation of some of the *Critique*'s central themes to Sartre's earlier philosophy.

## 1. MARXISM AND EXISTENTIALISM
### i. Sartre and Marx

After World War II, Sartre's practical relation to Marxist thinking was conditioned, on the one hand, by his popularity as an existentialist thinker and, on the other hand, by the complex milieu of intellectual excitement and political movement, which in France were not easily separable. After the Liberation, the spectrum of thinkers and political activists from the Left became popular because the Left alone had consistently fought against the Germans and the Vichy government. Although Sartre probably never fired a gun, he had been in the army and was captured by the Germans. He taught his fellow prisoners Heidegger, the only philosopher the Germans allowed.[6] He managed to talk the Germans into letting him go, claiming that he was never really a soldier because of his poor eyesight. He joined the Resistance, in which, he says, he was little more than an errand boy. If this is not exactly the picture of a hero, Sartre had at least placed his body on the side of the Resistance and, of course, he was always writing. *Nausea* and *Being and Nothingness* were published before the Liberation, and Sartre had produced *The Flies*, a thinly disguised attack on the Germans.[7]

---

5. This remark is in the preface to the French editions of the *Critique* and it is placed at the conclusion of the English translation of the *Critique* proper (E, 821; F, 9). In her translation of the *Question de méthode*, Barnes included this preface but apparently deleted those paragraphs that referred only to the *Critique*.

6. While a prisoner, Sartre kept a journal, of which a considerable part was lost. One section has been published as *The War Diaries: November 1939–March 1940*, trans. Quintin Hoare (New York: Pantheon Books, 1984). This diary clearly shows that Sartre was concerned with the theme of nothingness that would be central to *Being and Nothingness*. Although he was allowed to teach only Heidegger, Sartre's diary entries substantively distinguish his thought from that of Heidegger and not from that of Hegel.

7. *The Flies and No Exit*, trans. Stuart Gilbert (New York: Alfred A. Knopf, 1947). My re-

The French Communist party (FCP) had also fought on the side of the Resistance. The FCP was close to Moscow with its Stalinist political platform and its imposition of a rigorous dialectical materialism. But many Marxist thinkers rejected the FCP's theoretical limitations and were rethinking not only the Marx of *Capital* but the early Marx, particularly the Marx of the *1844 Manuscripts* that were just being introduced and translated. Here, the emphasis was not on dialectical laws but on alienation. This backward introduction of the early Marx was paralleled by the late introduction of Hegel. The scene was further complicated by the fact that Hegel was now being read through both Marxist and existentialist eyes. Alexandre Kojève, who began lecturing on Hegel, had first come in contact with Kierkegaard and Heidegger; Jean Hyppolite translated Hegel's *Phenomenology* and even used exact phrases from Sartre's *Being and Nothingness*.[8] What emerged from this new look at Hegel and Marx was the centrality of the theme of alienation and the indebtedness of Marx to Hegel, not only for the dialectic, but for the analysis of the master-slave relation in the *Phenomenology*.

There was another consistency in the French rediscovery of German nineteenth-century thought: a gradual transition from a Cartesian, atemporal approach to reality to a realization of the need to consider both the historical placing of thought and the historical moment of the thinker. Thus, Sartre takes a new look at the notion of "ideology," namely that what an age takes as "universal reason" is basically a notion of reason defined by a rising class to fit its needs. In the *Critique*, the notion of ideology becomes an aspect of a more complex distinction between analytic and dialectical reason.

On the practical level of political activity, there was, of course, the constancy of the FCP; as diverse as was the intellectual spectrum of the Left, the political reality after the war was that the Party represented the masses of the French workers. The tensions in choosing between joining the one party that had effective political strength and retaining intellectual integrity could be agonizing for the French intellectual. In order to stay within the Party, Lukács was made to recant his *History and Class Consciousness*, with its emphasis

_____

marks in this section are a simplification of a rich and complex time in Sartre's life. Immediately after the war, Sartre founded *Les Temps Modernes* with Beauvoir, Merleau-Ponty, Aron, and others. During these years, he also attempted to become involved in leftist politics without becoming a Communist. There was the aborted attempt in *Socialisme et Liberté*, and his participation in *Rassemblement Démocratique Révolutionnaire* (Revolutionary Peoples Assembly), which he later considered to be merely anticommunist and not viable. See his *Situations*, trans. Benita Eisler (New York: George Braziller, 1965), 248–49; Mark Poster, *Existential Marxism in Postwar France: From Sartre to Althusser* (Princeton, N.J.: Princeton University Press, 1975), 134–35 n. 61; Sartre, *Sartre by Himself*, trans. Richard Seaver (Interviews by Alexandre Astruc and Michel Contat) (New York: Urizen Books, 1978), 51–52.

8. See Poster, *Existential Marxism*, 3–71. For a slightly different emphasis, see Perry Anderson, *Considerations in Western Marxism* (London: Verso, 1979), 52.

on alienation rather than the dialectic.[9] Sartre and Merleau-Ponty were to quarrel, first because Sartre did not join the Party, then because he did.[10]

Within this intellectual and political context, it is not always easy to retrace Sartre's own philosophic development. In order to teach philosophy, Sartre had taken the formal training for the *agregé,* and he had read *Capital* as early as 1927; he had also spent a year in Berlin reading Husserl in German, and he read Heidegger soon after. He must have read Hegel in the original at least prior to writing his *Being and Nothingness,* because in that work Sartre frequently arrives at his own position by first examining the views of Hegel and Heidegger. But, for Sartre, there was the important distinction between academic reading and the reading that changed his thinking and his life. In the case of his early reading of phenomenology, he had been searching for a philosophy of the concrete himself. In this early period, however, it is clear that not only Marx but also Hegel occupied a secondary role. In *Being and Nothingness,* despite the use of the Hegelian terms "for-itself" and "in-itself," there is no real use of a dialectic, truncated or otherwise, nor is there a meaningful confrontation with Hegel or Marx.[11] After the war, spurred by the changing intellectual climate and the political tensions, Sartre began a complete reading of Hegel, Marx, and Freud. He also began reading Kierkegaard in depth.

But now Sartre's approach was not academic. He saw that his earlier existentialism had not provided a bridge between theory and political practice, and also that he had not considered the status of the intellectual within culture. Implicitly, he had accepted from the early Husserl the conviction that the genetic components of a phenomenon, its diachronic depth, could be discounted for the purpose of philosophic analysis: the nature of human relations was philosophically important, but their historical reasons and roots were not. The tie between the historical depth of human relations and these relations as a presence before us was to become an integral aspect of the *Critique,* with its progressive-regressive movement. Through this method, the *Critique* aims at revealing what in analytic terms can be called "the condition for the possibility" of human relations. That is, Sartre attempts to show us the *large-scale, objective conditions* that allow *these* human relations, rather than others, to be possible. He has in mind the objective possibility of such phenomena as colonialization, racism, and revolutionary action.

9. Georg Lukács, *History and Class Consciousness,* trans. Rodney Livingston (Cambridge: MIT Press, 1971).

10. Sartre, *Situations,* 225–36; Poster, *Existential Marxism,* 145–46. There was also, of course, the friendship and final break with Camus; see *Situations,* 71–111.

11. See Klaus Hartmann, *Sartre's Ontology: A Study of Being and Nothingness in the Light of Hegel's Logic* (Evanston, Ill.: Northwestern University Press, 1966). Hartmann's general thesis is that the internal development of *Being and Nothingness* should be understood in light of Hegel's logic and that the basic relation of the for-itself to the in-itself is one of a truncated dialectic.

By the time Sartre wrote the *Method* in 1957, Marxism had become for him the philosophy that weds theory and action. He was experiencing the proletariat, those " 'sub-men conscious of their sub-humanity,' " (*Method*, 19, F 23, NF 29) not merely as a tragic problem that had not yet been resolved, but as a historical phenomenon that was being maintained in existence by present practices. But, unlike many of the Stalinist Marxists of his time, Sartre had a firsthand knowledge of the texts of Hegel and Marx. There were also Kierkegaard's and Sartre's own existentialism. And most importantly, Sartre was not a historian but a philosopher; everything would be rethought. This was to become clear when Sartre, in the *Method*, interpreted Marx as bringing together Hegel and Kierkegaard; while Marx and Kierkegaard each developed his philosophy in relation to Hegel, neither was aware of the other's thought. In the *Method*, Sartre's situating of existentialism within Marxism is a philosophic interpretation with ambiguities that I will soon consider. But I would first like to examine some of the background that preceded the writing of the *Critique*.

At first, Sartre's position was that of an intellectual of the Left who could not join the Party. In "Materialism and Revolution," he distanced himself from the Party by insisting that humans make history and not laws. "The revolutionary, on the other hand, is defined by his *going beyond* the situation in which he is placed." [12] He was, of course, proposing that the FCP incorporate existentialism within its intellectual program. But one aspect of the argument was to become crucial for the *Critique,* namely, that one dialectic cannot apply to both nature and history. How important such a unified dialectical materialism was to Marx is debatable. [13] In general, Sartre plays Engels and Lenin against the "true Marx." Regardless of Marx's own view, Sartre explicitly denies that we have a neutral perspective from which we can see both history and nature. On the other hand, he accepts on a commonsense level our obvious ties with animals and minerals, but he rejects the idea that we have the philosophic tools to elaborate these connections. This position is not a rejection of science but a perspective on science as a set of intellectual tools constituted by praxis for the purpose of controlling nature. Sartre's insistence that the dialectic be located only within history has led some commentators to speak of an implicit Cartesian dichotomy between human praxis and nature. But the question that must be addressed is the implicit idealism in an a priori

Hartmann is, of course, correct in observing that Sartre frequently states Hegel's position on a particular topic, such as negation or objectification, but Sartre's statement of the opinions of others is external to the development of *Being and Nothingness*.

12. Sartre, "Materialism and Revolution," in *Literary and Philosophical Essays,* trans. Annette Michelson (New York: Collier Books, 1962), 225.

13. See William L. McBride, *The Philosophy of Marx* (New York: St. Martin's Press, 1977), 46–48, 60, 110–14, 124–25.

transcendent perspective that delineates nature and humans as objects of a unified study.[14]

The claim of many Marxists that dialectical materialism is valid in the realms of both nature and history leads Sartre to reject materialism in the *Method,* because, in this context, it is equivalent to an idealism. "There are two ways to fall into idealism: The one consists of dissolving the real in subjectivity; the other in denying all real subjectivity in the interests of objectivity" (*Method,* 33 n. 1; F, 31 n. 1; NF, 39 n. 1). This type of materialism does not question the relation of the materialist to materialism; it assumes that the movement from the human organism to nature is the same as the movement from nature to the human organism. This assumption is itself the result of praxis, a series of historical activities that constitute materialism as a positivism with its reverse side of "spiritualism." Indirectly, we here encounter the distinction between "dialectical" and "analytic" reason. Reason can constitute itself as a tool. In this sense, analytic reason can be an instrument in two senses: it can recognize that it is molding and limiting itself as an analytic tool, in which case it is dialectical reason operating, as it were, in good faith; or it can present itself as the universal reason of a neutral observer, in which case it is the tool of an ideology that, for Sartre, masks its goal of limiting humanity. This will be discussed at some length as we proceed with our study of the *Critique.*

With "Materialism and Revolution" in 1947, Sartre felt that he had indirectly given aid to American capitalism. Further, the political situation was changing. The strength of the FCP was diminishing, and the cold war was intensifying. Sartre feared the presence of Washington in Paris more than the presence of Moscow. A final stupidity on the part of the French government tilted the scale: there was a general crackdown on socialist groups. Sartre defended the Party as a protest, and, between 1952 and 1953, wrote a series of articles for *Les Temps Modernes,* which were to become *The Communists and Peace.*[15]

*The Communists and Peace* is an occasional work, loosely argued. The main problem was still the union of theory and practice. Sartre writes on two levels: On an empirical level, there are the arrests of dissidents in the Soviet Union and the arrests of Communists in France. But, on a broader, more historically significant level, there are the series of praxes in both countries that made the arrests possible. The present philosophic situation is not a mere epi-

---

14. As early as 1937, in *The Transcendence of the Ego,* Sartre had rejected the need to postulate a theoretical bond that explained the union of consciousness to the organic *from the perspective of the inorganic,* saying that "it has always seemed to me that a working hypothesis as fruitful as historical materialism never needed metaphysical materialism." (trans. Forrest Williams and Robert Kirkpatrick (New York: Noonday Press, 1957), 105.

15. Sartre, *The Communists and Peace with a Reply to Claude Lefort,* trans. Martha H. Fletcher and Philip R. Berk (New York: George Braziller, 1968) (hereafter cited as *CP*).

phenomenon. There is a class struggle, but it is not between ideal categories. "I don't concern myself with what would be desirable nor with ideal relations which the Party-in-itself (*Parti-en-soi*) sustains with the Eternal Proletariat; I seek to understand what is happening in France today, before our very eyes" (*CP,* 120). There are two issues: the FCP as a political organ under persecution, which Sartre still sees as viable despite all its faults, and the distinctive history of the French worker, a particular oppression that did not exist in American capitalism, namely "Malthusianism." An enlightened capitalism would be content with exploitation and with buying off a section of the middle class by raising its standard of living at the expense of the lower classes. But the French had added oppression to exploitation. Consequently, each class struggle has its own "truth." It is impossible to know critically and a priori that a single class struggle exists throughout the world. Sartre credits Marx for this emphasis on the need for separate historical analysis of class struggles.

In the last third of *The Communists and Peace,* Sartre also investigates the notion of class, which was later refined in the *Critique.* The reality of a class is not that of a superentity that unites individuals into some quasi-organic whole. On the other hand, a class has more reality than the sum total of individuals who are concerned about each other. One of the main purposes of the *Critique* is to elucidate the ambiguous reality of a class, and Sartre clarifies in *The Communists and Peace* that he is attempting to evaluate classes from the perspective of the most disadvantaged.

The United States and the USSR could debate an elitist notion of freedom. As for the French worker, "she too wants liberation. But her freedom doesn't resemble yours; and I think that she would gladly do without the freedom of expression of which such fine use is made in the Salle Gaveau if she were freed from the throbbing rhythm of the machine" (*CP,* 228). Sartre, of course, always defended freedom of expression, even when the Communists had tried to censor their own members. The issue here, however, is that the goal of freedom of expression is being used as an excuse for tolerating injustices that could be eliminated. On their part, the Communists held that the future liberation of the worker is a justification for tolerating present oppression. The liberation promised by capitalism is less oppressive, but, in the long run, it is also more alienating and inhuman: "At the end of the last century, Taylor said *to* the workers, 'Don't try to think; others will do that for you.' Thirty years later, Ford said *of* the workers, 'They don't like to think for themselves'" (*CP,* 193).

When the USSR invaded Hungary in 1956, Sartre broke with the Party and again wrote three articles for *Les Temps Modernes,* which were later to become *The Ghost of Stalin.*[16] Although it is also an occasional work with a ca-

16. Sartre, *The Ghost of Stalin,* trans. Martha H. Fletcher (New York: George Braziller, 1968) (hereinafter cited as *Ghost*). This book appeared in England as *The Spectre of Stalin,* trans. Irene Clephane (London: Hamish Hamilton, 1969).

sual discourse, it is still timely, arguing that "nothing is served by arresting the free development of a country by force: it is up to it to overcome its contradictions" (*Ghost,* 61). Again, the work proceeds on two levels. Empirically, there are the historical events and tensions, both internal and with the West, that led to Stalin's power; there are his death, the talk of de-Stalinization, and the practices of a specific Soviet de-Stalinization. On another level, there is the attempt to comprehend the relation of the empirical events to the original Soviet socialist program. On this level, Sartre attempts to reveal a socialism that betrayed its own goals. Some critics have interpreted the book as implying that all socialism must have its Stalin and lead to failure. But the opposite is, in fact, the case. Sartre does emphasize that the Soviet Union is a socialist experiment turned sour. Whatever pressures the West may have brought to bear, it was *Soviet* Communists, *Soviet* praxes that ruined socialism for the USSR and its satellite countries. "Must one give the name of socialism to this bloody monster which tears itself apart? I answer frankly: yes" (*Ghost,* 81). Sartre's concern here, as in the latter third of *Critique I,* is to uncover the "reasons" why Soviet communism became alienated from its original goals. The implication in Sartre's analysis is that the Soviet Union could and should have developed a socialism superior to Western capitalism.

The background to Sartre's analysis of the difference between a "successful" bourgeois capitalism and democracy and a socialism that has failed was also integrated into the last third of *Critique I* and was to become a substantive part of the *Critique II.* In general, Sartre's point is that capitalism is alienating in its very intention: it sets out to cultivate a privacy that renders group political involvement nonviable; the vote is a chimera that leaves the power groups of the elite classes free to set their own goals. Socialism, on the contrary, aims at making viable the political power that resides in the people through group praxes. It operates within the tension between the individual's present needs and the needs and goals of the nation and humanity.

The Soviet failure, however, resulted not from an error in policy, nor from the wickedness of Stalin, nor from class conflict. Soviet socialism broke its ties to its people by a series of free practices that gradually alienated the Party from the people. But, again, even as a failure, it was still an original effort toward freedom and, as such, radically different from bourgeois democracy:

> A young Russian, in a conversation which a French friend reported to me, began by accepting criticisms in good grace and by admitting the defects of the regime. But after a moment, he asked, irritated: 'And you? What else do you have to offer us?' My friend made the response which we all would have made: 'Nothing. The West has nothing to offer.' But it is necessary to add today: 'And you Russians, if you succeeded in making us believe that your barbarity in

> Budapest is only a normal episode of socialist construction,
> no one in the world would have anything to offer any more.
> To anyone.' And I particularly notice, as a matter of fact, that
> Merleau-Ponty doesn't get very upset over the Soviet interven-
> tion: if the U.S.S.R. is worth neither more nor less than capi-
> talist England, then, indeed, not much is left to us except to
> cultivate our garden. In order to preserve hope, precisely the
> opposite must be done: to recognize, through and beyond er-
> rors, monstrosities and crimes, the obvious privileges of the
> socialist camp and to condemn with all the more force the
> policy which endangers these privileges. (*Ghost,* 120–21)

In *Ghost,* Sartre outlines a progressive-regressive study of Soviet socialism that reveals the relation of praxis to "inertia," and to what in the *Critique* he calls the "practico-inert." In the early years of Soviet development, the people understood the conflict between their need for bread and the country's need for industrialization. The "leaders" expressed the tension between the demands of the industrial worker and the hardships of the farmer. This contradiction was also understood by the people themselves; it was the specific way the So-viet people lived the tension between the concrete and the universal dialectic. The Party members worked hard and long hours. They received a few privi-leges, which of themselves meant nothing. Gradually, however, *their* hard work, *their* long hours of dedication began to have a value of themselves. A hierarchy of functions, which was not of itself alienating, became a hierarchy of values and privileges, with the Party members on top (*Ghost,* 66–76).

The institutionalization of the Soviet Communist party points to a *danger* present in any socialist enterprise: hard work, dedication to a general plan, small economic advantages that of themselves are harmless and even de-served, begin to legitimize a privileged perspective on the country's real needs and its international relations. "Some men, by placing themselves *in a certain political perspective,* based on an evaluation *which is their own* of the inter-national relations, judged it preferable to refuse the socialist forces of the new Hungary their chances and to plunge this country into chaos" (*Ghost,* 63 [Sartre's italics]). And, a little further on, he adds:

> Born of the Plan, it is the Plan which legitimizes their
> privileges: their personal ambition is not distinct from their
> devotion to socialism conceived as abstract economic plan-
> ning, that is to say, ultimately, as the continuous increase of
> production. This total alienation allows them to consider
> themselves as organs of the universal to the extent that the
> Plan must be established by their own efforts; the demands of
> the masses, on the contrary, even if they take them into ac-
> count, are for them particular accidents of a strictly negative
> character. (*Ghost,* 71–72)

This alienation is distinct from that which occurs in capitalist countries such as the United States, where subtle propaganda creates the illusion that anyone could be a public figure if *chance* were on their side. The play of power groups is kept hidden. The unique alienation in Soviet bureaucracy, however, led to a peculiar form of the "sacred" and to a specific "cult of personality." "By subordinating his person to the group, the Soviet man avoids the absurd vices of bourgeois personalism but, by the same token, the even more imperious necessity to maintain and reinforce unity causes his individual reality to go underground" (*Ghost*, 76). This alienation provided *the objective possibility* of a cult figure such as Stalin, as well as the need to de-Stalinize on a superficial level. Stalinism is the failure of a group praxes and is thus distinct from bourgeois individualism. It is a group pushed to the limit of becoming identified with a person. "Stalin alone is pure unity: He is the act" (*Ghost*, 78). The Party as a group has abandoned the complexities, the gambles, and the tensions of working in diverse ways for a common goal, without any privileged status and in close connection with the organized groups of the people. It has ceased to be a channel of power and has become an instrument of power with its own army and its own police.

Sartre does not apologize for his earlier "defense" of the Soviet Union. Historical events change, and judgments must change with them. He acknowledges that during the time of Stalin the "sores" were covered over (*Ghost*, 93). But more basic to his change of view is the implicit judgment that the persecution of a literary and political elite, while never justifiable, did not, of itself, indicate the total failure of Soviet socialism. The invasion of Hungary, however, was an attack on the workers and the people of a country. It represented a betrayal of the very purpose of socialism. This invasion could not have occurred as a mere political error; rather, it was the sign of a basic alienation of the Party from the people. Stalinism was itself an unstable state that demanded its condemnation, if civil war was not to break out. But, at the same time, Soviet de-Stalinization was aimed at retaining the Soviet Party, as it was, at all costs: "by making Stalin a devil, they had replaced white masses with black masses and they had not at all gotten out of the cult of personality" (*Ghost*, 110).

The invasion of Hungary, with its sloganlike justification, made a true de-Stalinization impossible; the new leaders now closed the system in on itself so that a cult figure would always be needed in order to be raised up by the system. After this had occurred, it was possible to see Stalin as the original symbol of this cult. But the fault was not only with Stalin but also with those who followed him. Here again, Sartre refuses to be merely deterministic. As he is to repeat frequently, history makes humans, but humans also make history.

Sartre concludes by turning his attention to the Party in France. Here, at this time, he sees that a true de-Stalinization may be possible for the French Left.[17]

> For our part, it's been twelve years that we have been debating with the Communists. At first with violence, later in friendship. But our goal was always the same: to cooperate with our feeble forces in achieving this union of the Lefts which *alone* can still save our country. Today, we return to the opposition: for this very simple reason, that there is no other position to take; alliance with the C.P. as it is, as it intends to remain, can have no other effect than to compromise the last chances of the United Front. Our program is clear: through and beyond a hundred contradictions, internal struggles, massacres, de-Stalinization is in process; it is the only effective policy which serves, in the present moment, socialism, peace, the rapprochement of the workers' parties: with our resources as intellectuals, read by intellectuals, we will try to help in the de-Stalinization of the French Party. (*Ghost*, 142)

At the time of writing the *Method*, Sartre sees his task as primarily directed not to giving a direction for political action but to elucidating the historical dimension of daily life—for example, the relation between the petit bourgeois who buys a newspaper and stands in line to wait for a bus on his way to work for wages, and that war that he, through his government, is waging in Algiers. There is also another dimension to the problem of how theory is related to action, namely, that of the status of instruments. Here the point is not merely that we need a hammer to drive a nail into a wall in order to hang a picture. Rather, it is the fact that the hammer was bought and manufactured by workers and that the picture is a luxury in a private apartment that exists within a world where a third of the inhabitants are undernourished. A theory of action thus concerns the relation of a network of instrumentality to the ideologies of the times.

17. For a different exposition of the preceding three works, see Thomas R. Flynn, *Sartre and Marxist Existentialism* (Chicago: University of Chicago Press, 1984), 43, 53, 78–80; Peter Caws, *Sartre* (London: Routledge & Kegan Paul, 1979), 131–43; and Ronald Aronson, *Jean-Paul Sartre* (London: New Left Books and Verso, 1980), 214–33. See also Perry Anderson, *In the Tracts of Historical Materialism* (Chicago: University of Chicago Press, 1984), 69–73. Anderson remarks: "*The Ghost of Stalin*, which in and through its very excoriation of the Russian intervention in Hungary, held firm to the prediction that 'deStalinization will deStalinize the de-Stalinizers'" (71). But the import of *Ghost* is that the condition for the possibility of de-Stalinization was already destroyed by the leaders that followed Stalin (*Ghost*, 100–107). After the invasion of Poland, Sartre had definitely given up on Russian communism, but not on socialism or French communism (*Ghost*, 121–29). Anderson's interpretation of the *Ghost* leads also to a pessimistic reading of the last third of *Critique I* and the unfinished manuscript of *Critique II*.

When we turn to the *Method* to see how the relation between existentialism and Marxism weds theory and action, we must keep the occasional character of the work in mind. The discourse is not as loose as in *The Communists and Peace* or *The Ghost of Stalin,* but it is also not as rigorous as in the *Critique.* In a sense, Sartre is still trying to discuss an issue on two levels: to hold a dialogue with Marxists at home and abroad, while working out a philosophic position. Sartre's remarks are thus ambiguous. For example, he claims: "And since I am to speak of existentialism, let it be understood that I take it to be an 'ideology.' It is a parasitical system living on the margin of knowledge" (*Method,* 8; F, 18; NF, 22). On the other hand, he also states, "Existentialism and Marxism, on the contrary, aim at the same object; but Marxism has reabsorbed man into the idea, and existentialism seeks him everywhere *where he is,* at his work, in his home, in the street" (*Method,* 28; F, 28; NF 35).

Indeed, if we go through the *Method,* we can distinguish several senses of "Marxism" and "existentialism." There is the "philosophy of Marx" in its concrete relation to nineteenth-century Western civilization; there is the "dead Marxism" of the official Communist party, which continues to apply Marx's philosophy as if it were a system of a priori principles that merely needs to be adjusted to contemporary society; and finally there is a "living Marxism," for which Marx's thought gives merely heuristic principles or guides and of which Sartre sees himself as the *only* representative.[18] Somewhat parallel to these senses of Marxism are three senses of existentialism. First, there is a "historical existentialism," of which he had reluctantly agreed to speak. In this context, Sartre writes approvingly of Kierkegaard. Second, in a loose analogue to "dead Marxism," Jaspers is dismissed as an unoriginal thinker who covered up the fact that his philosophy was developed within a suprahuman framework. Sartre leaves Heidegger in limbo, claiming that his case is too complex to consider at this time. Finally, there is a third sense of "existentialism," one that is allied to the "living Marxism." This existentialism is obviously Sartre's own, and it is true that he seems willing to consign it to a secondary place within his Marxism.

In the *Method,* Sartre begins with a quasi-Marxist view of the role and the division of philosophies. He denies the existence of "Philosophy" except as a

18. Perry Anderson believes that Sartre and others who were working on Marx independent of Soviet influence were remarkably unaware of each other's works (*Considerations,* 69). In the same work, commenting on Sartre's view of Marxism in the *Method,* Anderson remarks, "Thus, from 1924 to 1968, Marxism did not 'stop,' as Sartre was later to claim, but it advanced via an unending detour from any revolutionary political practice. . . . The hidden hallmark of Western Marxism as a whole is thus that it is the product of defeat" (42). This may indeed be true, but, for Sartre, this defeat arises not from the economic power of capitalism but from the Soviet betrayal of socialism. In the *Tracts,* Anderson reaffirms his view (20–21), but adds, "By and large, a line could be drawn below the original Western Marxist experience by the middle of the seventies. . . . What succeeded it? A sudden zest, a new appetite for the concrete" (21).

hypostasized abstraction. There are, he says, only "philosophies." Nevertheless, in certain historical situations in which a *specified kind of totalization* clarifies the self-consciousness of the rising class, *a* philosophy exists for that time. Since the sixteenth century, we have had the philosophies of Descartes and Locke, Kant and Hegel, and, finally, Marx. "At the time of the *noblesse du robe* and of mercantile capitalism, a bourgeoisie of lawyers, merchants, and bankers gained a certain self-awareness through Cartesianism; a century and a half later, in the primitive stages of industrialization, a bourgeoisie of manufacturers, engineers, and scientists dimly discovered itself in the image of universal man which Kantianism offered to it" (*Method,* 4; F, 15; NF, 19–20). Throughout the *Critique,* Sartre will return to these different ways human beings become conscious of themselves. In each case, he will note that a different type of self-consciousness arose because human beings had established a new relation to matter.

Although this division is very general, it does challenge the notion that philosophy develops as a history of ideas. In this present view, a philosophy reflects and focuses the rights and duties of a rising class. In a later work, Sartre indicates that, in fortunate times—when the oppressed class is also rising class with certain cultural advantages—the intellectual is not alienated from the new philosophy that is being developed. In the "Golden Age" of bourgeois humanism, thinkers like Montesquieu, Voltaire, Diderot, and Rousseau brought the tools of analytic reason against "the traditions, privileges, and myths of the aristocracy, long founded on an irrational syncretism." [19] But intellectuals today must recognize that this same humanism has its own myths that now serve to keep the majority of human beings exploited and oppressed. Today's intellectuals, born of this ideology, must attempt to distance themselves from it. "The only way the intellectual can really distance himself from the official ideology decreed from above is to place himself alongside those whose very existence contradicts it." [20]

### ii. The We- and Us-Relations

One of the central themes running through the *Critique* is the nature of our bond to each other. [21] Heidegger, in *Being and Time,* had claimed that this union is an internal relation, a "being-with" another. Cooperation is thus an integral part of the human reality, whether we empirically put it in

---

19. Sartre, *Between Existentialism and Marxism,* translated by John Mathews (New York: Pantheon Books, 1974), 234–35.

20. Ibid., 256.

21. Although Sartre refers to his task as establishing a "structural anthropology," this again must be understood in the context of the occasional nature of the *Method.* Sartre uses some structuralist insights, but the overall movement and program of his dialectic cannot be reduced to structural techniques. In regard to Sartre's use of the term *structurelle,* see Caws, *Sartre,* 143.

practice or not. Each of us is both an "I" and a "we." Many Marxists have sided with Heidegger on this point, seeing in the "we-relation" the type of union among peoples needed for the success of class struggle.

In Sartre's critique of Heidegger in *Being and Nothingness,* he maintained that the "we" is only a psychological state. We thus cooperate with each other only when and if we are actually doing the cooperation. To the extent that our cooperation is not actual, our bond, as a subject to others as subjects, exists only as a personal conviction that others are concerned with our lives.

On the other hand, Sartre claimed that the fact of our cooperation is objectively inscribed *in things.* The slots in a rowboat, for example, are, for the rower, the objective means for cooperating as a team. Each participant's team spirit and willingness to endure fatigue are personal, but the condition for the possibility of cooperation is in the object. In *Being and Nothingness,* Sartre thus insisted that "being-with" is an "us-relation"; that is, cooperation exists *in the world* insofar as praxes produce a unified work, for example a racing boat, which then enables others to cooperate among themselves, for example a team in a race.

Nevertheless, even in *Being and Nothingness,* Sartre never claimed that human relations arose from the confrontations among *isolated* individuals. On the contrary, in his earlier work on phenomenological ontology, Sartre described that our being-for-ourselves is also our being-for-others. It is true that, in the abstract, the existence of others cannot be deduced from the nature of consciousness. An infant growing up in a forest would not discover by any privileged, interior reflection a need for a relation to other humans qua human, nor would such a child be human in our sense.[22] But we are born into a world where we encounter the existence of others as a brute given. This does not mean that the existence of others alters the structure of consciousness and behavior in a merely superficial way. On the contrary, once the existence of other persons is given, consciousness is internally altered and structured to be the concrete humanity that we encounter in our everyday lives.

Here we see an instance of the unique relations of the abstract to the concrete, referred to in the Prefatory Remarks. The existence of others is neither deducible from nor reducible to the abstract. Once the concrete is given, however, the abstract no longer exists as a quasi-essential state underlying the concrete. Given the existence of other people, we cannot say that de facto our consciousness has a more fundamental relation to itself.[23] Claiming that might

22. Sartre rejects the Neo-Aristotelian perspective which claims that the higher, human organism, by its "virtual-power," sees, hears, smells, tastes, and touches in the same formal way as lower organisms. If the "child of nature" makes sounds, they are not the sounds of our humanity nor of our domesticated animals nor of wild animals. They are a new facticity of a different humanity.

23. See *BN,* 252–303. I interpret the "look" as referring both to the concrete existing other

be effectively equivalent to maintaining an Aristotelian nature, except that even this concrete situation may be abstract in relation to more concrete circumstances, in which a new facticity could once again internally restructure consciousness and behavior. Indeed, in regard to our historical relation with others, this restructuring is precisely what happens in the *Critique*.

In both *Being and Nothingness* and the *Critique*, Sartre describes our human bonds nominalistically. If there is a general perspective, it is that our interpersonal relations and our social organization are not *by nature* positive. A neurotic love can deepen each partner's tragic condition, and, as we shall see, reciprocity can lead to oppression as well as to an opening into a more expansive human life. Insofar as our union with each other is positive, it has been established by our own praxes. For who or what else could bring about the objective possibility of positive human social relations? God, Thou, or the Transcendent? Indeed. But this would evaporate the human adventure. Nature or Being? Sartre's answer, consistent with a philosophy that develops from a human perspective, is a definite no.

Sartre's denial that we have a priori positive bonds to each other raises the question of whether our historical situation will always allow us the possibility to recognize when we have fallen away from our humanity. A genuine we-relation could guarantee that our privileged and private reflections would give us a perspective from which to judge the degree of humanity within a certain situation. But did the children of the Third Reich realize the horror in the goal of exterminating the Jews? Do we recognize the inhumanity in our own exploitation of others and in our direct or indirect colonialization? For Sartre, the possibility of becoming aware of alienation exists only to the degree that praxis has established the condition for that possibility. Some of us can thus escape, to some degree, the general historical alienating dimension of our lives in our daily occupations, that is to say, in our local relations with our books, our friends, and our organizations. Still, our own praxis may eliminate the possibility of this reflection.

In support of the we-relation, critics point to the cooperation among the members of a family, and to the pain, sweat, and suffering of people when they act for a common goal. But if a husband leaves his wife before their child is born and the wife gives the child to an orphanage, where is "the family"? And every conquering army suffers in pain and sweat. A we-relation should guarantee that the cooperation is truly human *by nature*.

To repeat, Sartre does not deny that we cooperate with each other. In the *Critique*, his emphasis is on the objectified structures that make both conflict and cooperation possible. A visitor from another planet, or an archeologist of

---

and to the meanings inscribed in things by others. Thus, I see it as both singular and plural. For a different interpretation, see Flynn, *Sartre and Marxist Existentialism*, 25.

the future, could "read" about our conflict and cooperation without reading our books. Our conflict would exist in the locks on our doors, in the objective arrangement of social institutions such as courtrooms; our cooperation would be present in our hospitals, or in something as humble as a four-oar rowboat. For Sartre, needless to say, the individual element is also crucial. The alteration of our natural environment into a world of competition and cooperation has itself been brought about by past human praxes. We each spontaneously interiorize these past structures, interpreting them in our own project. Either we support and retain them by our chosen passivity, or we attempt to alter them for better or for worse. In one sense, the *Critique* can be summarized as an attempt to elucidate the symbiotic relation between the human organism, both as an individual and as a member of a collective, and the environment, laden with the objectified meanings of our history.

Although Sartre will deny the existence of a we-relation, in the sense of an a priori positive bond uniting humans, he implicitly redefines this notion in the *Critique*. The result is that something like a we-relation emerges in the group-in-fusion, where each individual is also the common individual. We will see that such an individual can perform an action that is distinctively individual but that also surpasses the power of any one individual.

Sartre's view of the we-relation is thus a change from his position in *Being and Nothingness*. In his ontology, the historical dimension was considered to be merely an aspect of the human situation. "Conflict" was, therefore, given in the fact of wars and oppression, and the human roots of these situations were not examined. This explanation alone, however, is too simple; it does not account for the description, in *Being and Nothingness* of love as a conflict between freedoms. From the perspective of the *Critique*, however, Sartre's descriptions of interpersonal relations take on different meanings. As will become evident, the distinction between the abstract and the concrete in the *Critique* relates, in general, to the distinction between the local significance of our actions and their historical import. It is now possible to interpret interpersonal relations, such as love, in an abstract but positive way. Our relations with our friends are usually abstract because they do not concern historical change. Sartre must have had in mind his own relation with Simone de Beauvoir, in which positive reciprocity was a bond that simultaneously united them and moved them to fulfill their own uniqueness. The seeds of failure exist in this healthy conflict; there is always the danger that one person will either attempt to dominate the other or surrender the possibility of change and growth.[24]

On the wider, historical level of the *Critique*, however, it is also clear that "conflict" is real and oppressive. From this perspective, the claim in *Being*

24. In *Being and Nothingness,* Sartre implicitly distinguishes two different ways in which human relations may "fail" (379). See *Commentary BN,* 183; see also Book I, chapter IV, section 4.

*and Nothingness* that "conflict" is the essence of human relations can now be seen to say something else about human relations: we have made an environment in which our large-scale relations to each other are such that we naturally must have another group of humans as our enemy. Sartre's general recognition of this historical phenomenon is shared by Christians, Marxists, and many others. What is common is the awareness that historical evil is not explained either by accidents or by the presence of a few wicked men. The Christian points to original sin, the traditional Marxist to economic laws, and others to such explanations as the violence of our evolutionary history. But, for Sartre, the cause of our large-scale "falling from grace" is due to the way human praxes have slowly altered our environment so that conflict is part of the world's objective structure.

There is, to repeat, one constant in Sartre's philosophic view of our social relation: only individuals exist. Social unities, therefore, are not like gelatinous organic substances. On the other hand, "individual" does not mean "isolated," and social realities are not merely subjective. Social unities do exist in the world, but they require the active participation of an organic consciousness, not merely to recognize them but also to sustain them as unities. This is a substantive claim about the relation of knowledge to reality, and, as such, it can be substantiated only gradually as we proceed.

Our investigation of the relation of praxes to history concerns both our actual history and what Sartre terms "the condition for the possibility" of our history. This phrase, however, must not be understood in an analytic sense of validating criteria for existence or in the early Kantian sense of discovering the active human components in our thinking about the world. Sartre begins with the concrete world, and he is trying to describe how large-scale cultural conditions establish the parameters for our possible actions. The phrase "condition for the possibility of" also refers to the "who" seeking to uncover the way praxes establish the condition for freedom and its future development. The underprivileged are too hungry to examine their own historical condition. The dialectic operates within the conscious tension of a study aiming to be world-historical even as it knows it originates from an elite segment within this history. Sartre, however, does not consider his perspective to be merely ethnocentric, because to be bourgeois is to be more than ethnocentric. Again, this is a substantive claim; it requires seeing how freedom is both situational and transcendent of its situation. In this respect, we can again see an evolution in Sartre's thought.

### iii. The Social and the Historical

Sartre has always described human freedom as situational; it is the way we surpass our given conditions. At first, however, Sartre had little realization that transcending a tragic situation could itself be tragic. A tragic situation can be described as one in which a group of people attempt to make someone else the a priori limits of their own freedom. For example, in fear of their own freedom, anti-Semites fix on the Jew as the object of their hate. They are afraid of the ambiguities of the free life. Good, for them, becomes the mere elimination of an easily identified evil, and the purpose of their lives thus becomes simple to define: it is the elimination of this definite object, the Jew. For Jews, the situation is tragic, for they are not free to live in a world devoid of anti-Semitism. Nevertheless, if they live in a community where many people are not anti-Semites, the effect of anti-Semitism can be more or less overcome.[25]

In a more detailed way, Sartre's study of Genet draws attention to the way in which a closed, local environment tragically limits the objective possibilities for expressing one's humanity. From Genet's childhood, everyone saw him as a thief.[26] Genet, previously an orphan and now adopted, wishes to be accepted by his family and his community. But for them Genet was tainted from birth. His evil, again, defines their good. The townspeople need evil, and Genet personifies it for them. In the studies of both the anti-Semite and Genet, Sartre introduces his notion of Manichaeism that he is to return to throughout the *Critique*. At present, we need only note that, for Sartre, "Manichaeism" is not primarily the name of a fourth-century heresy but rather an objective, potentially actualizable social structure in which both good and evil can be made into positive forces. Thus, the present-day Manichaean believes that good is, as it were, dammed up by the force of evil. One needs merely to blow up the dam to be inundated by good. Society thus produces the criminal precisely in order to eliminate him.

The point of this digression is to dispel a rather general misunderstanding of Sartre's philosophy as individualistic, in the sense that "individual" means "isolated." There was always a "social" or interpersonal dimension to Sartre's thought, but his reflection on Hegel and his encounter with Marx made possible his distinction between the social and the historical. The social is local and regional; the historical is worldwide, or nearly so. Furthermore, the historical is qualitatively different from the social. Thus, for example, if world poverty is a historical phenomenon, it is a distinct aspect of all our lives that cannot be reduced to local, social dimensions. This, in a most general way, is the technical meaning of praxis as distinct from mere action: *praxis is action precisely insofar as it is historical.*[27]

25. Sartre, *Anti-Semite and Jew*, trans. George J. Becker (New York: Schocken Books, 1948), 90–113. This book appeared in England as *Portrait of the Anti-Semite,* trans. Eric de Mauny (London: Secker & Warburg, 1948).

26. Sartre, *Saint Genet: Actor and Martyr,* trans. Bernard Frechtman (New York: George Braziller, 1963).

27. For a different perspective, see Flynn, *Sartre and Marxist Existentialism,* 18–30. I am,

Compared with Sartre's earlier works, the *Critique* adds the realization that historical phenomena, such as poverty, are sustained by human praxes. When the freedom of some limits the freedom of others by creating objective, seemingly natural conditions that cannot be transcended, then this constricture causes inhumanity, rather than mere obstacles to overcome. In Sartre's study of Genet, these untranscendable situations created by human beings are local and somewhat elitist: Genet seems to have been well fed and to have had leisure; he could not transcend his thiefhood, but he could seek salvation in writing. However, historical alienation, precisely because historical, cannot be transcended by the individual qua individual.

### iv. Hegel, Kierkegaard, and Marx

In the first section of the *Method*, Sartre situates his own Marxism between Hegel's ambitious totalizations and Kierkegaard's emphasis on the individual. It has already been noted that this historical placing is an interpretation of the thought of Marx.

In general, Sartre is here in sympathy with Hegel's attempt to explain the relation of knowledge to reality as well as his efforts to acquire a general perspective on reality. Sartre, however, rejects Hegel's idealism. For Hegel, there was movement, a "dialectic," within both knowledge and reality that accounted for the progressive unfolding of nature and history. More specifically, Hegel maintained that our actions objectify our thoughts and that this process, of itself, produces both alienation and a higher form of self-consciousness. We do not completely recognize the way the products of our actions reflect our selves. Work thus produces alienation, but alienation in turn dialectically moves our consciousness to a higher level. We are, in this way, later united with the selves from which we have been alienated. The entire process is supposed to move us to a higher form of humanity that participates in the higher form of nature and history. Finally, situated like Hegel at the end of this history, we should be able to understand how we have been produced by the historical process and how we are one with this dialectic. The Hegelian dialectic thus aims at a concrete that is also an absolute; that is, the goal is to comprehend an existing individual and a historical world in which being is mean-

---

however, in general agreement with Flynn's approach to the *Critique*. He has given one of the most comprehensive descriptions of the role of the third in historical relations. If there is a substantive disagreement between us, it will depend on the significance of distinguishing interpersonal and social relations from historical relations. Michael Theunissen also maintains that Sartre's early ontology gives the basis for "social relations" (*The Other: Studies in the Social Ontology of Husserl, Heidegger, Sartre, and Buber*, trans. Christopher Macann [Cambridge: MIT Press, 1984]), 204–5. Still, Theunissen projects a transcendental problem onto Sartre's philosophy; Sartre's nominalism, in *Being and Nothingness*, is able to cope with the relation of the ontological other to the ontic other. Furthermore, for Sartre, the world is not constituted by consciousness.

ingful, in which all that appears isolated is united, and in which movement and finality are one.[28]

Sartre has two major objections to Hegel's reduction of the uniqueness of being to the intelligibility of the historical process. First, he agrees with Marx that objectification does not of itself lead to alienation. Rather, objectification is simply the process through which we alter the world after our own image. We discover ourselves in our own products, and this knowledge expands rather than contracts our self-consciousness. Alienation, on the other hand, is a contingent historical event that cannot be deduced from our ability to alter the world through action; where alienation occurs it is an irreducible phenomenon that cannot be deduced from or reduced to a more general historical process.[29]

Second, Sartre accepts Kierkegaard's critique of Hegel, namely, that the irreducibility of each human life cannot be incorporated within a system. It is important, in this context, to understand Kierkegaard's objection to Hegel correctly. It is more than the mere insistence on the importance of the individual, as Hegel also emphasized the relation of the individual to the historical process. In a footnote, Sartre says that it is thus possible to follow Hyppolite and attempt an existentialist interpretation of Hegel (*Method*, 9 n. 6; F, 18 n. 1; NF, 23 n. 1). But for Hegel, the uniqueness of the individual is always surpassed and rendered meaningful by the dialectic, and history itself gives rise to the type of self-consciousness needed to realize and express the historical process. For Kierkegaard, however, the individual can transcend, by subjectivity, the entire historical process as it can be known by any philosophic system.

Still, Sartre notes correctly that Kierkegaard's view would be impossible without Hegel's thought. In a very real sense, Kierkegaard is willing to accept the validity of the entire Hegelian system, but he insists that nowhere does it express the irreducible uniqueness of an individual's life. Kierkegaard further maintains that by leaving out subjectivity one omits *everything* of significance

28. It will become clear that, for Sartre, the dialectic includes a constant restructuring of a phenomenon in relation to its increasingly concrete states and the positioning of the dialectician, in relation to the dialectic.

29. Sartre's view on objectification is more complex than this sample formulation. In *Being and Nothingness*, Sartre had already distinguished, in a somewhat different context, his view on objectification from that of Hegel. For both Sartre and Hegel, people see us in ways that are different from the ways in which we see ourselves. Nevertheless, according to Hegel, we can learn exactly how other people see us. Sartre terms this an "epistemological optimism," and he maintains, on the contrary, that other people's free interpretations of our behavior prevent us from ever learning how we objectively appear. To state Sartre's position more radically, we do not have an absolute objectivity that can in principle be recovered by knowledge. This lack of identity between knowledge and being does not throw us into alienation; it is rather the origin of the healthy way we depend on others to know about ourselves. See *BN*, 238–44.

as far as human life is concerned. Nevertheless, it is important to realize that Kierkegaard is not referring to a popular, loose notion of subjectivity, for example, that of having an opinion about something.

Indeed, for Kierkegaard, subjectivity implies a dialectical "affair" with objectivity. I have deliberately not attempted to state what a dialectic is, because I wish to avoid early conceptualization, preferring instead to let Sartre's notion unfold *in use*. And I do not wish to impose a simplistic method onto Hegel's thought. Sartre never accuses Hegel of having a dialectic that mechanically explicates the negative aspect in every positive quality, uniting the two in a higher reality, a "synthesis," or, more accurately, a "for-itself-in-itself." What is important for our purposes, however, is that Kierkegaard maintains— and, on this point, Sartre agrees—that the significance of Hegel's thought is his *attempt* to form a philosophic system that embraces the development of knowledge and reality.

In *Concluding Unscientific Postscript*, Kierkegaard acknowledges that Hegel considered the relation of knowledge to reality by beginning with immediate experience. But Kierkegaard objects that Hegel's thought does not take immediate experience immediately; that is, Hegel's system does not justify its own movement to immediate experience. Rather, it is evident, Kierkegaard continues, that Hegel arrives at the importance of immediacy through reflection. Is Hegel's personal relation to his dialectic important? Kierkegaard's answer is yes; the explication of the relation of knowledge to reality must reveal the movement of subjectivity itself.[30] In agreeing again with Kierkegaard, Sartre situates himself within his own dialectic: "To seek the beginning of knowledge is to affirm that the foundation of temporality is, precisely, timeless, and that the historical individual can wrench himself free of History, desituate himself and relocate his fundamental timelessness by a direct vision of being. Temporality becomes the means of intemporality. Naturally Hegel was aware of the problem since he placed philosophy at the end of History, as truth-that-has-come-into-being and retrospective knowledge. But this is the point: History is never finished, so this atemporal reconstitution of temporality, understood as the unity of the logical and the tragic, becomes in turn an object of knowledge. From this point of view, there is no being at all at the beginning of Hegel's system, but only the person of Hegel, such as it had been fashioned, such as it fashioned itself"[31] (Sartre, *Between Existentialism and Marxism*, 153).

30. *"How does the system begin with the immediate? That is to say, does it begin with it immediately?* [Kierkegaard's italics] The answer to this question must be an unconditional negative" (*Concluding Unscientific Postscript*, trans. David F. Swenson [Princeton, N.J.: Princeton University Press, 1941]), 101.

31. Sartre also distinguishes between the universal singular and the singular universal (168– 69). For example, what is important about Genet is not that he took a universal condition of lan-

To further expand on Sartre's discussion, in *Fear and Trembling,* Kierkegaard interprets the Hegelian dialectic as a movement of subjectivities. All
that is significant for human existence occurs on a higher level than objective
truth, which is assumed to be valid. Thus beauty, virtue, and faith are the result of subjectivities that are irreducible to their objective conditions. Further,
these subjectivities are *contingent* events that *might never be.* Beauty is the
result of a "leap" brought about by the "aesthetic knight." In analytic terms,
the objective, historical situation may provide the necessary conditions for
beauty, but without aesthetic subjectivity, beauty would not exist for humans.

Of course, Kierkegaard's goal was to show that faith is not reducible to a
system, and it is here that his view is clearest. Abraham might never have been
the father of faith, and faith itself exists only when the subjectivity that brings
it about exists. *Objectively,* Abraham's faith can be pointed to as consisting of
a synthesis of the subjectivities of the aesthetic and ethical knights. The aesthetic knight's life is his commitment to a beauty that is embodied in the temporal and the finite. The ethical knight, on the contrary, renounces worldly
happiness for eternal rewards. In this context, Abraham's faith can now be
pointed to as a synthesis of the subjectivities of the aesthetic and ethical
knights. Abraham is totally committed to the present. He lives to have a son.
On the other hand, he is totally committed to the eternal. He will renounce the
son who gave meaning to his old age, the son who justifies his life on this
earth. In Kierkegaard's view, Abraham never renounces his conviction that he
will be happy in this life even as he gives up the only thing that can make him
happy in this life. It is faith, not the historical process, that brings this objectively unintelligible synthesis into existence. And this faith is not a monu-
mental act that, once made, no longer characterizes the individual. It is a continuing effort by which the individual synthesizes in life what is objectively
inconceivable.

Thus, the real dialectic, for Kierkegaard, is an affair between interiority
and objectivity. The "truth" of a Don Juan is not an interior disposition locked
in his mind, but a continuing, delicate balance between his pursuit of beauty
and his seduction of women. For Kierkegaard, it is possible to distinguish the
behavior of a Don Juan from that of a mere flirt, but one would have to have at
least the equivalent degree of subjectivity. Thus, Kierkegaard tacitly recognized the need to introduce the observer into the act of observation.

Still, as Sartre notes, Kierkegaard has given a great deal over to Hegel. He
has granted to Hegel that the entire making of history is not the task of individual lives. For Sartre, the true dialectic must bring together the insights of
Hegel and Kierkegaard. That Sartre sees Marx as doing precisely this, is, as

---

guage as poetry and expressed it in a singular way but that, on the contrary, he used language to
universalize the contingency that he was an orphan whose adoptive parents labeled him a "thief."
See also Robert Denoon Cumming, *Starting Point: An Introduction to the Dialectic of Existence*
(Chicago: University of Chicago Press, 1979), 38–48, 188–89, 261–72, 466–67.

already noted, clearly a historical reconstruction for the purposes of placing his own effort in the *Critique* in historical perspective.

### v. Being and the Meaning of Being

In two long footnotes, Sartre introduces the question of the relation of knowledge to reality. Although the following sections can be skipped, or returned to after a reading of the *Critique,* they are important for placing Sartre's study on a proper philosophic level.

From another perspective, Hegel's dialectic can be viewed as reducing being to meaning, or existence to a knowledge of existence. Sartre will return to the relation between being and knowledge frequently, for it is crucial to distinguishing an idealistic dialectic from a materialistic one. Here, he emphasizes that rejection of the Hegelian dialectic implies not that existence is irrational but only that existence is not a meaning. His remarks here are consistent with what he maintained in the introduction to *Being and Nothingness.* There, he was careful to show that *being* is never reducible to knowledge, even though, on another level, knowledge itself is a type of being: my concept of a triangle, insofar as it exists in my consciousness, is a type of being. But this being is not its three-sidedness: the *being* of my triangle is that of transcended matter; it is a quality of the unique materiality of my body. Nevertheless, for Sartre, being and knowledge are not separated, as Kant's noumenon and phenomenon are generally understood to be. In distinction to the Kant of the *Critique of Pure Reason,* who seems to maintain that the way things appear to us is not the way they are in themselves, Sartre insists that we directly perceive empirically existing things.[32]

### vi. Realism and Idealism

Sartre's view of the relation of being to knowledge is closely allied to his distinctively realist position. He has always recognized the insights of both traditional idealism and realism, although he considers their separate positions to be extremes. In the present context, he notes that the idealism of Hegel is valid insofar as it recognizes that being must be related to knowledge if explanation and truth are to be possible. The error of this idealism, however, lies in concluding from this relation that being can be reduced to a *knowledge* of being.

Thus, Sartre agrees with the general realist's position that the realm of being is different from the realm of knowledge. Nevertheless, he objects to any form of Cartesian realism that completely separates these realms. For Sartre, consciousness is not a mere mirror of existence; consciousness is rather part of the very fabric of the world.

This important point warrants some comment. The entire movement of

32. See *Commentary BN*, 4–13.

Sartre's earlier *Being and Nothingness* can be understood as a consistent attempt to avoid what he there terms the "extremes" of idealism and realism. In his earlier work on ontology, Sartre maintained that idealism is right when it insists that there cannot be a world without humans but wrong when it maintains that this world originates from human knowledge. On the other hand, realism is right when it insists that the world exists independently of human knowledge but wrong when it maintains that the world exists independently of human *reality.* Sartre's position, therefore, is that matter is internally altered into a world through the original fact of human existence on this planet. That is, the world exists independently of our knowledge but not independently of our being. If we briefly note that "being" for Sartre refers to our primary material condition, we can say that the world is the way it is because of the unique matter of the human organism.[33] The *Critique* unfolds within the framework of a position between idealism and naive realism already established in *Being and Nothingness.*

### vii. The Various Senses of Reflection

In the present context, the distinction between idealism and realism is also the question of the extent to which knowledge is active, altering the subject known. Since, however, philosophic knowledge is obtained by reflection, this issue brings us to consider the status of reflection. In a crucial footnote in the *Method,* Sartre examines the relation between the type of reflection present in the dialectic and armchair reflection. Sartre's notion of consciousness and reflection are important for a proper understanding of the *Critique,* and it may thus be useful to review his general position.

In *Being and Nothingness,* Sartre distinguishes between the prereflective and reflective cogito, and he further separates what he calls "pure reflection" from "impure reflection." All these distinctions are perhaps best understood through an example: When we are truly engaged in an activity such as reading, watching a movie, or playing tennis, we are not explicitly aware of ourselves as performing the activity; rather, we are aware of the activity itself. We say that we are "out of ourselves," and the time passes without our being aware of it. The spontaneous activity—watching a movie or playing tennis—Sartre calls the "prereflective cogito." It is a characteristic of these activities that their spontaneity tends to disintegrate. No matter how much I am, as it were, thrown out of myself into the very activity of playing tennis, every now and then there is a fleeting awareness that *I* am playing tennis. I may suddenly hear the sound of the tennis racket hitting the ball as the right sound of a good shot, and I am immediately thrown back to myself. These fleeting aware-

33. I plan to develop this distinctive anthropocentrism in a forthcoming book. The basis is found by reading the chapter in *Being and Nothingness* entitled "Transcendence" (171–218) together with the chapter entitled "The Body" (303–59).

nesses Sartre calls "pure reflection"; they do not interfere with the activity itself, but accompany it and disappear with it.[34]

If I should pause and concentrate on these fleeting moments of pure reflection, or later turn my attention to them, I then cease the activity and make it an object of my "impure reflection." Thus, after the game, I may question whether in fact I was playing tennis as well as I usually do. I become aware of myself as an object among other objects in the world. The "I" is the object of my activity, which is here the activity of reflection. I may come to some very mistaken conclusions as to why this self that I am examining played tennis poorly, just as I may come to some mistaken conclusions as to why another person played tennis more poorly than usual. From his earliest monograph, *The Transcendence of the Ego,* Sartre rejected the privileged status that is usually attributed to introspection. He insists that we have a more intimate knowledge of ourselves than others have, but not a more objective one. Thus, the prereflective cogito refers to spontaneous activities with their fleeting moments of pure reflection. The reflective cogito, on the other hand, is so-called armchair reflection; we cease an activity and stand back to examine it.[35]

These distinctions are complicated, because it is also clear that Sartre views all human activities as reflexive. The term "reflexivity" refers to both pure and impure reflection, insofar as they are distinct from a mechanical process. The distinctive characteristic of reflexivity is nothing other than awareness itself. Here our efforts to elucidate the nature of consciousness run into the limitation of language; our efforts to explain our own reality by reflecting on it must of necessity be imperfect and imprecise. Normally when we speak of awareness, we tend to refer to the moments of either pure of impure reflection, that is, to our more or less explicit awareness of *ourselves.* But, for example, when we are absorbed in watching a movie, we have not thereby become machines or robots. Spontaneous human activities are not blind; rather, we frequently maintain that our true character is revealed by our spontaneous behavior. Thus, the term "reflexivity" calls attention to the distinctive character of every act of consciousness, whether prereflective or reflective. Speaking

---

34. *BN,* l–lvi, 150–70, 333–39.

35. I am here considering consciousness in a very abstract, that is, local, context. Thus, I am not viewing the subject from the perspective of emotions, or self-deceptions. In a deep neurosis, or emotional state, the subject will seldom be aware of his prereflective condition. See Sartre, *Sketch for a Theory of the Emotions,* trans. Philip Mairret (London: Methuen & Co., 1962), 56–94; *BN,* 557–75. There is an evolution in Sartre's understanding of the relation of spontaneous behavior to the prereflective cogito. In the early works, from the *Emotions* at least to *Being and Nothingness,* the emphasis is on the significance of the individual's general prereflective project, so that a person who is prone to anger may at times behave joyfully, but the joy is not genuine. Later, Sartre will say of the bourgeois that although he can be characterized by his class consciousness, he does indeed enjoy such things as his family or fishing; the relation between the individual and class consciousness is, as we will see, a dialectical tension between one's local and one's historical existence.

metaphorically, every act of consciousness tends to bend inward, to collapse on itself, even while going spontaneously out toward its object. But, of course, this way of speaking about consciousness, while it may clarify some aspects, is too Cartesian to truly reflect Sartre's view. Consciousness, for Sartre, is not a mind; consciousness is the organic body precisely as it acts humanly.[36] A tall body may incline a young athlete toward playing basketball, but the playing of basketball is not tallness, but what consciousness does to tallness. Indeed, the consciousness of basketball playing is the human organism as playing basketball.[37]

In distinguishing between the prereflective and reflective cogito Sartre radically alters the Cartesian cogito, and, indirectly, acknowledges Hume's insight. Descartes was wrong in his assumption that the "I" reflecting is the same as the "I" found in reflection. The prereflective cogito is not our ego; it is not a self that unifies all our activities. Rather, it is the very activity of awareness. Thus, from this perspective, Hume is correct in insisting, contrary to Descartes, that the "I" that thinks today is not reducible to the "I" that thought yesterday.[38] Still, Descartes was correct in indicating an area in which certitude truly exists. In our moments of pure reflection we become simultaneously aware of our consciousness with its "nonthetic object," that is, we are aware of living in the world but we do not explicitly delineate the things of the world as objects of our reflection. For example, when I become aware of the sound of the ball hitting the tennis racket, I am simultaneously conscious of the act of being aware and of the sound of which I am aware. Within these fleeting moments of pure reflection, the bond between knowledge and being is perfect, although they are still not reducible to each other. The act of being

36. The use of such terms as "nausea" is meant to call attention to the fact that the cogito, for Sartre, is visceral; it is the body as negated and transcended. Some critics, such as Marjorie Grene, admit that Sartre speaks of consciousness as bodily, but Grene interprets this as an unsuccessful attempt to resolve an original dualism (*Sartre* [New York: New Viewpoints, 1973], 44–67, 229–239). Rather, Sartre's emphasis on consciousness, before his examination of the body, is only a methodological procedure. See *BN*, 305–6, 358–59; and see note 41 below.

37. Of course, for Sartre, from the perspective of the individual's freedom, it is also true to say that the consciousness of basketball playing is not basketball playing. A player may suddenly toss the ball aside and start fighting another player. Actually, the situation, for Sartre, is more complex than indicated here, for there is an internal relation between the prereflective cogito and the ego.

38. Sartre himself does not implicitly develop his notion of the cogito as distinct from those of Descartes and Hume. Nevertheless, as early as the *Transcendence of the Ego*, Sartre makes his position on the Cartesian cogito very clear: "In a word, the Cogito is impure. It is a spontaneous consciousness, no doubt, but it remains synthetically tied to consciousness of states and actions" (92). For a somewhat different interpretation of Sartre's *Transcendence of the Ego*, see Caws, *Sartre*, 50–61. Also, for a study of Sartre's notion of person in relation to the analytic tradition, see Phyllis Sutton Morris, *Sartre's Concept of a Person* (Amherst: University of Massachusetts Press, 1976).

aware of the sound is not the sound of which I am aware. Certitude does not exist here as a separate judgment; it is the very quality of the bond itself.[39]

Still, we are faced with an important problem concerning philosophic reflection. Sartre does not elaborate the relation of philosophic reflection to pure and impure reflection, but the philosopher must be engaged in some kind of armchair reflection. In *Being and Nothingness*, the implication is that philosophic reflection originates from earlier moments of pure reflection to which the philosopher can return. In this respect, Sartre's continual use of examples, both in *Being and Nothingness* and throughout the *Critique*, are not mere illustrations of a philosophic position, but invitations to test his conclusions within our own experience.

Sartre's position on consciousness can be restated by calling attention to his emphasis on what he terms the "being of consciousness," that is, the kind of reality a consciousness is. It is not possible to review here in detail his meticulous study in the introduction to *Being and Nothingness*.[40] Briefly, Sartre acknowledges Husserl's insight in describing consciousness as an intentionality; all consciousness is an awareness of something other than consciousness itself. For example, when I am engaged in watching a movie, I am not directly aware of *myself* watching the movie but of the movie itself. But Sartre goes further than Husserl in insisting that there is absolutely no content or unity to my consciousness other than the content or unity that comes from the object. Nevertheless, consciousness is not a blind force or a mechanical activity; it is the very awareness of, for example, the movie being watched. We can express this only inadequately, by saying that this watching is a *nonthetic self-awareness*.

Again, we must note that this distinction between consciousness and material activities does not imply that consciousness is *substantially* different from matter. Consciousness is not "a mental activity." Sartre rejects all forms of Cartesian dualism. There is only matter, although, because of consciousness, there are various states of matter, including consciousness itself.[41] Sartre de-

---

39. There is no need to speak here of an infinite regression. Every activity, including impure reflection, is from another perspective, a prereflective cogito. That is, reflexivity is an aspect of pure and impure reflection.

40. See *Commentary BN*, 19–48.

41. Compared with "inert matter," consciousness is the negation and transcendence of "matter." In this context, which is the context of the first part of *Being and Nothingness*, Sartre speaks of consciousness as a "nihilation," that is, a continual disintegration of inert matter and the coming-to-be of the world. Still, it is clear that the in-itself and the for-itself are, for Sartre, abstractions. Indeed, the for-itself cannot *even be considered* apart from the in-itself. The for-itself is the in-itself as already nihilated. The in-itself has a logical priority over the for-itself, but we never encounter it as such; pure, inert matter could be an object only for an angel or for God. Consciousness is thus not some activity distinct from that of the human body when it acts humanly, that is, for a purpose. Sartre did not need Merleau-Ponty to teach him this. The fundamen-

scribes this unique materiality of the human organism by stating that it brings negation into the heart of inert matter. This negation, as already noted in the Prefatory Remarks, brings about the distinctions of things, just as it allows for the unique "distance" that must separate a knower from the thing known.[42]

Thus, when Sartre refers to the "being" of the human reality, he is calling attention to this unique materiality of the human organism, a materiality that negates and transcends inert materiality, altering it into a "world." This "negation" is not a relation that can be explained once and for all. Sartre's notion of negation is crucial for understanding his philosophy, as it is developed both in *Being and Nothingness* and throughout the *Critique*. However, it seems best to develop this notion gradually as we proceed with our study.

Throughout the *Critique,* Sartre focuses his attention on the relation of knowledge to reality, and, in this respect, he distinguishes his approach from those of both Hegel and Marx. The first part of the *Method* makes it clear that Sartre is concerned with history from the perspective of its *being*. Here, in a long footnote (*Method,* 32–33; F, 30–31; NF, 37–39), he criticizes Marx and Lenin for their epistemological views. Once again, the issue arises of a dialectic unifying nature and history. Here, Sartre does maintain that Marx identifies both human beings and nature within the same materialistic dialectic. Sartre claims that a human being, for Marx, is not an alien being added to nature; knowledge and trees, subjectivity and history are all on the same order of being. All are objectively *there*. Lenin, Sartre continues, correctly sees that this view eliminates the possibility of knowledge and truth. Sartre insists, therefore, that knowledge is a reflection of what exists objectively. But this also eliminates the unique significance of knowledge and subjectivity. For Sartre, subjectivity is neither everything nor nothing. The irreducible uniqueness of an individual life may not alter the general course of history, but much of the particular content of history is made only by individual lives. In a different context, Sartre will agree that history demanded someone like Napoleon but point out that without Napoleon, *these* wars, with *these* deaths, might never have occurred. Furthermore, for Sartre, the "comprehension" of the dialectic is an essential aspect of it. Thus, as we will see, the unique being of the subject is an aspect of the being of the dialectic.

---

tal difference between Sartre and Merleau-Ponty is found on the level of being. For Sartre, all the meaning within being comes from the human reality. Sartre has never deviated from this position. For Merleau-Ponty—and, indeed, for Heidegger—there is at least an opening through which being can point to a meaning (in the loosest sense of this term) beyond that originating from the insertion of organic consciousness within the fabric of matter.

42. In this sense *only,* Sartre's position on the materiality of consciousness recalls Aristotle's distinction between the matter present in nonknowing and knowing beings. For Aristotle, the unique matter present in knowers receives forms as *other,* that is, as not forming a third composite. Sight does not become a red object when it senses red.

Sartre thus maintains that Marxism and indeed existentialism are midway between Hegel's emphasis on system and Kierkegaard's insistence on individuality. The philosopher must aim at comprehending totalization, but we will see that these totalizations are open-ended and that they incorporate but do not dissolve the irreducibility of either individual lives or historical events.

## 2. THE PROBLEM OF MEDIATIONS AND AUXILIARY DISCIPLINES

Throughout the *Critique,* Sartre is very much concerned with the crucial problem of reductionism, that is, the claim that an apparently unique phenomenon can be explained completely by reducing it to more basic elements. For example, those who maintain that thought is totally comprehensible in terms of the neurological and chemical activity of the brain are reductionists. Reductionism is very closely allied to foundationalism, the position that seemingly higher, complex realities can be deduced from a few basic fundamental principles. For example, a foundationalist would maintain that, given an understanding of human nature, one can deduce how an individual should behave in a particular circumstance.

In his rejection of reductionism and foundationalism, Sartre develops his own position between traditional Marxism and analytic and pluralistic philosophies. On the side of the Marxist, he insists that philosophy should be a totalizing effort. There is, for Sartre, *a* history and *a* method for comprehending this history. But on the side of the analyst and pluralist, Sartre insists on the irreducible uniqueness of an individual life, the local autonomy of a collective, and the basic significance of a specific historical event. The true philosopher does not shrink from the task of acquiring a single perspective and is also sensitive to the empirical findings of the "auxiliary disciplines," such as psychology, sociology, and anthropology. The philosopher, for Sartre, is well aware that the empirical findings of auxiliary disciplines are themselves interpretations. There are no isolated facts; every factual finding of the empirical sciences exists within an accepted scheme that is in itself not questioned by the sciences. Still, the realization that facts are interpretations does not justify reducing them to, or deducing them from, the scheme itself.

According to Sartre, reductionism is a form of idealism. We have already noted that idealism can appear in one of two forms. First, the usual forms of idealism attempt to dissolve all that is real and unique into subjectivity: the human contribution is all-important, and the world is viewed as a projection of human consciousness. Second, subjectivity can be reduced to objectivity. This seeming realism is also actually an idealism; the consciousness that supposedly contemplates this completely objective world would have to be a pure mind with no intrinsic relation to matter. Sartre, on the contrary, maintains that the real exists independently of subjective interpretations, and yet he also insists that epistemology must model itself after the truth of microphysics, namely, that the observer is intimately bound with the act of observation.

The problem of mediations is important, because reality is complex; the philosopher is not justified in considering individual lives and events only from the perspective of their ultimate significance. The traditional Marxist mistakenly believes that we know everything important about a life if we know it is bourgeois. "Valéry is a petit bourgeois intellectual, no doubt about it. But not every petit bourgeois intellectual is Valéry. The heuristic inadequacy of contemporary Marxism is contained in these two sentences" (*Method*, 56, F, 44; NF, 53). Furthermore, if we are to understand the true significance of an individual's life, we must consider the person not only as an adult but also as a child. The philosopher must use the discipline of analysis, and for Sartre this means existential analysis, the principles of which he laid down in *Being and Nothingness*. Thus, we cannot deduce the concrete significance of an individual life from the general clashes of history, although it is indeed true that history gives the abstract meaning of a life. Indeed, we must not assume that the importance of an individual life is merely a private affair and that history moves of itself on its own level. Rather, both the individual life and the general historical process reciprocally influence each other and are integrated into a complex, open-ended totality. Where, for example, a life is lived "privately"—as is frequently true today—that life is a historical event that says as much about the age as about the person.

Mediations are also needed not only to reveal the uniqueness of an individual life, but also to elucidate the distinctive reality of a "collective." Again Sartre introduces in the *Method* a theme that he later develops at length in the *Critique:* One of the distinctive features of human historical existence is that it is lived amid collectives. A collective, for Sartre, is not a mere aggregate; it has its own unique existence, an existence that possesses less reality than an individual but more than that of a mere aggregate or concept. A newspaper, for example, is a collective; its unity is more than that of a pile of rocks, but less than that of an animal. Also, its existence has less reality than an organism but more than a concept. One of the essential points in the *Critique* will be to establish that these collectives do indeed have a distinctive unity and existence and to show that totalizations must respect this uniqueness as well as that of individuals. For example, in examining the stock market, the dialectic must study not only the individuals buying and selling stocks but also the elusive reality of the "stock market."

Finally, Sartre notes that mediations are needed because we must expect to encounter discontinuities in our study of history. For example, the movement from individuals to the objective meaning of their work, and from individuals to collectives, is not continual. Discontinuities are irreducible happenings that must be studied as they appear.

## 3. THE PROGRESSIVE-REGRESSIVE METHOD
### i. A Sketch of the Method

The progressive-regressive method allows one to respect the individual uniqueness of each action and event as well as its place in the open-ended totalizing movement of history. This method is an extension of the natural way we comprehend a human action. Sartre gives the following example: If I am studying with a friend and he suddenly gets up to walk toward the window, his action both unifies and clarifies our situation. My comprehension of his action is "progressive," because I spontaneously grasp the goal of his action, to open a window. At the same time, by a "regressive" movement, I become aware of the room being too hot. Previously, when I was absorbed in reading, I had passed through this heat and experienced it only as a vague discomfort. But now a new action has been introduced into the room, an action neither reducible to nor deducible from the heat of the room. We both could have continued reading, and a third person entering the room might have called us "library rats" because we seemed unaware of the heat. Not only is my "comprehension" of the cause and of the effect simultaneous, but the phenomena themselves—heat-as-cause and opening-of-window-as-effect—came into being simultaneously.

After this initial comprehension, the progressive-regressive movement begins again: My friend's action of opening the window is not an abstract behavior but a very specific way of opening the window. If he *flings* the window open, I comprehend his action on a more concrete level. Then by another regressive movement, I recognize something very fundamental about his personality and his project: I see the exuberance of his behavior. Thus, my attempt to explain my friend's action mechanically as resulting from a chain of stimuli would miss the concrete meanings of his behavior.

Technically speaking, "to comprehend" a situation and to grasp it through the progressive-regressive method are one and the same. However, the English term "comprehension" has too intellectual a connotation. For Sartre, the term implies both an intellectual knowing and a personal experience: I introduce my own reality in the very act of knowing an object. For example, as I see my companion heading for the window, I pass from my vague realization of discomfort to an explicit awareness that the room is "hot." I further internalize his behavior as directed toward the relief of this heat. The abstract possibilities of my friend's actions are dissolved when I consider them in the concrete, and I consider them in the concrete only when I introduce my own existence in the situation. Theoretically, I could imagine someone going toward a window and merely looking out of it. From a positivistic viewpoint, from the perspective of a neutral observer of "atomistic facts," I should suspend all judgment about the meaning of my companion's action until I actually see him open the window. But this abstract possibility dissolves in the light of my own concrete experience in *this* heated room with *this* companion.

To repeat, the first movement of the dialectic as praxis is necessarily progressive and synthetic. The intentionality of consciousness requires that human actions be understood initially as directed toward a goal, a goal that is itself a synthetic whole of which the individual and the situation are merely moments or aspects. Afterward, a regressive movement can attempt to analyze the components that brought the action about. This distinction between a synthetic and an analytic approach to phenomena separates Sartre's philosophy from much of contemporary analytic philosophy.

The analytic, reductionist philosopher maintains that only what can be reported by instruments exists objectively; but if wavelengths exist objectively because they are reported by a machine, why do not colors exist objectively, since they are reported by the eye? It seems strange to call "subjective" what every human being experiences when placed in the same situation. If every human being sees a stick in the water as "bent," it is strange to say that this is a subjective judgment. Indeed, the analytic stance implies an idealistic perspective of a nonhuman mind knowing in a nonhuman way: we imagine how a stick would appear to an observer in a vacuum. The stick in water indeed appears the way it should appear when the light from it passes through the medium of water to the medium of air and reaches a human observer.

The reductionist would regard Sartre's view as anthropocentric, but, for Sartre, there is nothing wrong with being anthropocentric where humans are concerned. A picture is, for example, a human artifact, and to see it in a human way is to see it "objectively." Of course, the brute material components are also objective, and on each of these different levels the phenomenon can be completely described. Given an analytic approach and scientific equipment, the reductionist will indeed describe all that is *there,* and what is there is not colors as they are seen by any human eye but a quantity that is the proper object of a machine.[43] A scientific apparatus does indeed report an aspect of reality. By maintaining, however, that this aspect *is* reality, the reductionist converts a realist philosophy into an idealist one. Nature becomes the Cartesian world known by a pure mind. Matter is an idea. On the contrary, Sartre insists that pure extension is only an abstraction that we never encounter in human experience.

### ii. Levels of Reality and Comprehension

Sartre retains his initial phenomenological approach to reality as he develops the dialectic in the *Critique*. The phenomenological approach to reality can be described loosely as a "return to things," that is, a return to

43. For the present purpose, there is no need to adopt a more critical perspective on art or to consider Sartre's own views of the activity of the imagination in the forming of a picture. Fur-

the world as it is experienced by human beings. The prereflective awareness of an object and the phenomenological description of it are, however, only the first steps in the progressive-regressive movement. A human action or a historical event does not have a simple basic structure; it is a multileveled phenomenon. As we have noted, these levels must be integrated, and the uniqueness of each level must be respected. Here again, an example may clarify what I understand to be Sartre's program.

Following R. D. Laing's lead, it is possible to give a Sartrean interpretation of certain forms of madness as resulting from early childhood choices occasioned by unbearable family conditions. Parents who regret having had their child may make no effort to hide their feelings. If the child is raised in relative isolation, with no close friends, he or she may feel that living in the real world is unbearable. The child spends more and more time in a fantasy world, a world that becomes more real as the environment is experienced as increasingly intolerable. The child gradually abandons himself to a private world and language. The parents do not recognize what is happening; their attitude toward the child is primarily dictated by their economic situation. Because of the child, for example, both parents may have had to drop out of school and accept menial jobs.

A traditional Marxist interpretation would see the child's insanity as resulting from the economic conditions and bourgeois goals of the parents. But Sartre would insist on the uniqueness of the child's tragic choice. Another child might have been able to "wait out" the experience, or, more tragically, might have committed suicide. This child's insanity, with its unique world and its unique language, is an individual project. It cannot be explained by the general, alienating, economic conditions of the adult society. Sartre claims that the condition of alienation can modify the result of an action but not its profound reality. Given the initial circumstances, the child's behavior must be affected by some type of alienation, but this general condition does not explain the insanity itself.

To explain what occurs in the child's action, Sartre, as we will see, claims that we should describe "the internalization of the external and the externalization of the internal." We must see praxis as a movement from objectivity to objectivity through intentionality. In our example, the child externalizes his internalizations by gradually projecting a more pleasant fantasy world as "there."

The study of the child's situation must reach the child at his own level, and at this level the psychoanalytic interpretation is the most concrete. From a more general, indeed more "basic," perspective, it is true that the child's in-

thermore, as we have already noted, Sartre's anthropocentrism is on the level of the being of the world.

sanity is produced by his general historical situation. This situation can now be brought in, but it must be introduced in a way that retains the significance of the child's choice. The progressive-regressive movement thus begins from an understanding of a phenomenon on each of its levels. It continually goes back and forth between these levels, attempting to achieve a totalizing knowledge that retains the irreducible uniqueness of each level.

In the *Method,* Sartre sketches several examples of the progressive-regressive movement, but the one he returns to most frequently is the example of Flaubert and *Madame Bovary.* I will mention here only a few of the highlights of this example. Flaubert's *Madame Bovary* was regarded as a realist work. A traditional exposition, an exposition that Sartre calls "lazy," would have attributed the success of *Madame Bovary* to the fact that the age demanded works of realism. But a closer look at Flaubert's life reveals that the activity of writing was his unique way of coping with his family environment. Also, in *Madame Bovary,* Flaubert describes a feminine aspect of his personality: *Madame Bovary* is a description of a masculine femininity. Finally, Flaubert hated realism. What we have to ask ourselves, then, is what kind of realism did the age in fact create for its own needs, and how did it alter *Madame Bovary* for its own purposes? Flaubert's work thus illuminates not only his own project but also the age in which he wrote.

The individual's behavior is thus considered as a "spiral," and the union is more one of tension than one of homogeneity. As with Flaubert, the individual may relive an early "wound" on different levels, and the concrete significance must be examined differently in each situation. The "truth" of an individual's life is thus a complex unity of the historical truth of his class and the concrete truths of his daily life.[44]

This brief exposition of the *Method* is but an introduction to the task of the *Critique,* and its main purpose has been to provide a correct perspective on Sartre's philosophy. For Sartre, the task of philosophy is to raise the consciousness of the average person so that history can be made self-consciously. At present, a great deal of our history is the result of inhuman forces directing our destiny. Marxism, for Sartre, was a gigantic effort in the nineteenth century to create a unified, self-conscious proletariat that could direct its own history. Sartre notes that it is too early to achieve this goal. There are many proletariats because there are many national production groups. But both the *Method* and the *Critique* were written, Sartre says, to help us achieve the understanding that we need to make our history in common.[45]

44. See Hazel E. Barnes, *Sartre and Flaubert* (Chicago: University of Chicago Press, 1981), 78, 82–84, 87–88, 90, 363–66.

45. The *Method* has a brief conclusion. Some of its material has already been discussed, and some of it will be integrated throughout our discussion.

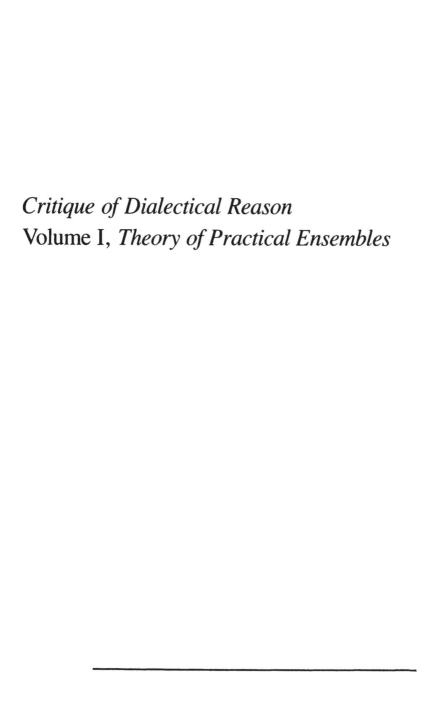

*Critique of Dialectical Reason*
Volume I, *Theory of Practical Ensembles*

# INTRODUCTION

# 1    The Dogmatic Dialectic and the Critical Dialectic

## 1. (DIALECTICAL MONISM)[1]

The main purpose of the argument in the two parts of the introduction is to present a framework for establishing the validity of the dialectical
method; this also entails solving the general problem of the relation of historical knowledge to historical reality. It would be convenient if we could simply
accept the existence of historical events and then look about for a method to
describe them. But every method tailors its object to itself. Thus, even the
progressive-regressive movement introduced in our preceding study of Sartre's
*Problem of Method* accepted uncritically the existence of historical events.
But here we must question whether, for example, the existence of the Boston
Tea Party or the fall of the stock market in New York during the Depression are
indeed events with their own unities. The dialectical method thus works on a
different level than the progressive-regressive movement. Speaking metaphorically, the dialectical method knows itself to be an interpretation and accepts the challenge of validating itself.

The claim that the dialectic validates itself and thereby establishes itself as
*the* method for studying history puts it in conflict with the seemingly modest
claims of positivism.

To restate what was said in the background chapter, the task in *Being and
Nothingness* was to show that all conceptual and reflective knowledge is subsequent to a more primary bond of consciousness to being. This bond *to* being
is itself a bond *of* being; this means that all reflective and conceptual knowledge is based on the link between the unique materiality of the human body
and the distinctive matter of the world. It has already been noted that this
bond is not amenable to a foundationalist interpretation; there is no single,
univocal relation to which all conceptual relations can be reduced. Rather, in
each case a separate study will reveal that a particular conceptual explanation
of phenomena—such as the scientific description of color as either a wave or a

---

1. The original French text gives subdivisions but no subtitles.

movement of protons—originates, in some way, from a lived relation between the matter of the human body and the matter of the world. This does not imply that a phenomenological reduction can be the basis for scientific knowledge: the fact of the relative densities of molecules of wood and water cannot be mapped onto the commonsense knowledge that pinewood floats.

The two terms of the relation, the unique matter of the body and the unique matter of the world, are both material but nevertheless irreducible to each other. Moreover, in their separate states they are both abstractions, although in different ways that are not important to elaborate at this time. Thus, we never experience either the isolated human body or the brute matter of the world. We live within the totality that is our being-in-the-world, and philosophic reflection accepts this totality as a given.

As we have seen, Sartre always rejected the critical stance of Cartesianism, namely, that ideas are the immediate object of knowledge and that we know the world only through the mediation of our ideas. For Sartre, we experience the world directly, as when our hand touches the metal of a doorknob or the bark of a tree. The sense of touch not only reveals our bond of materiality with the world but also highlights the fact that the observer is always involved in the act of observation. The very act of touching a thing alters the thing touched: a rose picked is no longer a rose.[2]

Although the heuristic principles of the *Critique* are not deducible from those elucidated in *Being and Nothingness*, they are within the same general context of negation and materiality. Sartre begins the *Critique* with the claim, "Every thing we established in *The Problem of Method* follows from our fundamental agreement with historical materialism" (E, 15; F, 115; NF, 135). It is Marx's materialism as well as the social dimension of his thought that attracts Sartre. I believe it will be clear that Sartre radically reinterprets Marx's historical materialism within the context of his own unique realism. In *Being and Nothingness*, this realism implied that the world is the way it is because consciousness "happened" to matter, and in the *Critique* Sartre will say that nature is a human adventure. To describe the event of human consciousness as

2. See Thomas R. Flynn, *Sartre and Marxist Existentialism* (Chicago: University of Chicago Press, 1984), 197–98; Pietro Chiodi, *Sartre and Marxism*, trans. Kate Soper (Atlantic Highlands, N.J.: Humanities Press, 1976). Flynn is correct in noting that the dialectic must be able to distinguish what is given from what is taken. But criteria for this distinction cannot be given in advance, and Flynn himself has indicated this difference between the given and the taken in his excellent study of the three generations of the bourgeoisie (157–67). (See below, chapter 8; 2, ii.) Chiodi agrees that the Marxist attempt to apply the dialectic to nature and history is, at present, on questionable ground (112–23). In other respects, however, Chiodi attributes a Cartesianism both to Sartre's earlier philosophy and to his dialectic, which effectively eliminates the distinctiveness of Sartre's dialectical nominalism (xii–xiii, 14, 18–19, 23–25). Chiodi disregards the crucial distinctions between alienation on local and historical levels and instead gives his own criteria for a univocal notion of alienation (90).

a contingency, or "happening," is to emphasize that, while events retrospectively may appear to lead up to the appearance of consciousness, they do not account for its successful appearance. Given that Melville produced *Moby Dick,* his earlier works can be seen as leading up to his masterpiece, but these earlier works did not of themselves imply the production of *Moby Dick.*[3]

Sartre's philosophy thus emphasizes the appearance of novelty, but this emphasis does not imply that novelty is irrational. Prior to the advent of consciousness and its unique mode called "reason," nothing was rational; the human organism—whose praxis is, from different perspectives, reason, will, and action—establishes the parameters within which things appear as rational or irrational, contingent or necessary. Necessity does indeed exist but only as a consequent of the primary contingent event, the happening of consciousness.

In *Being and Nothingness* the philosophic procedure for describing the totality, consciousness-within-a-world, was a modified phenomenological description. Phenomenological descriptions are particularly suited for describing the nonhistorical. These nonhistorical phenomena are nevertheless temporal: they have a past, present, and future. But temporality is not of itself historical; historicity is a de facto, regional, human phenomenon. Some primitive societies are not historical, and, for Sartre, there is no way to deduce historicity from the abstract condition of human consciousness. Still, where it occurs, and it is fast occurring throughout the globe, this historicity is not an epiphenomenon; that is, it is not a superficial modification of some more basic human condition. Rather, when and where historicity occurs, it intrinsically alters the very mode of consciousness so much that, in respect to it, members of primitive societies are an alien species.[4]

For Sartre, historicity introduces into the world a complexity that can only be properly examined by the dialectical method. This method, to repeat, is not constituted in a vacuum and then applied to objects. The critical validation of the dialectic is the topic of these two introductory parts and, to a great extent, the topic of the entire *Critique.* At this time only a general indication can be given as to why the study of an historical consciousness should require a distinct method: in the world of so-called nature, we cannot alter the primary structure of things because we cannot change our bodies with their given

3. In this context, Sartre hints that all evolutionary theories *assume* the existence of a drive for sustaining life. This drive appears as a radical "happening"; *Given* the successful appearance of a new species, biological theories can then be said to "explain" their appearance from lower species.

4. One can, of course, point to the fact that members of primitive societies easily become acclimated to civilized society. But civilized human beings could just as easily become acclimated to an extraterrestrial society without denying the "alien" character of extraterrestrial life. Nevertheless, all humanity shares the distinctive modes of consciousness characteristic of the human body. These modes are not an essence but rather a general context in which consciousness can develop in radically different ways.

senses. Freedom thus confronts certain givens, such as the redness of the rose. This redness can be reinterpreted but it cannot be eliminated. A bunch of red roses may signify love in our society and hate in another. A historical object, however, such as the French Revolution, is more complex, because it is itself a reification of freedoms; it exists not because the body is the way it is, but because innumerable individuals made certain choices. A distinctive approach is thus needed to reveal freedom in action within the object itself.

Clearly, the above explanation is itself debatable. Some historians would say that chance or necessity causes history, and not free human actions. We seem to be caught in a dilemma of first having to prove that history is the result of individual free choices and then needing a method to reveal that history is caused by the action of separate freedoms. This dilemma, however, is nothing but the healthy circularity of the dialectical method, a circularity that works both because we are within it and because it is conditional. Thus, in *Critique I*, Sartre says that he is accepting uncritically the existence of one history for humanity. The existence of *a* history rather than many histories was to be established in the second volume. Accepting uncritically a single history for humanity, Sartre establishes in this volume the validity of the dialectical method for examining human historicity, and he reveals the existence of distinctive objects such as "collectives." Nevertheless, it does not follow from this caveat that the entire *Critique I* is conditional; it may still be a valid description of a more regional history, such as that of Western Europe.

## 2. (SCIENTIFIC AND DIALECTICAL REASON)

In this second section, Sartre continues his efforts to establish the suitability of dialectical reason's self-validation. As in *Being and Nothingness,* the task is to develop a position that avoids the pitfalls of idealism and naive realism, but the task here is more complicated because Sartre is considering the more concrete situation of human historicity.

Within the perspective of the *Critique,* we can say that idealism is right in accepting the task of reason's justifying itself. In this respect, a naive or scientific realism pretends to mold itself according to the characteristics of the object being studied. These realisms accept a correspondence theory of truth: the mind is a tabula rasa within whose neutral passivity the object unfolds with the identical characteristics it has outside the mind, and truth is nothing more than the reflective recognition of this de facto conformity. The mind is thus like a camera, truth like a well-developed picture. But the idealism of Kant and Hegel have always correctly pointed to the activism implicit in this passivity. Returning to our analogy: The chemicals in a photographic plate actively discriminate among the innumerable waves that impinge upon it, reacting only to the small segment of the electromagnetic spectrum that is visible to the naked eye. A photographic plate sensitive to infrared light would show a completely different picture. Although idealism correctly emphasizes the active aspect of knowledge, it has lost sight of the material context of knowledge. Consciousness for the idealist is the consciousness of the active intellect, and truth is nothing more than the intelligible form of the object. The idealist has lost what was correct in the realist attitude, namely, that matter is not produced by knowledge and that its intelligibility cannot be reduced to the activity of an intellect. The activity of the chemicals in a film implies waves or photons existing independently of the film.

Historical materialism, for Sartre, insists both on the active role of consciousness and on the irreducible materiality of its objects. Dialectical materialism must thus develop a notion of truth that is distinctive to itself, one that describes a monism in which the two distinct materialities of knowledge and object operate. Because traditional Marxists have failed to do this, they have naively accepted the correspondence notion of truth, and they conceive of knowledge as illuminating its object within an idealistically neutral background. Our study is thus on the level of a study of being, not in the sense of an ontology which questions, for example, what it means for a tree to be a thing, but in the sense of a dialectical study that constantly questions the bond between praxis and its object.

### 3. (HEGELIAN DOGMATISM)

Unlike the Hegelian dialectic, our dialectic must show that there is a dialectical relation between ourselves as dialecticians and our entire dialectical procedure. We must thus be aware that our critique of Hegel is itself dialectical. For example, we must not think that our examination of Hegel's position is merely an objective recognition of a philosophic error. This recognition exists, but it is within our own project of establishing the validity of the historical dialectic. Thus, what becomes significant is that Hegel saw himself at the *end* of a history. He did not have to prove the dialectic, because it had already occurred. The grand totalization, the unification between knowledge (*savoir*) and being, had already been effected, and thus Hegel clearly did not see himself as an "idealist" in our present sense of the term.[5]

### 4. (THE DIALECTIC IN MARX)

Unlike Hegel, Marx regarded himself as still within "prehistory," in which, for example, the meaning of *the* proletariat was not yet fixed. He interpreted the dialectic for his own time; he recognized a genuine future with completely new events. According to Sartre, Marxists, however,

---

5. In the text, Sartre claims that in Hegel's own time there existed seeming indications of the unity of knowledge and reality. These included the success of science in controlling nature and the critical accumulation of historical knowledge that made the present appear completely intelligible.

have not taken up the task of rethinking the dialectic for our time but instead have applied it as if it were some form of Kantian "a priori" that merely needed new contents.[6] But the dialectic must be validated again, and positivists must be shown that totalities do in fact occur.

## 5. (THOUGHT, BEING, AND TRUTH IN MARXISM)

Sartre has been objecting that pluralistic and positivistic attitudes actually hide an uncritical monism. This objection, however, seems to present a dilemma, because a critical and conscious monism appears to be idealistic. Hegel could thus affirm that the dialectic was the single method for understanding itself and its object, because the real for him was the same as the rational. Knowledge and being were on the same level. Thought was thus both constituting and constituted; that is, the content of thought was constituted by its object, and, reciprocally, thought thereby became aware of itself as constituting the intelligibility of the object.

Sartre objects to Hegel's idealistic monism, and he agrees with Marx that being is irreducible to knowledge and that praxis outstrips knowledge. Nevertheless, the dialectic is indeed a knowledge, and, precisely as a knowledge, it does not seem capable of encompassing the irreducible uniqueness of action. Again, the Hegelian, idealistic dialectic eliminated this dilemma by the insight that thought is itself being. The dialectical character of being was thus established by the identical act that captures the dialectical movement of knowledge. As we have noted, Sartre has always rejected this idealistic perspective because it does not distinguish between the being of knowledge and the knowledge of being. That is, it does not respect the distinctive materialities of both knowledge and being.

In one sense, Hegel is right, thought *is* being. But this statement hides an ambiguous use of the term "being." The term can refer either to the existence of something independent of our thinking about it or to the distinctive *way* in which something exists, as when we search for the "being" of X. In the first sense, a thought is a being; for example, my thought of a triangle is a being because it exists in my consciousness independently of another's awareness. Sartre's important point is that "being" can also mean the being *of* something, and in this sense it refers to the distinctive way a quality "exists." In this sense, the being of thought is not reducible to the being of things. For example, the materiality of my perception of the existing red rose is not the materiality of its existence, nor is the redness as an intelligible quality reducible to the state of being red. Both the perception of red and the red existing outside my perception are materialities, but they belong to different orders.

The contradictions within idealism do not of themselves solve the dilemma

---

6. See below, Introduction, chapter 2, note 4; book I, chapter 4, note 5.

inherent in a correct dialectic. We must confront the paradox that the historical dialectic is *monistic precisely because it is dualistic:* thought is material but is not reducible to the materiality of things. We could easily sidestep the dilemma by affirming that thought and action are separated but merely happen to move along parallel courses. This Leibnitzian harmony would eliminate the reality of the mutual way thought and being react. What we have to aim for is a monistic relation that accounts for and reveals both the relation and irreducibility of knowledge and being. The Hegelian dialectic ceases to be dialectical when it affirms the final reducibility of knowledge and being. The dialectic, however, must always, at each instant, retain its dialectical character; not only must thought and being be dialectical, but the relation between them must also be dialectical.

Consequently, Sartre insists that the dialectic is different when the aspects related are different. *In this sense only,* his view is reminiscent of the analogy of proper proportionality. This analogy is *not* illustrated by the usual example that two is to four as four is to eight. There is no analogy exhibited here, because two is half of four *in exactly the same way* as four is half of eight. A true illustration would be that a loud, piercing sound is to the ear what a loud, bright color is to the eye. Here, the analogy is a proportionality between proportions. One can never abstract from these proportions a univocal quality, such as "loud." In a universal concept, however, the Aristotelian notion of "man" for example, it was given that a notion of humanity could be abstracted from Socrates and still include Socrates as one of its instances. Referring to this comparison, we can say that for Sartre the dialectic can never be abstracted from the things that are related dialectically. Nevertheless, this "analogy" must be used only as a guide. In the classical context, analogy properly referred to terms, and it operated within a clear distinction between terms as signs of concepts and concepts that were themselves signs of things. In Sartre's nominalism, however, language is a praxis, and the distinctions between "concepts" and "terms" is something established by human reflective practice.

### 6. (THE EXTERNAL DIALECTIC IN MODERN MARXISM)

According to Sartre, Marxists adopt an easy solution to the problem of the relation between knowledge and reality. They eliminate knowledge as a distinctive phenomenon. For them, the dialectic is a univocal dialectic of pure nature; that is, matter unfolds by itself through laws that are intrinsic to it. Human beings are simply the spectators of nature's development; knowledge is simply a mirror of reality.[7] Effectively, the traditional

7. See "Background" chapter, section vi.

Marxists eliminate knowledge as a distinct phenomenon by resolving it back into the world. This "abortive" attempt to understand the world Sartre calls "*external,* or transcendental, dialectical materialism" (E, 27; F, 124; NF, 146): it applies the dialectic to humanity from a position outside human history.

### 7. (THE DIALECTIC OF NATURE)

For Sartre, the external dialectic is not truly dialectical, although it was referred to by Engels: "The materialistic outlook on nature means nothing more than the conception of nature just as it is without alien addition" (E, 27; F, 124; NF, 146).[8] That humanity is referred to as "an alien addition" gives the clue to the way this scientific realism views human knowledge: any distinctive quality to knowledge is regarded as "alien." The ideal here is that knowledge should evaporate itself in its object. All the insights of Kierkegaard are lost. Subjectivity is viewed as distorting our awareness of history rather than as contributing toward history. Indeed, for Sartre, the Marxists have no realization that the totality, "natural history," may itself be a human phenomenon. True, we accept hypotheses that have been tested by facts as objective laws. But the totality, the "fact-hypothesis," is to a great extent correlative; facts and hypotheses reveal and support each other.

Sartre does not elaborate here on how science develops from human freedom. Rather, his efforts are to show that the dialectic must develop between two extremes. An idealistic dialectic is rejected because it would attempt to show that nature and science are solely products of knowledge and reducible to the intelligibility of knowledge. Thus, against Hegel, Sartre insists on the irreducibility of being to truth: the materiality of things is not reducible to the materiality of knowledge. At the same time, Sartre rejects the scientific monism of Marxists who would reduce history and knowledge to aspects of a grand, materialistic dialectic of nature. He calls attention to a different aspect of the unique quality of truth and its irreducibility to being. Truth is what happens to being when we are inserted within its fabric. Thus, the human phenomenon is neither all of being nor an epiphenomenon in being.

### 8. (CRITIQUE OF THE EXTERNAL DIALECTIC)

In sections 2 and 3, Sartre criticized the idealistic dialectic of Hegel; here he examines in more detail the scientific dialectic of Marxists. Most of this criticism has already been mentioned, but because scientific

---

8. Sartre credits this remark to Marx, but the editor of the English translation notes that it appears instead to be from Engels, from "an unused section of a draft of [his] *Ludwig Feuerbach and the Outcome of Classical German Philosophy.* The text of this unused section appears as a section of *Dialectics of Nature,* trans. C. P. Dutt, Moscow, Progress Publishers, 1934, pp. 195–9" (E, 27).

thought is so frequently and uncritically accepted as the ideal of human knowing, these arguments warrant restatement and a brief elaboration.

Effectively, Sartre's argument is that both scientific and traditional Marxists' realisms are hidden idealisms. First, although these apparent realisms talk about matter, they are concerned with the idea of matter rather than the living complexity of matter. Although Sartre does not make his remarks from the perspective of Berkeley's critique of Descartes, this approach would seem to be appropriate. Descartes claimed that qualities such as color and sound are merely subjective. What exists outside the mind are simple, extended, solid bodies that are interpreted by consciousness as qualities. Berkeley, however, correctly noted that we never experience pure extension and that a quantity without qualities is merely an object to satisfy the mind. Of course, Sartre would reject Berkeley's conclusion, namely, that matter is indeed only an idea. But I believe that he would accept the implicit critique: if matter exists, it is the proper object of a living body and not directly an object of a thematic study.

Descartes's position was consistent insofar as he saw a need to justify a supposedly certain knowledge of pure matter. Consciousness could contemplate pure extension because consciousness belonged to another realm of being, the spiritual. (Descartes was aware of the scholastic view that consciousness could know all material bodies only if it were itself not material.)

Sartre does not develop these sections precisely along these lines. In the previous section, he objected to Pierre Naville's claim that "a *subject* is only an object considered as the center of particular reactions." Here he continues his criticism, noting that this apparently modest claim actually hides an a priori foundationalism and that it is a dogmatic postulate of absolute truth. We must question from what perspective one can defend Naville's claim. If consciousness is *merely* a center of delayed reaction, consciousness is not itself a delayed reaction; it is rather a superhuman description of the human condition. Indeed, the apparent humility of positivism hides the desire for a superhumanity, namely, the desire to know how the world would be without human beings. Sartre asks what kind of doubling of personality is represented by persons who see themselves as *merely* moved along by the external dialectic of matter and yet are *sure* of the movement. If thought is nothing but the manifestation of a mechanical dialectic, it cannot think itself or us. What appears to be merely a recognition of the necessary way reality works is really a form of alienation: *it is one's own living thought conceiving itself as a universal consciousness that in turn understands itself as if it were the consciousness of another.*

According to Sartre, Engels also falls into this trap: Engels criticizes Hegel for imposing the dialectic on matter, but he himself effectively does the same when he claims to deduce the dialectic from nature. If the dialectic were deduced from nature, it would be a scientific hypothesis. It would be determined as a scientific law by an analytic reason. This reason could recognize the dialectic only as a contingent happening. Thus, the dialectic as an intelligible law of history would be imposed on history by analytic reason, that is, by a pure reason that could study the dialectic as one object among many.

The continuing development in the *Critique* will make it clear that Sartre is not simply opposed to analytic reason. He does question the acceptance of such reason as the "natural reason" for understanding the world. For Sartre, analytic reason is rather a tool to fit human needs arising from a historical situation. On the other hand, analytic reason may mask its historical origins and thus become an ideology; pluralism and the correspondence theory of truth may appear to flow from human nature itself.

## 9. (THE DOMAIN OF DIALECTICAL REASON)

In this last section, Sartre summarizes the first part of the introduction and sketches the plan of the book. The parameters of historical materialism are determined by distinguishing it from the scientific, monistic materialism of Marxists. It is indeed conceivable, Sartre notes, that some day the dialectic may be shown to be valid in the inorganic realm; but at present our information does not warrant this assumption. These Marxists thus invert the proper order of certainty: the present, historical condition of humanity establishes the validity of the dialectic in the social realm. Here, and not in the realm of the inorganic, historical materialism reveals itself as a dialectic from within; it exists because the praxis of individual human beings brings it about; "it must be the same thing to produce it and to have it imposed on one, to live it and to know it" (E, 33; F, 129; NF, 151).

We can, Sartre continues, indicate at this time some of the conditions that have to be fulfilled if we are to attain a knowledge of the historical dialectic. These conditions will, in different ways, reinforce the single requirement, namely, that *nothing can ground the dialectic except the dialectic itself.* Sartre goes on to list conditions:

1. The dialectic must be able to be validated in our everyday experience. This grounding must sustain the contradictory relation between everyday facts and rational necessity: there is no historical necessity that I arise from bed at 8:05 A.M., and yet all historical necessity arises from individual facts such as these. The idealist solutions of Kant and Husserl explain away this contradiction: Kant maintains that the mind *imposes* necessary structures on facts; Husserl claims that the essential structures of facts are revealed by their relation to pure consciousness. But the dialectical method works within the contradiction that necessity exists in our contingent, historical experiences.

2. The dialectic rejects spiritualism, affirms materialism, and yet insists on the irreducibility of knowledge to being.

3. We must accept Marx's claim that "men make their own history . . . but under circumstances . . . given and transmitted from the past" (E, 35; F, 131; NF, 154).⁹ Sartre interprets this statement to be a rejection of both analytic reason and determinism. Even where analytic reason affirms freedom, it treats history as an *average* of the innumerable action of individuals. Determinism claims that history results completely from prior conditions. If the dialectic exists, we should be able to find a dialectical rationality that is more than an average and yet not produced by blind laws of necessity: Individual praxis should be revealed as producing totalizations that in turn produce a history, and this history produces human reality.

4. The above-mentioned reciprocal determination must not be understood in a Hegelian sense; praxis outstrips knowledge and creates genuine novel events. Events work on human beings, but human beings rework events. In this reworking, Sartre will later distinguish superficial relations of exteriority with things and persons from deeper relations of interiority.

5. The dialectic must accept the idealist goal that reason founds itself, but it must reject the foundationalism of this view. There is no wider, nondialectical perspective from which the dialectic can be justified. Nevertheless, the dialectic does not validate itself in one stroke as an abstract schema that is then imposed on facts. If the dialectic is true, it is so because material conditions are such that it must be true. From this perspective, the dialectic is a nominalism; that is, what exists are individuals and totalities produced by individuals. But from another perspective, this same nominalism must justify intelligibility and necessity as well as establish the contexts for the analytic meaning of "necessity."

More generally, dialectical reason must show that analytic reason is a moment within its own development. Here Sartre simply indicates that, to the extent to which the scientist adopts a passive attitude of a neutral observer of nature, nature responds as the totality of neutral events. Thus, if the dialectic exists, it can become apparent only to those of us who see our actions contributing to the meaning of our present epoch and who also see the epoch acting on us. We must be able to see in each of our actions something bigger than our actions, and we must be able to return and see both as simply our praxis. The dialectic must be shown to be perfectly "translucent" because it is us, and it must also be shown to escape us. This will not be a mystifying experience but simply our dialectical understanding of ourselves.

The term "translucent" has caused a great deal of confusion in Sartre's philosophy. Neither here nor in *Being and Nothingness* has it ever meant a clear,

---

9. The editor of the English translation gives the following reference: Karl Marx, *The Eighteen Brumaire of Louis Bonaparte*, vol. 1 of *Marx and Engels: Selected Works* (1962), 257 (E, 35).

reflective understanding of ourselves as objects of thought. It is also not to be understood in the analytic sense of possessing clear and distinct ideas. Negatively, the term implies a rejection of the Cartesian thesis that ideas are the immediate object of knowledge. Thus, consciousness is translucent in the sense that it is an *immediate* awareness of things, an awareness that does not occur through the mediation of ideas. Returning to our earlier example of playing tennis: translucence simply refers to the fact that while absorbed in playing tennis we *are* the awareness of tennis playing. This awareness does not mean that our reflective understanding of what tennis playing means for us is translucent, but simply that consciousness flows directly into every action that is distinctively human. Tennis playing is neither an explicitly reflective endeavor nor a blind, automatic response; it is rather the translucent union of consciousness with its nonthetic object. The term "translucence" indicates not only a rejection of Cartesianism but also a denial that empirical existence can be bracketed. Sartre's notion of intentionality, therefore, is a repudiation of both Descartes' methodical doubt and Husserl's bracketing of empirical existence.

# 2  Critique of Critical Investigation

## 1. (THE BASIS OF CRITICAL INVESTIGATION)[1]

The main point of the first part of the introduction was to show that *if* the dialectic exists it must be a monism that is also a dualism; that is, the dialectic must itself be a materiality that can respect the irreducible unique materialities of knowledge and being. The second part of the introduction focuses attention on the conditional aspect of this critical investigation, the question of whether the dialectic *does* exist. It is, however, important to keep in mind that the present introductory critique of the critical "experience" does not attempt to establish the truth of our dialectic. This task is not separate from the content of our critical investigation. Rather, our constant goal here is to avoid pluralism's illusion of neutrality by preparing ourselves to recognize the degree to which the *type* of questions we ask determine the *kind* of objects we may find.

A bond of being, that is, a bond of materiality, exists between dialectical reason and its dialectical object. In the concrete, dialectical reason and its object exist separately only as abstractions. The term "abstract" always implies a relation to the term "concrete"; for Sartre, the context gives the different specific meanings of both terms. Here, the concrete is the synthetic totality, dialectical-reason-dialectical-object, and the abstractions are the moments, dialectical reason and dialectical object. In the present sense of the terms "abstract" and "concrete," only the synthetic totality exists. Thus abstraction here means what can be examined apart from its whole but cannot exist as such. Since we cannot examine everything at once, our study here is on the abstract moment, dialectical reason. Failure to recognize that all of Sartre's major philosophic writings proceed from the abstract to the concrete, in the above sense of these terms, accounts for much of the present misreading of these works, as we have already noted.

1. We must recall that the titles of the subdivisions are added by the editors. The French title of this chapter is *"Critique de l'expérience critique."*

The distinction between the method of investigation and the existing realities being investigated is not crucial in an analytic or pluralistic approach; these methods naively assume that they merely happen to come upon the object if it happens to exist. Use of the dialectical method includes an awareness that, to a great extent, the method brings its object into existence. As we have seen, the dialectic accepts from idealism the insight that consciousness is active, although it rejects the idealist's claim that reason produces either the material content of the object or its a priori structures. We must also recall that the bond between dialectical reason and its dialectical object is itself dialectical. This bond is a materiality that respects and reveals the irreducible materialities of its own synthetic moments, dialectical reason and dialectical object. Finally, we must keep in mind that when we are suspending critical judgment on the existence of *a* history, although we accept naively that, to some extent, we are within *a* history.

Sartre will frequently return to note the conditional status of the critical investigation throughout the *Critique*. Although no true example is possible prior to the unfolding of the *Critique* itself, a very loose illustration may be useful at this time.

If we return to our examples of tennis playing, we can observe that it is a material phenomenon: The balls, rackets, and court are organized into a synthetic totality through the activities of the people playing tennis. Within this synthetic whole, playing tennis, we can regressively distinguish two "moments": the physical bodies, human and inorganic, precisely as physical, and each player's consciousness of playing tennis. Each individual consciousness, however, is nothing other than a human body precisely as it is human. *Thus, the material monism that is tennis is composed of two irreducible materialities, the bodies as physical and the bodies as consciousnesses.* While these two orders of materiality can be separated only by an act of abstraction, this distinction is genuine. Thus, the height and weight of the players and the specific materials that make up the tennis rackets, balls, and the matter of the court all contribute their own irreducibly unique quality to the playing of tennis. If the players are heavy and slow, the tennis rackets weakly rather than tightly strung, the balls dead rather than lively, and the court made of cement rather than of clay, the materiality of the game would be different that if, for example, the players were light and swift, and the other material conditions the same.

Thus far, our illustration does not imply a dialectic because it does not consider tennis playing as *historical*. We now have to question to what extent tennis playing is not only a whole, but also a totalization, that is, an open-ended totality that is included in ever-widening circles of totalizations until we reach *a* historical "tennis playing." Here we encounter the dilemma spoken of above: *this* tennis playing is historical only if there is *a* historical tennis playing, and, reciprocally, *a* historical tennis playing exists only as the totalization of individual games of playing tennis. Sartre's procedure is, as it were, to temporarily suspend *critical* judgment on the existence of *a* worldwide tennis playing. We recognize on a naive level that this game is called tennis because there are rules applicable throughout the world to every game of tennis. Furthermore, there seems to be a procedure for ranking tennis players throughout the world. Nevertheless, at this time we suspend critical judgment as to the status of world tennis playing. We critically investigate only whether this tennis playing is indeed a totalization. We still remain aware that we are continually operating within the synthetic totality, regional-tennis-playing-world-tennis-playing. Failure to keep the synthetic whole in mind would cause the dialectic to degenerate into an analytic, or positivistic, approach based on a correspondence theory of truth in which the human mind is merely the passive mirror reflecting reality. Also, there is no attempt here to "bracket," in a Husserlean sense, world tennis playing, which remains as the horizon of the investigation.

Our illustration of a tennis game may now suggest some reasons why the game is not merely a synthetic whole but a totalization. Let us assume that both the players and those watching are implicitly aware that they are not professionals. Their order of rank may not be spelled out, but it is implicit in the activity of playing and watching the game. One is spontaneously aware that one is a beginner or advanced amateur. Tennis playing, with all its rules, is not a game that arises naturally on a desert island. One is initiated into it *serially* and *hierarchically,* and this initiation is a quality of the game itself. We are ranked as soon as we begin to play; we are aware of ourselves as learning quickly or slowly, as having a naturally good or weak forearm or backhand. Every stroke we make and every reflective judgment about our playing participate in a hierarchy of totalizations that lead to and are influenced by a world meaning of tennis playing, *assuming uncritically that there is such a meaning.* But, even if there should not be *a* world meaning for tennis, there would have to be a meaning to some extent, for example, throughout America or Europe, to explain our hierarchical comprehension of the game. Finally, the circularity of this investigation works only because we either play tennis or can imagine ourselves playing. We must see ourselves within the investigation if its circularity is not to be a vicious one. Tennis playing is consequently a dialectical comprehension insofar as it is the spontaneous way we enjoy watching an international competitive match between players whose distinctive movements embody the rules of the game in its hierarchical, competitive order of totalization.

This illustration is meant to highlight four points: (1) totalizations are characteristic of our historical life; (2) we comprehend these totalizations only by being within them; (3) totalizations are aspects of a monistic dialectic that is also dualistic; and (4) the proper method for studying totalizations is "critical investigation" that works within the totalization, critically examining the totalizations that are regional while uncritically assuming, for the present, the existence of a historical one.

The hypothetical nature of this critical investigation gives it a certain superficial similarity to the validation of a scientific hypothesis. An important difference is that a scientific hypothesis hides the degree to which it determines the very facts that are sought in its support.

## 2. (DIALECTICAL REASON AS INTELLIGIBILITY)

Our procedure here will superficially seem to follow a positivistic approach, in that we will indeed, Sartre remarks, look to the object as the guide of this study. In this respect, we acknowledge that dialectical reason exists, if there are regions in which totalizations do in fact occur. But, as we will see, our study is not analytic or pluralistic. An analytic approach could never recognize "dialectical objects," if they existed. At the very least, an analytic perspective brackets the tension and feedback between the observer and observed. We must be conditionally open to the fact that we are uncritically using dialectical reason, even as we look for dialectical objects.

According to Sartre, totalizations characterize *our* history. We are accustomed to speaking very generally about history as starting with the invention of writing or city life. The practice of writing and the development of city life may indeed be necessary conditions for our history, but they do not indicate what is specifically unique in living our historical lives. We frequently assume implicitly that there exists a human nature which becomes superficially different because it happens to live in a society that practices writing and is in general civilized. It is useful to recall from the *Method* the influence of Kierkegaard on our approach. Kierkegaard's objection to the traditional approach toward Christianity was that it viewed a good Christian (or Jew) as merely a good Greek who happens to believe differently. In this view, Abraham just believed different objective truths than did Socrates but lived the same type of ethical life. Kierkegaard's point was that if Christianity does not intrinsically alter an individual, then it is not worth talking about. In a sense, Kierkegaard turned the Hegelian dialectic within the subject, and he claimed that where the dialectical moments were synthesized, they were done so not by abstract thinking but by the way we live. In a similar, but not identical, way Sartre's important point is that *we speak meaningfully about our historical life only if our history is a quality that affects our every spontaneous and seemingly natural thought and action.* Sartre says, "It is therefore necessary for the critical investigation to ask the fundamental question: is there a region of being where totalisation is the very form of existence?" (E, 45; F, 137; NF, 161).

But, although we may turn our attention to the object of dialectical study, our approach is only superficially positivistic. The dialectic, in fact, must manifest a double intelligibility. First, the dialectic must include its own intelligibility; it must be able to validate itself dialectically. A positivistic approach does not justify its own intelligibility, because it does not validate its own correspondence theory of truth. It assumes that there are "things" and that they are reflected in the mind as in a mirror. Second, the laws that elucidate historical facts must be themselves dialectical. Thus, the traditionally understood Kantian approach is eliminated, because the (a priori) forms would be imposed on a brute matter that is given but not itself explained by the forms.[2]

In opposition to positivism and the Kant of the *Critique of Pure Reason*, Hegel seemed to maintain that the dialectic encompassed both itself and its object. But Sartre maintains that Hegel himself ultimately adopted a nondialectical perspective on his dialectic. Because he thought that he stood at the end of the dialectic, Hegel could see the dialectic of history. In this respect the dialectic appears as Hegel's objective *description* of the dialectic. He reverts to the correspondence theory of truth: his exposition of the dialectic is a mirror of the dialectic. But if there is a dialectic, Hegel must be within it, and he must show us how his own awareness of the dialectic is dialectical. In this respect, Kierkegaard seems to be right: Hegel is nowhere to be found within his system. In the context of our present study we can ask how the thought of a well-educated, well-fed German is related to the consciousness of the average person of his own time. Did other people pay a price for the "condition for the possibility" of Hegel's existence?

I have here somewhat interpreted Sartre's critique of Hegel. In the text, Sartre mainly notes that, taken in isolation, Hegel's dialectical laws, such as that the negation of a negation is an affirmation, appear gratuitous when stated as laws of reality. What Sartre seems to mean is that these laws cannot explain the origin of reality from the law that the negation of a negation is an affirmation. Furthermore, we do not see how Hegel's own praxis forms the dialectic. Sartre, on the contrary, places himself explicitly within his own dialectic. For example, we will see him maintain that his *Critique* would have been impossible prior to Stalin, and, more importantly, that he is explicitly aware of his own status as a French bourgeois intellectual.

### 3. (TOTALITY AND TOTALIZATION)

We have already seen that we can be said to live within totalizations insofar as our lives are historical. In this section, Sartre distinguishes a totalization from a totality. A totality is a being that is distinct from the sum of

2. Sartre notes: "I am thinking here of the *Critique of Pure Reason* rather than of Kant's later works. It has been clearly demonstrated that, in the very last part of Kant's life, the requirement of intelligibility led him right up to the threshold of dialectical reason" (E, 43 n. 21; F, 136 n. 2; NF, 160 n. 1).

its parts and yet, from a certain perspective, wholly present in all its parts. For example, an organism is a totality: a tiger is distinct from the sum of its parts in the sense that its integral parts, such as its paws and ears, are, in their severed state, the paws and ears of a tiger only analogously. Furthermore, insofar as the ears and paws are truly parts, the tiger is wholly present in them. When hidden danger approaches, the ears are the tiger as listening; in chasing a prey, the paws are the tiger as running.

In the *Critique*, however, we are not interested in organic totalities, but in humanly created ones, such as symphonies and paintings. Sartre regards these as obvious but extreme examples because their unity exists only in relation to the activity of a consciousness. In his *Psychology of the Imagination*, Sartre has shown that we project, through the successive notes and dried paints, the totalities of *the* symphony and *the* painting.[3] These extreme cases help us to have a proper perspective on the totalities we are concerned with in the *Critique*, such as *the* machine. For example, an automobile differs from an organic totality because its unity is in relation both to past human creative acts and to future human uses. But this relation is not translucent; machines have an inertia of their own, and they tend to have a purpose of their own. In the abstract, an automobile is an extension of our legs, but in the concrete, a car has purposes and needs of its own, such as fuel and space. Sartre will continually return to discuss the characteristics of these man-made totalities that have a life of their own. They are part of the "*practico-inert.*" On the other hand, unlike all types of totalities, a totalization is continually being formed by a present activity. Thus, as long as a totalization exists, it is an open-ended process. Furthermore, in a totalization, the parts and the whole are simultaneously being developed by the totalizing act itself. Sartre will give examples of totalizations in the *Critique* proper. Here, following a hint in the *Critique*, we will merely sketch an illustration.

A house or apartment in our historical society differs from a dwelling in a primitive society in that the apartment implies a hierarchy of totalizations. A primitive dwelling and a historical home have in common that they both mutually define themselves and their inhabitants; that is, by making one's home in a shelter one makes it into a dwelling, and, reciprocally, the shelter-made-into-a-dwelling alters the individual into a dweller. A renter of an apartment (or a purchaser of a house) differs radically from a simple dweller in that initially and prereflectively the renter's act of dwelling involves a hierarchy of totalizations; moreover, there is a unique reflective awareness of this hierarchy of totalization. In renting an apartment or purchasing a house, one enters a hierarchy of totalization, such as purchasing furniture, taking out loans, and, in

---

3. Sartre, *The Psychology of the Imagination*, trans. Bernard Frechtman (Secaucus, N.J.: Citadel Press, 1966), 74–77. The sounds and pigments function as analogues.

general, entering the series of renters and house owners. In this respect, Sartre notes that the dialectical intelligibility is the very movement of totalization. Thus, *the consciousness of renting is an integral part of the act of renting.* Finally, the rented apartment, the renter, and the act of renting form a dialectical totalization, such that the entire ensemble is wholly intelligible in each of its parts from a certain perspective. If we understand what paying rent means for this person, we would understand, from a certain perspective, the concrete significance of the life of a renter and the apartment as something that is rented. The ability to pay very high rent characterizes the social standing of the person as well as the social status of the apartment. Furthermore, this totalization participates in a hierarchy of totalizations that characterizes social standings throughout a good part of the world. A room becomes an apartment not only through the behavior of the individual but through large-scale economic and social forces as well. These forces are open-ended, and it is one of the tasks of this study to show their relation to praxis.

### 4. (CRITICAL INVESTIGATION AND TOTALIZATION)

In this brief section, Sartre emphasizes what he has already indicated, namely, that our present *critical investigation* cannot be regarded as an attempt at a nondialectical justification of the dialectic. If the dialectic carries its own intelligibility, then the critical investigation must be a moment of the dialectic itself. Sartre notes: "In practice, this means that the critical investigation can and must be anyone's reflexive experience" (E, 48; F, 140; NF, 165). In the following sections, Sartre will clarify the meaning of the terms "reflexive" and "anyone."

### 5. (CRITICAL INVESTIGATION AND ACTION)

The editor's subtitle is here misleading, for this very brief section deals mainly with clarifying the term "reflexive" used above. In this respect, Sartre makes it clear that his present study develops from the more abstract position on consciousness taken in *Being and Nothingness.* We have already seen that in *Being and Nothingness* Sartre characterized consciousness as reflexive, and that he showed how this reflexivity can be either a pure or an impure reflection. Furthermore, we have also seen, in general, how reflexivity—pure and impure reflection—occurs in a historical consciousness. When Sartre notes here that reflection is not parasitical but is instead a distinctive structure of consciousness, he is referring to impure reflection, that is, to armchair reflection, which is itself a distinctive praxis. His point is that just as armchair reflection produces thematized objects appropriate to it, such as my concept of myself as a good or poor tennis player, dialectical reflexivity will produce its own distinctive, individualized universals, such as the notion of bourgeois respectibility explained in book II. Sartre interestingly adds that all the concepts forged by history, including that of humanity, are individualized and must be understood in reference to an individual praxis. But again, we must recall that "individual" does not of itself mean an isolated individual.

The unique reflexivity characteristic of the dialectic cannot, therefore, arise in a nonhistorical context. If it is to be historical, the moment of reflexivity must itself be historical; that is, the critical investigation can only arise when the general historical totalization has reached its own moment of reflexive self-understanding. We must recall that this investigation is aimed at comprehending our specific history, not just any possible history. It thus leaves only the characteristics of unknown areas of totalizations, although Sartre notes that he will later consider to what extent extrapolation can be made. Such extrapolation, however, can never be dialectical knowledge, although it may yield useful information.

### 6. (THE PROBLEM OF STALINISM)

In section 4, Sartre said that this critical investigation can and must be anyone's reflexive experience, and in section 5 he clarified the term "reflexive." Now he elucidates the term "anyone."

This section will be understood only if we constantly keep in mind that we are attempting a *historical* study of history. If we are to reveal true historicity, it cannot be studied from a nonhistorical perspective. We must always situate ourselves within history while examining it. We must know the *who* of the investigation.

For Sartre, the dialectical awareness of totalizations did not occur before Hegel and Marx. Nor did the need and possibility of a *critique* occur before Stalin effectively put the dialectic on a wrong path. By attempting to obscure the very notion of dialectical rationality, Stalin put the final touches on the separation between thought and action that is characteristic of our time. Sartre seems to mean that, prior to Stalin, alienation was merely a lived alienation that could, in principle, be redirected by a direct knowledge of Hegel and, especially, Marx. Stalin, and Stalinist Marxists, so effected a "divorce of blind unprincipled *praxis* and sclerosed thought" that there no longer exists a possibility of rethinking directly the thought of Marx, as a practical affair. The thought of Marx is not a Platonic form that can be recaptured by a reading of his works. Indeed, a "personal" attempt to understand the "real Marx" would presuppose a type of alienation that the writings of Marx could not exhibit, namely, the alienation of a private life encountering history.

Anyone situated within history at the present time can give a critique of totalizations, more or less explicitly. Sartre notes that many such critiques are being made, and all, including his own, are debatable. Furthermore, the separation between thought and action that is characteristic of our age requires us all to reexamine our intellectual tools. The problem is deeper than a lack of a "will to act." A separation between thought and action is embodied in our institutions and general environment.[4]

## 7. (THE PROBLEM OF THE INDIVIDUAL)

This important section makes it clear that Sartre will retain his earlier interest and concern with the individual throughout the critique. He reminds us that, in the *Method,* he had maintained that our approach requires us to situate ourselves in relation to the ensembles that we are investigating. He also recalls briefly the general features of consciousness that were laid out in *Being and Nothingness,* namely, that the reflexive bond, as opposed to reflective union, between consciousness and its nonthetic content is a bond of being and thus apodictic. From our present perspective, this is simply our prereflective awareness of our lives as historical, that is, an awareness of our lives insofar as we continually totalize ourselves from birth to death.

Our approach will be successful if we can show that as we become more concretely aware of our lives, we become more conscious of the extent to which we are included within a hierarchy of totalizations. We must be able to go from our individual lives to history and see how our selves dissolve in history, and we must also be able to return and see how our selves have been formed by history. This requires that we see how our individual praxes are dissolved in the praxes of groups and series, and how our individual praxes are realized in group praxis. In this way, we will be able to understand to some extent the "truth" of our praxes.

Our approach, Sartre notes, will thus be the opposite of that indicated in the *Method,* where the dialectic as a praxis and a comprehension proceeded progressively: In the example given in the *Method,* the meaning of walking to the

---

4. "Far from plunging into dialectic at the start, he relies on analytical reason to inquire whether dialectical reason exists" (Marjorie Grene, *Sartre* [New York: New Viewpoints, 1973], 192). On the contrary, Sartre begins within an uncritical notion of the dialectic arising from both common sense and the historical tradition. In this historical sense the dialectic begins "a priori." Lévi-Strauss has also missed this important distinction in methodology: "In reading the *Critique* it is difficult to avoid feeling that Sartre vacillates between two conceptions of dialectical reason. Sometimes he opposes dialectical and analytical reason as truth and error . . . while at other times these two kinds of reason are apparently complementary, different routes to the same truth" (*The Savage Mind* [Chicago: University of Chicago Press, 1966], 245). As a "tool," the analytic reason of science can be a source of either benefit or harm. A scientist who attempts to show that "intelligence" is "naturally" found in a higher degree in a certain race or sex is indeed using analytic tools for oppression. Lévi-Strauss himself, to his credit, does not have a univocal notion of "analytic." Again, it may be useful to recall the medieval scholastic notion of analogy. The very distinction between analogy and univocation is that if the former is valid, one can never abstract the analogates from the analogon. In an "analogous way," if the dialectic is valid, one would never be able to formulate dialectical criteria that are independent of the act of dialectical comprehension. But this comparison between analogy and the dialectic assumes a distinction between terms, concepts, and things that does not apply to Sartre's dialectical nominalism.

window is the intention of opening the window to let in fresh air. In this simple regional case, the method and the praxis coalesce, because the behavior is limited to its immediate context; there is no process or hierarchy of totalizations. In the *Critique,* however, the object of the investigation is the unity of history itself, a unity that cannot be accepted as critically given. The *Critique uncritically* assumes the existence of *a* history, while critically turning its attention to those regressive steps that could justify a single historical outlook, if one indeed exists. Thus, our critique, as a method, starts with the existing individual *as already formed by totalizations.* It tries to elucidate these totalizations, retracing the levels of our present praxes in order to show how they include a hierarchy of totalizations without a totalizer.

The *Critique* therefore begins with the existing individual, but it does so abstractly. The existing individual is, of course, not abstract, but the individual's self-awareness frequently is. For example, when we awake in the morning, we may be aware simply of the need to prepare for another day's work. This awareness can become more concrete as we reflect that it is raining and we should leave earlier in order to get a space on the bus. Again, when we leave the apartment and purchase a newspaper, we can become aware that we are not only commuters but members of worldwide groups and series, such as consumers, investors, tenants, or homeowners.

## 8. (TOTALIZATION AND HISTORY)

This second part of the introduction is thus called "Critique of Critical Investigation," to indicate that from the very beginning we are adopting a critical attitude toward our own dialectical approach. As we have seen, this critical attitude implies our explicit recognition that we are within history as we are examining it. Specifically, this critical attitude implies that we must attempt to introduce a concrete, lived notion of the past within our critical investigation.

In *Being and Nothingness,* Sartre had already distinguished the lived past of temporality from the abstract past of time.[5] Briefly, my lived past is the nonthetic context of my consciousness; it is the "weight" of all that I have experienced and learned. It is also, according to Sartre, my body precisely as that which I continually surpass. My lived past is my thoughts, gestures, and actions insofar as they come from the context of my past actions. My lived future is the specific goal toward which these thoughts, gestures, and actions aim. My lived present is not a moment but a presence of things to my consciousness. Temporality is thus an aspect of consciousness itself.

Time, on the other hand, can be conceived as a linear projection into an

---

5. In *Being and Nothingness,* Sartre interpreted Heidegger's original contribution in *Being and Time.* Temporality can be imagined as a three-dimensional temporal spread, within which consciousness appears as a directional line, a vector.

imaginary horizon, in which the past is the origin of a movement, the future is the point toward which the movement is supposed to go, and the present is the point where the moving object actually is. Here an example may highlight this distinction. It is to this linear notion of time that we refer when we say that last year we visited Paris. On the other hand, temporality is indicated by the phrase, "I have never been the same since my trip to Paris." The difference between temporality and time can degenerate into a difference between a synthetic and analytic approach. Thus, the statement "I have never been the same since my trip to Paris" would be explained analytically as indicating a state of consciousness existing in a present moment that includes an extrinsic relation to a past event through an act of memory. A synthetic approach might now attempt to bring together these analytic aspects as a unity of perception. Through memory, for example, I perceive myself to be the one who has visited Paris. But as lived temporality, the phrase points to a modification of my organism such that the prereflective past of my present is my former trip to Paris: I now live so that my trip to Paris spontaneously affects at least some of my thoughts and actions.

Sartre's point is that if history is indeed a series of totalizations, then it should be an aspect of our present consciousness. We must recall that we are working under the uncritical assumption that history is *a* totalization. *In the abstract,* the positivist and pluralist could be right: there is no a priori reason why our lives could not have developed as a series of independent and unrelated endeavors. But our present experience does not support this interpretation. When we examine primitive societies, for example, we appear to have *a* historical perspective from which we identify them as nonhistorical. If there is *a* history and if history is indeed characterized by totalizations, then all of history must in some non-Hegelian way be present in each of our lives.

In our attempt to understand how history is present in each of our lives, we must not imagine that we are attempting to reconstruct events as they occurred. Historical events do not exist within us as geological layers, and we are not attempting here an "archaeology of knowledge."[6] What we wish to reveal is the presence or influence of historical events in our lives, what Sartre terms the "relations of interiority" between praxis and its historical object. In this respect, we must recognize, Sartre says, that a friendship in Socrates'

6. Michel Foucault, *The Archaeology of Knowledge,* trans. A. M. Sheridan-Smith (New York: Harper & Row, 1976), 126–31. As we proceed, Sartre may appear to be maintaining that the conditions for the possibility of our history are similar to Foucault's historical a priori. But it will become clear that any type of historical a priori is merely one moment in the dialectic, namely as an aspect of the counterpraxis of the practico-inert. Foucault has perceptively shown that, during certain epochs, broad analogies exist among the accepted modes of discourses in apparently disparate disciplines, such as economics and biology. Sartre would not deny this authorless praxis, but he would insist that this is one movement in praxis, and, more significantly, that the changes in epochs are due to changes in praxis.

time did not mean the same as a friendship today. Nevertheless, if there are totalizations—even if there is no essence to friendship—we must be able to recognize, within our present bonds of friendship, the influence of those bonds that existed during the time of Socrates. In my critical attempt to understand the meaning of *my* friendship, I reconstitute the earlier bonds of friendship that existed, and I also recognize my own present bond of friendship as reciprocally reconstituted by those earlier bonds. It is true that my lived past is what I transcend or surpass in my praxis. Nevertheless, critical investigation makes me aware that I am able to deepen my comprehension of my lived past by recognizing how it has been reconstituted by earlier totalizations. This investigation also shows how, in my present attempts to understand these reconstitutions, I am reconstituting my lived past.

I understand the distinction between past as past and the past of our present to be one of the most crucial points in the *Critique*. It implies (1) that we can have only probable knowledge of what friendship actually meant in the time of Socrates, a knowledge that can always be made more accurate through analytic studies; and (2) that we can have *certain* knowledge of a "historical" Socratic meaning of friendship *that we presently sustain in existence*, as well as a certain knowledge of the relation of this historical friendship to our present notions of friendship. The first meaning of Socratic friendship is determined by historical studies and concerns the *past as past*. The second, the object of the *Critique*, concerns the *past of our present*. The progressive-regressive movement operates primarily within the second meaning of friendship. The dialectic aims at comprehending why we sustain a particular perspective as "a historical event," and how this illuminates our present goals. To return to our example, we commonly refer to "Platonic" friendship as asexual. Why do we do this when it is also part of our present historical awareness that the Greeks frequently united the intellectual and the sexual in their relationships? We may indeed be mistaken about our understanding of Greek sexuality insofar as it concerns the issue of the past as past. But the question remains: Why do we sustain a notion of Platonic friendship as "asexual" when we are also aware of a historical notion of Socratic friendship that implies sexuality? What does this past of our present tell us about our views of friendship and sexuality? The progressive-regressive movement, or to use the more fitting term in relation to the *Critique*'s investigation, the regressive-progressive movement, attempts to reveal the dialectical ties among all our notions of friendship, although, to repeat, the emphasis is on the past of our present. Failure to recognize this distinction between the past as past and the past of our present has occasioned misreadings of the *Critique*, for example, in regard to the notion of scarcity, which is examined later.

Unfortunately, these analytic distinctions do not convey the *Critique*'s aim exactly. The dialectical perspective simultaneously considers the fact that the study of the past as past is itself an aspect determined by our present human relations, relations that tend to posit "events" as given prior to interpretation.

The dialectic thus moves diachronically, that is, deeper into the past, as it moves synchronically, that is, within a present participation in a hierarchy of totalizations. If history is still happening, it must be present in me and I in it. I must see myself not as merely carried along with the history, but as tied to history with bonds of interiority.

In the body of the text, and in a long footnote in this section, Sartre initiates what is to be a continuing critique of analytic reason: the implicit context of analytic reason is that it is possible to approach a study with an objective mind free of all preconceptions and, furthermore, that it is possible to have a super-perspective on all our own learning. But the myth of an untutored mind innocently examining its objects is, Sartre notes, as dangerous as the myth of the noble savage.

In general, Sartre's thesis is that the entire edifice of analytic and scientific reason—with its rules, concepts, and objects—is produced by a broader notion of reason, dialectical reason. The purpose of this production is to satisfy our needs, such as the need to control and manipulate the world. Thus, Sartre notes that science is like a machine in that it is also the exteriorizing of interiorization and the interiorizing of exteriorization: we thematize and externalize our prereflective awareness of the world into both laws and machines. From this perspective, dialectical reason is also the claim that reason, even insofar as it appears naturally to have the characteristics of universality and necessity, is the result of praxes.

We must not think that the dialectic produces analytic reason in an idealistic or Cartesian sense. The very view that consciousness produces concepts as its natural object of study is itself a construct of consciousness. We must keep in mind that consciousness, for Sartre, is the body as *human;* it is the diverse modes of reflection, perception, and praxis. Consciousness is a transcending and negating materiality and not a mind constructing objects.[7]

### 9. (PRIMARY AND SECONDARY INTELLIGIBILITY)

This difficult section is concerned with the intelligibility of the dialectic. We are so accustomed to accept the models of intelligibility from science and analytic reason that it requires an effort to think in other terms. As

---

7. From this perspective, dialectical reason is the claim that all reason, even as it appears to be a universal mode of thinking, is itself the result of praxes. In an extended footnote, Sartre elaborates on how geometric proofs are consequent upon a lived encounter with space. For example, the geometric proof that a line which intersects a circle at one point will, as it continues, intersect the circle at another point, is consequent upon the lived perception of the circle as an enclosing space and of the line as a static movement that goes through obstacles.

we have seen, Sartre's thesis is that the analytic and positivistic notions of intelligibility are themselves moments within the intelligibility of the dialectic. This claim, of course, follows on the condition that the dialectic exists. But it is also true that *if* the dialectic exists, then the understanding of its own intelligibility and that of analytic reason must already be present as the uncritical and lived context of our lives and thought.

Indeed, the very formulation of the problem distinguishes dialectical from analytic intelligibility. Analytic reason attempts to formulate each of its steps precisely and clearly in such a way that they do not imply each other; it attempts to reduce intelligibility to a few basic principles. Geometrical proof is the ideal. The intelligibility of the principle is either accepted as a brute given or it is relegated to a metasystem. The goal is to show how a whole can be explained as a combination of simple parts.

Dialectical reason, however, claims that intelligibility is dialectical practice itself as a totalization. This is its primary intelligibility. Its second intelligibility will be the intelligibility of partial totalizations. Sartre notes, at the end of this section, that primary intelligibility of the dialectic rests on there being *a* history and *a* totalization without a grand totalizer. The dialectic proceeds by recognizing the primary intelligibility to be, at the present stage of the investigation, the uncritical content of its movement. The critical study of this content, the existence of *a* history, can be conditionally suspended, but it cannot be abstracted from or bracketed as if it did not exist.

In comparison with the dialectic, analytic and positivistic reason pretends to be describing atomistic facts as if they were pure forms existing in some eternal heaven. Furthermore, it views the laws by which and through which it examines these facts to exist in some nonhuman space. Analytic reason does not encounter the disturbing fact that intelligibility is a human enterprise. Dialectical reason, on the contrary, recognizes not only that intelligibility and novelty are the result of human praxis but also that the very notion of human reality is "itself a synthesis at the level of techniques, and at the level of that universal technique which is thought" (E, 58; F, 148; NF, 174).

The claim that intelligibility and novelty result from praxis does not, for Sartre, lead to subjectivism. A few examples may illustrate Sartre's point: The intelligibility of the "electric light bulb" was Thomas Edison's very search for and discovery of a filament that would sustain an electrical charge and would glow for a suitable time. Madame Curie's growing awareness that a new element was being discovered was the series of her efforts and techniques with pitchblende. And Helen Keller's realization that what was being tapped on her hand by Anne Sullivan was a *symbol* for water, was the *praxis itself* of tapping, precisely as this particular event of tapping was a member of a series of previous endeavors. In each case, intelligibility and novelty arose because these endeavors were temporalizations included within a hierarchy of totalizations. Each experiment, each act of learning, was not an isolated act; it arose from a definite past and aimed at a definite goal. The goal of each effort was abstractly the same; success was achieved because the praxis involved a fortunate emphasis or use of materials. And where novelty came about it was primarily because of free praxis. Once the novelty existed, it gave intelligibility and temporalization to the entire series. For example, on the synchronic plane, Helen Keller's realization that this tapping was a symbol is within the series of other endeavors by her teacher. On the diachronic plane, the explicit realization that something stands for meaning arose because language is a praxis that carries the weight of historically won meanings. *But the realization might never have been.* Without the free praxis that happened to succeed, the student-teacher relation would not have been given, and the entire preceding series of endeavors would not have been part of an "instruction."

Thus, by abstracting from praxis, analytic reason leaves behind the very intelligibility it tries to explain through basic principles. The present critical investigation requires us to recognize that intelligibility implies temporalizations. Without temporal continuity, there would merely be isolated moments that are completely unrelated. A law that would supposedly relate these isolated events would require for its own formulation the very temporality that it denies to the events. The temporal continuity required to formulate the law is an aspect of the intelligibility of the law itself. So fundamental is this temporality that we easily pass through it even when we think we are reflecting on discrete events. In fact, it is impossible to think in completely separate, discrete thoughts, and no science fiction has been able to describe what such "thoughts" would be like. Meaning is an unfolding, and such unfolding could not occur without human beings. For Sartre, we do not merely witness this unfolding of events; rather, by our being and praxis, we provide the possibility for the unfolding. In this respect, Sartre notes that temporalization and totalization exist within machines. A machine embodies the weight of our history, and, in principle an alien culture could reconstruct our history from a single machine.

### 10. (THE PLAN OF THIS WORK)

Sartre's ambitious goal in this work is to show that we have reached a stage in our historical development where we can control our destiny and history. We can direct our individual lives to the extent that we are living within *a* history that has a distinct intelligibility. If true, this claim should not appear bizarre to us; rather, it must be shown to be the implicit content of our life. Uncritically, the existence of *a* history in our lives seems indicated by such things as the present state of communication, the interdependence of world currencies and productive systems, international corporations, and the condition for the possibility of both global destruction and world peace.

Sartre here sketches the plan of his *Critique*. As we have seen, the *Critique* proceeds regressively; it retraces totalizations and their relations to individual praxis so as to reveal not only the intelligibility of praxis and totalizations but also the relations between them. Thus, both praxis and totalizations must be seen as moments of a dialectical reason. If this attempt is successful, it will reveal the a priori reasons for there being *a* human history, conditions that are a priori both because past praxes have made them so and because we now sustain them as the conditions of our history. The unfinished second volume was to have established that we are, in fact, living in *a* history.[8]

This enterprise is ambitious, because on every level we must show that our actions are contained within a hierarchy of totalizations. A positivist could very well admit that on one level we are contained within a totalization, but that on another level we live privately. We have to show, for example, that even when we live alone we do so within the totalizing group of those who live alone.

Furthermore, in order to avoid idealism, we must show how both totalizations and universal concepts are consequent upon individual praxes. For example, Sartre notes that the concept of alienation is consequent upon alienating praxes. Praxes thus form concepts that reciprocally elucidate their character, rather than the concepts bringing about the praxes. (Indeed, the present mode of speaking, insofar as it distinguishes praxes and concepts, is itself the result of our present praxes of alienation.)

When Sartre claims that this study will be successful if it reveals a priori structures, this must not be interpreted in an idealistic sense. The a priori structures will be shown to have been *established*. His remarks, however, are aimed at those Marxists who claim that the dialectic can be built up a posteriori. But, as we have seen, such an approach necessitates adopting a nondialectical attitude toward the dialectic. It assumes the validity and truth of a hyperempirical approach, and it is idealistic in the extreme. Sartre notes that we can parody Kant and say that this present endeavor is an attempt to lay the foundation for a "Prolegomena to any future anthropology" (E, 66; F, 153; NF, 180). It can also be said to reveal, in a very broad sense, the structural foundation for the possibility of there being a history.

Sartre notes that the main division of volume I is into the *constituent* and

8. As noted in the Prefatory Remarks, the incomplete second volume of the *Critique* has been published by Gallimard (see Bibliography, below, under "Writings of Sartre"). A translation is planned by Verso (London), publisher of the translation of *Critique I*. See also the forthcoming work by Ronald Aronson, *Sartre's Second Critique: An Explication and Commentary* (Chicago: University of Chicago Press, 1986).

the *constituted dialectic*. This division is more or less coextensive with the division of volume I into its two books. In the first division, we will see how the dialectic reveals itself in praxis and finds its own limit in an *antidialectic*. In the second, we will examine the interplay between praxis and totalizations and the ways in which forces directed by agents and those without agents bring about results.

## 11. (The Individual and History)

In these last two sections of the introduction, Sartre would again have us reflect on the extent to which we tend to accept the concepts of analytic reason as the parameters for any discussion. This second part of the introduction, as a *critique* of this critical investigation, must attempt to keep us continually within dialectical reason itself. Specifically, our task is to see if there are internal relations between an individual life and human history. This effort confronts us with the relation between freedom and necessity, concepts forged, however, by analytic reason. Thus, even if we concede that we are free as individuals, we tend to believe that we are determined to the extent that we are moved by the forces of history.

It seems natural to oppose freedom and determination, because we compare the concept of a pure freedom to the concept of an objective necessity. In the light of these analytically clear concepts of pure freedom and objective necessity, we further identify intelligibility and certainty with necessity. For example, a circle is intelligible, and the truths about it are certain because they are necessary. If we are free, then we see that our actions are unintelligible and that we cannot be certain of them. As Sartre elucidates in the long footnote to this section, the very opposite is true. We may be able to understand his claim if we return to our example of tennis playing.

When we are actively engaged in playing tennis, we are aware, particularly in those moments of pure reflection, that we are playing tennis *freely*. That is, we are certain that the praxis we are engaged in has the intelligibility of tennis, not through external criteria but through the very bond of being that connects us to the activity itself. We *are* this tennis playing and not a series of necessary, mechanical movements produced by a robot playing tennis. We are this tennis playing as the translucent consciousness of tennis playing, and as a negation that surpasses this playing toward goals of our own. In this respect, necessity does not follow upon intelligibility but is opposed to it. If we thought that we were moved by external forces to play tennis, we could not understand our own activity. But insofar as this consciousness of tennis playing is also a totalization, we can regressively understand it as a hierarchy in which freedom and necessity intermingle. For example, on reflection, I see that I necessarily needed a tennis racket, which had to be purchased in some store and manufactured by some group of individuals. This interplay between freedom and necessity will be developed throughout the *Critique*. Sartre states, "In any case if my life, as it deepens, becomes history, it must reveal itself, at a deep level of its free development, as a strict development of the historical process so as to rediscover itself at an even deeper level, as the freedom of this necessity and, finally, as the necessity of freedom" (E, 70; F, 157; NF, 184). But again this freedom must not be conceived as analytic; it is not a pure freedom that happens to act on matter. We will see that individual praxis is both free and necessary, because it is the interiorization of the external and the externalization of interiority. We will soon become very familiar with these terms "interior" and "exterior." At present, it is useful to keep in mind that a machine originates from our interiorizing aspects of the world and that its production is an embodiment of these interiorizations.

Human beings thus place their objectifications within nature, or more accurately, nature is a human adventure. Nature, Sartre says, can be understood as our essence to the extent that essence is our transcended past. Indeed, if we were nothing but objects within a perfectly objectified nature, we would be robots. That is, we would go to a future that would appear free but would simply be our determined destiny.

## 12. (INTELLECTION AND COMPREHENSION)

In comparing the terms "comprehension" (*la compréhension*) and "intellection" (*l'intellection*), Sartre is further clarifying in what sense praxis is intelligible. The term "comprehension" is restricted to praxis precisely as it originates from an agent. In our study of the antidialectic, we will see that there are "actions without an agent, productions without a producer, totalisations without a totaliser, counter-finalities and internal circularities" (E, 76; F, 161; NF, 190).

If there are totalizing activities that produce *a* history, then these "vagabond and authorless" actions must be included within dialectical intelligibility. The term "intellection" is the broader term including all partial totalizations, whether they are praxes, and thus produced by an author, or "antipraxes," and thus authorless.

This second part of the introduction, as a critique of the present investigation, reminds us that there must be a reason broader than analytic reason. Analytic reason recognizes actions that have authors, but experience teaches us that we are frequently exposed to historical forces that seem to originate from nowhere and that seem to oppose our best plans. To the extent that we can talk meaningfully about these antihuman forces we must be able to incorporate these notions within a broader notion of reason, a notion that Sartre calls dialectical reason.

# BOOK I

From Individual Praxis to the Practico-Inert

# 1     Individual Praxis as Totalization

(1. NEED)

Like *Being and Nothingness*, this first volume of the *Critique* proceeds from the abstract to the concrete. Book I of this volume shows how individual praxis totalizes and thus unifies the environment. The import of this first book, "From Individual Praxis to the Practico-Inert," is that group praxis would be impossible unless the environment were altered so as to "mediate" praxis; the unity of a group could only come through a unified matter, and thus both the group and the historical aspects of the practico-inert come into existence reciprocally. Book II, "From Groups to History," examines the reciprocal relation between groups and history from a limited perspective, specifically, that of France during the nineteenth century.

Sartre's procedure of beginning with individual praxis may seem to prejudice his procedure. We might ask, "How can individuals effectively become a 'we'?" This objection, which is also frequently made against Sartre's early existentialist philosophy is largely due to a misunderstanding concerning Sartre's general philosophic procedure. Sartre begins, in fact, with the complete human condition, including, here in the *Critique*, the fact that we act effectively in common. But, for Sartre, neither common praxes nor isolated praxis are a priori aspects of a human nature; both are de facto conditions that arise both from freedom and the environment. We will examine this in more detail as we proceed. Here an analogy may help us to understand Sartre's initial perspective on the individual and the we.

A complex organism is a novel event, but we can, nevertheless, comprehend it as a unity resulting from the interaction of individual cells. To speak of individual cells within an organism is not to refer to isolated cells. To what extent an individual cell within an organism resembles an isolated cell is an open question. This analogy is meant only to illustrate that "individual" does not *of itself* mean "isolated," and it does *not* imply that society, for Sartre, is a quasi organism. As we will see, Sartre completely rejects the organicist theory of society.

Sartre begins this first part by noting that if the dialectic exists we must be able to find answers to the following four questions:

1. How can freedom and necessity be grasped in an empirical process?
2. How are we to understand the seemingly paradoxical claim that totalization both effects unification and can only be effected if there is a unifying principle?
3. How can there be a true historical future, since the dialectic requires us initially to comprehend the present in terms of the past and the future?
4. How are we to comprehend the materiality of praxis in relation to other forms of materiality?

These four questions highlight the distinctiveness of our regressive approach, and Sartre here gives a first, abstract answer to all four questions. He also reminds us of the circularity of our approach; we must be at least open to the dialectical method prospectively (*à titre prospectif*) if we are to see the possibility for the reciprocal relation between the human organism and the environment at every level of our investigation. As we proceed we shall see that free praxis imprints a simulacrum of itself into inert matter, so that ultimately the dialectic is between praxis and antipraxis. At this abstract level, however, Sartre's effort is to show that even our so-called biological functions are elementary forms of praxis.

Sartre does not attempt to answer these questions systematically; indeed a systematic approach might give the impression that the critical part of our investigation is an epistemological issue that must be settled before we can proceed. Rather, the critical endeavor is the investigation (*expérience*) as it seeks to understand and justify itself. Still, Sartre will devote an explicit study to each of these issues, as they appear as problems within the investigation itself. With this in mind, it may be useful to say a few introductory words about all four questions.

The first question initially focuses our attention away from concepts and onto praxes. Indeed, Sartre will indicate that human "biological" needs automatically adumbrate aspects of an experience that is both necessary and free. Thus, we must eat to live, but these lives we must live, even on a biological level, are not given in nature; for example, we eat to live longer, healthier lives than our parents did. But the second question raises the issue of whether this experience of freedom and necessity is indeed dialectical, that is, whether praxis establishes a hierarchy of totalizations. The task will be to show that even though only individuals exist as entities, totalizations are not thereby subjective. Here, on the first abstract level of praxis as the satisfaction of biological needs, we will see that nature itself is totalized in relation to our organic unity. Even on the molecular level, inert matter is not a pure in-itself but a humanized matter that takes its unity from the human biological unity.

The third question requires us to determine the relation between time and temporality. In this context, we see the distinctiveness of praxis as historical action, even on the human biological level. *Our* biological behavior is not a linear function that satisfies biological needs of maintaining our existence as a *repetition*. The actions of primitive societies serve to sustain and repeat the biological life of the past. Our historicized biological behavior, however, is toward a health that has not yet existed. Primitive societies experience hunger, but not malnutrition. The issue of temporality is crucial, and it will arise at every level of our investigation. In a more concrete context, we will see that scarcity is an aspect of temporality, and the possibility of a new "historical" picture will arise toward the end of this study.

The final question reminds us that praxis is a materiality and thus that our dialectic attempts to elucidate the relations among diverse forms of matter. Here, at this abstract level, Sartre notes that the evidence seems to indicate that the molecules of organisms and inanimate things are the same; we thus seem to be involved with two states of the same materiality. But even if this is true, there is still a priority of the matter of the human organism in relation to inanimate things. For the unity of a molecule is still the exteriorization of our biological interiority. Thus the molecule as *higher* complexity is given, because the human organism is accepted as an organic unity that results from complexity. The molecule is thus already accepted as an exteriorized interiority; it is a transcendence with immanence.

We must clarify all four issues as we develop our critique; here Sartre's early point is to establish that historicity is not an epiphenomenon superimposed on a more basic, biological nature. Rather, it is a distinctive process that alters both human existence and things at every level of their existence. Sartre says that we must keep in mind throughout our investigation that "man is 'mediated' by things to the same extent that things are 'mediated' by man" (E, 79; F, 165; NF, 193). All private, subjective world-making is based on this primary reciprocal relation between the being of humans and the being of things. The elucidation of the internal relations between our being and the being of historical objects, assuming they objectively exist, is the task of the regressive movement of the *Critique I*.

Sartre does not always make it explicitly clear that we are primarily concerned with the *past* of our *present* and not with the past as past. The two parts of the introduction, however, have already established this perspective, which must always be kept in mind. This view might be emphasized by a reminder that our approach is regressive because we accept our successful jump to civilized life as a radical contingency. The mere fact that we developed a history from a life that we now recognize as "primitive" means that a term like "need" signifies a different reality when it refers to our primitive life than when it refers to life lived in a primitive society today.

Nevertheless, we must not go to the other extreme and claim pure equivocation for terms such as "primitive" and "need" as they apply to the early stages of our own development and to the present stage of undeveloped peoples. We all inhabit the same planet and share common biological needs. On an abstract level, we can identify similarities between ourselves and members of present-day primitive societies, although we can never be certain of what these similarities mean concretely.

"Everything is to be explained," Sartre says, "through *need (le besoin)*; need is the first totalising relation between the material being, *man,* and the material ensemble of which he is a part" (E, 80; F, 166; NF, 194). Need, however, is not first in a foundational sense; rather, our regressive study reveals that, on an abstract level, and from the perspective of our history, need is the first relation of the human organism to matter. Here again, it may be useful to attempt another indirect explanation of Sartre's regressive approach, as it operates in conjunction with his distinct nominalism.

In the concrete, such realities as my weight have all the complex meanings of our technological society. These "meanings" are not superimposed on some nature; they are aspects of my human flesh in its concrete reality. If I am large, my weight is for me an excess and a danger to my health, or it is the weight of my flesh as I attempt to bear it in conscious opposition to the prescriptions of society. All my weight is flesh; all my flesh is historical. Still, if someone needs a "weight," for example, to hold a helium balloon from rising, I can serve as well or as poorly as a sandbag of equal weight. My weight is thus ambiguous vis-à-vis inanimate objects, animals, and even members of primitive societies. In an Aristotelian philosophy, this ambiguity would be recognized, and one would explain it by saying that the higher, human form can do *virtually* whatever the lower forms can do. That is, in the concrete, what extends my body in space and gives it weight is human flesh; nevertheless, I affect through my flesh what extended inanimate objects affect in space. My substance is different, an Aristotelian explanation would continue, from the substance of inanimate things, but I can abstract from these different natures a common property referred to by the univocal term "weight," or "body."

From the perspective of this problem only, Sartre can be understood as "deconstructing" the Aristotelian position.[1] In place of the Aristotelian a priori hierarchy of formed matter, that begins from the inanimate and proceeds up to human beings, Sartre establishes a hierarchy that originates from the unique materiality of human beings and proceeds *downward.* In place of the forms themselves, Sartre describes praxes and levels of materialities. These levels are real because the human level is real. Thus a radical but unique nominalism

---

1. Sartre never speaks this way about his philosophy. He seems to have had little interest in the thought of Aristotle.

arises.[2] The term "weight" can no longer be understood univocally as referring to a common property. From the perspective of holding down a balloon, I can imagine that I do what a sandbag does. But the "doings" are radically different: Only human, conscious flesh can "hold" or "weigh." Physics may try to remove these anthropomorphisms, but for Sartre they are always there.

As already noted, a nominalism was already present in *Being and Nothingness*. Here, this nominalism is complicated because of a dialectical tension between the terms as they are being examined in this early section and as they will be examined in the later sections. For example, the "need" that we are analyzing here is already modified and to some extent determined by the "need" that will be elucidated in the concluding sections on class struggle.

Sartre's nominalism is, as we have seen, different from traditional nominalism. Universality is not exclusively a property of names. Language is a human relation; universality is something that human relations achieve. Within this perspective, Sartre is thus claiming that "history" arises from *our human, historical needs,* and not from a possible evolution from abstract, animal needs, such as the need for food. We would like to be able to say that the needs of animal life are a necessary but not sufficient condition for history, but this analytic principle implies a common, organic nature that can develop either historically or nonhistorically. For Sartre, on the contrary, whatever community might exist between our human organic life and animal or primitive human organic life would have to be established by a rationality that is not yet available to us. In the concrete, our organic life is different because of the novel event of its becoming historical. The way I have been fed as a child makes me chew my food differently from an animal or a member of a primitive society, and this difference *is* my chewing. Of course, in extreme hunger, my chewing may seem to approximate what it is for a nonhistorical organism. And this similarity is not subjective; it forms the basis for our scientific universals, such as the universal notion of an organism. But science is a praxis; its objectivity is not independent of human needs.

Sartre thus distinguishes need as (1) a biological function, (2) a nonhistorical action, and (3) a historical praxis. These distinctions, however, must not be understood in an analytic sense, that is, they are not given from a neutral perspective. To repeat, the entire discussion is *from the perspective of need as praxis.* Thus, when Sartre is examining biological needs, they are our biological needs as historical organisms. The same is true when Sartre is examining need as function. There are indeed similarities between our biological needs and those of a dog, for example. Again we confront the issue of a unified dialectic, which was examined earlier. Sartre implicitly denies that we

2. Sartre does not develop either his nominalism or anthropocentrism. Such elaboration is useful but not necessary; the justification of the language of the *Critique* is not separate from the task of the *Critique.*

have constituted a general notion of "need" or "animality." Our biological needs are thoroughly human, despite their similarities with the biological needs of other organisms. (Failure to keep this perspective constantly in mind is one of the major sources of confusion in reading the *Critique*.)

Thus, even on the level of biological needs our comprehension is a praxis. For example, in hunger, what we are most certain of is our need for money to buy food, and the need of our stomachs for food is the need for food purchased by wages. On a more abstract level, where there is *less* evidence and certitude, the satisfaction of need is also a mere action. Thus, abstracting from the need to *buy* food, food must also be made digestible, just as members of primitive societies must, for example, cook meat. Finally, on an even more abstract level, need is a function, such as in the need of the stomach for protein. On this biological level, human needs appear similar to all organic needs. And this similarity objectively exists, but it does not, as commonly thought, give rise to the most evident and certain knowledge of our needs.

But our regressive approach is actually more complex than I have indicated. For while it is appropriate for biology to study need only as a function, we must look for the adumbration of the dialectic, even on the most abstract level of need. For this is precisely what a historical approach means. We must not fall back into the errors of a seemingly modest positivism that actually hides a superempiricism. If we could understand our need as built up from abstract layers, as if these were some materialized version of Neoplatonic forms, then we would be outside our own need, describing it objectively in accordance with a correspondence theory of truth. Rather, we must look to see how our need is dialectical, even on its most abstract level of function.

While our method is regressive in the overall context of a progressive movement to *a* history, it is, in every local context, also progressive in respect to the immediate historical context. Thus, even while discussing the relation of molecules in a biological function, Sartre also reminds us how need totalizes the environment through human labor and machines. It is not accidental that Sartre sets the context of this study by returning continually to the *satisfaction of need through labor*. Nevertheless, labor is here considered as abstract in relation to the activity of machines. Sartre notes that, through needs, human beings totalize their environment as a field that may possibly satisfy those needs. Rivers and forests are given as sources of fish and game. But we will see that machines totalize the environment for themselves as well as for humans. This in itself does not mean that machines are alienating. We will see that, for Sartre, alienation is the result of a distinct praxis not brought about by machines in their abstract state.

These introductory remarks give merely the context for Sartre's comments on how individual praxis totalizes the environment. Sartre's main point is that, even on an abstract level of satisfying needs, human beings totalize their environment by using a controlled inertia to alter it. A human being does not become a fixed inertial system, as, to use Sartre's example, a spider does when it makes a web. This is most clear in the division of labor, but it is also apparent in need as function and action. Even on an abstract level, human needs are directed toward a humanity that is not given in nature. Our need to alter our environment is a need to establish a humanity that does not yet exist: our need for efficient farming methods is our need for a life of leisure as well as our need for food.

It is from our historicized biological needs that nature receives its first objective unity as a quasi organism. This totalization also reveals the environment in its natural state to be impossible for civilized life. We rework this impossibility so that our future humanity is now a future possibility. For example, tools become not merely instruments to sustain a humanity that repeats itself, as in primitive societies, but also instruments that can adjust to an environment being altered to sustain a humanity that does not yet exist. Civilized farming is *initially* a transcendence of nature; it is the human project of producing food quickly and cheaply.

We thus satisfy our basic "biological" needs by totalizing our environment differently than do members of primitive societies. Specifically, our relation to the inorganic is, Sartre says, "univocal" (that is to say, "unilateral") and of interiority. It is unilateral in the sense of being one-directional; the totalizing on this level moves from our organic nature to the inorganic realm that is now unified as a field of possible satisfactions for our "biological" needs. Our relation is of *interiority,* because the inorganic is now the exteriorization of our interiority.

It may be useful here to sketch some background for Sartre's uses of the terms "interior" and "exterior," and the related terms "immanence" and "transcendence." For Sartre, our body has interior and exterior aspects. In our Cartesian language, the term "consciousness" unfortunately seems to refer to a mind existing within a mechanized body. Correspondingly, "flesh" is taken to be only the appearance of consciousness. In this context, "immanence" *seems* to refer to what goes on inside our body, our private thoughts and feelings, "transcendence" to the external manifestation of these thoughts and feelings. We could, of course, try to invent new terms, but this would have the deceptive appearance of placing us beyond a language within which we in fact always exist. We must, for the most part, use these terms, but we must constantly attempt to avoid the Cartesian dualism inherent in them. We must not be deceived into thinking that one grand effort can place us beyond our tradition.[3]

In this context, it is also important to recall that terms, for Sartre, do not

---

3. Pietro Chiodi and other critics have misunderstood Sartre's use of terms such as "interiorization" and "exteriorization," believing them to imply a Cartesian dualism that fractures the dialectic. (See Chiodi, *Sartre and Marxism,* trans. Kate Soper [Atlantic Highlands, N.J.: Humanities Press, 1976], 52–54).

refer to concepts within which individual cases are contained as instances; rather, they refer to what he calls "particularized universals," from which we abstract not a nature but heuristic principles and tenuous similarities. If these terms are to be understood concretely, they must be continually reinterpreted within each new context.[4]

With this caveat in mind, we can now outline the meanings of the terms "interior," "exterior," "immanent," and "transcendent" in relation to our present abstract examination of consciousness and flesh.

In the concrete, the human body is a unique material reality. From a biological perspective, our interiority is our materiality precisely as it is a unity irreducible to the cells and molecules that "exteriorly" appear to compose it. Within this context, "immanence" and "transcendence" refer to two closely related aspects of our materiality. "Immanence" is our materiality precisely as it seems to bring together disparate parts into a new, irreducible whole. Immanence is the organic unity of our "biological" multiplicity as it directs the environment toward our own historical ends. "Transcendence" refers to the same unity as it unfolds outward into the environment. In the same context, "interior" refers not to an intimate awareness, but to both our prereflective awareness of our relations to our environment and our ability to thematize these relations. Reciprocally, "exterior" refers to the environment as unified by both our spontaneous and our reflective behavior. Needless to say, "spontaneous" means humanly spontaneous. Before returning to our more technical discussion of need, an example may help to relate these two sets of terms. A woman who "needs" to get to work on time to keep her job establishes an immanence-transcendence situation between the organic unity of her body and the unity of the transportation system. Her body *is* an immanent tense quickness; it *is* the cultured need to be moved rapidly. And the transportation system *is* rapidly moving bodies as a transcendence. When the woman oversleeps one morning, she interiorizes this exteriorized transportation system as something already given to her.

Returning now to our *regressive* discussion of need, we note that given the successful appearance of our historical, organic life, a true objective unity enters the world with its corresponding objective negations: the organic is unified; the inorganic is not. But the organism is not a self-contained unity; it continually requires the inorganic for its preservation. Furthermore, its own unity is maintained by continually using up the inorganic in order to avoid returning to the inorganic. Thus, the organism both lacks and needs the inorganic. From the perspective of our own historical, organic unity, we can see

4. Of course, my entire "explanation" is circular. It begins by accepting the analytic distinction between "terms" and "concepts" and then, on another level, tries to show that this distinction does not hold. This circularity, however, is consistent with the dialectic as it proceeds to gradually establish itself critically.

that need is thus a negation of a negation. The organism is not the inorganic, and it is not the mere absence of the inorganic, since it needs the inorganic. Consequently, we can regressively understand the unity of our organic life as composed of two negations that result in an affirmation. But it must be always understood that the *affirmation,* the de facto existence of organic life, is given to us first, and we then regressively comprehend it as resulting from two negations.

*From our historical perspective,* we can also understand the distinction between time and temporality to occur first on the level of the organic. If need existed in an abstract realm of a "now," it would lack intentional unity and thus degenerate into a system of exterior relations characteristic of the inorganic. Our organic need for food brings about a lived future that opens the environment into a horizon of possible satisfactions. On this organic level, we can also distinguish our temporality *from what appears to be* the temporality characteristic of primitive societies. In a primitive society, the satisfaction of needs is repetitious and exists either in nature or in the recalling of techniques of the past; these satisfactions are disrupted only by a type of scarcity about which Sartre later will have a great deal to say.

We are now in a position to distinguish a little more fully nonhistorical action, called simply "action," from historical action, called "praxis": *action is purposeful behavior directed toward goals that exist in nature.* Specifically, our goals arise from a project, a free interiorization of our own flesh and a corresponding alteration of our environment. To climb a mountain is an action, because the goal of arriving at the peak is given in nature. Even on this level, our project is not an act of the will; it is a movement of our body as it directs itself toward intentional goals. *In a praxis, however, such as building a factory, the goal is not given in nature; the "need" for profit is a goal we establish in the world.*

Of course, this discussion is abstract; we will see how the environment, thus totalized, has "needs" of its own. But what is clear at present is that we direct inert matter to goals not given by nature and that we use this "interiorized matter" to satisfy needs that, again, are not in the world.

## (2. THE NEGATION OF THE NEGATION)

The dialectical "principle" that the negation of a negation is an affirmation is valid only from a regressive perspective. Given organic matter as totalized into nature through the human organism, one can *then* see that this unity results from a double negation. But before turning his attention to the significance of the "double" negation, Sartre reminds us that negation comes to matter only through human existence. The context makes it very clear that Sartre is reaffirming here the general perspective on negation that he held in *Being and Nothingness.* There he showed how "negations" in the world, such as absences, are not mere psychological projections onto matter. These alterations of the environment come to it through the fact of human existence, but the environment thus altered is not dependent on human knowledge. Indeed, on a deeper level, Sartre further showed that the fundamental differentiation of things came about through the human reality as it is an ontological negation. But even in *Being and Nothingness,* Sartre emphasized that this negation was a "happening" to the fullness of matter.

Negation always presupposes an existing reality. Here in the *Critique,* the emphasis is to show that the distinctions within our humanized environment are there objectively, although they are introduced into matter only through praxis. Again our approach is regressive. What is given first is that, even on an abstract level, praxis as labor is a negation of a negation. That is, the human organism, through labor, spontaneously negates the totality of the inorganic as nature, even as nature is itself a negation of matter as inert. What the contemporary farmer spontaneously aims for is a wheat that is not given in nature even as wheat itself is not given by the inorganic.

Regressively, we thus see that nature with its laws is a totality only in relation to our successful leap to human organic life. Atoms form molecules as a *higher* reality, only because our body is a unity of complexities. We are thus *not* the exterior unity of the inorganic, although we are in danger of returning to the separateness of the exterior relations characteristic of the inorganic. And furthermore, we are not the goal of an evolution, for this goal is the way we have exteriorized our relation to nature.

### (3. LABOR)

Here, and throughout the English edition of the *Critique,* the subdivisions provided by the editor must not be taken too literally. In fact, Sartre discusses need, negation of negation, and labor throughout this chapter, and these concluding paragraphs are more a summary than a separate section.

Through labor, the environment becomes a humanized thing and a dialectic emerges between the human reality and nature as humanized. We are here concerned with a theoretical formulation of this dialectic, in the sense of theory not as an analytic category separate from praxis but as an elucidation of the dialectic in words. We must make many efforts to reveal the relation between the analytic and the dialectical, and we must not expect that one grand, epistemological effort will clarify our linguistic task once and for all.

What we have revealed, Sartre notes, is a relation of interiority between human beings and things. The dialectic may be difficult to see on the level of function, but Sartre notes that it is still certain. We are accustomed to interpret the biological process, such as digestion, as a more fundamental objective reality than labor. But we must remember what was said at the beginning of this chapter, namely, that we mediate things to the extent that things are mediated by us. Not only is biology as a science a human thing, but the thematization of the body as a combination of pumps, tubes, pressure, and so forth, is an objective organization of consciousness for the purpose of healing. It is conceivable that a society might not be interested in health. One could assert that the human stomach, for example, would still be a stomach, but this attitude hides a naive realism that implies the existence of a transempirical mind observing its body as a machine. Our stomachs are rather our own exteriorizations of our internal projects for health. This is not to be understood idealistically, as if our stomachs were produced by our will power. It is again a question of praxis: matter acts on matter, and the way we practically "live our body" in relation to our interior is our stomach: our praxis, in this context, is that we spontaneously want more than a stomach given by nature; we want a stomach suited for a long, healthy, civilized life.

We have thus seen that the individual totalizes the environment through praxis as labor. Labor, however, is as much a relation among human beings as between human beings and matter. Here again, human relations must not be considered idealistically. Human relations are distinct materialities, and, as such, they both alter and are altered by the matter of the environment.

2　　Human Relations as a
　　　Mediation between Different
　　　Sectors of Materiality

## (1. ISOLATED INDIVIDUALS)

"Immediate experience," Sartre begins, "reveals being at its *most concrete*, but it takes it at its most superficial level and remains in the realm of abstractions" (E, 96; F, 178; NF, 208).[1] If I start a casual conversation with a stranger on a bus, this meeting is concrete but superficial. We talk about the weather or crowded conditions as if we were isolated individuals, each having no particular set of personal relations. On an abstract level, to be isolated seems to refer merely to the fact of bodily separation. Isolation, however, is a specific mode of human existence, with a special materiality and praxis. Sartre refers to the semiemployed agricultural day laborers in southern Italy who eat once every day or once every other day. Hunger and need exist in them not as a specific demand for food but as a chronic ailment that is their life. Their isolated habits alter their entire consciousness so that all their relations have the specificity of being isolated.

Sartre's opening remarks make it clear that our regressive analysis does not aim at revealing how history results additively from innumerable isolated individual praxes. The possibility for isolation arises from the material configuration of the environment. From this perspective, one could be tempted to reduce the full significance of human relations to historical conditions, as do traditional Marxists. But, for Sartre, as we have seen, praxis remakes historical circumstances even as these same circumstances make human beings historical. It is, indeed, the material environment with its mode of production that provides the necessary condition for agricultural laborers to work as isolated individuals. But, as we will see, their life is also the result of particular, oppressive praxes that do not arise merely from exploiting and alienating modes of production. An enlightened exploitation of labor should aim at keeping bodies well fed just as it should seek to keep machinery in good con-

1. This insight is usually a claim of an idealistic philosophy. But one of the distinctive features of Sartre's materialism is that it also affirms that significant human phenomena are not built up foundationally from the elements of our immediate, concrete experience.

dition. Furthermore, the specific way the laborers interiorize their oppression, by living their hunger as a chronic illness, is their distinctive praxis as a response to their historical environment. Their response is neither reducible to nor deducible from their environment.

We must thus remember that at any one time we are performing only one aspect of a dialectical movement; each aspect becomes idealistic if it is not considered with reference to the whole. Thus, a particular regressive analysis reveals praxis as a transcending relation of the individual to the environment. A converse study would show how the individual and the material content of his praxis is constituted by history. The entire dialectical procedure attempts to reveal both the individual as constituting history and history as the constituted milieu that conditions the individual. In the total process, the individual will appear as constituent reason (*la Raison constituante*) working within history as constituted reason (*la Raison constituée*).

Sartre's materialism can be understood here as an attempt to avoid both an individualistic and an organismic view of society. Society is not a collection of atomized, totally free individuals who mutually consent to live together. Nor is society an organismic whole in which the meaning of an individual life can be found by merely examining the whole. The atomistic view does not explain the unique phenomenon of history; the organismic view does not show how an individual life can contribute to history. But both views have an implicit thesis in common, which Sartre terms "the liberal view." They both start with a homogeneous notion of the human being as something that either exists by nature in isolation or is by nature subsumed in the structures of society.[2] Marxists, for Sartre, fall into the liberal trap by accepting the productive forces of society as the starting points. They think that by beginning with the whole they avoid a formalism, but they implicitly accept both a formalism and a foundationalism in their very stance of beginning with the total, complex whole as something that determines the meaning of an individual life from every significant perspective. We have seen above that we must indeed have a loose kind of formalism, in the sense of a distinctive monism. Furthermore, our formalism must allow the distinctiveness of individual praxes to emerge as something new. Sartre says, "My formalism, which is inspired by that of Marx, consists simply in recognizing that men make history to precisely the extent that it makes them" (E, 97; F, 180; NF, 210).

The interaction between individuals and history is itself a materiality. Sartre uses the example of language. We can study language just as we study money, namely, as an exchange of inert quantities. Words can be taken as jot-

2. This view is consistent with that in Sartre's *Anti-Semite and Jew,* trans. George J. Becker (New York: Schocken Books), 55–58; 146–47. The liberal saves the Jew as human being but eliminates him as Jew. Cf. Joseph H. McMahon's excellent discussion in *Human Beings* (Chicago: University of Chicago Press, 1971), 99–105.

tings on paper or vibrations in the air that seem to carry meanings. Insofar as these meanings involve a network of meanings with complex historical nuances that are beyond the individual's grasp, language appears to separate individuals. But this incommunicability is based on a more primary communicability that reveals language as the very life of an individual. Language does not come to us as a given; it is rather an aspect of life in its specific condition, whether we live this life alone in silence or united with others in a common enterprise. Every word we speak is the entire language, and all of the language is in every word. But in every word that is used, each individual totalizes the language differently, and this individual totalization reveals a life with its projects and alienations. Thus, as we speak within language, we alter it.

Here, again, we must be careful not to fall into Cartesian dualism. The individual is not a substance with clear ideas trying to use words to express his inner thoughts. Words, like gestures, are an aspect of our materiality; they reveal our primary dialectical relation both to the matter of the world and to other people. Language is a human relation; it is a distinct materiality mediating our relation to institutions and people. Our comprehension of language can be broken down into two aspects of a dialectical movement. First, we encounter words as a complex of exterior sounds and symbols, and we interiorize this exterior complex in such a way that we are aware that the words of *our* thoughts are *not* those exterior words. Second, language reciprocally emerges as an exteriorization of innumerable interior thoughts, each of which is *not* our thought even as it is the language of all of us. Thus, language is the interiorization of exteriorities and the exteriorization of interiorities. That is, language is praxis.

In a more general way, we use ourselves, as well as other people, not as ends but always as a means to accomplish our goals. Although we can never perfectly recapture our own objectivity, we find our *selves* as objects in the world amid other objects, and we use our present awareness of our selves and other selves as means for new projects. Of course, this relation has the double negation characteristic of the dialectic. We can comprehend the dialectic here, on this abstract level, as composed of two negative moments within the positivity of an ever-escaping totalizing field: we *discover* ourselves and others within a unified practical field, and we then *interiorize* this exterior plurality. We now, as it were, rediscover ourselves within the world as interiorities that are *not* like others. But we are also not those interiorities, for we transcend, in our present projects, our unique selves as we understand them to exist in the world. This process is clearly seen in children: The child discovers himself in the eyes and behavior of his parents. He then thinks about this complex of self and others and projects a *new* complex of self and others, those who are thinking about themselves. Finally, the child secretly denies that he is like those *other* thinking selves.

Reciprocally, the world emerges as an exteriorization of interiorities, each of which transcends and uses the other. That is, we comprehend that what we interiorized in the first place was a plurality of exteriorities, each of which was a unique center of interiority. Moreover, we recognize that we are not *these* transcending selves, but a more intimate transcending objectivity whose complete meaning eludes us. Our relation to other selves is thus a praxis: it is an interiorization of exteriorities and an exteriorization of interiorities.

But we have not yet attempted to reveal the uniqueness of praxis as a human historical activity. We must break from an analytic perspective that tends to see the whole as built up additively from individual parts, like a string of separate mutual relationships. On a more synthetic but still relatively abstract level, the first distinctive aspect of a historical human relation is that it is always in reference to a *third*. This will be our basis for comprehending that a concrete, interior, historical relation to all human beings is hidden even in our apparently exterior relations to strangers.

## (2. DUALITY AND THE THIRD)

Our historical society is actually formed in a much more complex way than either an atomistic or organismic theory imagines. In reality, reciprocity between individuals always occurs through matter and through the mediation of a third (*tiers*). Sartre's example reminds us of the importance of introducing our own being into our comprehension of the dialectic.

From my window, he says, I see a road mender and a gardener, separated by a wall and thus working unaware of each other. But who is this I? It is that of a petit bourgeois intellectual, taking a few moments' rest from his work. My initial relation to the workers is thus negative, because I do not comprehend their work and I am not a member of their class. But, Sartre notes, my negative relation to them has two aspects.

First, these class differences exist only against a synthetic organization of human ends that is our very material environment. In certain pathological cases, such as those of depersonalization, people may see themselves as members of an alien species, as angels, for example; they thus do not see their ends as human ends. Second, these negative relations with the workers affect my very being; they are thus relations of interiority. Things are laden with meanings given them by the work of others, and through my behavior, such as writing, I organize them in line with my own project.

In the concrete, however, I am aware of the distinctiveness of my project only through its separation from the projects of others. I am aware of my own objectivity by visualizing it alongside everyone else's objectivity, precisely as each is an objectivity-for-the-other. The work of each of the two workers is *not* the work of the other and *not* my work. I thus become explicitly aware of what my work has always been: a limited engagement with the real. Nevertheless, we must recall that we can never know ourselves exactly as we are known by others. Thus, although I interiorize my limitation in the face of these two workers, the full meaning of this lack escapes me. I do not know how their unique transcendings would see a petit bourgeois intellectual. My own limitation exists within innumerable pluralities, within which I must continually discover the meanings of my project as limited. But, at present, these two workers appear to me, Sartre says, to be two "slips" (*glissements*) within the world through which meaning escapes me. These remarks, however, must not be accepted in a completely negative way. The meaning of these worker's lives escape me from my lazy "idealistic perspective." But, if the circumstances are right and if I am willing to put forth the effort, I may indeed be united with them in a genuine "we." For example, I may take the trouble to know them and to help them form a union.

But reciprocally, I experience these workers in their act of working as a loss of meaning only because there is already a world of meanings. Here, we can only begin to see how this is possible. First, it is through me that each worker is ignorant of the other. For example, on a desert island of only two people, where each is separated by an impassable mountain from the other, ignorance would not exist. Ignorance, however, is not a subjective state. Ignorance is real because it can be used; if, in a farfetched example, I try, for a price, to interest the road mender in hiring a gardener, I can use each one's ignorance of the other's existence for my own profit. Sartre's example is that of a general who plans a strategy based on the fact that two enemy forces are ignorant of each other's position.

It is not merely as losses of meaning that I perceive the road mender and the gardener. *Through each,* I perceive the totality of the same world: I perceive my world being mended and gardened. I am thus neither a mind agreeing with other minds to form a society nor a member of some organic totality arising from the family to the state. Our history is a unique reality in which each of us is an individual in the same world, because our world is initially given as a plurality of unifications.

We are still, however, on an abstract level, for much of what is said here *appears* regressively to be common to primitive society. What we are describing is instead an abstract level of our historical life. In our historical world, a diversity of professions is embodied in the very materiality of our environment as something mediated. In the abstract, we can imagine two persons talking to each other without mediation. A conversation within history, however, presupposes the existence of a third as a mediator. We will continually return to this crucial point. Here, Sartre simply states that reciprocity could be perfect only if God were the transcendent epicenter. But the epicenters are materialities, and reciprocity is thus always conditioned and limited by matter.

In the text, Sartre uses Lévi-Strauss's description of potlatch to illustrate mediation. The equivalence of the exchange of gifts implies a third evaluating and witnessing the equivalence. But more importantly, an irreversible temporality is established in the gift through the mediation of the third. The gift is something that is *given,* and it embodies a real, irreversible temporality because there are always *thirds* through whom this givenness is objective.

Nevertheless, we must not interpret a ternary relation as a foundation from which we can deduce binary relations. *On its own level,* reciprocity is a bond between two persons. We must not imagine mediation idealistically. Two persons do not talk to each other through the mind of a third. Rather, they communicate through the materiality of words, and thus through the materiality of the passive presence of others in their use of language. Thus, when I speak with a friend in the privacy of my home, the character of our language as private is through the mediation of language as public.

### (3. RECIPROCITY, EXPLOITATION, AND REPRESSION)

We began this chapter by noting that although our immediate experience is of concrete reality, this experience is nevertheless abstract, in the sense of being superficial. For example, the superficial reality of a conversation is that it is a reciprocity between only two persons, but when we examine this reciprocity in detail we see that it always involves a mediation through a third. In this context, we must keep in mind the complexity of the dialectic, remembering particularly that, on a certain level, the abstract is real and the concrete must always be rethought within the context of the abstract.

We may recall that the first chapter of book I began with an abstract description of how totalization results from individual praxis. On this level, the dialectic is completely translucent, because it is the life of workers in their work: while pruning the rose bush, the gardener knows that he is gardening. But, moving to a more concrete, synthetic level, we see in this second chapter that each worker's direct relation to matter is simultaneous with the relations of other workers: while pruning the rose bush, the gardener knows both that he is not mending the road and that he and a road mender are workers. For Sartre, however, all personal relations are possible only because their schema already exists in matter; gardening and road mending are possible jobs only because there is a specialized world in which gardens and roads need to be maintained by specialized jobs. It is a de facto occurrence that these schemas also imply mediation; that is, they have entered into a hierarchy of totalizations that make history.

Since the concrete reality of being human is determined by praxis, that is, by a specific historical relation to matter, reciprocity will differ according to its historical circumstances. No *definition* of reciprocity is thus possible. We can give what may sound like a definition, but the words must be interpreted heuristically. We can say that reciprocity is a bond of interiority between individuals, arising from a unification in matter, that preserves the distinctiveness of each subjectivity. This description is not a definition, for at least two reasons. First, it does not and cannot give us the various abstract and concrete levels to which it applies. It may apply on an abstract level but not on a concrete level. It may be that, in this case, the abstract is more important than the concrete. Second, a phrase such as "unification in matter" is, in this case, but a shorthand for the ambiguous totality of instruments, institutions, and pluralities of people that mediate reciprocity differently in each case. For example, in the concrete, reciprocity can exist within alienation, exploitation, and repression. We shall see later on, Sartre says, that these forms of inhuman behavior are dialectically produced out of their opposites. Thus, of itself, reciprocity is not a guarantee of human dignity.

Here Sartre gives a few examples to show how reciprocity always occurs through the mediation of a third, and how it can exist within such relations as exploitation. For example, workers who sell themselves as a commodity in exchange for wages, enjoy, at the moment of the exchange, a bond of reciprocity in the freely drawn contract. The free contract, however, hides the historical situation, which requires that the workers, because of poverty, sell themselves in this way. Sartre says, "absolute respect for the freedom of the propertyless is the best way of leaving him at the mercy of material constraints, at the moment of the contract" (E, 110; F, 190; NF, 222).

Also, the way in which the third is present affects the reciprocity. Sartre uses the example of two workers performing a task together. We must not imagine that their union exists in some disembodied "getting together of minds," so that instead of two subjectivities there is now an idealistic bond between minds alone. Each subjectivity is separated simply because each body is separate. In this respect, Sartre parenthetically mentions that the complexity of history exists because of plurality. This plurality is real; it occurs differently with different effects. Returning to our example, the unity of the two workers originates from the unity in the object. Each one's project is to be included in the other's. But this reciprocity of projects is already given in the workers' tools and environment. The explicit awareness of their mutual bond requires the existence of another, as a third, to activate the reciprocity embodied in their tools. If two persons were raised alone on a desert island, they would not have reciprocity as we know it. Each would see the distinctive ways in which they have *separately* objectified themselves in matter. They would not be able to see the community of their objectifications. Indeed, the community could not exist, because there could be no material means through which it could occur. Only through a third could the two establish and then recognize a common objectification that both would see as common. That is, only through a third could each see that both were seen by another in a common way.

We might, on the other hand, picture a desert island with three inhabitants. *Regressively,* we could picture this trinity as the "basis" for our historical reciprocity, in that any one of the three, at any time, could be the mediator for the other two. Nevertheless, Sartre notes that this relation of the dyad (any two) to the third would be an interior relation, but *not reciprocal and not totalizing.* It might be interior, because it could conceivably define the subjectivity of each, either as a mediator or as within the reciprocal bond. It could not be reciprocal, because there could be no reciprocity between the mediator and the other two *as a couple.* The relation between the mediator and the other two could not be totalizing because the subjectivities do not exist in the world as interiorities that are united. Only as being in matter could they be negated, transcended, and totalized. Perhaps an expansion will clarify this important point. Let us imagine the three on the island to be an old man living alone and a young couple setting up house together. Sartre is here making two related points: First, the couple cannot have reciprocity as we know it, because they do not see themselves in the world as a "couple." Second, the old man cannot provide this mediation. He can only contribute another private opinion about their togetherness, an opinion to consider along with their own. Reciprocity as we know it, however, requires that there be in the world, for example, in the institution of marriage, an objective couple, and that our couple negate and transcend this objectively given couple. In this context the "third" is any couple as married.

The way the mediator is present affects the bonds of interiority. For example, Sartre notes, if we imagine the mediator to be a timekeeper clocking the movements of the two workers in our earlier example, his mediation effectively removes the distinctiveness of each worker's subjectivity. Through the presence of the timekeeper, each worker sees his individuality to be inessential; it is the activity that is essential. The two workers become very aware that their personal lives are private, and although they are working in common, conscious of sharing each other's fate, they are also aware of the inessentiality of their individualities.

The above analysis is of course still very abstract, and we are not maintaining that history was additively built up by a hierarchy of thirds. Regressively, however, a ternary relation is seen to be fundamental to our historical existence. This ternary relation is an aspect of our materiality and not a Hegelian synthesis of two individuals as thesis and antithesis. In the concrete, our material environment is very complex. Groups as well as individuals can have a type of reciprocal bond through other groups. We must also see how class relations affect reciprocity and indeed make it possible. The workers are members of a class, and we have no knowledge of what history would be like without class distinctions. We must establish gradually more sophisticated tools that can cope with historical complexities. Our next step will be to show how human relations affect a material milieu. Of course, we are working within the dialectic. If history is a totalization, then the individual praxis totalizes a practical field, and, reciprocally, this practical field should now be revealed as a field totalized by innumerable human relations.

# 3    Matter as Totalized Totality: A First Encounter with Necessity

## 1. SCARCITY AND MODE OF PRODUCTION

This may be a useful place to recall that the entire book 1 is entitled "From Individual Praxis to the Practico-Inert." "Practico-inert" is Sartre's term for matter as totalized by praxis in such a way that it is imbued with an inertia enabling it to react to praxis with a "counterpraxis," or "antipraxis," of its own. That is, practically speaking, our "world" has interests of its own that are not in harmony with our interests. There is no a priori reason why this had to be so; it is de facto the way we have worked matter. The elucidation of this reciprocal, multilayered interaction between praxis and antipraxis is the task of this *Critique*. Sartre's procedure, sketched in the two introductory parts, requires us to reexamine our tools, at each level of our investigation, that is, to reconsider in what way the dialectic is dialectical. Furthermore, we must examine how praxis constitutes its object even as it is being constituted by it.

As a guide, one can point to at least seven sections in the *Critique* where, as the dialectic becomes increasingly concrete, our regressive method reveals praxis and antipraxis to have new characteristics not deducible from the earlier abstract stages of the dialectic: in book I, the sections on need (*le besoin*), duality, scarcity or rarity (*la rareté*), and serial behavior (*la série*); and, in book II, the sections on the apocalyptic moment of group fusion, the pledge or oath (*le serment*), and institutional praxis. At each level, the regressive study reveals that freedom has altered matter to create our present historical milieu. Our regressive approach identifies certain internal relations between praxis and matter as more abstract than others, but all these material relations de facto exist at every level of our lives. Thus, in the concrete, our needs are complex, mediated, historical needs that clash, as we will see, with the needs of machines. But it is still true that need can be identified on a most abstract level—for example, the need for food.

Our needs, however, do not become more concrete in a neutral context. Thus, we saw that labor as a praxis to satisfy needs is a relation not only to matter but also to mediating thirds. Moreover, mediation and labor do not develop into technology in a neutral environment. At this level, our regressive approach identifies *scarcity* or *rarity* as the specific milieu that gives our modes of production their antihuman inertia. Of itself, technology is neutral; if it turns against us, it is because we have constructed, as it were, an inertial system in which machines project their destiny beyond our own projects. In this milieu of scarcity, we encounter not obstacles to our freedom but a necessity that overrides our praxis insofar as our praxis attempts to have historical weight.

In each of the pivotal dialectical moments that I have mentioned, it is thus important to recognize that we are not examining some neutral, factual situation to see how it has influenced history. Such a nonhistorical attitude would contradict everything that was said in the introduction. Rather, we are elucidating structures that are already historical. Thus, scarcity, or rarity, does not refer merely to some objective shortage of food, for example, but rather to this shortage precisely as it is an aspect of our modes of production. Here, the subtitle—"Scarcity and Mode of Production" ("*Rareté et mode de production*")—is one of the few given in the French text. Once again, Sartre's perspective must be kept in mind. We are concerned, therefore, primarily with the scarcity that we sustain in existence *as the past of our present*. Everything that has been said about Sartre's nominalism must also be recalled, particularly that this scarcity is already connected to a scarcity resulting from class struggle and colonialization, a scarcity yet to be examined.

The term "scarce" in English is more objectively neutral than the term "rare." Book dealers, for example, call a book "scarce" if there are few of them available, regardless of whether anybody desires them. A book is rare, however, if it is desirable and expensive. *Usually* this means the book is also scarce, but not always. There are certain "rare" books that are always available if one is willing to pay the price. Sometimes the price of rare books is the result of supply and demand; that is, there are not enough book collectors who would buy the book at a higher price. But the price can also be artificially established. One book dealer may own many copies, or several dealers may establish the price together. Rarity as the result of praxis is even clearer in the instance of the production of lithographs. An artist now has the technology to produce an almost unlimited number of "original" lithographs of identical quality, but a dealer will tell an artist to do a very small number in order to keep the price high. These trivial cases are not really what Sartre is concerned about, but they do raise the question of why a society should so spontaneously accept the desirability of possessing rare objects. Mere individual psychological preference does not explain a history that requires rarity. Sartre's point is that even where we have the means to eliminate rarity we do not do so, because that would abolish history as we know it.

The opening paragraphs of this section set the context for the discussion of "scarcity," a term that we will now accept as a translation of *la rareté*. The world is not an objective arrangement of atoms that is altered merely extrinsically by human relations. Such a world might be the strange, temporary abode of a pure mind, but it could not be the world of a human organism. Everything that human beings encounter is matter intrinsically altered by praxis as a totalization of the environment. The world is the interiorization of the human organism and is the project as transcendence. This world is a world of struggle, because there is not enough for all. But it will become clear that this scarcity is also the world as made scarce by praxis.

Indeed, one distinct aspect of the *Critique* is that it examines the way matter as "passive activity" is a counterpraxis to human praxis. Sartre notes that others, including Marxists, have studied how human beings fight against nature, the social structure, and each other but that no one has tried to study how human beings fight against their *own* praxis. For Sartre, a historical environment receives our praxes and, by its passive activity, acts on us by counterpraxes.

### i. Scarcity (and History)

Scarcity, Sartre says, is "a fundamental relation of *our* history and a contingent determination of our univocal relation to materiality" (E, 125; F, 202; NF, 237).

Sartre's description of scarcity as both fundamental and contingent is consistent with the general elucidation of the relation between necessity and contingency given in *Being and Nothingness*. There he also described such phenomena as the "look" as contingent and yet radically altering our consciousness. Indeed, for Sartre, there is no reason why consciousness itself has to exist, but, given its existence, it establishes necessary relations within matter. In a similar way, scarcity is an aspect of "both the necessity of our contingency and the contingency of our necessity" (E, 124; F, 202; NF, 236).

Scarcity is contingent because we have no a priori way of knowing whether another organism could exist in an environment without scarcity. Scarcity is not simply finitude; it is not merely the fact that we cannot do everything at once. If there were only a few million people existing throughout the world, with all their needs and comforts provided for mechanically or easily by the environment, scarcity would disappear. These people would be finite, but not "human" as we know humanity. So radical would the elimination of scarcity be that, according to Sartre, we cannot conceive what a consciousness existing outside the milieu of scarcity would be like.

There is a very abstract sense of scarcity that describes the condition of any organism in relation to its planetary environment. Still there is no reason why scarcity as we know it had to occur.[1] Once scarcity became the milieu of our

---

1. The regressive method points to an abstract notion of scarcity arising from the limited con-

history, however, it altered both the bonds of reciprocity that unite us to our fellow human beings and the interior but unilateral bonds that unite each of us to our material environment. Indeed, insofar as scarcity alters our consciousness, it internally affects our body, or, in the language of *Being and Nothingness*, it radically changes the way we *exist our body*.

Since some primitive societies have a condition of scarcity apparently similar to what may have led to our own history, we cannot say that scarcity is, of itself, sufficient to produce history. Rather, our regressive analysis reveals scarcity as the basis only for the *possibility* of our history. If we reflect upon it, it becomes clear that everything we do is in the milieu of scarcity. Three-fourths of the world's inhabitants, Sartre says, are undernourished, and millions are actually starving. The hungry and the unsheltered of the world are always present to each of us. William James said that if we but broke down a few of our walls, we would see the hungry of the world staring at us. But Sartre's view is more radical: scarcity alters our every prereflective thought and gesture. Whether we are reflecting upon it or not, we always act in the milieu *that there is not enough for all*. And the crucial point is that *we are responsible for the condition of scarcity* in the strict, historical sense.

Although historical circumstances can alter the particular way scarcity may appear—giving a higher standard of living now to this group, now to another—scarcity exists at any one period as a *hexis* (in the *Critique* and in *Being and Nothingness*, Sartre consistently but mistakenly writes *exis*), that is, as the habitual, unspoken judgment on the human condition, such as the belief that man must work by the sweat of his brow.

As the basis for the possibility of *our* history, scarcity affects all our totalizations. Our praxis imprints a seal upon matter, embedding meanings in it, as, for example, when we build a highway. Through our organic needs, the environment thus becomes a totalized totality—a city, a nation—but, because of scarcity, this totality has a nonhuman aspect. Overpopulation becomes a constant threat; in numerous ways, implicit as well as explicit, scarcity chooses its undernourished and its dead. The unborn are already unwanted. This totalized environment thus divides humanity. The first structure of this totalized matter is negative in regard to humanity as a whole. There is not only the possibility of universal destruction but also "the permanent possibility that this destruction through matter might come to any individual through

dition of our organic existence within a planetary existence. But this "scarcity" is not the scarcity of our history, and there is no reason to conclude that a scarcity arising from our finite condition would lead to alienation. Critics such as Raymond Aron have distorted the entire development of the *Critique*, by failing to distinguish a sustained scarcity as the past of our present from an abstract scarcity. In particular, Aron projects a transcendental deduction onto Sartre's dialectical nominalism (*History and the Dialectic of Violence*, trans. Barry Cooper [Oxford: Basil Blackwell Publishing, 1975], 34–36).

the *praxis* of other men" (E, 127; F, 204; NF, 239). Although we will see that collective and group praxes are possible, they can never arise as such from scarcity, which is always divisive. Thus, the seed is sown for totalized matter as antipraxis, and the unity of group praxis will have to confront this non-human praxis.

Our discussion of scarcity, Sartre notes, is of course very abstract, and our main purpose is merely to note the dialectical intelligibility within scarcity. We can thus recognize that the totalizations within the milieu of scarcity are circular. The environment as scarce produces individuals as survivors. Furthermore, scarcity as the condition for the possibility of our history reemerges in our very efforts to transcend it. It appears as the nonhuman aspect of every praxis. I may wish only to buy food, be employed, buy a house, or have a friend, and I discover that I have taken something from someone else. Even if I buy a house that no one else wants, I have a home amid the homeless. Their inability to buy a house is the ever present nonhumanity within my humanity. Conversely, as a potentially starving and homeless person, I am a threat to my fellow human beings. I am even a threat to myself, because I never know what I might do because of scarcity. I thus always face myself as *other;* that is, as nonhuman. Humanity in the milieu of scarcity is an alien species that plots to kill human beings, and I am one such alien.

The concrete form of our reciprocity, that is, our reciprocity in its historical dimension, is altered by our sustained scarcity. Our regressive analysis indicates that wherever there is that historical entity of a "human being," reciprocity is always conditioned by this scarcity. When I try to make the goals of my companions my own in a common praxis, the nonhumanity in each of our ends turns to face us, dividing our action from us. Nevertheless, on an abstract, local level, the alienation resulting from scarcity can indeed be eliminated among particular interpersonal relations.[2]

2. As the dialectic develops in its spiral movement, the notion of alienation appears in ever-widening contexts, which in fact have always been present uncritically. It is thus contrary to Sartre's procedure to attempt to give one criteria for eliminating alienation. According to Pietro Chiodi, a viable notion of alienation requires that "the 'subject,' the bearer of alienation, is so conceived as to be capable of both losing, and eventually recovering, his own being" (*Sartre and Marxism*, trans. Kate Soper [Atlantic Highlands, N.J.: Humanities Press, 1976]) (82). This claim, however, is ambiguous. To the extent that a distinctive alienation appears on a local level, an individual may be able to remove it: for example, a mother may be able to eliminate a generation gap between herself and her daughter. If the context is wider, group or national effort is required to eliminate alienation: the American Civil War as an attempt to eliminate slavery. But if alienation is historical—because, for instance, our cultivated society makes each of us to be the competing other—then it can be removed only through collectively altering our historical environment. Sartre's point in the *Critique* is that dialectical comprehension allows us to become conscious of this historical alienation, even while we are within it.

In our search to reveal the intelligibility of totalizations as they occur in the milieu of scarcity, we can note, Sartre says, the first stages of ethics insofar as they are a praxis. Ethics are here seen as unfolding within the context of a Manichaean conception of evil as a force to be eliminated.

In a general way, the problem that Sartre faced in attempting to construct an ethic is that the rights and duties that any ethic would elucidate refers to the relations among elitist classes that in fact oppress lower classes. Traditional ethics never really address the problem of the totality of these rights and duties as they are related to the condition of the underprivileged. Moreover, Sartre's understanding of the Manichaean aspect of the history that we have constituted for ourselves must have presented an obstacle to the satisfactory construction of an ethic. Thus, it must have been evident to Sartre that our practical fundamental ethical principle is *that evil must be destroyed,* and that this principle merely makes explicit an aspect of the human condition that needs to be explicated. In *Being and Nothingness* and *Anti-Semite and Jew,* this fundamental aspect was referred to somewhat abstractly as a project in bad faith. Here, in the more concrete discussion of the *Critique,* the orientation toward destroying evil is seen as an aspect of the special ways in which scarcity reemerges, even when we attempt to transcend it. In the concrete, our projects emerge in the context of scarcity, and therefore within the permanent threat of falling into a form of Manichaeism. Sartre's brief but complex remarks touch very broad themes, and I can merely suggest what I think is the general direction of his thought.

Prior to the *Critique,* I believe that Sartre's most general and abstract matrix for an ethic could be described as follows: A moral life should be oriented to accomplishing good. But good is ambiguous; it is never clear what is the right thing to do, and we can never be certain that the results are as we intended them. Still, a moral life is one that accepts the attempt to put good in the world, even in the face of despair, anguish, and abandonment. This "despair," this "abandonment," this "anguish" is simply the willingness to act in the direction of the more human even though there are no guarantees for success. Some may object to those who embrace this human condition, saying, "How can you aim at doing something that is more or less good if there is no maximum, no ideal good by which things can be judged to be more or less good?" The proper answer would be that this theoretical, analytic problem disappears in the concrete. For example, it is sufficient to take my own well-fed, well-clothed, well-housed body as the "more human" and a starving, naked, homeless body as the "less human," and it is sufficient, at this level, that my praxis aims at allowing the other to live as I live.[3]

3. The emphasis here is on a collective responsibility. Past practices have established a pattern, given inertia, and produced large-scale objective conditions for the possibility of praxis, but, at present, we are responsible for our historical situation to the extent that we sustain, fur-

But many people are frightened by such freedom and ambiguity. Lazy, and demanding final success and security, they hypostasize the human aspects of good and evil into the forces of Good and Evil. Moral action is thus made to appear easy: Destroy the force of Evil that dams up Good, and good results will overflow into the world. Those in bad faith thus see the human struggle to occur within nonhuman dimensions. They would not hesitate to destroy whole populations as Evil. No one, however, can live continually with the nonhuman dimension of this antihumanism, and such people thus live their everyday lives on a more human scale. But their bad faith, as a project radically different from good faith, is always present, a permanent threat of destruction.

In *Being and Nothingness,* Sartre had already made it clear that good and bad projects were more basic than any ethical judgments. Ethics involve choice and responsibility in some way, and Sartre insisted that he was working in an ontology that could not judge responsibility. Thus, we can describe the radical difference between a life of good faith and one of bad faith, but we cannot say how responsible individuals are for the general direction of their lives. A child growing up during the Third Reich would no doubt believe that Jews should be destroyed. It is impossible to know to what degree the child could awaken to the inhumanity of this view. The question of ethical choice, the question of authenticity, concerns those in good faith. Thus, in *Anti-Semite and Jew,* it is the Jew who must respond either authentically or inauthentically to the bad faith of the anti-Semite.

An analysis of Manichaeism in Sartre's *Saint Genet* would be the next crucial step both in tracing Sartre's efforts in formulating an ethic and in understanding the elliptical remarks in the *Critique.* A situation can be in bad faith, and a project in good faith would be tragic in such a situation. In good faith, we try to learn about ourselves from others. We try to balance our intimate awareness of ourselves with our understanding of how others see us. In a healthy community, we can judge among several objective views about our

---

ther, or try to alter the inertia of the practico-inert. For an excellent study of how collective responsibility is consistent with Sartre's rejection of an organismic notion of society, see Thomas R. Flynn, *Sartre and Marxist Existentialism* (Chicago: University of Chicago Press, 1984), 52–169. Aron, on the contrary, begins his *History* with a caricature of Sartre's dialectic— *"Probably for the first time a philosopher discovers the dialectic in solitude"* (25, author's italics)—and he continues his self-imposed Cartesian interpretation of Sartre throughout. For example, Sartre's point about scarcity is not that each of us as an individual would be different if we fortuitously lived in an environment of "unlimited products" (Aron, *History,* 32) but rather that our humanity would be different if we could collectively relinquish our hold on scarcity, our praxes that sustain the poor as poor. Also, Aron strangely attributes to Sartre and to Simone de Beauvoir a lazy Cartesian perspective, saying that "one wonders what is the proper classification for minds capable of grasping the social whole without analyzing its elements" (*Marxism and the Existentialists,* trans. Helen Weaver, Robert Addis and John Weightman [New York: Harper & Row, 1969], 80). Sartre and Beauvoir are in fact careful about details; one has merely to read their works unbiasedly.

behavior. In Sartre's interpretation of Genet's situation, everyone in his small community saw him as a little thief. Genet initially had no awareness of himself as a thief, but he took seriously the views of others, seeing them as the more justified. His project became to interiorize this objective statement of guilt and crime. Genet's good faith was his openness to his environment; his authenticity was his willingness to interiorize what he understood to be his objective situation. The situation itself was in bad faith; that is, those around him were in bad faith and imbued bad faith into their institutions. Genet's project was thus tragic. If he wished to remain in good faith, he had no choice but to encounter his objective "thiefhood." For Genet, this appropriation of his situation was also his transcendence, his life as a writer. Genet wrote not as an innocent in a cruel world, but as one continually attempting to transcend the thiefhood given him by others.

In the *Critique,* the projects of good and bad faith become subsidiary to the Manichaean context of the environment. Furthermore, Manichaeism is seen to originate from the milieu of scarcity and thus to be an aspect of the history that has made us human. Because of scarcity, the inhuman has become a part of our humanity. I thus seek to destroy humanity as humanity when I seek to destroy it as enemy and as evil. This inhumanity becomes embedded in our institutions and is an aspect of the antipraxis of totalized matter. A complex matrix exists in which Manichaeism is now a habitual aspect of our history, always capable of being actualized.

Individual praxis is ambiguously situated within this matrix: although we should avoid operating within the context of good and evil as hypostasized forces, these forces *do* passively exist, as embedded in our environment; they are *objective.* Thus a praxis that attempts to operate in the openness of a good and evil of human proportions operates also in the context of an institutionalized, absolute evil. The alien who might activate the mechanism of armament and destroy an entire world is myself.

But a "choice" must be made. We either abandon the ambiguous fight in its human proportions—allowing ourselves to be moved passively by the antihuman forces brought about by past human actions and creating more inhumanity by our inactivity—or we operate under the constant threat of Manichaeism, but never accepting it, never allowing our lives to be guided by either absolute good or absolute evil. Indeed, the essence of Manichaeism is that there is no practical difference between the two.

This explanation is, of course, very abstract, because it is at this stage that *violence* arises. Are we then to submit passively to those who have embraced Manichaeism and see us as the evil to be destroyed? Sartre has never condoned passive submission. But we must be careful not to embrace Manichaeism ourselves. The choice of violence is difficult because violence always appears, Sartre says, as counterviolence. It always appears as justified by the potential violence of others and by the passive presence of absolute evil as an aspect of our situation. But there is a genuine counterviolence, one that does not use the inhumanity that is a part of our humanity as an excuse for initiating violence. This counterviolence truly responds to the actual violence of others and not merely to threats; it accepts the anguish of destroying humanity in the enemy.[4]

Thus, the relation of an individual to the environment through scarcity gives, Sartre says, "the abstract matrix of every reification of human relations in any society" (E, 132; F, 208; NF, 244). Because of scarcity, there exists the permanent threat that the bonds of reciprocity between myself and others will degenerate, and that we will each see ourselves as alien beings fighting over the same planet. Moreover, scarcity creates the permanent possibility of personifying my fellow human being as Evil incarnate. Here Sartre alludes to an important but ambiguous point: armies, classes, and lesser groups seem capable, *in principle*, of transcending scarcity. This remark, within the context of the discussion of Manichaeism, seems to mean that when an army or group is organized against an enemy as Evil, it transcends within itself the bonds of scarcity. Nothing seems to unite us so easily as the belief that we are fighting absolute evil. In our efforts to defeat the enemy, we pool our resources and diminish our own condition of scarcity. But this unity of action is deceptive: the enemy is a *human* army, and we hate and kill human beings when destroying the enemy as Evil; when we hate the enemy, we hate ourselves. But in our daily skirmishes with the enemy, the mystifying haze of Good and Evil disappears and we recognize the enemy's humanity.

It is also at the level of violence and war that power relations most clearly emerge. War, Sartre says, is a "labour of man upon man" (E, 136; F, 211; NF, 248). When one individual or a group has an advantage, praxis becomes *power.* In the context of Manichaeism, this power can become as absolute as the evil it apparently combats. But the power, in its Manichaean context, does not create any human good: when war is over, the real problems of life return with even more telling force.

The important point is that we can be united in groups to fight the conditions of scarcity, and one wonders what would happen if an army fought to remove scarcity instead of another army. William James had a similar thought in his essay on the moral equivalent of war. But Sartre's conception and reservations are again more radical than those of William James. A sustained scarcity is the basis for the possibility of our history; thus, whenever it is fought in one area, it will reemerge in another. We will see that, for Sartre, it is an aspect of our mode of production, although it is not caused by a mode of production. But, before continuing, it seems appropriate to make two observa-

---

4. Cf. Simone de Beauvoir, *The Ethics of Ambiguity,* trans. Bernard Frechtman (New York: Philosophical Library, 1948), 129–55.

tions. First, one can always use this ambiguity as an excuse not to fight against scarcity. Sartre is certainly not suggesting passivity, for this would be to live within the simple goal of Manichaeism, and to desire a clear evil to destroy before attempting to create good. Second, it seems that we must operate on two levels. We must attempt to relieve hunger and suffering when it occurs locally. But we must also be aware that some global perspective and praxis is needed.

At present, our history emerges within the context of a scarcity of essential goods for all. But this scarcity is complex: workers and consumers are both expendable and scarce. Luxuries are overproduced, while whole populations starve. Indeed, capitalism has been historically constituted so that *over-production requires this level of the needy*. For example, it seems clear that the constant movement of fashions throughout the world is to a great extent made possible by the silent constant that millions should go naked. Historically, we also know that nations have exported necessities such as bread, keeping vast populations underfed, while they imported luxuries for the few.

A sustained scarcity is thus an aspect of every totalization of our environment. It presents the perpetual threat of dividing us against each other and thus against ourselves; it has also brought about those very territorial totalizations that characterize our history. Sartre uses the example of the Chinese peasants and nomads. To the nomads, the peasants are seen to be continually encroaching on the nomads' land. To the peasants, the nomads are invaders, constantly threatening to confiscate the land the peasants have tilled. *Regressively*, we see from our present historical existence that the scarcity of land "caused" the tension that made the environment of both nomad and peasant a common field of action.

### ii. Scarcity and Marxism

In a footnote at the conclusion of these pages, Sartre states: "It must be clearly understood that the rediscovery of scarcity in this investigation makes absolutely no claim either to oppose Marxist theory, or to complete it. It is of a different order" (E, 152 n. 35; F, 224–25 n. 1; NF, 263 n. 1). But Sartre adds that Marx did realize the impossibility of interpreting history from a nonhistorical perspective; he knew that we must always be correcting our understanding of how the past actually occurred and was further able to show—this for Sartre was one of his main contributions—that "labour, as a historical reality and as a utilisation of particular tools in an already determined social and material situation, is the real foundation of the organisation of social relations. This discovery *can no longer* be questioned" (ibid.).[5] Marx

5. Nevertheless, the entire discussion makes it clear that this remark must be interpreted in a context in which labor, of itself, is not the sufficient cause of human relations' being the way they

did not explicitly formulate or strictly abide by a regressive attitude, nor, according to Sartre, did he explicitly examine the significance of scarcity, which he took for granted; he seemed to view scarcity as an accidental condition of humanity that resulted from ignorance.

For Sartre, however, it was Engels rather than Marx who claimed that an abstract necessity existed in history. Engels tried to show that, given the modes of production, the clashes among classes had to occur. But, according to Sartre, *there is no reason, in the abstract, why a capitalist or any mode of production should necessarily lead to the development of class societies, precisely as they are antagonistic groups.* One can easily imagine a technological society in which more than enough for everyone is always produced, although we cannot concretely imagine what kind of humanity would live in such a society. Division of labor would no doubt arise, but there seems no reason why this should have to develop into a struggle of classes. That it did so in our past is true. Thus, a positive historical circumstance must have occasioned changes that later established necessary relations through totalizations. Although we cannot be certain that society always produced less than was needed, it is conceivable that an underfed and expendable population became necessary if others were to live well. This inhumanity became accepted as a necessary, objective structure of humanity, and then it indeed became objective. In this sense, we might say that the biblical comment "The poor you have always with you" is a judgment about what human beings have done to each other in the milieu of scarcity, and not an a priori condition of humanity.

Sartre also briefly locates his thought on scarcity in the context of Engels's dispute with Eugen Dühring. Engels, Sartre explains, correctly chided Dühring for foolishly claiming that property relations were always based on violence. Engels was able to show that property relations frequently exist without actual violence. But Dühring, according to Sartre, saw something that neither Engels nor Marx perceived, namely, that in all our relations we see the other not only as one of us but also as the one who threatens us. Dühring was wrong in interpreting this to be *actual* violence. Violence does not have to be either actual or even intended for there to be the possibility of violence as a permanent but passive aspect of the environment.

The error of Dühring and that of the classical economists of the time who stressed scarcity, such as Adam Smith and Malthus, are, according to Sartre, exact opposites. The economists held that scarcity was an accidental characteristic of human nature. Dühring, however, claimed that our wills were enslaved and that we thus had a spontaneous impulse toward violence. But if the

---

arc. For example, the division between skilled and unskilled labor established an objective condition for a division within the working class. The following discussion makes it clear, however, that this division did not require the substantive, cultural alienation between skilled and unskilled workers that de facto occurred.

insights of both sides are retained, we recognize that, since there is no human nature, historical circumstances, if they are basic enough, can alter the very meaning of humanity.

It thus becomes evident that Marx's historical laws work only when we grant the content of history. *Given* class struggle, we can see how diverse modes of production define human relations and alienation. The modes of production can account for the origin of classes only when these modes are seen as working in the milieu of scarcity. That is, the milieu of scarcity explains the general reason for conflict; the modes of production explain the particular manifestations of conflict in any society.

Marx's thought, according to Sartre, stops short of explaining the origins of the negative in history. There is no reason, in the abstract, why our attempts to objectify ourselves in matter should be alienating. Praxis is alienating because, in the milieu of scarcity, everything that we do has an aspect of inhumanity. For example, in the abstract, there is no reason why an artist's production of a piece of sculpture should be alienating. In the concrete, however, the artist's work is time and energy spent on a luxury when millions are starving. The artist's demand for supplies is de facto a demand for luxuries amid scarcity. Nor would it help for the artist to stop sculpting and start farming. There are no easy answers. What we must do is to at least attempt to understand the intelligibility of our history, if we are to control it.

### 2. WORKED MATTER AS THE ALIENATED OBJECTIFICATION OF INDIVIDUAL AND COLLECTIVE PRAXIS

Alienation, for Sartre, exists because praxis occurs in the milieu of a sustained scarcity. He thus distinguishes his view not only from that of Hegel, but also from those of Marx and Engels. We have already seen the general context of these remarks: *there is no a priori reason why either reciprocity or the capitalist's mode of production should result in alienation.*

Sartre, however, does not object to Marx in the same way he objects to Hegel. Aside from the fact that Hegel dialectically deduces the master-slave relation from the nature of consciousness itself, his descriptions are idealistic because *the* master and *the* slave do not exist. At any one time, there are many types of masters and slaves with complex relations within their own classes as well as with each other. Marx, however, correctly sees alienation to originate from material situations. Specifically, Marx's own descriptions reveal alienation as resulting from the constraints of tools. Thus, the concrete means of producing coal during the late eighteenth and early nineteenth centuries restructured the entire society, producing new human types, such as "iron and coal men."

For Sartre, the descriptions of Marx are correct, on their own level. But these descriptions point to a more basic negation about which neither Marx nor Engels were concerned. Sartre's point is that Marx and Engels pass over the strangeness of the fact that the discovery of a new source of wealth should produce more extreme conditions of poverty and fatigue for groups of humanity. Regardless of the means of production as such, the condition of all should have been improved. Coal was produced by nature, and there was no reason why human beings should try to acquire coal all at once. Sartre seems to be implying that it would make no sense to say that the greed of a few capitalists caused an entire inhumanizing complex to come into existence. Rather, a non-human milieu already existed, namely the condition of scarcity. Thus, this new positive wealth developed in the negative context *that there would never be enough for all no matter what improvements were made.* Iron and coal developed in the *objective* situation of a society whose general historical existence required a segment of its population to be disposable. In this way, every positive cultural advancement redefines rather than eliminates its poor and oppressed. Modes of production do explain the specific ways scarcity disappears in one area only to be found more deeply in another area, affecting other groups. They do not, however, explain why an increase in wealth should of itself lead to class antagonisms. In the abstract, the same means of production could have produced a bettering of conditions for all amid the accumulation of wealth by a greedy few.

Nevertheless, we must not think that every individual praxis translucently experiences the milieu of scarcity as such. Indeed, it is on this level that we encounter the first genuine complexity within praxis as distinct from mere action.

To indicate the direction of this complexity, it may be useful to return to the example of tennis playing. Insofar as I play tennis for my own purposes, for example, to please a friend, I transcend the international sport of tennis. This negation and surpassing is an aspect of the translucent activity, my tennis playing. Nevertheless, this does not imply that I thematically or explicitly transcend tennis as an international sport. Such quasi thematization may be present when, for example, someone plays in the context of a choice not to play tennis for money and professional competition. Regardless, however, of such thematization, the international "sport" of tennis is within every game of tennis, escaping the translucent bond of knowledge to being. When I hit a tennis ball, I am implicitly aware of being either an amateur or professional. In an analogous way, the historical transformation of action into praxis causes a fundamental alienation to occur on the prereflective level. *Locally,* my praxis may not occur in the milieu of scarcity. I may be aware of my praxis only as improving my condition, and, on this local level, my experience is real. But, in our present historical situation, our praxis is also received in a matter totalized by past human actions. Through these totalizations, every praxis occurs within a broad milieu of society, within which it participates, as Sartre says, in society's choice of its own dead. On the historical level, every praxis takes place *in* violence, although not *by* violence. We will see shortly that this occurs because matter has been so totalized that it both receives our praxis and also acts on us with an inverted counterpraxis. From this respect, the purpose of Sartre's *Critique* is to enable us to comprehend the alienated aspect of our praxis through the dialectical understanding of the relation of praxis to antipraxis.

This comprehension of praxis and antipraxis will, of course, always be from a perspective within our history and language. We may thus note, for example, some of the strangeness in our way of referring to machines without implying that our own observations and comments are neutral. Sartre approvingly quotes Lewis Mumford's remark that "steam power *fostered* the *tendency* toward large industrial plants" (E, 159; F, 230; NF, 270).[6] The anthropomorphism in the terms "fostered" and "tendency" draws our attention to the general way machines produce their own kind of machine-like human beings. The exact meaning of these locutions is, for Sartre, ambiguous and difficult to determine, but they indicate the necessity of examining in detail matter precisely as it is an inverted praxis (*praxis renversée*).[7]

### (i. Matter as Inverted Praxis)

The following pages stand as a pivotal movement in the dialectical development of the *Critique*. Here the discussion explicitly turns from the previous abstract discussion of human action to the distinctiveness of praxis. Of course, this present description of praxis is abstract in relation to the more concrete study of class being and group praxis that is to follow. Nevertheless, Sartre notes that we here reach one of the concrete characteristics of our historicity.

"*Every praxis,*" Sartre says, "is primarily an instrumentalization of material reality" (E, 161; F, 231; NF, 271). Praxis is not merely the human use of tools within nature; it is rather the very means of converting "inert matter" into that instrumentalized matter called "nature" and "culture." Here, everything that has thus far been said about Sartre's unique materialism and what I have called his "anthropocentrism" must be kept in mind. Specifically, the term "inert matter" is a relative term indicating matter as it exists prior to a praxis. From another perspective, so-called inert matter is always altered by the human organism from which it receives inertia and unity. Although matter becomes totalized by receiving numerous individual praxes, it never achieves

6. The editor of the English edition provides the following footnote: Lewis Mumford, *Technics and Civilization* (New York: Harcourt, Brace and Co., 1934), 162. The italics are Sartre's.

7. This section should be compared with what Sartre has to say about "forces" in nature in *Being and Nothingness*. See *BN*, 186–204; *Commentary BN*, 137–43.

the organic unity of the human organism. But so-called natural facts that disrupt cities, such as gravity or volcanic eruptions, are "socialized facts." It is the city's unity that unites otherwise separate actions into, for example, the thing called "erupting volcano." To repeat what has been said earlier, this unity of nature is not subjective; it is rather a unique exteriorization of the interiority of human praxis, possessing its own appropriate unity. On the other hand, if so-called natural facts are humanized, it is also true that social facts have their own unique unity and "thinglike" existence. Both "an atom" and the historical unity of "the Mediterranean" during, for example, the Spanish hegemony of the sixteenth century, each have their own distinct kind of existence independent of conceptual and reflective judgment. In this respect, Sartre maintains, it is possible to agree with both Durkheim, who said "treat social facts as things," and Weber, who said "social facts are not things." Social facts *are* things, Sartre says, "insofar as *all things* are, directly or indirectly, social facts" (E, 179; F, 246; NF, 289).

We must also keep in mind not only Sartre's unique materialism but also the fact that his method is regressive. More than most philosophers, Sartre kept himself well informed about current history and economics. His goal, however, is not to attempt to reconstruct the past as it actually happened but rather to comprehend the present historical ties between human beings and their environment. Our perspective thus takes place not within the abstract coordinates of time, but within temporality. Every praxis is a surpassing of the present from a past. As my every gesture toward an object is from the past "weight" of my body, every praxis is laden with our historicity. It is these *present ties with the past* that Sartre wishes to elucidate.

One of the distinctive aspects of praxis is that it acts in the face of an authorless counterpraxis. Thus, Sartre here examines: (1) how matter becomes totalized by receiving human finalities; (2) how totalized matter then has finalities *of its own;* (3) how one aspect of the distinctiveness of our history is that these new finalities are counterfinalities, that is, they act against our original intentions; and (4) how certain powerless groups suffer from these counterfinalities and how others use them for their own finalities. The point of Sartre's discussion is not to *deduce* class antagonism from the fact of counterfinality, but, working within the context of class antagonisms, to retrace a regressively "originative source" for these antagonisms.[8]

To repeat: in the abstract, there is no reason why our alteration of the environment should have resulted in a counterfinality. Conceivably, totalizations could have arisen in which matter's "passive action" was only secondarily a

8. I have borrowed this term from Calvin Schrag's *Radical Reflection* (West Lafayette, Ind.: Purdue University Press, 1980). As a *regressive* originative source, Sartre's position is different from that of Schrag.

counteraction. This state of affairs would have lead to a different history and
to a different humanity. This is not now possible, but it is conceivable that
by being aware of this counterfinality we can learn a new praxis that originates from an awareness of its own future counterpraxis and thus alters or
eliminates it.

Sartre develops this section through three examples: a rather short description of Chinese peasants cultivating land; a more extended analysis of the role
of precious metals during the Spanish hegemony of the sixteenth century, specifically during the reign of Philip II; and a reference to the iron and coal complex during the eighteenth and early nineteenth centuries.

To a great extent, the history of China is to be understood in relation to the
constant threat of floods. How were these floods caused? Their intensity was
certainly due to deforestation by the peasants in their cultivating of the land.
The goal—or praxis— of each peasant was positive, namely, to plant crops.
For every peasant, cultivation demanded eliminating trees. Inexorably, vast
territories were deforested. The actions were not planned by the peasants as a
group, but they were carried out serially by each peasant.[9]

The cultivated land was thus also an easy route for water; floods became
intensified, and this counterfinality began to restructure the life and praxis of
the peasant. The flooding also united the peasants, but their unity was basically negative. The peasants realized they were each helpless in the face of the
floods. If some enemy, Sartre says, had wanted to persecute the peasants, they
could not have been more effective than the peasants themselves.[10]

The presence of inverted praxis (*praxis renversée*) requires a *disposition* in
matter. Sartre notes that some flooding would have happened even if the land
had not been deforested. To have prevented flooding altogether, reforestation
would have to have been planned from earlier times. Furthermore, in order for
counterpraxis to occur, the praxis, such as deforesting, has to have an aspect
of fatality. That is, it has to be seen as the obvious thing to do by all. Thus,
each peasant saw eliminating trees as the natural way to cultivate land.

At this abstract level, however, we have not yet uncovered the characteristic
of inverted praxis. Praxis, we recall, interiorizes matter, giving it unity and
meaning. Here, however, the peasants are united only negatively; they are an
atomized group facing nature as an antihuman force. Inverted praxis occurs as
this threat of floods alters the very consciousness and life of the peasant,

9. See book I, chapter 4, section 1.

10. A similar condition exists today in the Himalayas. The peasants are being taught to see
deforestation as the cause of flooding. The task of reforestation would be hopeless, were it not for
the fact that reforesting can occur serially as the original deforestation occurred. But it is important to note that this teaching is through the historical consciousness of others; the totalization of
deforestation was not available to the early Chinese peasants. In a later interview, Sartre reiterated
the fact that the present example is only virtually dialectical. See his *Between Existentialism and
Marxism*, trans. John Mathews (New York: Pantheon Books, 1974), 52.

bringing into existence, for example, the reality of a "river civilization."
"Thus nature, though transcended, reappears within society, as the totalising
relation of all materiality to itself and of all workers to one another" (E, 165;
F, 235; NF, 276). Nevertheless, it is again important to note that Sartre's example illustrates counterpraxis regressively, that is, for us. We cannot claim
that deforestation was a counterfinality for the peasants; we do not know what
it meant for them. To the extent that we see them more or less successfully
reacting to the threat of deforestation, we already see them within our history.
But this last aspect, that of counterpraxis, or inverted praxis, by which totalized matter restructures our lives and our environment, is more evident in a
more complex example, where the forces are social, such as the role of precious metals during the reign of Philip II of Spain.

The Spanish discovery of Peruvian gold appeared—and indeed was, from
one aspect—a positive enrichment of wealth. Yet this enrichment produced a
higher cost of living and a deeper poverty for the underprivileged. Again, in
the abstract, there seems to be no reason why such an increase in wealth
should not have benefited all, although perhaps unequally. Rather, Philip's intention of accumulating gold in Spain led ultimately to the counterpraxis of
the outflow of gold and the eventual decline of Spain and its influence in the
Mediterranean.

The minting of gold coins established real relations with other coins and
with various activities of minting. A minting of a coin was more than what the
praxis of minting put into it. (Of course, from another viewpoint, this "more"
was itself produced by other praxes.) The complex significance of the coin
arose both from its quality as a precious metal and from its seal. To the extent
that it signified Spanish wealth, it was at times worth more than its value as a
precious metal. As a metal, its value was also used as a commodity that could
be stored. Spain was the vessel that *contained* gold; thus, the outflow of gold
was conceived as a loss of wealth. This is not mere imagery: the unified policies of Spain, as well as its frontiers, acted as a container.

The ambiguous entity "Spain" began to have complex relations with the
equally ambiguous entity "gold coin," relations that were only dimly understood by the individual merchants and by Philip II. First, insofar as gold was
both a sign of wealth and a commodity, it became less valuable as it became
more plentiful. Money can thus lose value without leaving one's possession.
The value of my money is not under my control, and I relate to it precisely as
something controlled by forces that are sometimes authorless. Thus, as gold
became more plentiful, prices rose, and one needed more gold to buy the
same item. The individual merchant may have indeed increased his wealth by
a thousand pieces of gold, but the value of each coin was diminishing. Although it was not understood that the devaluation was produced by the desire
to accumulate gold as wealth, inflationary prices were indeed realized locally,

and they produced numerous anticipatory practices that worsened the overall situation. Thus, to keep prices down the merchants kept wages down. In the wake of an increasing wealth was an increasing poverty.

Later, even this wealth was lost by a more general antipraxis, or authorless praxis. Spain needed gold, and it became for itself a vessel to store gold. But Spain also desired an empire, and an empire required the outflow of gold. These contradictory needs were realized separately, and their contradiction was not included in a single praxis.

The value of the Spanish gold coin must not be understood either idealistically or subjectively. The *idea* of matter that we are concerned with, Sartre says, is not Hegelian; it is "naturalistic and materialistic because it is matter itself producing its own idea" (E, 171; F, 239; NF, 281). Gold is a commodity because in the praxis of the times it was taken as a commodity. But there is a contradiction within the praxis. As a unit of measure and as a precious metal, each unit of gold was identical with every other unit, and more units meant more wealth. Nevertheless, as a commodity within a system of international trade, gold acted as any commodity, decreasing in value as the supply increased. In this respect, gold can be seen as having an antipraxis in relation to the human attempt to establish a synthetic, unified praxis, here the accumulation of wealth by Philip II.

From another viewpoint, the mediation between Spain and gold was brought about by people acting serially as "other" on the margin of society. Spain was seen as wealthy because gold was coming into its resources. Yet, through innumerable illegal and legal means, gold was going out of Spain. Although this outflow was occurring all over Spain, it was not seen as essential. The only purpose unifying Spanish activities was the influx of gold. All Spaniards engaged in exchanging gold for other commodities saw themselves on the margin of this essential activity, as foreigners. They did not see themselves as traitors, believing simply that their activities did not interfere with Spain's essential accumulation of wealth.

We can learn three things, Sartre adds, from this example: First, the employers, by lowering wages, did not save themselves from further inflation but did weaken the population, producing a manpower shortage. Second, as with the case of the Chinese peasants, this counterfinality united the masses negatively, as a helpless mass of individuals facing the common danger of low wages. Here, Sartre says, we can see the true meaning of reification. It is not the metamorphosis of an individual into a thing. Rather, it occurs because society through its structures requires individuals to live their membership in a group in such a way that their praxes are predefined. An anti-Semitic praxis tries to structure the meaning of every action of the Jew. In a similar way, every argument of the worker for better conditions is interpreted as inflationary and as a sign of unrest. Thus, in their weak and depopulated state, a quasi totality is formed by the workers; they act as a general strike.

Inverted praxis is thus possible because individual praxis can become engraved within matter. Matter becomes being; that is, it receives and thus reduces human praxes into *things*. Here we may recall that Sartre uses the term "being" in two senses. First, "being" can mean the unique materiality in question. In this first sense, "being" refers either to the way praxis surpasses its given situation or to the passivity of things, specifically their inertia. But the term "being" can also refer to *a* being, or *a* thing. For Sartre, *a* being or *a* thing is matter as sealed with praxis and as having a passive action. A gold coin is *a* thing; a flood is *a* thing; an erupting volcano is *a* thing. Things are part of totalizations of things. Complexes of passive actions take place, all in a milieu of scarcity, and thus the inverted praxes that result are an aspect of a nonhuman process.

Still, Sartre says, we must not exaggerate the significance of the nonhuman forces of history. History does point to something Other than human forces controlling humanity. But, according to Sartre, those who, exaggerate this Other, like Heidegger, have a hatred of humanity at heart.[11] This Other has been created by human beings, and human beings are responsible for it. This responsibility is no doubt different for different groups at different times. Sartre does not elaborate on this point, but it seems clear that the Chinese peasants had to cultivate land to survive. The Spaniards did not have to keep wages down with the same urgency. And in the more obvious example of the coal-mining industry, which we will return to later but will not examine further here, the employers of coal miners had the general knowledge and ability to improve air quality and conditions. Here, it is clear that the employers took the counterfinality within mining as their own finality. The smoke and noise was a sign of their power. Ultimately, a larger counterfinality would engulf them—for example, unionization, the depletion of mines, and the cost of

11. In the footnote (E, 181 n. 56; F, 248 n. 1; NF, 291 n. 1) Sartre refers to Walter Biemel, *Le concept du monde chez Heidegger* (Paris and Louvain: Nauwelaerts, 1950), 85–86. Sartre continues: "Biemel adds that, in his writings after *Sein und Zeit*, 'Heidegger begins with Being and ends up with an interpretation of man' (Ibid.). This method brings him close to what we have called the external materialist dialectic. It, too, begins with Being (Nature without alien addition) and ends up with man; it too regards knowledge-reflection as an 'opening to Being (*l'Étant*) maintained in man by the Been (*l'Été*).'" Regardless of the accuracy of Biemel's interpretation of Heidegger, it is clear that, in his later writings, Heidegger did hold that the human reality might be redeemed from its technological epoch by an openness to being. "We are thinking of the possibility that the world civilization which is just now beginning might one day overcome the technological-scientific-industrial character as the sole criterion of man's world sojourn. This may happen not of and through itself, but in virtue of the readiness of man for a determination which, whether listened to or not, always speaks in the destiny of man, which has not yet been decided" (Martin Heidegger, *On Time and Being*, trans. Joan Stambough [New York: Harper & Row, 1972], 60). For Sartre, *only* human praxis could be responsible for such a "readiness," and we are the only guide for this praxis. In this context, Aron reduces Sartre's subtle view of the relation of praxis to Manichaeism to a simplistic notion of an isolated Hobbesian nature caught in the social web of absolute evil (*History*, 135–37).

cleaning whole cities like Pittsburgh. Here, we see a group of people who have chosen an inhuman other to advance their own situation. They will, of course, dehumanize themselves by increasing the inhumanity that is part of humanity.

As we have seen, one of the purposes of the *Critique* is to show how a project can include within its wider totalization the contradictory movement of praxis and antipraxis. But before developing this notion, Sartre notes a further important aspect of antipraxis, the creation of "exigency-man." Tools and machines—the complex of things created by human beings—now create new human "needs." "Vampire objects" come into existence that demand attention, that call for our very sweat and blood. Once a machine has been built, a demand is set up not only for its care but for other machines. It becomes difficult in any situation to distinguish our true needs from the needs of our products. Machines demand from us a certain rhythm and alterity. Anyone can serve them, and each worker is simply an inessential aid to the essential working of this machine. Workers become united as inessential units, each worker a someone who might be anyone, united to other workers in alterity and passivity. Indeed, in this alienating context, the very preeminence of human beings becomes their ability to activate machines.

In the abstract, all the exigencies of matter and machines appear to be conditional: "if the worker needs wages . . ." or "if the goods are to be produced. . . ." The concrete reality is different, however. The demand exists *in* the situation. The exigencies, Sartre says, are both "man as practical agent and matter as a work product in an indivisible symbiosis" (E, 191; F, 256; NF, 301). This symbiosis explains those locutions referred to earlier, such as the fact that the performance of steam engines "required" them to follow valleys and water courses. Indeed, complex industries such as coal mining required the inventions that were later "discovered," such as Watt's steam engine. In this regard, exigency-man is one who bridges the gap between the objects required by an industrial complex and the production of the objects. Exigency-man works on a new kind of being, namely matter as *it* transcends individual praxis. This counterfinality has been caused by human beings and can be used by others for their own purposes. During certain times, the use of this counter-finality characterizes groups. The unwillingness to see that what was happening to the miners could indeed be remedied characterized the praxis of the bourgeoisie at the beginning of the industrial revolution.

### (ii.) Interest [12]

In this subsection, Sartre continues describing the counter-finality of totalized matter. In one respect, his procedure can be understood as

---

12. The division is given in both French editions, but the numeration was added by the editor of the English translation.

an attempt to rethink, within the materialism of the dialectic, our relation to our environment. Our analytic prejudice inclines us to think of ourselves as monads that decide our fate while floating above our environment. When we recognize a common interest, we imagine it is because we have examined the situation disinterestedly and then recognized an advantage common to all. Thus, a worker is seen as selling his labor power as a commodity in exchange for wages. The contract is viewed as open for all to see, and there is apparently no mystification involved. True, unfortunate conditions can bring about unjust contracts and incidental inhuman conditions, but, in general, capitalism *apparently* allows the worker and the capitalist to determine their own interests and destinies through the free exchange of labor power for a fair wage. Following Marx, Sartre's point is that mystification has been taken from religion and the state and put into the marketplace of the capitalist. The true meaning of Calvinism and Puritanism, Sartre says, is that the capitalist is the elite of God who carries on the work of creation by increasing wealth. For Sartre, what we call "capitalism" is not merely an economic system. It is a marriage between an economic system and a system of values.

Sartre again explicitly notes that his dialectic and his materialism are on a different level than those of Marx: "But my remarks, though they are possible only on the basis of this reconstruction [Marx's *Capital*] . . . belong logically, *before* this historical reconstruction, at a higher level of greater indeterminacy and generality" (E, 216; F, 276; NF, 325–326). The fact that the capitalist owns the means of production does not, of itself, explain the possibility for the distinctive mystification and alienation characteristic of class struggle. In a sense, Marx elucidates the content of the class struggle without attempting to explain how it could exist as a totality. It is inconceivable, for Sartre, that individual capitalists *independently* all decided to be greedy, to give only a "fair wage" for labor, and, more importantly, to pass over the inhumanity that was involved in treating labor power as a commodity. It is further inconceivable that their structure as a class arose simply because they each saw that they had an interest in common. The realization of common interest, Sartre notes, can just as easily lead to disputes as to agreement. Part of the mystification of the marketplace is that just as exchange *appears* as reciprocity between two free individuals, so too class struggle *appears* as a clash between the subjective agreements of the workers on the one hand and the interests of the capitalists on the other hand. *But what has to be explained is how classes could have arisen in the first place.* To repeat, Sartre's point is that classes could have arisen only if matter had been so totalized that conflict *first* existed in a totalized form within the environment. We are not yet ready, he comments, to explain exactly how classes can come about, but we are describing that preliminary stage in which each sees himself in the world as other-than-himself. In analytic terminology, we are concerned here with the "condition for the possibility" of classes.

In this context, "interest" refers not to an interior, subjective decision about what we are going to do with our lives, but to the discovery of our being-outside-ourselves as worked matter. Consequently, we can see (regressively) a continuity of Sartre's thought from *The Transcendence of the Ego* to *Being and Nothingness* and finally to the *Critique.*[13] In *The Transcendence of the Ego*, Sartre showed that the "I" is a fragile object in the world. In *Being and Nothingness*, Sartre clarified the thoroughly situational aspect of consciousness as a being in the world: I am my place, my language, my country, in the sense of *not* being these; that is, in the sense of being a free relation to these aspects of my situation. Freedom, for Sartre, has always meant freedom in relation to the givens of our materiality. In this sense, consciousness always discovered and negated the *self* that it saw in the world. Furthermore, the way that I see myself is not the way another sees me, and I am both of these ways of being. But, at this abstract level, this self is not a being-outside-itself in the sense of the *Critique*. For while freedom demands objectification, it does not of itself require that our objectivity should be a self as *other-than-ourself*. But this is precisely what happens within the symbiosis that takes place between us and matter within our history. The world gives us our interest and our destiny as categorical imperatives, as demands. Embedded and totalized within a milieu of scarcity and alterity, the freedom of others *first* acts on us, structuring our very personality; then we must restructure our personality and become conscious of our freedom "in the shifting hell of the field of practical passivity" (E, 219; F, 279; NF, 329). Interest is thus another form of *exigency*. But over and above the general form of exigency, "interest" connotes that one's *personality is itself within the objective complex of things that determines the practico-inert*. Nevertheless, we must also keep in mind how local situations, such as one's family, affect personality. In this respect, Sartre's study of Flaubert is an important counterweight to the *Critique*.

We can note a form of quasi interest within the simple ownership of property. The "man of property" is literally a man who has so interiorized external things that they become his consciousness. When he rearranges his property, he rearranges his ideas. Consequently, he sees himself and others as *things:* People, like tables and chairs, are impenetrable monads that occupy space. Reciprocity degenerates into forms of external relations. Strictly speaking, however, interest occurs only on a more complex, historical level. First, interest implies what Sartre calls "massification," the dispersal of people as a collection of atoms, each one guarding part of themselves as private. There is no natural reason why we should not spontaneously tell all that we know about ourselves to others. Massification is not our natural, primitive state, but an

---

13. Sartre was always aware of the danger of describing the world from an apartment *over-looking* Paris. See *Between Existentialism and Marxism*, 228–85.

aspect of our particular historicity. It is especially through the complex of machines that each of us sees himself as *other* amid a collection of *others*. The capitalist decides what he is going to do by imagining first what other capitalists will do. The special mode of his objectivity is that he sees himself as a competing *other* among a collection of competing *others*. Yet he needs these others even as he competes with them. Thus alterity is in the social milieu; it is the special way scarcity has manifested itself through machines. What also becomes evident here is a form of rationality soon to be examined, namely, seriality.

The interest of the capitalist comes from the factory insofar as his factory is one among many possible factories. If he installs a machine, it is because he sees himself as one of a collection of competing capitalists. (Still, Sartre observes, his choice is not between installing a new machine or begging for food.) Once the new machine has been installed, however, *it* has interests. No longer is factory production aimed at meeting a demand; rather, new markets must be found to satisfy the supply, for "the machine cannot stop." Luxuries are overproduced, while necessities are underproduced. The capitalist does not question the process, taking it as self-evident that regardless of what advances are made the poor will always be with us. Here the issue of historical need is treated as if it were a biological one. The capitalist's *need* to increase productivity is like a hungry man's need for food. Indeed, need is treated as an opaque force, like the wind to which a person happens to be subject. Sartre finds it surprising that even Marxists are willing to make need into an unintelligible force and then project this unintelligibility as a part of the objective world.

Within the milieu of scarcity and alterity that has determined our history, the operations of the machine are seen as essential. The increasing efficiency of machines may incidentally alleviate burdensome labor, but its main object is to be cost-effective. A machine is made to eliminate human workers; thus, even while requiring them, it proclaims their inessentiality. Within the milieu of scarcity and alterity, the workers emerge as a collection of inessential, disposable labor units that are unfortunately needed here and now. The implication in this section is that the capitalist's heaven is a world in which he can be allowed continually to compete with other capitalists, using robots to "man" his factories. These robots produce every conceivable necessity and novelty, and there is a continual *need* for all of these. The worker, however, now unemployed and without a purpose, justly suffers the life of the damned, starving amid the plenty reserved for the elite. The point is that there is no a priori reason why machines should function for their own purposes. This relation has been established by praxes, although, as we will see, in a much more complex way than through the scheming of a few capitalists. What is clear here is that the worker cannot find his interest in the machine as it threatens to eliminate him. Rather, the machine is the *destiny* of the worker; it is his objective inessentiality.

Of course, there is a contradiction in the capitalist's unspoken ideal. Commodities are commodities only if they are purchased. A capitalist needs consumers other than himself. The worker's hell has to be revised. Somehow, *some* of the workers will have to be given enough money to buy the products so that the capitalist heaven can continue. Thus, workers who are industrious and respectful will receive money as a sign of the capitalist's mercy; others will suffer as a sign of his justice.

If capitalism can exist despite its contradictions, it is, for Sartre, because matter exists as "bewitched matter." Marx, as we have seen, realized that capitalism brought mystification into the marketplace. He thus spoke of commodities as fetishes. But I believe that Sartre's point here is that such fetishism could not work if it were a mere subjective projection onto commodities. Mystification exists within the commodity itself. The commodity is part of a totalized material system and this system delineates human beings as objects and chooses its dead amid a milieu of scarcity. The personality of the capitalist as a capitalist moves within this mystification; he sees himself as other than himself, and he chooses this other. He competes, producing new luxuries amid scarcities of essential goods because others will do so if he does not do so first. But, as a capitalist, he is already this competing other even before he judges it necessary to compete. This point will be expanded on later, but what is important here is that the interests of the capitalist, *his* concerns, become the destiny of the worker. On another level, the destiny of the worker can dialectically become the destiny of the capitalist. When the workers strike, the capitalists become conscious of themselves as having their fate determined by the workers. But the strike is originally a true counterviolence. It implies the milieu in which machines are for the interest of the capitalist. The workers respond to a destiny made for them by others.

### 3. NECESSITY AS A NEW STRUCTURE OF DIALECTICAL INVESTIGATION

"At its most immediate level, dialectical investigation (*l'expérience dialectique*) has emerged," Sartre observes, "as *praxis* elucidating itself to control its own development" (E, 220; F, 279; NF, 329). As the historical situation of the agent is revealed to be more concrete and complex, involving ever-widening historical consequences, everyday praxis is seen to encounter the authorless antipraxis of totalized matter. The question now arises whether, in the face of antipraxis, individual praxis can continue in its effort to control its own development. Sartre's answer is a qualified yes; in principle, individual praxis, with the proper intellectual tools, can comprehend, if not alter, the effects of counterpraxis.

We must be careful to recall that Sartre is *not* suggesting that a "higher" praxis emerges, one that is a Hegelian synthesis of a simple, immediate praxis and its antipraxis. True, a new realization of the dialectic arises, one that not only reveals the presence of antipraxis but also begins to comprehend the relation between praxis and antipraxis. Sartre thus speaks of two dialectics: one that until now has operated and revealed the existence of antipraxis and another, wider and more encompassing, that incorporates the first. Nevertheless, this second, more complex dialectic does not allow the individual to perform a new praxis that absorbs in its translucency the counterpraxis of totalized matter. Rather, as we have earlier noted, praxis appears now to be complex: it is translucent on its own immediate level, and, simultaneously, it is continually eroded by a foreign antipraxis on a wider, more historical level.

What characterizes antipraxis, and distinguishes it from the ordinary reaction that any agent encounters when acting on matter, is that antipraxis simulates the intentionality and freedom of another agent. Antipraxis appears as a powerful, foreign freedom that controls individual freedom. Within a broad historical perspective, an individual can know that the historical consequences of a praxis will be engulfed by the effects of antipraxis. On this level, the individual operates within the awareness of a new type of necessity that is "that of a retroactive power eroding my freedom, from the final objectivity to the original decision; but nevertheless emerging from it; it is the negation of freedom in the domain of complete freedom, sustained by freedom itself, and proportional to the very completeness of this freedom" (E, 226; F, 284; NF, 335). Ultimately, for Sartre, this negation of freedom has been put in matter by the innumerable free praxes of other individuals. A quasi freedom greater than individual freedoms exists because we have caused it to be in matter, and it exists as an antipraxis because, operating in the milieu of scarcity, we have made it an alien counterforce.

All this is background for the main point of this present section, which is that knowledge, whether theoretical or practical, requires the awareness of necessary structures. To be more precise, this dialectical study requires its own specific type of necessity if it is to avoid accepting uncritically analytic or foundational notions of necessity. Dialectical necessity must be an aspect of our investigation itself, revealed by the dialectic itself. Such a procedure would be idealistic were it not for the fact that this necessity emerges from the material field of our investigation. Nevertheless, although our investigation is not idealistic, it is dialectical; that is, we must not fall back to an analytic or pluralistic view that naively claims merely to discover its material objects. It is true both that individual praxis encounters the passive action of totalized matter as something given and that it recognizes this given to be something brought about by other humans. Here we must also recall the conditional status of the entire investigation of the *Critique I*. We are assuming that history is *a* totalization of totalizations; we are, at present, accepting uncritically the grand totalization that seemingly results in *a* history in order to study critically the innumerable totalizations that could have made our history possible.[14]

To return to our present discussion, Sartre distinguishes necessity from both certainty and constraint. Certainty is an aspect of praxis as it appears translucent in those fleeting moments of pure reflection referred to earlier.[15] For example, while I am playing tennis, I may have a fleeting awareness of myself as playing tennis, an awareness that is my very tennis playing as it momentarily becomes a presence to itself. This moment of pure reflection is also the indubitability of my tennis playing. In relation to Sartre's own earlier examples, we can note that each Chinese peasant was translucently aware of cutting trees down for the purpose of planting crops. On this immediate, abstract, but nevertheless real level, the peasant saw his purpose accomplished. Again, the individual merchants during the Spanish hegemony were all indubitably aware of their individual acts of buying and selling.

Necessity must also be distinguished from constraint. Constraint acts as an external force inhibiting our intentions, whereas necessity occurs only when the action is allowed to unfold. The necessary result of deforestation occurs only when the peasant is allowed to cut down trees to cultivate the land. Furthermore, Sartre explains, necessity is not the narrowing of multiple means to one mean. The elimination of means occurs naturally as our free intentions become absorbed in their result.

Necessity, as a new structure of our dialectical investigation, occurs rather when I realize that my free, responsible praxis will fall into a network of world relations and be given meanings foreign to my intentions. Nevertheless, it is possible for peasants to be aware of deforestation and for merchants to realize that their individual transactions contribute to the rise and fall of the value of the monetary unit. Such knowledge can be the basis of control, particularly when it is unified in a group action.

The situation is, of course, more complex than has been suggested. Indeed, the above presentation can easily be misunderstood to be the simple analytic claim that individuals should learn how to cope with their complex historical existence. From an analytic or foundational perspective, human beings are,

14. Still I think it is clear that local "grand" totalizations exist, for example, the United States, France, and, perhaps, Western civilization. Furthermore, this limited totalization seems to be all that is required for *Critique I*.

15. Sartre does not here explicitly refer to the distinction between pure and impure reflection. See "Background" chapter, section vii. What is clear, however, is that both certainty and necessity arise from praxis in its relation to the practico-inert. I see no basis in the *Critique* for Chiodi's claim that "in this way the structure breaks up into opposing branches: on the one hand *physis* as the realm of necessity; on the other *anti-physis,* the realm of freedom" (*Sartre and Marxism,* 51). On the contrary, both certainty and necessity arise from the symbiotic relation between praxis and the practico-inert.

by nature, *either* isolated *or* social beings. The de facto historical structures are epiphenomena. They modify, but do not intrinsically alter, either individual consciousness, with its analytic reason, or human nature, with its positive interpersonal relations. From a dialectical perspective, however, it is simultaneously true that we de facto have a fundamental mode of existence, whether isolated or social, and that this basic mode of existence is brought about by both our individual behavior and the social system. We are, by nature, *neither* private individuals *nor* social beings. All human relations are established by praxes; that is, praxes produce the social webbing through which, in turn, other praxes receive their necessary structures.

Our very relations of interiority—the ways we love, know, hate, and possess—are de facto based on a primacy of exteriority. We are separate from each other not merely by the localization of our bodies in time and space but also by the different ways we exist our bodies. Our interpersonal relations to others thus spring from a primacy of privateness and seriality, a primacy that we both sustain and receive from the passive action of our totalized material environment. It is not God, the Devil, or nature, but rather the history that we have made that has brought about our specific alienations. With this in mind, we can now regressively see that the concrete relations with others described in *Being and Nothingness* is a description of the way the practico-inert affects interpersonal relations, even when these occur in private. A world in which doors to apartments and houses have locks to keep out the rest of the world is a world in which even personal relations degenerate into privacy and alienation.

Sartre comments perceptively, "the plurality of human actions is still a negation of the dialectical unity of each *praxis*" (E, 220; F, 280). That is, the specific character of our actions, their aspect of being one among many, does not originate from the mere separateness of our bodies from other bodies. This separateness could exist, and we might have an I-thou relation such as described by Martin Buber. But de facto our unity with our fellow human beings originates from privateness and antagonism, because historically each of our actions has become internally divided by these objective, negative qualities. Moreover, as will become clear in the following section, these internal relations, such as privacy, are reciprocally the interiorizations of our environment. Nevertheless, given the reciprocity between praxis and antipraxis, the priority, according to Sartre, must always be given to individual praxis. That is, *regressively* we recognize that our history is the way it is because individual praxis is the way it is.[16]

---

16. Of itself, negation does not have to be "negative" in the popular sense of the term; history did not have to develop antagonistic relations simply because of the ontological negation of consciousness.

In a footnote to this section (E, 227 n. 68; F, 285 n. 1; NF, 336–337 n.1), Sartre briefly relates his position on necessity both to Heidegger's position in *Being and Time* and to his own in *Being and Nothingness.* According to Sartre, Heidegger maintains that we experience necessity in our external objectifications of ourselves. Such objectification is the basis of the way we experience ourselves as objects with necessary relations of distance to other objects. For Sartre, on the contrary, true necessity is encountered when we experience ourselves not merely as objects, but as *others.* We experience necessity when we encounter ourselves as foreign agents with an alien freedom. The mere objectification of one's self does not mean that the self is encountered as a foreign agent: when I rearrange my room according to my taste, I encounter my own freedom as objectified and not as alienated; relations of distance are indeed established through my objectification, but only insofar as my objectification is an aspect of my free intention.

Sartre maintains, however, that the true *abstract* formulation of necessity was given in his own *Being and Nothingness:* our every action is an attempt to raise inert matter to the level of a justified existence. We attempt not merely to give matter a meaning but to make it *be* a meaning. That is, the for-itself attempts to make the in-itself into an in-itself-for-itself. On the level of immediate action, this goal is nonthetic. As I am hanging a picture on the wall, for example, I transcend the instrumentality of the hammer, nails, and picture in my project of beautifying my room. Momentarily, however, I may become fleetingly aware that my simple action is also an attempt to make matter into a world; that is, to make matter reason-incarnate. Here, on a very abstract but real level, I encounter my simple action of hanging a picture on the wall as the action of an alien freedom attempting to create a world. That is, I encounter not merely my existence as objectified but also my existence as it would be justified. In the section "Concrete Relations with Others" in *Being and Nothingness,* Sartre showed how the thematizations of this aspect of action lead to the various ways human relations can "fail." [17] Sartre's implicit view in *Being and Nothingness* is that our actions are healthiest when they pass through this godlike aspect of consciousness, neither thematizing nor fleeing from it. Necessity exists because we have no choice in the fact that our freedom consists in the attempt to justify matter's inert existence. For Sartre, we mistakenly thematize this necessity to be a requirement that God exist.

Sartre's position on necessity in the *Critique* cannot be deduced from *Being and Nothingness.* Regressively, however, we can now see that *Being and Nothingness* gave the abstract formulation and "basis" for the view in the *Critique.* The reader must be reminded that what is abstract is still real on its own level. While I am hanging a picture on a wall I can, despite the historical com-

17. See "Background" chapter, p. 34.

plexities of the times, experience that general alienation of my action as something godlike. For an individual, this "abstract" alienation could be decisive; we are not always on every level affected by the specificity of our historical situation. Nevertheless, the alienation we experience in our daily lives is frequently that of antipraxis. We experience, on the historical level, our own actions returning to us *not as godlike but as inhuman.* As I am beautifying my room, I can be aware of the millions of hungry and homeless. My action returns to me as an inhuman act of luxury.

Historical alienation is more complex than the alienation referred to in *Being and Nothingness,* because here we encounter necessity on different levels. We must recall that Sartre's radical nominalism requires that the concrete is not a mere instance of the abstract. With this caveat in mind we can note the following: Both "necessities" originate from a de facto occurrence: the abstract, from the way we thematize our natural tendencies to create; the concrete, from the way we have allowed praxis to become an antipraxis. Both necessities result in an alienation that is more than objectification, and, thus, they differ from a Hegelian or early Heideggerian form of alienation.[18] Nevertheless, historical alienation has been quasi thematized in the passive action of totalized matter: inhumanity is a force that can be awakened as an absolute evil. Here we face the complex issue of Manichaeism referred to earlier. At present, however, Sartre's concluding point is that necessity and alienation is more radical than even the Marxist conceives. Alienation does not result from exploitation, but rather it is alienation that makes exploitation possible on a large scale.

## 4. SOCIAL BEING AS MATERIALITY—CLASS BEING[19]

The experience of necessity is also the experience of our class being. For Sartre, the reality of class is more than a subjective awareness that we are united with others and less than a supraconsciousness in which we all share. As already stated, Sartre's realism, both in *Being and Nothingness* and here in the *Critique,* has always tried to avoid both an idealism that views the qualities that constitute the world as mere projections of consciousness and a

18. Heidegger's later position is more complex, and it was apparently Sartre's intention to develop this notion in the second volume of the *Critique.* Still, it is clear that Sartre would reject Heidegger's claim that something other than collective human praxis could lead us out of alienation. For a discussion of the later Heidegger on this point, see William J. Richardson, *Heidegger: Through Phenomenology to Thought* (The Hague: Martinus Nijhoff Publishers, 1967), 222–28, 240–43.

19. The English translation takes unnecessary liberty in shortening the French title, "De l'être social comme matérialité et, particulièrement, de l'être de classe." In this context, "social being" is a wider term than "class being."

realism that views these qualities as existing independently of human reality. All things are social because their unity as things comes about through their relation to the human organism. Thus, when our experience reveals ways of both thinking and practically dealing with our environment that cannot be concretely and practically transcended, this limitation is not due to a mere subjective attitude. If we cannot practically transcend our anthropocentric ways of thinking, it is because the mirror image of these anthropomorphisms is embedded in matter, thereby constituting concrete qualities within the world.[20] From this perspective, what we recognize as our interior life is the subjectification of objective structures of matter. And, reciprocally, these very material structures are the reception in matter of a pseudointerior life brought about by the alienating practices of others. Specifically, Sartre is here referring to the machine and the concrete way it has developed in our history within the milieu of scarcity. We thus experience our membership in a class, because our class structure already exists as a fundamental structure of our world.

Sartre's view on class being is consistent with his claim that we do not have a nature. In denying a human nature, Sartre never meant that we are free to do or to be anything we choose. Rather, because we do not have a nature, our situation is the origin of our internal relations to the world and to others. If we are equal, it is because we each have a situation that we can equally transcend. From this very abstract perspective, the one elucidated in *Being and Nothingness,* a rich person and a poor person have equal freedoms because each situation has similar limiting structures. A person born rich, for example, is free to be independent but can never become "self-made." On the more concrete level of the *Critique,* however, we experience, within our free praxis, the necessity of an alienating freedom transcending our own initial attempts to escape our situation. In this respect, our every attempt to escape our class returns to us as the alienating experience of fulfilling our class being. The important point, however, is that this alienation differs radically according to which class we are in.

In one of the few places in the *Critique* where he explicitly relates his position to his earlier views in *Being and Nothingness,* Sartre proposes the question of whether his claims here in the *Critique* contradict his earlier "existential" views. He used to claim, he says, that there are no a priori essences and that we are not born cowards but make ourselves cowards. Is he now maintaining that we do not make ourselves a bourgeois but that we are born bourgeois? Sartre's answer is that we are both born bourgeois and make ourselves so.

Sartre's response may seem unduly ambiguous. But his remarks are consistent with his own antifoundationalism and nominalism. We are indeed thor-

---

20. Nevertheless, we will see that the purpose of group praxis is to cope with those alienating mirror images of our own past praxes. See book II, chapter 1.

oughly historical, but, as we have often noted, this does not mean that in every circumstance and on every level our historicity is of primary importance. Sartre's radical nominalism requires that we constantly rethink what is important on each level. For example, we recognize very clearly that questions of historicity are not relevant when someone is choking or drowning. One saves someone who is choking by treating him "analytically," as a living organism that must be allowed to breathe. The analytic perspective on humanity is wrong only when it is universalized to cover the specifically human characteristics as instances within a universal. Analogously, Sartre can be interpreted as maintaining that the local enterprise of becoming a coward can indeed be a choice, as described in *Being and Nothingness.* One can indeed make oneself to be a coward in a situation in which historicity has little weight. From our present perspective of the *Critique,* however, a perspective that is concrete in relation to *Being and Nothingness* but abstract in relation to what is to follow, we see that we do not choose to belong to a class in the way that we choose to be a coward or to save a choking victim. And this distinction is more complex than a simple assertion that the nonhistorical is on a secondary, reflective level and the historical on a more fundamental level. Rather, it depends on the situation and the perspective: not only individuals but even groups, such as doctors in their relation to patients, can encounter freedom and its limitations on a nonhistorical level.

The perspective of the *Critique,* however, is on the historical person qua historical. On this perspective, our free praxis confronts itself as the authorless other of antipraxis. We experience our objectification as alienated and already embedded in matter. As our free praxis aims at its goal, we discover our *truth* and our *reality* as already awaiting us within the active passivity of matter. We further recognize that our very efforts at transcending our situation have been the means of realizing it. On the historical level, we realize what we implicitly knew all along, namely, that from birth our freedom had, at its heart, an inertia given to it by the concrete structure of our environment. We recognize that we are free in the way we realize our class being but that we can never escape from this class being. From this perspective, we live in a practico-inert hell in which our freedom is outwitted by an antipraxis, somewhat in the way that an enemy might outwit us by using the knowledge of our own free decisions to lead us into a trap. A middle-class person who attempts to escape the rat race of "keeping up with the Joneses" may discover that he has made himself a middle-class recluse. Given the fetishism of commodities, there may be only various alienating ways of possessing things. It would indeed be strange if an individual or group could eliminate the alienations introduced into matter by innumerable past praxes. Such historical alienation can be removed only through a historically unified effort. Still, the context here allows us to distinguish authentic attempts to escape our alienation from acts that directly contribute to it. As his own example of the anarcho-syndicalists will show, the attempts to escape historical alienation do indeed lead individuals and groups back to alienation, but they may also be the means whereby future generations escape at least one particular form of alienation.

Sartre develops two examples illustrating the relation of freedom to class being, one taken from Claude Lanzmann of a woman handling Dop shampoo, and the other of the anarcho-syndicalists. Both examples, Sartre warns, refer to capitalism of the nineteenth century. But although contemporary capitalism is more complex, Sartre maintains that the basic features of class being still apply.

A poor woman of the nineteenth century, who was born in a small town dominated by a large Dop shampoo factory, had her future existence already awaiting her as a component of the factory. Practically speaking, her only choice is to become the monotonous source of energy needed to run the factory's machines. If this woman tries to escape the monotony by indulging in private reveries, the escape is but another form of interiorizing her environment. She cannot become actively involved in thinking about her children or in planning an enterprise that involves creative energy, for this would distract her from her duties. Her thoughts must run, in Sartre's term, "laterally," in the rhythm of the machine's motion. She can indulge in fantasies, such as those of seduction, in which she is being passively carried along. She is both aware and unaware of what she is doing. (In this sense the woman can be said to be creating a "sub-conscious.") She is explicitly aware of her "choice" of fantasies, and she may indeed think of these as the way she has freely chosen to escape her position. And, from this perspective, her free praxis is indeed the choice of sexual fantasies as an escape from monotony. But it would be practically impossible for her to become aware that the machine has required her to adopt a passive attitude toward her own consciousness. In the abstract, such a possibility logically exists, but in the concrete, she and every woman of her class accept their possibilities as given by the factory. Such an "acceptance" by one of these women is more than a reflective decision; it is her very life.

On the historical level, there exists a split between being and doing that does not exist on local, nonhistorical levels. In *Being and Nothingness*, Sartre explained that *doing* ultimately resolves itself into *being*. Our actions reveal the primary way our bodies are related to the world and others. One person experiences tiredness as something to yield to rather than fight against, because his primary project and being is "to exist his body" as an object comfortably related to his environment.[21] The *Critique*, however, shows that from

---

21. See *BN*, 453–64; *Commentary BN*, 196–202. "Earlier I posed a question: I could have yielded to fatigue, we said, I *could have done* otherwise *but at what a price?*" (*BN*, 464 [Sartre's italics]). Of course, the fundamental project is not a "choice" in the sense of resulting from reflective judgment. Given our project not to change, our actions are relatively predictable and can be

a wide historical perspective our praxis can be in contradiction to our being. From a historical perspective, we see that the activity of the woman working the Dop shampoo factory is merely her interiorization of the mechanical iner- tia of the factory. That is, she has not "chosen" the relationship of her body to her environment, the way a person in *Being and Nothingness* is described as actively choosing not to physically conquer the environment.

Sartre recalls that in *Being and Nothingness* he claimed, following Hegel, that essence was past being.[22] We can thus never annul our past being, our "essence"; rather, our freedom is the way we transcend it. If we retain our distinction between local and historical perspectives, we can say that this is still true from a local perspective. But within our present historical perspec- tive, past being as our essence exists outside us as the untranscendable struc- ture that is our class being. The exigency of the machine has been made our destiny.

In the second example, Sartre shows how a specific form of humanism ad- vocated by the anarcho-syndicalist arose from the development of universal machines, such as the lathe. These machines required skilled labor and thus divided the working class into the skilled and unskilled. It seemed natural for the skilled workers to advocate a humanism in which they were viewed as having a higher level of humanity than their unskilled colleagues. Practically, the skilled workers did not comprehend that their own advantages resulted from accidents of birth. Abstractly, the inhumanity within this humanism could have been transcended. Practically, even if the transcendence was theo- retically envisioned, it would, Sartre says, have led to rationalization and jus- tification rather than to a humanism that advocated equality for all workers.

Class being is thus not something added to our lives; it is rather the very substance of our lives as they are lived in relation to others within our histori- cal environment. Inertia and exteriority, the exteriorization of interiority brought about by the machine, led to an economics that aspired to become like physics, and, in general, to an analytic perspective on humanity. Further- more, the existence of an objective, alienating structure somewhat justifies the individual's claim that he cannot change the inhuman state of affairs. These claims of impotence do have a justification within the inertial system of our environment. It is clear from Sartre's entire *Critique* that our present posi-

---

more or less in accord with this project. The mountain climber who yields to fatigue could perhaps have gone on another ten yards without changing his project. Also, Sartre is not claiming that we change our projects without prior events leading to the change, but rather that these events never *cause* the change. This analysis of freedom, while abstract, is still valid in local contexts; that is, Flaubert was free and did as a matter of fact change his project when he turned to writing as a way to cope with his father's view of him as an "idiot." To repeat, Flaubert had to be a bourgeois, but to be a bourgeois is not necessarily to be Flaubert.

22. See *BN*, 107–20; *Commentary BN*, 111–16.

tion is ambiguous: we cannot transcend our class being, and we do not concretely know what such a transcendence would be like. But, at present, we can begin to comprehend our history as a whole and to control it. We do not know what a humanity without inhumanity would be like, but we do know aspects of our inhumanity that can be eliminated.

In a long footnote to this section (E, 247–50 n. 75; F, 301–3 n. 1; NF, 355–358 n. 1), Sartre rather cryptically describes how, because of class being, praxis has a contradictory relation to value. His remarks should be interpreted as part of the running commentary on the way a Manichaean ethical structure has characterized our history. Indirectly, his remarks also supply an answer to the question why an existential ethic is so difficult to formulate: no ethics can completely transcend the inhumanity within our humanity. For Sartre, it is today impossible to live a truly moral life directed by truly ethical principles; nevertheless, there is, to repeat once again, a radical and fundamental difference between the acceptance and the furtherance of our inhumanity and the steady but ambiguous attempt to free ourselves from it. The implication of Sartre's thought in this extended footnote is that we should not need or require an ethic, at least in the accepted sense of that term. Values should arise from a free, creative praxis unfolding within the world. Ethics, however, presents values as hypostatized and as already given. Praxis thereby degenerates into an instance within a class: virtue is a class of actions, such as speaking the truth, and an unethical act is one that falls outside this class. More generally, good and evil are projected as forces, and ethics becomes a study of the principles of avoiding evil so that the force of good can act.

In this context, Sartre says that value is the contradictory unity of praxis and exigency. First, let us note that, in the abstract, praxis is the translucent way each individual transcends a situation. From a local, nonhistorical perspective, we have seen how an action can unfold in this way: a person who spontaneously saves the life of a drowning person transcends the physical act of swimming; the *value* of the act is the act of saving the one drowning. But here, value presents itself as an archetype, *already* justifying praxis as praxis unfolds and fulfills itself. From this abstract perspective, the value of saving this drowning person is stolen from the praxis insofar as the praxis is already given in general principles, such as "man has no greater love than to lay down his life for his fellow man." Thus, even in the abstract, value and praxis have a contradictory relation.

But, in the concrete, historical context, this contradictory relation between value and praxis is more complex. Value is a *double* contradictory movement embodying praxis and exigency, and it presents the added dimension that is both the covering up and the revealing of the contradiction between free praxis and the exigency of the practico-inert. In the first contradictory movement of value, I see that the lathe, for example, requires skilled workers, and I see this need as coming from the lathe itself. But the value of the skilled work, as something higher than that of unskilled work, is not in the lathe; it is rather in the technical skills of the skilled worker. Value thus appears as both the exigency of the practico-inert and the merit of acquired skills. But if this were the only contradiction in our social structure, it would not result in the deep alienation that is in fact an aspect of our society. Thus, a second contradictory movement arises, which simultaneously reveals and hides the fact that the machine demands that I see myself as the other who must be skilled to operate it. *This revealing and covering is at the heart of value.* Skilled labor becomes more than the exigency of the lathe; it becomes a human value. And as a human value, it is not myself as other but as I should be. It is not the machine that requires me to be skilled, but my own nature. There is something wrong with me if I am not skilled. Value attempts to hide that this exigency is the requirement of a technology that preordains the slots into which humanity should fall. But value's own attempt to hide is also that which reveals exigency, on a deeper level, as a requirement of the practico-inert hell. Exigency is not the simple demands of the machine, but the demands of a technology that initially operates within the milieu of scarcity to sustain the wealthy and retain the poor. True, the ethical superstructure arises from the economic base, but the superstructure would not arise and could not be supported unless the economic base originated from a more fundamental material condition, the milieu of sustained scarcity. It is a question not primarily of economics, but of an alteration of the fundamental materiality of our environment. It is not the machine itself, but the machine in the milieu of scarcity created by our past praxes.

The situation is even more complex, because value appears also as the very goal of praxis. Value thus thematizes the aspect of praxis as a free transcendence, presenting itself as that which should transcend all past transcendences, including the untranscendability of class being. But this is again value as both a revealing and a covering up. There is thus, Sartre continues, a fundamental ambiguity in all morality, past and present. "Every system of values rests on exploitation; every system of values effectively negates exploitation and oppression" (E, 249 n. 75; F, 303 n. 1; NF, 357 n.1). Thus, technology is indeed a means by which the underprivileged classes can attain a better standard of living. Technology is also the limit of their humanity. Implicitly those who possess technology regard themselves as having a higher and more nobler humanity than the underprivileged. But although our entire notion of colonialization operates within this perspective, there is no a priori reason why the possession of technological advancement in itself implies a higher humanity.

# 4    Collectives

This first of the two books of the *Critique* concludes with a study of the collective (*le collectif*). In Sartre's usage, the term "collective" refers to the passive aspect of the social structure, and the term "group" to the active aspect. Thus, the term "social" has the wider extension: a social object, or social state, can be either a collective or a group.[1]

Although groups arise from and fall back into collectives, the collective is not temporally prior to the group. In the concrete, a particular collective exhibits, as we will see, the characteristics of the groups that have both arisen from it and degenerated back into it. The main reason for beginning with a study of the collective is that our procedure has been to establish first the objective, material condition for praxis. This approach is aimed, in part, at making it clear that the distinctive features of action as historical do not arise untutored from the inner depths of one's subjectivity. On the other hand, Sartre also constantly emphasizes that praxis is not reducible to its material conditions.

In approaching our study of the collective, it is again important to think

---

1. This entire exposition of terminology is, again, analytic. Strictly speaking, words in a dialectical discourse are not terms; that is, they do not "refer to" or signify things. This analytic way of speaking implies a correspondence theory of truth that is itself critiqued by dialectical thinking. Nor do words signify aspects of a system, which would imply a coherence notion of truth. And words are not merely tools to be used in a pragmatic test of truth. In attempting to avoid the interrelatedness of Hegel's system, the pragmatic view accepts uncritically the independence of the local. (In this respect, pragmatism does not recognize its uncritical acceptance of a monism from which it can delineate its local, pluralistic regions, where novelty does indeed occur.) Finally, words do not signify merely themselves or other words in a structuralist sense, in which the entire realm of discourse has a life of its own. A structuralist's perspective on discourse implies that one is beyond discourse. On the other hand, all these ways of accepting and interpreting words are not "errors." They are aspects of our alienated historical existence in which discourse and praxis are no longer united within our historical existence. Consequently, we can never completely escape this separation, although we can become aware of it by examining its extreme instances. For Sartre, words are thus part of our entire material existence, reflecting within themselves the alienation within our lives; better, words are our lives from a certain aspect.

through the analytic and idealistic uses of this term. Thus, a collective is not a mere aggregate of individuals united through purely external means, such as people meeting accidentally at a crossroads. Nor is a collective a collection of isolated individuals united by their acceptance of a common purpose. The collective is rather the interpenetration of individuals and material environment considered from its relatively passive and inert aspect; it is "a structure of totalising or pseudo-totalising *interpenetration*" (E. 253; F. 306; NF, 361). The task of this chapter is to elaborate the concrete meaning of this abstract description, but Sartre gives an initial caveat: he warns us not to conceive of this passive structure as merely the way tools and machines passively determine certain uses and skills. There is an abstract sense in which the demands of a technological society give the "being-outside-itself" of our subjectivity by merely requiring certain kinds of skilled workers to keep it running. But this demand as such is not specifically historical; it exists also in the cultivated land of the primitive farmer. What is distinctive in our society is that our being-outside-itself structures our consciousness with an alterity that cannot be deduced from the requirements of a technology that has merely become more sophisticated. Thus, through a history of past praxes, there exists a *"real unity within Being"* (E. 255; F. 308; NF, 363) that structures our every prereflective thought and gesture with an alterity not deducible from the abstract relation of a human organism to a technological society.[2]

When human relations are viewed from their historical aspect, the structure of the collective is seen to alter intrinsically every relation of reciprocity or isolation. Reciprocity, as a relation of interiority, is no longer a direct relation either among individuals or between individuals as a unit and a third individual as another unit. The passive inertia of the collective interpenetrates every relation of reciprocity, so that all human relations become affected with relations of exteriority. On this level, even when a person talks to another, loves another, or works with another, these relations of reciprocity are intrinsically altered by the passive structures of the collective preexisting within the historical world. Also, every relation of isolation, such as writing or sweeping the floor, is altered by the same structure of collectivity into a pseudorelation of reciprocity.

Thus, the unity of a collective exists independently of the thoughts of the people who exist within it. This unity was, of course, created by the praxes of other humans, and, in a general way, we now sustain it by our own praxes. Nevertheless, of itself, the unity of a collective does not depend on active human involvement. Sartre asks us, for the present, to think of the collective as,

---

2. In conformity to what I believe is more proper English usage, I have not followed Sartre's usage in capitalizing the term "being." Also, the term "Being" has the connotation of an hypostatization of being.

for example, the totality of a factory rather than a tool whose purpose is surpassed by a human project. Thus, in a small coal-mining town, the mine, even when closed, is a real unity, intrinsically altering every relation of reciprocity of the miners, their families, and their friends.

As we examine praxis on more concrete levels, Sartre remarks that it develops as a "spiral" whose concentric encirclings point to an ever-escaping, historical, concrete situation. This spiral unfolding of praxis never achieves synthesis in a Hegelian sense, because praxis takes place within a milieu of scarcity. This milieu occasions each person's praxis to occur initially as the praxis of another. It is not merely that we see ourselves as another, but rather that our praxis is the praxis of the other as he is also other than himself. On this level, for example, we spontaneously buy a paper on the way to work precisely as we are the other purchasing a newspaper. Our praxis thus constantly eludes us; its significance is constantly elsewhere in the *series* of those who go to work.

The characteristics of the collective and the group can best be studied in their extreme, but not thereby rare, forms. To use Sartre's example, a small combat unit almost eliminates the passivity of its collective, including the total bureaucratic structure of the army. At the opposite extreme, the buildings of a political party may still be a collective, even though the party has only a few members.

The first aspect of the distinctive alterity that the objective unity of the collective induces in behavior is that it structures each individual so that he exists as a member of a series (*la série*) rather than as an instance of a general class. Consequently, we should not conceive of our membership in society as analogous to the way the numbers one, two, three, and so on, belong to the class of cardinal numbers. Rather, it is analogous to the way the numbers first, second, third, and so on, belong to the class of ordinal numbers. Let us now turn our attention to this serial structuring of our behavior.

### (1. SERIES: THE QUEUE)

Sartre's first example of a collective is of people waiting at a bus stop for a bus. This example, Sartre says, reveals the relation of seriality clearly, but it is a superficial relation, not altering praxis on a profound level.

Those waiting for the bus are a plurality of isolations; this is revealed in such simple acts as turning one's back on one's neighbor or reading the paper. Isolation is not the mere neutral gathering of individuals; it is a special type of reciprocity. The intensity of isolation, Sartre notes, expresses "the *degree of massification* of the social ensemble" (E. 257; F. 309; NF, 365).[3] Isolation is

---

3. In a note, Sartre says that he means this only in an "indicative way" (*d'une manière purement indicative*). I understand this to mean that a high degree of isolation does not of itself have to lead to massification. It is conceivable that individuals could devote themselves to a relatively

the way each individual interiorizes the false interiorization that already exists, exteriorized, within our environment. The simple phenomenon of a bus, with its limited number of seats and lines of people who, at least in France, take tickets assigning them their place, occasion a distinctive type of isolation. Here, each member is other than himself precisely insofar as every other member is other than himself. Let us see exactly what this means.

On an abstract, but nevertheless real, level, those waiting for the bus can be considered analytically as individuals within a class of people with a common interest: getting to work. From this perspective, the bus is merely the vehicle capable of conveying to work as many people as it can hold. Individuals can be put in a one-to-one correspondence with the places on the bus. On this abstract but real level, conceptualization, Sartre says, has a legitimate place. Just as we can conceptualize the cardinal number ten, we can also conceptualize ten people waiting for a bus. The basis of the conceptualization is the fact that each one here exists as negating his personal ties to specific groups. Everyone is simply one who is waiting to get on a bus. *At this level, true alterity does not exist:* each person is oneself just as every other person is oneself. At this abstract level, alienation does not occur, because the simple separation of our bodies in space from other bodies is the same for everyone. "In a concept," Sartre says, "everyone is the same as the others insofar as he is himself" (E, 262; F, 313; NF, 370).

On the more concrete level of the dialectical "experience," seriality and alterity are seen to characterize the collective of those waiting for a bus. Each person lives his isolation not as a simple member within a class of those isolated for some common reason, but in such a way that his isolation is experienced as imposed from causes that he cannot specify. Whether because of an unspoken "everyone for himself" or a more sympathetic "every person is very much alone" (E, 257; NF, 365; F, 309)—each lives his isolation as if he were another. Each person is linked to each other by a unique chain of isolations characterized by alterity and seriality. Nevertheless, we must here recall our general context; alienation does not always enter into personal relations on a local level. Thus, a family can indeed enjoy a meal at home without experiencing this unique historical seriality.

Seriality highlights the contradiction that exists between the uniqueness of each individual and the interchangeability of each as a commuter. It matters to me that I am fourth in line with a good chance of getting on the next bus, but I am so through no merit of my own and through no determination of my needs compared with the needs of others. The bus system has given me an ordering, one that gives me or denies me a priority and simultaneously makes me real-

---

isolated life for a common purpose. Our present material existence, however, does not seem to lead easily to this kind of isolation.

ize that any other person could be standing in my place. As an ordering, seriality "becomes a negative principle of unity and of determining everyone's fate as other *by every Other as Other*" (E, 261; F, 313; NF, 369). Also, the "*formula of the series* [*Raison de la série*] is a dynamic scheme which determines each through all and all through each." (E, 266; F, 317; NF, 374). Thus there can be no univocal concept of a collective, because the ordering and unity of the members of a collective consists in an indefinite approximation to a characteristic that is itself never fully realized. Sartre does not mean that there cannot be an abstract, mathematical ordering of ordinal numbers. But our ordinal numbering in a series that characterizes collective existence is qualitative as well as quantitative. If I am the twelfth in line, I may not get on the bus. Our behavior is serial even on a more profound level. To be a Jew, a soldier, a miner, or a bourgeois merchant is a mode of seriality. One is a Jew precisely insofar as one is the other who is a Jew. The anti-Semite makes a Jew to be a Jew; but it is our collective structure that makes the Jew to be a Jew as other than himself.[4]

On one level, the collective is the structural organization of our world; it is the inorganic, passive basis from which groups arise. From this perspective, the collective can be said to be the material condition of the possibility of seriality. Strictly speaking, however, the collective as the structural organization within the practico-inert and the members within it cannot be abstracted from each other. They form a symbiotic relation. But, whether we start from the members (those waiting for a bus) or the inorganic complex (bus, bus stop, tickets, etc.), what is revealed is the exigency of the material field. There are only so many seats, and we must be first, second, or third, or else we do not get to work on time.

"There are," Sartre says, "serial feelings and serial thoughts; in other words a *series is a mode of being for individuals both in relation to one another and in relation to their common being* and this mode of being transforms all their structures" (E, 266; F, 317; NF, 373). This objective alienating condition does not mean that individuals may not here and there engage in conversations and become acquainted. But a bus trip in a metropolitan city is radically different from a "bus trip" in, for example, an undeveloped nation. When I was taking a bus trip in Moshi, in East Africa, the destination was only an excuse for the enjoyment of the trip. Our need for efficiency is not given to us by nature.

## (2. INDIRECT GATHERINGS: THE RADIO BROADCAST)

These descriptions of seriality are good illustrations of Sartre's unique nominalism. For Sartre, all universality is practical. To repeat, at each

4. See Sartre's *Anti-Semite and Jew*, trans. George J. Becker (New York: Schocken Books,

level of concreteness, the abstract common characteristics must be rethought to see how the appearance of novelty may intrinsically alter the abstract structure.[5] We have thus seen that a serial ordering has alterity. In the concrete, however, alterity exists in qualitatively different ways. These differences are brought about by corresponding differences within the practico-inert field. Thus, there is a fundamental difference between the types of alterity experienced by those waiting for a bus and by those listening to a radio broadcast, and this distinctness is itself brought about by the difference between the material configuration of the bus, bus stop, sidewalk, and street and the material configuration connecting a radio broadcaster to the listeners of the broadcast.

Those waiting in line for a bus, or, indeed, those gathered in a lecture hall, have a distinct relation to each other insofar as they are capable of reciprocity and group praxis: if the bus is canceled, those waiting can talk to each other and decide to complain as a group; those listening to a lecturer can express, through applause or shouts, their approval or disapproval. But here we are concerned with the distinctive type of inhuman alterity that exists in gatherings brought about by instrumentalities in which *absence* and *impotence* characterize the seriality, such as a radio broadcast.

Mere distance does not cause a relation to be one of absence. Two people talking on a telephone can be distant but not absent, in the present sense of the term. Those listening to the broadcast experience absence, and thus impotence, because they cannot influence the broadcaster or the others listening. To turn off the radio is not to eliminate the broadcast but simply to return to one's isolation.

A radio broadcast has at least two levels of seriality. There is the broadcaster, who, no matter how personable, speaks within the power structure of the broadcasting system. Within this system, he speaks as a broadcaster, as

---

1948). Sartre is here refining his position by introducing the notion of seriality. The situation of Jewishness created by anti-Semitism is altered by the seriality within the practico-inert; one's Jewishness is always elsewhere.

5. In a classical notion of universality, to take the simplest example from geometry, the abstract structure of a triangle, three-sidedness, does not have to be reinterpreted when the novel feature of equal sides is added: an equilateral triangle *is* a triangle. Sartre's nominalism is also different from the classical notion of analogy, particularly as developed by Aristotle, Aquinas, and Cajetan. Here, for example, when a term like "rational" is applied to human beings and to artifacts, the term is analogous, and no common characteristics can be abstracted from the analogates, "human beings" and "artifacts," to form the analogon, "rational." But a single rule can be given that requires one to think laterally along a correspondence theory of truth: in the analogy of proportionality, a *similarity*, of proportions exists, although not an identity; in the analogy of attribution, causality or something like resemblance functions. The so-called analogy of inequality, which is frequently overlooked by medieval logicians, would, I believe, be the more fruitful path for understanding Sartre's use of universality in relation to classical logic. But Sartre never explicitly develops his nominalism, and this is not the place to attempt such elucidation.

one competing like every other to be better than every other. Everyone competes as the other. To be a broadcaster is to be other than oneself. One becomes other than oneself to fit into the few slots of broadcasters the system can maintain. (Here we may note that this system defines its own "oddball" broadcasters.) It is an inhuman other who broadcasts and to whom others must listen passively as ones absent from the speaker. Each listener may experience this absence in many ways, all of which reveal a form of impotence. Listeners may experience anger or fear that others are being misled by false arguments, or they may feel joy about arguments that they agree with but cannot strengthen or share. Sartre is here referring to the radio primarily as a means for political broadcasts. The listener can respond to the broadcast only by attempting the complex action of trying to reach millions who may have heard the broadcast. The radio broadcast brings about a double alterity: the broadcaster speaks as one other than himself in a series of those other than themselves, and each listener experiences absence and impotence, as the other who is like every other listener experiencing absence and impotence.[6]

Once again, these comments must be taken in the context of class antagonism that is implicitly present but critically to be examined. Thus, it would be politically dangerous for the establishment to encourage and to construct an objective situation that would make it easy to listen to political broadcast in common with others and to discuss the content. The right of assembly is a negative right, and it fosters what some have termed a "negative democracy."

### (3. IMPOTENCE AS A BOND: THE FREE MARKET)

Our investigation of seriality is proceeding from the more abstract to the less abstract. If each example were examined in its full concreteness, it would require a lengthy treatise that would reveal within its progressive-regressive movement the full significance of the present abstract studies. Nevertheless, these examples reveal different aspects of seriality, each of which has a definite significance within the local phenomenon studied. Thus, for those listening to a political radio broadcast, seriality manifests itself through a qualitative alterity in which each listener, within the series, experiences himself as the other who is weak or strong. The material configuration of the radio broadcasting system makes each isolated listener experience *alterity* as impotence and not impotence as a bond. Conversely, the radio system is the exteriorization of the interiority of listeners; it is the exteriorization of knowledge that awaits us when we walk into a room that has a radio. The radio awaits us as the other who will speak to us, and it is as the other who will listen that we turn on the radio.

6. The television news commentators of the major networks seem to fit the description of alterity. Even the token blacks and Orientals seem to be clones, whose personality is already *there*, in the system.

Within a more complex material configuration, where people are brought actively together, seriality is experienced through impotence as a bond. A market is such an example. A market has a distinctive synthetic unity that is more than an abstraction and less than an organic whole. The market is both the exteriorization of knowledge—namely, the marketplace, the corporations, and the unions—and the interiorization of this exteriorized knowledge by the individual buyers and sellers.

On an abstract level, a market, such as a market with numerous individual booths selling flowers or food, is experienced by those entering it as a homogeneous container housing goods. On this level, all buyers and sellers experience themselves as isolated free agents exchanging money for merchandise. One can study the market from this perspective by simply enumerating how many people attended the market and how much money was exchanged for goods. But this would not be the correct perspective for a sociologist or economist, for it abstracts from buying and selling as human relations. Furthermore, this abstraction is false insofar as it presents the free market as a state of nature within which free agents act. Rather, the free market and its individual "free agents" are both *constituted realities*.

The milieu of the market is thus distinctive and cannot be explained as physical atoms interacting quantitatively with the market as another quantitative force. Nor can this milieu be explained as a gestalt (Sartre refers to Kurt Lewin) resulting from the seeming common purpose of those wishing to exchange money for goods. Rather, the link between the buyers and sellers involves a complex hierarchy of series that are beyond the comprehension and experience of any individual buyer and seller.

When we purchase goods, it appears on an abstract level to be a direct exchange of money for goods. Actually, both buyer and seller, as well as the merchandise, are linked within the market by a serial bond of impotence. In a free market, the price of the merchandise is fixed not through mutual agreement of this buyer facing this seller but through the totality of potential buyers and sellers. In theory, there is a price that satisfies both demand and supply. At a lower price, more people would demand the product, but fewer manufacturers could profitably produce it. At a higher price, more manufacturers could produce the item, but fewer people could afford it. The manufacturer who makes a profit is the one who can produce the item at a price the majority of people can afford. But he has not fixed his price as an isolated free agent. Rather, he has been influenced by the possible actions of other manufacturers. Sartre notes that one does not have to accept this simple Marxist explanation of the free market. What is important is that the manufacturer's price in today's complex market is determined by a virtually infinite series that is beyond the grasp of the individual manufacturer acting as an individual.

We have also seen above that the value of the buyer's money is affected by constant change, so that the dollar is and is not a dollar. The individual buyer and seller are indeed linked to every other buyer and seller. The link, however, is one of impotence. The center of the market exists, but it is constantly "elsewhere."

The link within the series can be understood as somewhat like the way a property is assigned to a (denumerable) mathematical infinite: first, a property is formulated in a recurrent formula so that what is true of $m$ is true of $m + 1$; second, there is shown to exist a number $n$ that has this property; and finally, one can construct the class of all numbers having the property, for example, the class of even numbers.

In mathematics, the class of such infinite numbers would be considered to be closed. But since we are dealing with real people, the seriality is here a "detotalized totality." True conceptualization is not possible, because, unlike the mathematical property "odd," the property of a collective human series both formulates the series and is outside it. One could never conceptualize the class of buyers and sellers, because, unlike the members of a class, the members of a human series are linked to each other by the same relations that separate them. Insofar as I purchase this item at the given price, I am constituting the very laws of supply and demand that constitute me as a buyer. I am thus linked to every other buyer, and it may seem that we constitute the class of buyers. But I buy as the other, that is, as one already in the class of those who can afford to buy at this price. Sartre points out that in individual cases the seriality can be overcome by group action, on the part of either the buyers or the manufacturers. The general milieu of impotence, however, still exists.

### (4. Series and Opinion: The Great Fear)

With this fourth example, Sartre begins to answer explicitly the question proposed at the beginning of this section, namely, what is class being? In a very general way, class being is both a special configuration of our environment and a radical alteration of individual consciousness. Another attempt to put Sartre's answer in proper perspective may be useful here. He does deny the organismic view of society. There is no collective consciousness formed by the union of individual consciousnesses, and we cannot understand our social existence as a natural extension of the family unit; each individual consciousness within the family unit is already altered by the class structures within the environment. Primitive societies may be formed by a union of families, but we can only know this as a conjecture originating from our own historical perspective.

Even so, class consciousness is not merely an accidental bond originating from people uniting together for a common purpose. From this perspective, Sartre does not accept that our history is formed by a series of social contracts. Individuality, in its concrete form, with all its so-called natural rights, is a product of history. Still, Sartre is not a cultural determinist. Aside from the crucial issue of praxis as free, Sartre would not accept either a socio-biological or cultural view of human history, as these are usually formulated. The cultural view does indeed emphasize the distinctiveness of human rela-tions; for example, it attempts to show how antagonisms or crises experienced by adolescent males in certain primitive societies are culturally determined. Cultural determinists, however, implicitly accept that biology as an empirical science correctly describes the human organic life. It thus implicitly relegates its own descriptions to the level of epiphenomena; culture is something added to more basic biological functions. In accepting the standard division between sociological and biological sciences, and particularly in allowing the biologist to assume the role of the "hard" scientist in touch with the objective facts of nature, cultural determinists effectively remove the basis for their own posi-tion. In contrast, sociobiologists perceive that such relations as antagonisms have indeed been fundamental to the human condition. But they interpret this fact in a traditional, foundationalist way and attempt to reduce culture to biol-ogy. Antagonism becomes a genetic response. This foundationalist view is based on a model of science in which biology itself is reduced to physics and mathematics, thereby eliminating antagonisms altogether.

Sartre's position here is opposed to both culturalism and sociobiology as I have loosely described them. *For Sartre, terms such as "antagonisms" are thoroughly anthropomorphic; we understand the so-called conflicts in primi-tive societies and those of wild beasts only from our own historical perspec-tive.* Sartre's materialism requires that we experience, understand, and de-scribe all other materialities only from the perspective of our own distinctive, human materiality. We never experience the *purely* biological, as if it were some trait common to ourselves and animals. From the experience of our hu-man bodies, we make conjectures about other bodies, and regressively we es-tablish probable relations, as described earlier.

Sartre's use of the term "being" (*l'être*) is a key to help us think through the Aristotelian and Cartesian distinction between nature and culture. This term "being" is to be understood within the more humanizing thought of Kant, He-gel, and Marx. But Sartre avoids the subjectivism of the early Kant, by insist-ing that the a priori necessary ways of existing and thinking exist in the world through the praxes of other human beings. He also avoids Hegel's idealism—first, by generally insisting on matter as the only reality; second, by denying that historically worked matter is merely the self as objectified; and third, by denying that consciousness advances by achieving a synthesis with this objec-tified self as other. Finally, Sartre does not follow the traditional Marxists in their claim that the specific alienation we experience results from the capi-talistic mode of production. Class consciousness, antagonism, alterity, impo-tence, and seriality are both universal, a priori structures of matter and praxes that sustain and surpass these structures. From the perspective of structure, the economic is only one facet of the entire practico-inert system of our history. From the perspective of praxes, alienation results from oppressive serial and group behavior. But, from a historical perspective, we can change our history only by changing our *being*, that is, only by changing our practico-inert field, from which the condition of the possibility of our praxes arises. The entire thrust of the *Critique* is that such change is possible.

Sartre thus wishes us to experience the specific way *being* makes us human. We are still, of course, concerned with *individual praxis*, but we are finally reaching the point where we see the precise distinction between action and praxis: *praxis is our every thought and deed precisely insofar as it occurs within the practico-inert field of class being and is altered by that same field.* Thus, our every thought and deed is a praxis insofar as it is a spontaneous interiorization of the "exteriorized knowledge" called class being. Furthermore, precisely insofar as it is historical, every individual praxis is part of a collective. As we have seen, this implies that every individual praxis is part of a series in which alterity characterizes each member and in which each member is linked to every other through impotence.

In the body of the text, Sartre continues his discussion by referring to the Great Fear of 1789, particularly as this has been studied by Georges Lefebvre,[7] and, in an extended note (E, 300–6 n. 88; E, 344–49 n. 1; NF, 406–407 n.1), Sartre refers to colonialism as a form of racism. Both examples are given to elucidate the distinctive feature of praxis as class being, specifically its temporality.

The general distinction between time and temporality has been made earlier; here the important point is that temporality is an aspect of the practico-inert.[8] A distinctive past, present, and future exist within the world. To give a simple example, a lathe has a distinctive, frozen temporality. Its characteristics define the sequence of skills needed to operate it. But in a more complex way, as we enter and think within these frozen temporalities of the practico-inert, we can, given proper historical circumstances, actualize such phenomena as the Great Fear and colonialism.

In this respect, the spread of such fear cannot be understood either as mass hysteria or as reciprocal actions passed from one individual to another, nor can it be reduced to an organized praxis. Fear propagates itself serially as a material wave, and this propagation displays its own laws and temporality. In "normal" temporality, the future comes to me both as made by other human beings and as capable of being *remade* by them. When opinion actualizes seriality, however, I as other face the future as other. That is, the future is still

7. The editor of the English edition provides this reference: Georges Lefebvre, *The Great Fear of 1789*, trans. Joan White (1956; N.L.B., 1973) (E, 295).

8. See chapter 2 of Sartre's introduction, section 8, and note 5.

human, but it is an alien humanity, and I accept this alien humanity as my future. True, I do not recognize myself to be alien, but I take it for granted that a part of humanity is dangerously alien.

The law of this propagation is that I do not reflect critically within myself but rather accept whatever comes from others because these others are also other than themselves. I enter within a series in which each accepts as evident that human beings are by nature evil and that the good ones can survive only by making themselves other than they would be. The rule consists in believing the worst because the worst does in fact exist; the rule is not to require evidence, for evidence is the game of the alien other. I thus actualize the Manichaeism implicit in seriality. Within humanity's future, I see an incarnate evil; my good is purely negative, the blind commitment to eliminate this evil. I accept a very special belief structure, namely, that nonpersuasive evidence justifies precisely because it is nonpersuasive.[9]

We must remember that Sartre is here referring to temporality and belief as structures of the practico-inert. It may seem strange to speak about "belief" as an objective structure. But this is consistent with Sartre's view of the practico-inert as "exteriorized knowledge." We can easily accept a chair as a form of "exteriorized knowledge," but Sartre's point is that the material configuration of our world, its being, can contain within its web the exteriorization of nonpersuasive evidence itself. Phenomena such as the Great Fear of 1789, colonialism, and other forms of racism can spread and sustain themselves because this negative aspect of seriality exists as the *inertia* of the practico-inert awaiting to be actualized.

Thus, bureaucracies, as well as certain newspapers, contain a priori structures that, when one enters and thinks within them, make it natural to accept nonpersuasive evidence as the rule of thought. One spontaneously listens to and accepts as true what the other speaks about and affirms, because both the listening and speaking are already given as that which should not be tested. Sartre says that some intelligent people are attracted to this form of thought, particularly in the form of racism, because they desire thought to be like stone. Everything has been thought by some supreme Other, and each thought is eternal and unthinkable.

In the Great Fear of 1789, the unruly peasants were seen not as fellow countrymen by those in authority, but rather as foreigners and bandits. Bandits had always existed, and normally they would have been treated as local criminals deserving individual attention. Instead, these bandits became the occasion for propagating a wave of fear, in which each poor peasant was seen as a bandit. The condition for the possibility of this view already existed within the

9. This view is also consistent with what Sartre maintains in *Being and Nothingness,* and it is the clue to my conviction that implicitly Sartre advocates strong and weak notions respectively of good and bad faith. See Prefatory Remarks, note 35, and cf. *BN,* 67–70.

practico-inert, insofar as this was already imbued with alterity and seriality. Also, in colonization, each administrator must accept it as given that those colonized are subhuman, in order to justify the colonization itself. Each administrator thus enters a discourse and life-style in which his own good is to harness the inhuman energy of the alien natives. Sartre, however, will return to expand on the racism hidden in colonialism.

## (5. SERIES AND CLASS: THE FRENCH PROLETARIAT)

This last example, of the French proletariat of the early nineteenth century, brings us a step closer to comprehending the objective reality of class being. Again, it is important to note that we are explicitly concerned, in this first book, not with group praxis but rather with individual praxis precisely as it is historical. From a historical perspective, our individual praxis is neither the atomistic behavior postulated by a liberalistic philosophy nor an aspect of a common behavior originating from a common nature or a world spirit. We are thoroughly beings-in-the-world, and this implies that on every level of our behavior the unity of our action is specified by the unity of our environment. Spontaneously, we attempt to transcend, within our own projects, the unities and meaning embedded within matter. Within local environments, we have seen that we operate frequently on those abstract but real levels. For example, to change a light bulb we use a chair as a ladder. From this local perspective, our behavior is an action and not a praxis, because it is a simple negation of what is given us: the chair as an artifact for sitting made by others. Abstracting from whether it was produced by capitalistic or socialistic technology, an artifact such as a chair does not present us with alienation and alterity. A chair is indeed the objectification of another's consciousness, but such objectification is not alienating. From this abstract perspective, the chair is simply the reification of another's project or my own project at an earlier time, and action is the simple negation of what is given.

Primitive human existence probably was, and may still be, built on these simple negations of unities found preexisting within the world. And, conceivably, our history could have developed in such a way that our relation to the world would have been direct but complex. In such a world, matter would be the inverted bonds of reciprocity that reflected back both a human equality and a differentiation of skills. Also conceivably, a technological system could have developed with an inertia of its own without this inertia's developing into a counterfinality.

What actually occurred, however, was that a milieu of scarcity was produced, a milieu that retained itself even amid plenty. Human beings further worked matter so that other, false, inhuman bonds of reciprocity became embedded in matter as an essential part of the material environment. Then such universal machines as the lathe negated true reciprocity by calling for a division between the few, more human, skilled workers and the many, less human, unskilled workers, on the one hand, and the alien owners of the machines, on the other. Once again, we must note with care that there is no reason in the abstract why skilled and unskilled workers as well as owners of a factory could not work together equally as human, within a diversity of skills.

In this context, Sartre sees himself as departing from Marx. Even prior to capitalism, human beings had worked matter so that direct reciprocity on a social level was impossible. *From our regressive approach,* we can now point out that in the Middle Ages the hierarchy of the church established a serial relation between church officials that divided them as a class from laymen as a class.[10] Each layman considered himself as other than himself, because he first saw himself *socially* as the other who was a layman. These structures of laymen and church officials were embedded in matter: in the towns, churches, modes of dress, and so forth. Each layman experienced these objective structures as an active passivity whose counterfinality could not be transcended on a social level.

Thus, all social reciprocity precisely as social had to be a double negation: each layman had to negate the very seriality that negated him as a full human being and altered him into a mere layman, before he could negate and transcend the givens of his environment. Practically speaking, for the average person, not possessed of power and wealth, these negations were impossible on a social level. Each layman could have bonds of reciprocity on many abstract, local levels, for example, with his wife and children. But within the concrete historical milieu of the Christian age, each one spoke to his neighbor and worked the fields and metals as the other who was a layman.

Our entire history has, for Sartre, developed in a milieu of scarcity, within which some spontaneously see themselves as more human than others. This inhumanity has been reified within matter. Before an individual is actively antagonistic, "antagonism" as *inertia,* as an active passivity, preexists within the environment. Nevertheless, these latent antagonisms do not constitute class being. For example, a bureaucratic complex could, in principle, be transcended and negated by an individual project. Class being emerges because these latent antagonistic powers form a series within a series. They exist within an accepted and objective milieu of scarcity as a totality of indefinite and circular series. Class being thus has a counterfinality that no individual praxis can transcend. Nevertheless, as we will see, group praxis does locally, and for a time, overcome seriality and alterity. And Sartre says, "The worker will be saved from his destiny only if the human multiplicity as a whole is permanently changed into a group *praxis*" (E, 309; F, 351; NF, 415–416).

10. Sartre does not always make it explicitly clear that his approach is regressive. At face value, some of his descriptions seem to be historical in the traditional sense of an objective description of past events as past, rather than as the past of our present.

The important point for the present discussion is that, from a historical perspective, the sociality of the French proletariat could never be direct; it was always a second-order sociality, a negation of a negation. Such descriptions as Buber's I-Thou relation may describe local reciprocity, as, for example, when an individual consumer happens to respond to a salesclerk as a human being, but such idealistic descriptions do not reveal social existence as social. From a concrete historical perspective, with the exception of group praxis to be examined below, the sociality of the French proletariat, even when it was most positive, was characterized by impotence and seriality. "For the time being, what needs to be emphasized is that impotence, as a force of alterity, is *primarily* unity in its negative form, *primarily* action in the form of passivity, and *primarily* finality in the form of counter-finality" (E, 310; F, 352; NF, 417).

Here we can recall the distinction made earlier in regard to the collective. From the viewpoint of the complex of administrative buildings, offices, and factories, class being exists in the practico-inert. From the perspective of the symbiotic relation that exists between the individual consciousness and this practico-inert, class being is also a radical alteration of this consciousness. Locally it was caused by numerous common practices, such as building *this* factory, inhabiting *this* coal-mining town, starting *this* union. But, from a wider perspective, these practices formed a series; each worker, though isolated in time and space, was connected serially to every other worker. In the early nineteenth century, individual actions could not bring the workers together. Through the same technological system, every action was both connected and separated: the union paper, announcing the strike, in one town, the strike occurring in another. These series were indefinite, and even if individuals crossed class lines, the series remained as the passive activity of matter, that is, of being. As the example of the French proletariat illustrates, even before birth the worker's destiny existed in matter as a serial bond of impotence and alterity with other workers. Perhaps the people of Athens during the classical period of Socrates' and Plato's times had direct, positive bonds of reciprocities in relation to social matter. But the French proletarians were neither slave nor free. They were new beings created by their environment, which was itself created by other human beings. If they were unskilled workers, they could achieve "full humanity" only by transcending the inhuman way they were seen by both the skilled workers and the owners. But this "seeing" was not merely subjective. It was in the world—in the machine, in the dress, in the speech, in the *being* of their environment. Practically speaking, their sub-humanity was their untranscendable destiny.

We are now ready to examine in the next section how individual praxis, by virtue of its being within a class, is also a collective praxis. The collective is neither a group nor an individual in an abstract, nonhistorical situation. We will see that the collective is the individual as serially connected through matter with every other member of the class. To use a contemporary example: When we vote, using voting machines, we vote as a collective, and the collective is the ambiguous totality of ourselves and the voting apparatuses. These seemingly neutral apparatuses are produced by and reflective of the antagonistic division between classes and races. We vote neither as a group nor as truly socially free individuals. We each pull the voting lever, aware that our power and unity consist in our serial ties of impotence to our fellow human beings and not in our force as a member of a power group.[11] Still, insofar as it is possible to comprehend our class being, while still existing within it, Sartre says, "the working class in its contradiction represents the most resolute and visible effort of men to rescue themselves through one another, that is to say, *to rescue themselves from being*" (E, 317; F, 358; NF, 423–424).

## (6. COLLECTIVE PRAXIS)

These concluding pages are an important summary of this first book of our dialectical study. This study is itself an experience; that is to say, it is both an attempt to elucidate the dialectic within our everyday behavior and an invitation through the very act of reading to become aware of the dialectic. Sartre's constant use of common occurrences provides not just examples to be contemplated abstractly but types of our own experience that we must each substitute for ourselves. The dialectic is thus to be tested not only in the strength of its exposition, but also as it reveals itself to be an aspect of our everyday lives.

In a general sense, the term "dialectic" refers to the relation of experience to its elucidation. Negatively, the term is meant to reject the view that a true description constitutes a verbal map of reality, in which one puts the words or sentences in a one-to-one correspondence with the elements of the world. In this correspondence view of truth, the writer naively places himself in the privileged position of a mapmaker outlining newly discovered territories. The "dialectic," on the contrary, reminds us both that the one describing is within that which is being described and also that language is itself an aspect of the unique materiality that is the human reality. Just as a warm embrace is not an expression of consciousness but rather consciousness as expressing itself, so language is not a representation of consciousness but consciousness as representing itself.

Consciousness, as a unique materiality, can itself affect and be affected only by matter. Thus, when we speak of historicity as an "aspect of consciousness," we refer to the specific way we have habitually adjusted ourselves

11. See Sartre, *Life/Situations*, trans. Paul Auster and Lydia David (New York: Pantheon Books, 1977), 198–210.

physically to our environment. The woman referred to earlier, who worked in the Dop shampoo factory, adjusted her entire body to the rhythm of the machines, just as one does today riding the subways in a large city. But the practical field, to which every cell of our body becomes historically adjusted, has itself been made by human beings. "These transformations are wholly *material;* or rather, everything really takes place in the physico-chemical universe and the organism's power of assimilation and of a strictly biological selection exists at the level of consumption. But one will never understand anything of human history if one fails to recognize that these transformations take place in a practical field inhabited by a multiplicity of agents, insofar as they are produced by the free actions of individuals" (E, 332; F, 369–70; NF, 437).

Although Sartre does not mention it here, it is clear that the writing and reading of the *Critique* can reveal the same seriality, alterity, and impotence as any collective praxis. Indeed, this is clear about the publishing history of the book as a *product*. It is a commodity whose fate depends on the practico-inert field it critiques. More than this, as frequently mentioned, the language of the *Critique* is not above the specific alienations that it attempts to reveal. Terms like "study," "experience," "alienation," and "refer" all exhibit the alienation in our everyday lives, in which the product of our labor is a commodity to be sold and bought within a milieu of scarcity. (Not only does the term "study," for example, reflect a division between reflection as an occupation and praxes as labor power, but also, for the average person, time devoted to study is time taken away from earning a living.) Sartre is well aware that his attempt to escape his French, intellectual, bourgeois heritage is but a fulfillment of his class being as bourgeois. Still, to repeat, there is a crucial difference between struggling in good faith against inhumanity and directly aiming to increase it.

The necessity and intelligibility that counterfinality brings to free praxis is of a very special type. This necessity does not refer to the ordinary constraint or possibility of failure that we experience in action. Indeed, insofar as we are human organisms with needs, so-called constraints are really aspects of the humanizing of our environment. "Obstacles" and "failures" arise only within the perspective of a human project. If there is no need or desire to cross a river, the water is not an obstacle, and the possibility of failing to cross does not exist. Indeed, our freedom comes into existence only as a possibility of overcoming a given contradiction. We cannot walk on water, but it is not impossible that this impossibility could be transcended. We thus build boats. Sartre has always maintained that obstacles and the possibility of failure are aspects of our free choice as it unfolds.

Necessity, however, is the unique experience in which our freedom is being used to accomplish a purpose alien to our own intention. Our physical acts are the same, but, on this new level, we experience ourselves as simply one of the "others" doing what all the others must do, precisely insofar as they also are other than themselves. Everyone is looking for better working conditions; everyone, as the unemployed other, answers questions asked by the employer as other, and we are simply one of these others. The necessity of looking for a job is given to us by our environment, our practico-inert field. It is the way the world has been made by others. It is the freedom of those who have existed before us, embedded in matter. It is, to use Sartre's language, their "frozen voices" that call us to a work in which we as a thing produce other things.

> From this point of view, it must be pointed out both that the practico-inert field *exists,* that it is *real,* and that free human activities are not thereby eliminated, that they are *not even altered* in their translucidity as projects in the process of being realised. The field exists: in short, it is what surrounds and conditions us. I need only glance out the window: I will be able to see cars which are men and drivers who are cars, a policeman who is directing the traffic at the corner of the street and, a little further on, the same traffic being controlled by red and green lights: *hundreds of exigencies* rise up towards me: pedestrian crossings, notices, and prohibitions; collectives (a branch of the Crédit Lyonnais, a café, a church, blocks of flats, and also a visible seriality: people queueing in front of a shop); and instruments (pavements, a thoroughfare, a taxi rank, a bus stop, etc., proclaiming with their frozen voices how they are to be used). These beings—neither thing nor man, but practical unities made up of man and inert things—these appeals, and these exigencies do not yet concern me directly. Later, I will go down into the street and become *their thing,* I will buy that collective which is a newspaper, and suddenly the practico-inert ensemble which besieges and designates me will reveal itself *on the basis* of the total field, that is to say, of the Earth as the Elsewhere of all Elsewheres (or the series of all series of series). (E, 323–24; F, 362–63; NF, 429)

The freedom of others resides in matter as a "habitual" tendency whose structures we cannot transcend. Necessity is both the freedom of others embedded in matter and the field of others insofar as each has had his own freedom habitualized. We frequently go from a realization of our freedom as translucent to an explicit awareness of our freedom as manipulated. Someone looking for a job may be conscious during the day of numerous free choices, such as what advertisements in the paper to answer, and may be conscious at night of the plight and destiny of being one of those who must sell his labor. Sartre calls this manipulation of freedom a "mystification" for several reasons. First, this manipulation does not alter the physical action itself, although it gives it new relations and meanings. The farmer who worked on land to produce food for himself does the same activities after his farm has been bought by speculators. Before, however, he merely produced food to eat; now this same food is a commodity to be sold for profit. But the farmer's action is still there; it must not be disregarded, as traditional Marxists attempt to do, and it must not be considered to be unimportant because it is being used. Indeed, alienation exists only because the farmer's free praxis is *both* his working of the land *and* the fact that the product of his work has become a commodity. Moreover, he himself is both a free organism and a commodity, the product of his own product.

Second, the mystification is deeper than the above example illustrates. Necessity is normally not a direct object of our conscious behavior. The farmer whose land has just been purchased by speculators might experience a sense that the meaning of his work has been taken from him, but normally he takes the entire structure for granted. Things are already commodities, and we ourselves are given by them as producers of commodities. Mystification is usually so deep that, except in fleeting moments, we actually think we are acting freely, when we are rather carrying out a sentence imposed on us by the necessity within worked matter.

In fact, two extremes of awareness can occur. The first, one already referred to, occurs when necessity appears as an explicit object: we reflect on ourselves as being manipulated. The second occurs when our struggle is so close to the level of mere survival that we pay no attention even to those fleeting moments of awareness that our fate might have been different. Persons who labor for money just to buy food might imagine receiving higher wages to buy better food, but they seldom reflect that what is inhuman in their condition is that their labor is for sale as commodity in a situation where the scarcity of jobs is deliberately sustained by capitalists.

Usually, we become explicitly aware of counterfinality only in fleeting moments of awareness that life should not have to be like this. These reflections are not neurotic; they are a fitting response to a real inhumanity. From a historical perspective, *as individuals,* we can carry out the destiny imposed on us by the active passivity of matter. This active passivity makes us into a passive activity; that is, our free praxis becomes habitualized. The products of our labor no longer reflect our objectification but instead reflect that of a stranger, possessing an alien, habitualized freedom of counterpraxis. From this historical perspective, that is, from this concrete perspective, an artist's picture, for example, is no longer an objectification of his personality but a commodity for sale.

Of course, Sartre would not accept that we can recognize ourselves in our product merely by eliminating capitalism. The alienation exists in the very way we have historically worked matter in the milieu of a sustained scarcity. What has to be removed is the seriality in which each of us as other faces our fellow human beings as other. This seriality, however, is the very structure of our present history, although, to repeat, the seriality and alienation can be removed locally.

It is thus we who have made negation into not merely a transcending of inert matter but a relation of alterity and antagonism as well. Negation here means both the positive force of transcending matter and the weakening of praxis through seriality. Sartre observes that later, when we consider group praxis, we will examine the more positive element in praxis. He also says that we can now answer the question posed earlier about negation in the emergence of the "iron and coal complex": namely, how can the discovery of greater energy and wealth for humanity actually lead to the impoverishment of the average worker? The answer is that the individual praxis of discovering coal occurs within a collective whose objective destiny was that most workers would always be poor, no matter how much wealth existed.

We have now reached the stage in the dialectic where we are ready to comprehend group praxis. Before we proceed, however, we must note several important features of the dialectic thus far. First, there is no grand, a priori dialectic that encompasses individual praxis, the counterpraxis of matter, and group praxis. That is to say, we must not imagine that somehow group praxis will emerge from the ashes of counterfinality. Of itself, counterfinality gives rise only to necessity, and there is no guarantee that it will ever be overcome by group praxis. The active-passivity of counterfinality may be the *occasion* for a different type of freedom, group praxis. *Given group praxis,* the whole process—individual praxis, counterfinality, and group praxis—can *then* be understood through a dialectic that constitutes itself from these given moments. The dialectic is thus *constituted* from its moments, *if these are given*; it is not a dialectic *constituting* its moments from its own a priori structure. (One is reminded here of the two approaches to set theory, one constituting sets from isolated elements, the other attempting to avoid the paradoxes of set theory by claiming that a set must be known to exist before subsets or elements can be examined.)

Second, collective praxis is individual praxis, precisely insofar as it arises within a milieu of scarcity and is part of a seriality of praxes with alterity and impotence.

Third, every praxis is a unilateral, interior relation, through which an individual exteriorizes interiority. Of course, this exteriority already reflects another's interiority. All praxes are thus reorganizations of structures that have been organized by others. Of itself, counterfinality does not produce anything; it is merely the active passivity of matter and needs to be actualized by human beings. In the concrete, however, human beings are always there. The collective thus consists of serial structures in which the active passivity of counterfinality is always being serially actualized. This actualization by the other brings about a new, broader exteriorization that engulfs the local exteriorization of the individual. For example, when a country has been defeated, the individual praxes of those making clothes may remain physically the same. But the individuals and the products are altered; they are the conquered working for the conquerors.

Fourth, while counterfinality is always actualized by an individual within a collective, this individual is both other than himself and part of a series of those who are also other than themselves. Thus, a land is conquered not through one, individual freedom confronting and limiting the freedom of another in mutual reciprocity, but through a series of others conquering the other *as* other. That is why individual soldiers, when outside their serial structures, frequently do not recognize each other as "the enemy." "It is the war," they say of their enmity, and on this local, abstract level, they may behave as friends.

Fifth, counterfinality arises as a moment of the dialectic only when group praxis has been recognized to be part of our history. We must always remember that we are working within the totality of our historical experience. In this experience, groups arise from and degenerate back into seriality; both occur simultaneously. To state this another way, we must not interpret our procedure in a traditional foundationalist sense. Seriality is not the foundation of group praxis. In the concrete, we have seriality only because we have group praxis. Without group praxis, individual praxis and counterfinality would not exist as we know them, and our history would be changed. It is this group praxis, which has always been present but never examined, that we must now try to comprehend.

# BOOK II

From Groups to History

PART ONE   *The group—the equivalence of freedom as necessity and of necessity as freedom—the scope and limit of any realist dialectic*

# (1  The Group-in-Fusion)

## (1. THE GENESIS OF GROUPS)

In this second book, we are continuing our attempt to understand the intelligible structures of history. We have seen how individual existence is modified by participating in the seriality of collectives, and now we will examine how seriality is altered by group praxis. Finally, we will touch upon the last distinctive characteristic of our historical existence, namely the alteration of individual existence by its participation in *a* single history occasioned by the antagonistic interaction of large class groups.

Before proceeding, however, we should recall the earlier remarks about the misleading character of the English divisions of this second book. The English editors unfortunately divide the dialectical moments of the original French text into eight analytical chapters. But it must be admitted that there is some confusion in deciding how to divide this second book. The original French gives four parts, using each of Sartre's four subtitles for this second book as indicating separate parts. The critical French interprets Sartre's second and third subtitles to be subdivisions of the first, giving only two parts to this second book of volume 1. I have followed the critical French, while also indicating Sartre's four subtitles in relation to the English chapters. I have also kept the English chapters as subdivisions. The general dialectical progression of this last book is to reveal the intelligible structures of groups as they can be understood to develop from the extremely vital but temporary state of fusion to the more rigid but permanent state of institutions. Under Sartre's first subtitle (chapters 1–4), this development is examined regressively and abstractly as an internal development of groups. Of course, the relation of group praxis to its nonthetic object is indeed considered, but the delicate question of the status of the unity of groups is not explicitly raised. Sartre's subdivision of part one (chapter 5) briefly sketches how the being and the unity of groups arise from their initial purpose of altering the environment. In the second subdivision of part one (chapter 6), the interiority of the group is now examined more concretely as a process of perpetual detotalization. Part two (chapters 7 and 8) gives the first examination of concrete praxis, that is, praxis on the truly historical level. Here the issue of the reality of class conflicts and class being is examined.

We must recall once again the conditionality and materiality of our dialectical investigation (*expérience*): Our dialectic is materialistic; it must be shown how the materiality of group praxis can overcome the specific inertia of alterity. Indeed, we are not attempting to reveal any a priori intelligibility within collectives that requires them to become groups. Rather, because groups develop within, emerge from, and fall back into collectives, we are then able to reveal regressively the intelligibility of this dialectical movement. We have seen that Sartre rejects the "organismic" view of history. According to this view, groups are quasi hyperorganisms uniting individuals in a way analogous to that in which the individual organism unites cells. For Sartre, the organismic view is not a simple error of abstract thinking; rather, it is the first, uncritical way the nongrouped react to the grouped. Those who are not actually involved within a specific group are not explicitly aware of the complex differentiation within group praxis; they thus tend to project a unity onto groups that is a simple, homogeneous extension of their own individual actions. Of course, this means that on this level we miss the distinctive character of a group and falsely unite mere collectives into groups. "It is striking that our most elementary patterns of behaviour relate to *external collectives* as if they were organisms" (E, 346; F, 382; NF, 450).

Sartre's rejection of the organismic theory implies that we cannot conceive of society either as developing from a natural extension of the differentiated unity of family life or as emerging from the homogeneous unity of separate individuals united for a common purpose. Both existence within a family and life lived alone are secondary phenomena that are built upon the alterity and inertia of each individual life within a collective. In the concrete, the individual within a family unity has not abandoned a free, isolated existence to form a higher union. Both the adults who initiated the union and the children born within it are initially weighed down by the alterity and inertia of their participation in the larger historical reality of the collectives in which they were born. But, to repeat what has frequently been said throughout this commentary, Sartre's procedure requires us to constantly remember that from an abstract—that is, a local and limited—perspective, the concrete reality is not always the most significant. The father of a nineteenth-century coal-mining family may have genuinely experienced himself as its provider. And, on this level, his experience was valid. On this level, he thus passed through the collective existence of his life as a miner; that is, he lived his life as a miner as an accident of birth. He would have conceived it to be as impossible for himself to have the luxuries of the owners of the mine as for the blind to see. But this impossibility defined his possibilities: it is possible for the blind to live a life relative to the healthy, and it is possible for the miner to define his humanity by his approximation to that of the owners. As long as this order is recognized as merely the way things happen to be, life, no matter how hard, is bearable. There is always the possibility that the impossible will happen—if not for the miner, at least for his children. But when these de facto impossibilities become de jure impossibilities, the miner realizes that the impossible had *always* been the forbidden. A law forbidding the miner to own or participate in the owning of mines arises only in the context that the miner might transcend his established position. The law makes change itself to be impossible. The impossible is not merely that which could be transcended (*dépassé*) were it not for the accident of birth; it is that which is forbidden to the very humanity of the miner.[1] Sartre says, "The direct result of this is to make the *impossibility of change* the very object which has to be transcended if life is to continue" (E, 350; F, 385; NF, 454).

Nevertheless, neither external nor internal conditions can, of themselves, explain why or how groups arise from collectives. We are not trying to construct a transcendental dialectic to show how the collective is a necessary moment in the formation of groups. It is conceivable that a society could have remained on the level of collective existence. Nevertheless, such a collective existence would be different from our own.

What we call collective existence is that which we experience when groups disintegrate. Therefore, it does not make sense to claim that either collectives or groups historically came first. Such a perspective would imply a non-historical approach to history. Rather, we know that de facto groups arise from and dissolve into collectives; groups negate and transcend collectives, thus preserving the alterity and inertia of collectives in transcending them. But the converse is not true. A collective does not, of itself, point to a transcending group praxis. By transcending alterity in group praxis, a union of miners does reveal its collective origins in the serial connection of each miner to every other miner as other. But, of themselves, these collectives do not reveal how groups can be formed; they hide their collective existence in the flight of seriality. The miner who is unaware of his historical condition is also not aware of being part of the collective of miners.

Thus, it is only from a perspective in which groups are given that collective praxis can be seen to be prior to group praxis. Moreover, we know from his-

---

1. The English term "transcend" has two general meanings in Sartre's philosophy. The first, usually expressed by *dépasser*, means to surpass, as a short person might surpass the given quality of height in a project of becoming a basketball player by training to be fast and agile. The second meaning, usually expressed by *transcender*, means to be outside of consciousness, usually as a quality arising from freedom but now existing in the world. Thus we will see, for example, that oppression exhibits these two meanings of transcendence. It is a surpassing insofar as it is a praxis of the dominant class, and it is also an objective structure of laws and institutions.

tory that oppressed classes, capable of revolutionary praxis, have arisen from oppressed collectives. Nevertheless, Sartre observes that at this early stage we cannot assume that important social structures, such as classes, are groups. The approach in this study will be to examine ephemeral groups first and then examine the more basic social groups, along with the question of whether classes are groups.

Since the dialectic is not transcendental, it is important to note that group praxis is contingent; that is, it is a historical happening. This happening, however, gives rise to necessary, intelligible connections. Thus group praxis can neither be deduced from nor reduced to collective praxis. True, group praxis arises in a milieu of scarcity in which individual need is experienced as common need. But again, it is important to note that, in the abstract, there is no a priori reason why an individual should experience need as common. That victims of famine unite to share food rather than fight over scraps of food, Sartre notes, is neither deducible from their historical situation nor reducible to it. The power of synthesis is both everywhere, in the free existence of each life, and nowhere, in that each life may or may not transcend individual need. Once that synthetic moment is given, however, both the transcendence of individual need for common purpose and the unification of the practical field become intelligible.

Group praxis, Sartre notes, is a complex phenomenon that must be approached on various levels of materiality. From one perspective, it is true that the unity of group praxis is specified by its object. The object specifies the precise type of alterity and inertia that each experiences within the group: the specific means of production, such as the lathe, brought about the specific alterity and inertia that distinguished unskilled from skilled workers. Nevertheless, unless this inertia had been transcended by the realization of the inhumanity within this division between skilled and unskilled, the very division itself would never have been experienced as a specific phenomenon. Therefore, the converse moment is given: the unity in the material field arises only when group praxis arises; unskilled and skilled laborers recognize that the inhumanity in their condition is humanly caused only when they adopt a common praxis against the owners of the factories. Thus, *given* the synthetic moment that brings a group into existence, we can then delineate its genesis and reveal its characteristics from the object of its praxis. "In our investigation we shall therefore have to study successively the genesis of groups, and the structures of their *praxis*—in other words, the dialectical rationality of collective action—and, finally, the group as *passion*, that is to say, insofar as it struggles in itself against *the practical inertia* by which it is affected" (E, 348; F, 383; NF, 452).

## (2. THE STORMING OF THE BASTILLE)[2]

Sartre begins his study of groups with ephemeral groups, and the first of these is what he calls the "group-in-fusion" (*le groupe en fusion*). In general, a group-in-fusion is formed when both the external pressures of other groups and the material environment are the occasion for a gathering to adopt a common praxis spontaneously. In a group-in-fusion, seriality is overcome negatively, and not, as in pledged or organized groups, positively, by a self-determination that explicitly aims at a common praxis. In a group-in-fusion, there is a crucial external occurrence in which the gathering, faced with a common need, danger, or enemy, spontaneously interiorizes the common threat. A group-in-fusion thus forms as an "apocalypse" (*l'Apocalypse*). An apocalyptic moment of fusion could never be attained unless the "hodological space"—that is, the complex of roads and buildings as these are concretely related to the physical movements of the gathering—were such that a synthesis could be spontaneously achieved.[3] Furthermore, a group-in-fusion has a distinctive temporality within its hodological space, such as the need to reach a specific location quickly and protect it securely.

This introductory, abstract discussion reverses, for pedagogical reasons, Sartre's own nominalistic procedure of delineating the characteristic of a group-in-fusion by describing a particular instance: the people of Paris immediately after July 12, 1789.[4] Prior to this date, the people had suffered deprivation serially, that is, each in resignation, thinking it was his fate. There were local outbursts, but these soon dissipated back into the seriality of the people of Paris as a mere gathering. The material configuration of the city, the pressures of outside groups—the army surrounding the city, the militia formed within it, the king as a personification of the threatening government—all these would be the occasion for Paris becoming a new city, a group-in-fusion.

At first, it might seem that the electoral assembly, as the representatives of the people of Paris, signified a common praxis among its citizens. But Sartre comments that this type of assembly represents its constituents only insofar as the representatives usurp the capacity of the people to organize. Indeed, as an assembly, the representatives were as much afraid of the people who elected them as they were of the army who threatened the city. In general, Sartre says,

2. This subtitle is somewhat misleading, for, as we will see, the central theme is not the storming of the Bastille but Paris as a group-in-fusion.

3. Hodological space is space in relation to praxis. For an airplane about to land, it consists not only of the airspace and the runway but also the radar, the air currents and temperature, and the weight of the plane.

4. See Wilfred Desan, *The Marxism of Jean-Paul Sartre* (Garden City, New York: Doubleday & Company, Anchor Books, 1965), 137–48.

the process of election is passive, and it leaves in its inert seriality the gathering that is electing its representatives: each votes as the other, aware that every other is voting as an other. The electoral assembly was, in fact, one of the power groups that enabled the people to become a group-in-fusion. Supposedly to protect the people from unruly mobs, although there was no fear or danger of such, the assembly created the militia, and the people became aware of their distinctive unity. Nevertheless, once the people became united, they could then force the assembly to represent them. At first, however, the active unity of the electoral group established the people of Paris only as a unity or a being "outside itself of freedom": the people saw that their individual votes brought *the* assembly into existence, and they saw their freedom in this accomplishment.

This reflection of their own freedom need not have led to unity. Indeed, its first manifestations were "imitation" and "enthusiasm": The people responded to posters and rumors by running into the streets, by meeting, shouting, destroying the tollhouses. What made synthesis possible was the *weight* of the numbers and the fact that the crowd started to arm itself. The act of arming had a "double signification of freedom." First, the people wanted the individual means to protect themselves against the dragoons, and it was always possible that they would fight each other over the availability of rifles. But a second movement of freedom made common praxis immediately possible, namely, the gradual realization, within each, that they were arming themselves *as the people of Paris against the king.* The moment that occasioned the apocalypse, the fusion of the city, arose when rags instead of guns were found in the boxes sent by Jacques de Flesselles. Spontaneously, the gathering interiorized that *it* had been tricked; deception can be aimed only at those who have a common purpose.[5]

In the moment of trickery, seriality was lost. Those in the gathering saw their unity not as something escaping them but as something *there* before them, reflected in the boxes of rags. But this moment of unity could have dissipated itself. The temporal process of fusion needed a new, more permanent focus. It is in this sense that the Bastille becomes crucial. The Bastille was a source of guns both for the people and for the army. The temporal pace of fusion could be sustained because this fortress and sign of repression had to be taken quickly. As the ringing of the bells signified the birth of a new city and reminded the people to be on their guard, the Bastille became the inert idea of the apocalyptic moment. Thus a group-in-fusion is possible when external pressure groups provide the motive forces *and* the practico-inert signifies the possibility of unified praxis. Nevertheless, the moment of fusion is not caused by these possibilities; fusion is itself a moment of freedom.

5. Sartre notes (E, 357 n. 8; F, 390 n. 2; NF, 460 n. 2) that Flesselles seemed to have acted from group faith, but this did not change the effect.

### (3. THE THIRD AND THE GROUP)

But how does individual praxis become group praxis? Sartre sketches his answer within the context of the ephemeral group-in-fusion. In general, Sartre's point is that group praxis is not a mere extension of the relations of reciprocity among individuals. Sartre thus breaks with most, if not all, of the traditional formulations of the relation of the individual to groups, and of both to society. We have seen that, in the abstract, individual action is translucent; that is, action and its intelligibility coalesce, and this is revealed to us in fleeting moments of pure reflection: in running to catch a bus, I am prereflectively aware that my action is apodictically that of running to catch a bus. Nevertheless, in its concrete, historical context, the signification of my action is stolen from me by the antipraxis of the practico-inert field. In its local context, my action of running to catch a bus does not make me aware that I run as all others run who must catch a bus to go to work. Within this historical context, I am, in Sartre's terms, "mystified, alienated, and cheated" from the translucent meaning of my free actions. If group praxis were merely an extension either of the way individual praxis spontaneously totalized its environment or of the way reciprocity brings about a common result then the antipraxis of the practico-inert would be left unaffected, and group praxis would be unimportant. What makes group praxis worthy of study is that it resolves, at least for a while and from a limited historical perspective, the contradiction and tension between translucent individual praxis and the inert counterfinality of the practico-inert. That is, group praxis overcomes the *passive* activity of each individual praxis and "decodes" the *active* passivity of antipraxis.

Group praxis, specifically that which forms groups-in-fusion, arises from our individual praxis precisely as each of us is a third in relation to every other as third. Here we must keep in mind that we are not trying to reconstruct history from individuals in isolation. Isolation, to repeat, is a specific mode of life made possible only through a concrete historical situation. We start rather with the full complexity of a praxis that reveals others and tertiary relations to others. We have already seen that mediated reciprocity is one of the characteristics of action as historical, that is, of praxis. In group praxis, this mediation is of a special type, and its characteristics are revealed by a study of the reciprocal relations between group praxis and its object.

Group praxis brings about a totalization *both of the environment and of individuals*. Then we must examine this totalization as an object as well as a subject. The example Sartre uses is that of an exhausted person being carried down a mountain by a rescue group. He totalizes his rescuers not as a spectator but as a subject of a group praxis: he is the subject being rescued by the group as they also are subjects. Group praxis temporarily eliminates the difference each one experiences between subjectivity and objectivity; this difference is not of itself alienating, although seriality makes it so. In our original example of Paris as a group-in-fusion, we can imagine many of the gathered fleeing, fearing for their lives. While running, each is not only the other running serially with all others; each is also a third, within whom exists the possibility of totalizing the gathering as *those who flee*. Indeed, if I simply stop and hide by myself, watching the group fleeing, fusion through me would never occur. If instead I seize upon an apocalyptic moment—shouting "Hide here!" —I fuse the fleeing gathering into a group. In this manner, I dissolve the distinction between the way I see myself and the way others see me. I do not fuse the group from without; rather, I face every other person fleeing as a third who could also totalize both of us within the group. This will be expanded on in the next section.

The above description would appear magical, if we did not keep in mind that concrete, material pressures and tensions make group praxis possible. It is not sufficient that external groups, such as the army, the assembly, and the militia, pressured the gathering within the city of Paris. The material configuration within and surrounding Paris must also have a unity sufficient to pressure the gathering. In this case, the existence of the Bastille was crucial. Each fleeing person must interiorize the antipraxis of the practico-inert arising from the environment of the city and the other groups.

Fusion resulted as much from the organization of Paris as in response to the strength of the army and the actions of the government officials. Indeed, the government was weak, but the forces of its bureaucratic institutions' active passivity transcended the weakness of the government officials and the army. This transcendence is what is meant by counterfinality; the *system* of worked matter acts on each individual with a force beyond its individual components. Paris, as a city-in-fusion, arose as a response to the strength of this antipraxis, and not from the weakness of the government. The new Paris arose both from the possibility of synthesis within each individual praxis and from the reflected unity caused by the tensions within the practico-inert.

Of itself, however, the unity reflected from antipraxis onto seriality is negative. The French government, as an oppressive force, *externally* united the people of Paris, as the oppressed. But this unity does not unite them from within and does not dissolve their seriality. Each could still suffer his fate as his destiny. The means for affecting the positive unity within the group-in-fusion begins to arise when the members spontaneously becomes aware of their relation to each other. They go into the streets, Sartre says, with no definite purpose, aware that they will find others so gathered. At this stage, seriality is still not overcome. A moment must arise, from the pressures of the historical situation, when each is aware of being both immanent and transcendent in relation to the gathering. As transcendent, each could effect an external unity to the gathering by becoming the third who is watching either as subject being carried along or as the external spectator who sees the gathering as an object. As immanent, each is aware of being actively within the gathering. Group praxis arises when the transcendent and the immanent coalesce.

Again, we must not conceive of this union idealistically. We are referring to praxis, that is, to the habitual relations within the family, work place, or neighborhood. To repeat, group praxis is not merely the resolution of the contradiction between translucent individual praxis and the complex of lived relations within a society, as happens, for example, when family life is considered in its local context. Such a resolution would merely be an extension of individual praxis; it would not touch the counterfinality of the practico-inert. Rather, group praxis resolves another contradiction, namely, that contradiction between each person as a mediating third and all others in their otherness. Thus, a family could have a local unity and each of its members could still, from a historical perspective, be the third who is the other. This alienation always exists, and, with only a slight change in circumstances, it could be more important for the members of the family than their abstract, local relations. In a family with a sufficient income, the needs of each member can be met. If the breadwinner becomes unemployed, the ever-present milieu of sustained scarcity then touches each member of the family. It is this historical alienation that group praxis temporarily eliminates.

## (4. The Mediation of Reciprocity: The Transcendence-Immanence Tension)

We have studied the genesis of the group-in-fusion, and the task is now to describe its structures. This brief section is both difficult and crucial. Through an examination of transitory groups, in particular the group-in-fusion, Sartre lays the foundation for understanding the general problem of how group praxis can be both individual and common. Here, in particular, it is strikingly evident that Sartre has not abandoned the primacy of freedom in his philosophy.

All relations within a group are characterized by a distinctive mediation. Group relations are relations of reciprocity mediated by and through the group precisely as the group is a praxis. Even in the simple case of a group waiting for other members to join them, those who walk to join the group share the same activity as those waiting for their arrival. Through mediation, each one's waiting or walking is both his own and the group's. Each individual praxis is thus enriched with a new dimension by which it is simultaneously individual and common.

Of course, ordinary reciprocities, such as speaking to a friend, are mediated through matter, such as spoken words. Furthermore, the broad historical context of the language of these words exerts an active passivity on each speaker, alienating each of them from the meanings of his own discourse. In group praxis, however, the mediation is precisely through praxis, that is, precisely through action as it is historical. Each individual praxis mediates through the group praxis. Sartre notes that this mediated reciprocity within a group-in-fusion has two aspects or moments.

The *first* is the distinctive way each becomes a third within a group. Each individual is a third by participating in the group, and the group is a group insofar as it can be fused and moved by each third as a potential sovereign. To illustrate this moment Sartre asks us to imagine a group in flight, from which individuals have become separated. When those who have been separated begin to rejoin the group, their serial connection to the main body is radically different from that of those joining a line of people waiting for a bus. In the queue, each is the other who may be the last one to be able to get on the bus. Scarcity creates a situation in which each one's ordinal numbering on the line is alienating from every other. When two persons join a group, however, seriality enriches by strengthening the humanity of each one.

The crucial point is, Sartre notes, that relations within a group are ternary and not, as many sociologists think, binary. Each person approaching the group is not an individual other joining the group as a common other. Rather, each person is initially related to every other through the group itself. I approach the group with my friend not insofar as we are friends but insofar as we are separated members of the group, and I see others joining in the same way. This is a unique reciprocity in which numbers eliminate the inhumanity within the practico-inert brought about by scarcity.

In a group, each member's freedom has a new dimension because the other as a third is not a mere object. In ordinary reciprocity, the other objectifies and transcends me in his project insofar as I objectify and transcend him in my project. But, in group praxis, each as third is immanent to every other as third; each has the same relation to every other, through their relation to the group. From this aspect, the praxis of those walking to the group and the praxis of those awaiting their arrival are the same praxis. This new dimension of individual freedom is, Sartre says, *power*. This power destroys alterity. When I see both the other coming to the group and those waiting within the group, I see my own "lived objectivity"; "*I see myself come to the group in him*" (E, 377; F, 406; NF, 479). Thus, we recapture our lost objectivity before the other not through our ordinary relations of reciprocity but through the mediation of the group. Here, however, we must recall Sartre's dialectical nominalism; the term "objectivity" no longer has its abstract meaning of the self as objectified. In the present discussion, objectification takes place in the practico-inert field of seriality. And the present point is that alienation is overcome not through the general movement of a dialectic but through a contingent event in specific circumstances: the fusion of a gathering into a group.

Sartre then describes the *second* aspect of mediated reciprocity within a group-in-fusion: In ordinary seriality, I am at the mercy of the forces of anti-praxis. I see my action repeated not as mine but as the other's. For example, each Chinese peasant who tilled the land also deforested the land, and the hoarding of gold in Spain occasioned the devaluation of currency for each Spaniard. But in the group, I see my action repeated precisely as mine. Every person in the group can mediate between every other person and the group. In a group-in-fusion, this is obvious, because every person is a potential sovereign who can lead the group. Now one person gives a direction, now another. On this level, there is no ruled or ruler. At the proper moment, someone may shout "To the Bastille!" The group moves to the Bastille not because it has been ordered, but because its praxis was immediately oriented in this direction. Thus, in a group-in-fusion, temporality is both crucial and conditioned by events, as, for example, the need to capture the Bastille quickly.

Since each person is capable of being a temporary sovereign regulating the group, each is also potentially the transcendent other attempting to control the group for his own purposes. As long as fusion continues, however, this capability of becoming the transcendent other exists only as an "immanence-transcendence" and not as an explicit transcendence. Each individual is mediated through a regulatory third, and each is capable of being that third. Sartre says, "we shall call the individual's being-in-the-group, insofar as it is mediated by the common *praxis* of a regulatory third party, his 'interiority' or 'bond of interiority' in relation to the group" (E, 381; F, 409; NF, 483). In this respect, the law of the group-in-fusion is what Sartre terms an "alteration of statutes": each, as a potential regulatory third, can become equally an actual regulatory third, *without becoming a transcendent other to the group.* In this alteration of statutes, the regulator is simply the de facto means that gives the group its temporary, practical, and "biological" unity. Within this common praxis, actualized by a specific third, each one totalizes himself and every other as the third who could equally regulate the common praxis of the group. Whatever momentum the group carries is thus not that of inertia. Sartre concludes these paragraphs by observing that we shall soon see how this common unity, as a developing totalization, attempts "to realize itself as individuality."

## (5. THE INTELLIGIBILITY OF
## THE GROUP-IN-FUSION)

Throughout the *Critique,* Sartre is very concerned about the relation between the mode of exposition of a developing reality and the reality as it concretely develops. As a dialectically written work, the *Critique* aims at eliciting within the reader a dialectical *experience.* Or better, the *Critique* is a dialectical experience precisely as it is part of the synthetic totality of books and readers. A critical work must be aware of itself, for the work as a critique is not separate from what it studies. The *Critique* is thus part of the ongoing history that it is attempting to understand. This critical investigation accepts the whole of history; it assumes, as given, individuals, gatherings, and groups, as well as the entire literary discourse about them. Nevertheless, it is still true that no mode of exposition can perfectly parallel a developing reality. Indeed, as written, the *Critique* takes place not within the developing praxis it elucidates, but after it. An analytic discourse attempts to heal this breach between exposition and action by reconstructing the synthetic whole from its atomistic parts. But it necessarily tailors reality to fit its own mode of discourse. In its own logic, the conclusion necessarily follows from the premises and is reducible to them. Thus, the synthetic whole is interpreted as developing necessarily from the parts and as reducible to them. But, as we have frequently noted, this empiricist's perspective masks an idealistic viewpoint in which the observer becomes an untutored transcendent mind objectively noting the empirical happening of parts uniting to form a synthetic whole. An apparently innocent methodology is thus a total philosophy.

Unlike the analytic approach, Sartre's regressive method never loses sight of the novelty of the synthetic whole while attempting to elucidate the intelligibility of its genesis and structure. Again, we should recall an important point about this intelligibility: human relations are what is most intelligible to human beings. Ideas or inert matter could be comprehended directly only by a God or a pure mind. Despite its complexity and continuing development, or, rather, because of it, history is more intelligible than mathematics or physics. Sartre here reverses the entire philosophic tradition in which the unchangeable, the necessary, and the nonhuman are considered to be more intelligible than the transitory, the contingent, and the human. Sartre never quite states his claim this explicitly, but the direction of his thought is that we understand nonhuman relations only through an "analogy" with human relations.[6]

Group praxis has more intelligibility than individual praxis, precisely because, in the concrete, our lives take place within and surrounded by other, larger groups. As cautioned earlier, no exposition can perfectly parallel a developing reality. Although the *Critique* assumes the existence of all history, it proceeds, as we have frequently noted, from the abstract to the concrete. Thus, the group-in-fusion is studied first, because it is the simplest and the most abstract. That is, the moment of fusion can be examined as relatively autonomous from larger historical forces. Furthermore, the group-in-fusion is itself examined in an abstract way, because its temporary union does not actively incorporate the historical heterogeneity of each of its members. The group-in-fusion is specified by a definite goal, such as the taking of the Bas-

6. Strictly speaking, analogy implies a form-matter relation. This term, however, is here applicable insofar as it also signified, for Aristotle, a type of equivocation.

tille. From this perspective, each, as a regulatory third, is the same, and, as we will see, each is more free than when acting alone. Nevertheless, in the concrete, the differences in individual backgrounds do come into play and, in certain groups-in-fusion, they can be crucial.

The central problem in comprehending the intelligibility of group praxis is to grasp how it could be simultaneously individual and common. Briefly, Sartre directs us to see that group praxis is an activity that is specified by its object. When a group-in-fusion is "hot," each group member spontaneously recognizes that the circumstances demand common action. Needless to say, the circumstances do not cause each to act as if everyone's action is his own. The same circumstances could give rise to serial flight rather than fusion. The fusion is a unique event of freedom that brings about the unity of its object, just as the object reciprocally specifies the unity of the fusion. Thus fusion is not irrational or magical. It is not a substantive, "gelatinous" unity among individuals, nor is it a superficial bond of agreement emerging among individuals deciding to act in common. *It is rather a radical alteration of the individual's praxis so that it is no longer merely individual but also common.* As we will see, ontologically only individuals exist. Nevertheless, in and through their unfolding praxis each individual recognizes that he is acting for every other and that every other is acting for him. Each sees the praxis of the others as his praxis.

Thus, in the very act of regrouping, each individual recognizes the unity of the group. In my free act of joining the group, I see *myself* in the individuals I am joining. If I happen to give a direction, it is because chance has placed me at the proper position. But my being *here* is also my being *there,* through the unity of the group. A direction from *there* is not given by the other but by me as *there* through the other. Thus, Sartre says, the real problem in comprehending group unity is one of excess: everyone is unifying everyone and there seems to be too many centers of unity rather than too few.

But, Sartre continues, this problem is again one of formulation: we delineate the issue analytically and try to understand it synthetically. Moreover, an organism is a completed totality, but a group praxis is a totalizing process. The group-in-fusion is thus constantly restructuring itself as it absorbs and bypasses the unities within the practico-inert. The walls behind which it regroups and the streets through which it runs are all means by which it sustains its unity. And the goal itself is a process. The victory of the taking of the Bastille is the activity of the people walking up and down the corridors. Once this activity ceases, and the group-in-fusion as such collapses, the individuals are in danger of falling into seriality and alterity.

But we still have not answered how there can be many centers of praxis, each separate and common. "We must show," Sartre says, "in what way every *praxis* is a free individual development and in what way it could only be what it is as the *praxis* of the totalised multiplicity" (E, 393; F, 418–19; NF, 494). The second half of this formulation, Sartre states, is the easiest to explain. It is only as part of a group that each individual can do what he does. Each individual has the power of acting from the group; apart from the group, he would recognize that circumstances would make his action useless. For each person in the group, the size of the group is a means, the way a rifle is a means. The individual has the strength to attack or defend a threat *here*, because everyone is *here*. This power does not diminish freedom; rather, it makes freedom translucent, from a more concrete historical context than does individual praxis. If I, as a demonstrator, do not allow myself to be passively taken by the police, it is because I do not want to be taken. And I now have the power to do what I want to do.

We can now see how the first part of the question is to be answered, namely, in what way every praxis in the group is also a free individual praxis. In a group-in-fusion, each is most himself, but each sees that what he wants to do can only be done by many. I am aware that through me, as a third, the entire group totalizes itself *here*, and I spontaneously allow my act to be also the totalization of everyone else as a third. It is me acting *there* as it is me acting *here*. I am responsible for everyone's act, as everyone is responsible for me. Here, Sartre says, we see the first emerging of the "we" (*nous*). I do not see myself as the transcendent object of the other; rather, I see both myself and the other within the free unfolding of the group praxis as it accomplishes its result. *If I could be everywhere I would be, and through the group I am. It is not the other who gives me an order from there, but myself as a new source of freedom.* Each individual is a third through whom all are totalized *here*. But this must be understood as a practical response to a historical danger. A group-in-fusion does not arise by a reflective decision to become united. "The silk-weavers of Lyons did not unite against *alienation and exploitation:* they fought in order to prevent the constant lowering of their wages" (E, 401–2; F, 425; NF, 502).

# (2    The Statutory Group)

(1. The Surviving Group: Differentiation)

One goal of the *Critique* is to comprehend the permanent structures of large, historical groups in order to determine whether classes are groups. Sartre begins with the group-in-fusion not because it is chronologically prior but because it is the most abstract and simplest to understand. The pervasiveness of analytic thinking inclines us to believe that the simplest must have occurred first; it is, however, conceivable that the most complex type of group was historically the first.

The general outline of these sections is to show how the group-in-fusion leads to organization and then to the institution. More specifically, following the translator's three subdivisions of this chapter, we can say that first Sartre shows how the group-in-fusion survives its "hot" state of extreme active praxis by taking itself as its own object. Second, he shows how the group-in-fusion achieves a degree of permanence through the pledge. Third, he raises the question of intelligibility once again by examining the subjects of fraternity and fear. The English edition entitles this chapter "The Statutory Group," but its main theme is how both the pledge and terror give permanent structures to groups.

Sartre begins with a reference to negations, and it may be useful here to review his terminology. He states: "The intelligibility of the fused group depends, therefore, on the complex ensemble of a negative designation of its community, reactualized in the negation of this negation, that is, in the free constitution of individual *praxis* into common *praxis*" (E, 405; F, 427; NF, 505). The individual free project is a negation, because it is always a surpassing of what is given in order to accomplish what is not yet present. Individual praxis is a reorganization of the environment. In group praxis, however, I negate my praxis as individual in order to have it reemerge as common. I run to storm the Bastille not as an isolated individual—indeed, I could not "read" this possibility in the environment—but as a member of a group. I negate my individual running in order to be the regulatory third who has the power of the entire group *here*, in my running, just as I am *there* in each other runner.

Group praxis is thus a secondary negation presupposing the primary negation of individual praxis. Nevertheless, group praxis is neither reducible to nor deducible from individual praxis. From the viewpoint of intelligibility, individual praxis is that of constituent reason, whereas group praxis is that of constituted reason. This will be examined in more detail later. Briefly, constituent reason reveals my praxis to be, from a local context, translucent and certain. It is my practical organism accomplishing its goal: I am certainly and translucently the organism running to catch the bus. In group praxis, however, my praxis is certain but not translucent. In attacking the Bastille, I am attacking the innumerable frozen freedoms that are the power of its antipraxis. I meet more than individual enemy soldiers when I attack the institution of the Bastille. My action is certainly mine, but I do not understand its full historical significance. For my action to be historically translucent, I would have to understand history as a totalization of totalizations, *the goal of the Critique*.

A new type of object-being thus comes into existence with group praxis. As conquered by the group-in-fusion, the Bastille is totalized and surpassed as a means to an end just as a hammer is translucently "passed over" in putting a nail on the wall. But the Bastille remains still masked in passive inertia. The conquering of the Bastille does not dismantle the organization represented by and embedded within the Bastille. This is not merely because enemy troops may regain the fortress, but because the power of the fortress is not only in its bricks, mortar, and soldiers but also in the system of the government outside the fortress. The Bastille as an object-being of the group-in-fusion is neither a translucent means to an end nor an active passivity resisting my praxis. It is "passed over" the way a hammer is passed over to accomplish a carpenter's project, but it also continues to act on me. Of course, the hammer also has hidden meanings and "inertia," but these are on a level different from its use as a tool. In storming the Bastille, however, the group directly confronts the power of the Bastille, a power that is both translucent, insofar as it is being conquered, and possessing inertia, insofar as its collective ties, with the government, for example, remain untouched.

This conquering of individual impotence is a new unveiling of the world, and the individual within the group has not only group power but group thoughts. These thoughts and behavior are characterized by a certain lack of translucence, for they take place in a milieu that is both sovereign and violent. Individual praxis is sovereign, but it does not attack the necessity and the masked violence of the practico-inert. When I run to catch the bus to go to my job, I do not challenge my situation as an employee with its practical identity between creative human work and quasi-mechanical labor for which one receives a wage. Within a group, however, I may have the power to confront the practico-inert's active passivity with the group's constituted passivity.

We will soon see that the group uses violence to provide itself with a viable structure. At present, however, we are concerned with another transitory state. The group is no longer in the heat of battle, although it is prepared to be so at a moment's notice: the Bastille has been taken but the enemy may return. In the heat of battle, differentiation occurred spontaneously, but now a practical *reflexivity* occurs in which the group takes itself as its own object. If the group is to survive, it is clear to all that assignments have to be given, posts taken, watches manned. Since the unity of the group comes from its object, we can now question what actually occurs when the group that survives the heat of fusion takes itself as its own object.

We have seen that each person's being in the group is characterized by an immanent-transcendent relation. This relation involves a unique relation of interiority. Normally the interiority of the other person is hidden from me, in the sense that at any moment he can change his project. True, since the "I" is in the world, his present project can be grasped from his behavior. But in group praxis, I know him from within, that is, I know he will not change his project. This is evident when the group-in-fusion is in the heat of activity, but it is still true in what Sartre terms the "surviving group" (*le groupe survivant*). Through the pledge, we will see that it is also true when the group has a permanent structure.

When the group takes itself as an object, the immanent-transcendent relation, with its unique interiority, gives the group differentiation. I am watching *here,* assured that the other who is sleeping is also here with me. I do not effect this union by myself. This would lead to pure immanence and destroy the other's union. I effect the union by being within the group. On the other hand, we are not members of the group as separate individuals whose reflective decisions bring another to join the group. This would give rise to a superficial union in which each would still transcend the group, unaware of the other's true interiority. Rather, there are multiple centers, each united to each other through the group, just as the group itself was formed in the milieu of need. This need is still paramount when the group takes itself as its own object. The group is a means to demolish the exigency of the practico-inert. As a means, the group *is not;* it is an ongoing process that uses the environment to restructure itself. The unity of the group is thus the positioning of everyone within the group. But here we see the possibility of disintegration. The more time I spend watching at my post alone, the greater the possibility that this act of watching will become mine alone. This is a question not of my subjective state or my abstract reflection but of the environment. I may be far from the group and unable to communicate. The group will continue for as long as it remains a practical means for each one in the group. We have still not revealed how the group gives itself permanence by taking itself as its own object. The only permanence we have thus far encountered is that of either the organism or the practico-inert. The question of permanence is the issue of a new statute of being for the group, which we must now examine.

## (2. THE PLEDGE)

The group gives itself permanence by taking itself as its own object; the practical device that accomplishes this is the oath, or pledge (*le serment*).[1] As is true of all relations within the group, the pledge is also a *mediated* reciprocity. I am able to pledge to every other individual only through the mediation of the group and only insofar as I am already within the group. Furthermore, I can pledge only on the condition that every other in the group is pledging to me. The actual serial taking of the pledge is irrelevant; the first person taking the pledge takes it within the practical context in which all have agreed to pledge. I thus pledge as a regulatory third. I pledge here, within my project, my faithfulness and that of everyone in the group because it is already given to me that all the others are pledging me and themselves.

The pledge, for Sartre, is not a mere secondary phenomenon that leaves untouched the essential structure of our lives. It is not a mere collection of words or subjective thoughts. Nor is the pledge to be confused with some form of historical social contract, for this presupposes individuals whose free isolation is a product rather than a cause of society.[2] Instead, the pledge is a radical modification of that unique materiality, the human organism, precisely as this organism both totalizes its environment through freedom and, reciprocally, is totalized by it.

Within this totalizing process, two aspects can be distinguished, that of freedom, or praxis, precisely as transcending the inertia of matter toward new goals, and the inertia itself. In the text of the *Critique,* the terms "being," "ontological statute," and "inorganic" refer to the inertia of matter. But we must not interpret these terms in an Aristotelian or Cartesian sense. To repeat, all matter that we encounter in the world is humanized matter. A stone is matter already altered by the human organism. Furthermore, the terms "ontological," "being," and "inorganic" refer not to analytic classifications but to

1. The translation of *le serment* as "pledge" rather than "oath" can be justified because of the original meaning in English law of a person's *pledging* his body as security for an obligation, a connotation that is generally appropriate in Sartre's context. On the other hand, Sartre does speak of the "tennis oath," and from this perspective both translations are acceptable.

2. It may be true that the American Constitution was framed by individuals aware of themselves as separate or quasi-separate atoms of freedom uniting for a common purpose. But this condition of semi-isolation was produced by several conditions—for example, an expansive, fertile land being colonized by relatively few persons, seeking to establish religious freedom for themselves while excluding the American Indians and blacks.

everyday states of the human organism in relation to its environment. When these terms are applied to the group, they indicate the unique way the group gives itself permanence through the pledge.

The pledge establishes a unique type of inertia within the world, that of freedom's limiting itself. In *Being and Nothingness*, Sartre had already stated that the only limitation of freedom is another freedom. The other can comprehend my project and transcend it within his project. This limitation is very abstract, because I can change my project, transcending his transcendence. But in the context of the *Critique* it is clear that the antipraxis of the practico-inert field transcends both our freedoms. Through the pledge, however, we establish our own inertia to combat the inertia of the practico-inert.

The group-in-fusion survives as a pledged group by giving itself an organizational structure that imitates organic structure. The organic structure imitated is, of course, that of the practical human organism. The human organism is "practical," since it is given as working within the exigency and necessity of a practico-inert field altered by the praxis of other, larger groups. The Bastille is already given within the practico-inert reality of France. The members of the pledged group do not, therefore, invent organization. Rather, they interiorize this exteriorized interiority (the Bastille) and re-exteriorize it as a structure of their own permanence.

But what precisely is this unique inertia that the pledge establishes within the group? It is the limitation of my freedom from within itself. Let us recall that, for Sartre, circumstances do not limit freedom, because freedom is of itself thoroughly circumstantial. Nor does predictability limit freedom; it is accidental to my praxis that another, from an advantageous position, may be able to see the outcome of my action, for example, that I am walking into a trap. The other's freedom can indeed limit my freedom, but not from within my consciousness: the child Genet puts an object in his pocket; his foster parents see it as theft.

The only inner limitation of freedom would be a limitation of my project itself. This cannot occur on the level of individual praxis. My own limitation of my project would be a new project and not the former as limited: for example, I first decide to travel around the world and then decide to stay at home and save the money. But within the group, I limit myself from within, through the common limitation of every other. As I am making my pledge to remain in the group, I encounter the pledge of every other as a "common-other freedom" limiting my freedom. I freely pledge as one already freely within the group; I pledge to accept the limitation of every other freedom on my freedom, as I am the limit of every other. Again, we must keep in mind that everything is a question of praxis. The group has ceased its heated activity, but it is still in existence. The goal of victory has not yet been achieved. The group *in existence* now takes itself as its own object in order to continue. *The pledge could never establish a group*, for, at the moment of pledging, each must know that the other has already implicitly pledged.

Sartre distinguishes two moments, or aspects, in the pledge. First, I pledge so that everyone may pledge. I pledge to remain faithful to the group, to limit my freedom to the common project, so that everyone may remain faithful in order to insure victory. Second, I also pledge so that I may protect myself against my own freedom. The possibility of being a traitor arises only through the group, and this formal possibility exists even after the pledge. But, as the moment of pledging, I allow every other pledge to be my own guarantee against my future capability of changing. As I pledge, the freedom of every other comes to me as a unique other, namely, as a freedom limiting itself and me.

In a group-in-fusion, I encounter the other through our common object, such as the storming of the Bastille. But in the pledged group, I encounter the other in his freedom, that is, in his free project. Each pledge is able to limit himself, because innumerable other pledges have limited themselves. Each one gives the assurance not to betray the group so that this common-other freedom can protect the individual from his own betrayal.

### (3. FRATERNITY AND FEAR)

Through the pledge, each person freely commits himself to accept a common, untranscendable limit to his freedom. This common-other freedom is neither purely transcendent to each freedom nor purely immanent within it; it is a detotalized totality composed of epicenters of pledged freedoms. It has, Sartre says, a triple character of untranscendability: it is an exigency, insofar as it has a claim on each freedom; it is a framework, for it gives the context for praxis; and it is the basis of every praxis in the group. The question now arises of revealing the intelligibility of the triple character of this untranscendability.

Again, for Sartre, it is not the inorganic world but the practical human organism that is intelligible, first and foremost. Intelligibility is an aspect of individual praxis, and thus the question of how praxis can be both individual and common arises again, now at a different level. Specifically, the issue here is to understand the claim that this common-other freedom has on each individual. Sartre says that the problem has two aspects: First, we must see how individual praxis establishes the continuity of the pledge, that is, how the pledge is constantly recreated through praxis. Second, since the pledge occurs after the heat of action, we must see whence the pledge attains its force. Sartre responds to both issues together.

The pledge derives its continuity and force from its occurrence in and through violence. In the explicit form in which it occurs in the pledged group, this violence is qualitatively different from that of the group-in-fusion. The violence within the group-in-fusion aims at overcoming the necessity of the practico-inert, that is, it is directed outward toward combating antipraxis. In the heat of action, there is no practical possibility that someone will desert the group. Nevertheless, if one did attempt to betray the group, and not merely mistake its purpose, then a new violence that had always existed implicitly would become explicit, namely, *terror.*[3]

Terror is the "right" that each person in the group has over the life and death of every other person. Reciprocally, terror is the totality of epicenters of each person's terror, insofar as this totality is the common, untranscendable horizon of each person's freedom. The term "right" is not to be understood in any specific context of rights and duty, for these are a matter of custom and circumstances. The term here merely designates the general origin of all juridical power. Sartre also notes that terror is the origin of all the forms of the sacred. The sacred is a greater-than-human power over human life, and the origin of terror shows how this power is created by individual praxis.

We can comprehend the intelligibility of the pledged group by seeing that it creates fear of itself to replace the diminishing fear of the enemy. In the fused state, the group spontaneously fights in the face of fear in order to raise itself from inhumanity to humanity. (Sartre says that these abstract terms—"humanity" and "inhumanity"—are useful because they signify, at different stages, our attempt to free ourselves from necessity, that is from the forces of antipraxis.) *It is obvious but important to keep in mind that, throughout the* Critique, *Sartre is always considering the group insofar as its original purpose is to give greater freedom to each individual.* The pledged group makes explicit the juridical power of each member over the life of the others, which was implicit in the group-in-fusion. The pledged group does this by taking itself as its own object, specifically by creating fear in the form of terror. Thus terror, as the right of each one over the life of every other and of every other over the life of each one, is the intelligible structure of the pledged group.

Terror is a specific aspect of totalization, and it has its own temporality with its unique form of mediated reciprocities. Through the pledge, I am born into a new humanity that originates at the historic moment of the pledge with its concrete physical symbols, even if these consist of merely the place in which the group established its permanence. The new future is the specific goal of the group, a victory over some form of antipraxis. (The group also has a distinctive memory, which Sartre says is important but too complex to analyze at

---

3. It is clear that Sartre is trying here to compensate for what might appear to be a romantic notion of the group. Nevertheless, this section suggests important questions that cannot be examined here. For example, to what extent was terror the bond uniting the followers of Gandhi? That this bond arose from and was sustained in a milieu of terror is clear. (It is interesting that that revised French edition provides this section with the heading "*Intelligibilité du serment: la Fraternité-Terreur.*")

present.) Terror also creates the very context of all the concrete forms of mediated reciprocities, such as love, fraternity, and even hate. Within the context of individual praxis, love, for example, can occur only as nonhistorical, that is, as a local relation between individuals precisely insofar as they are isolated from their historical milieu. (This discussion is an interpretation of Sartre's views.) One loves at the price of being alienated from history. But, through the fraternity-terror that the pledge creates, love can be a historical phenomenon: a relation of reciprocity that is between individuals not as separate entities but as members of a group fighting against inhumanity. As an individual, no one can rise above the inhumanity created by necessity, that is, above the destiny in which antipraxis engulfs every praxis as individual. Furthermore, each individual is a possible center of rupture as well as a present center of continuity. Only by freely giving the juridical power of our lives to each other can we forge a common freedom, powerful enough to meet the force of counterfinality.

# (3   The Organization)

Sartre's procedure of going from the abstract to the concrete is aimed, as we have so often noted, at helping us to comprehend the historical richness and complexities of our everyday behavior, precisely insofar as it is historical. The *Critique* thus proceeds from the abstract, local, relatively autonomous level of simple nonhistorical action to the concrete level of group praxis. As each new level introduces an apparent density to the transparency of action, the question of intelligibility is raised anew. Here, we investigate the distinctiveness of group praxis; that is, we examine the question of whether organization and inertia alienate individual praxis, making it *being* rather than practical activity. This question also raises the issue of the distinctive character of common praxis. Sartre here considers the conditions of common praxis; later, in chapter 4, he examines the nature of common praxis.

Sartre's basic point is that organization is intelligible because it enhances rather than mitigates freedom. Organization is a distribution of tasks in order to accomplish a common purpose. If it is a fulfillment of the spontaneous differentiation that arises from the group-in-fusion, then it should reveal common praxis to be more concrete, rich, and free than individual praxis. If this is so, organized praxis will also be intelligible. We must thus study what Sartre calls the new "statute" (*le statut*) of the common individual, the state in which praxis determines its relation to its object by the way the group first acts on itself. The action of the group on itself is organization as praxis.

We must correctly place the issue concerning the common statute. The presence of what are normally called individual differences, differences of personality, does not of itself answer the question of how praxis can be free while also limited to a task assigned by the group. First and most obviously, if these differences are not related to the task to be done, then they are unrelated to praxis precisely as it is common. To be a devoted parent may affect personal relations at home but not necessarily one's participation in a group. The more important question, however, is whether the individual style of fulfilling one's task is the answer to how praxis can be both individual and common. But, as we will see, "style" of itself is not enough to make a praxis both common and individual.

Sartre illustrates the relation between individual praxis and the common result by two examples, a football team and an airplane pilot. When one joins a football team, one accepts a function that has already been specified by the rules of the game, such as being a halfback. At this level, rights and duties are not merely reciprocal, they are equivalent. The duty to be a good halfback is the right to be trained properly, and the team's right to have a competent player is its duty to provide training and equipment. The web of these lines of rights and duties gives rise to power that must be maintained, in some way, if the group is to continue.

The good halfback works within this web of power in such a way that by surpassing the abstract form specified by his function he fulfills himself as a halfback. He is better than the halfback on an opposing team not by going outside his assigned task but by the way the concrete choices he makes on the field transcend the schema of his functions. Only in an abstract situation is praxis reduced to function and routine, as when a very strong team plays a familiar, weak team on its home field. But generally, the difference between winning and losing is the difference between the concrete choices the players make on the field. The point is that praxis, while regulated by function, is not reducible to it. The "style" of the halfback is not something added to his playing; it *is* his playing. The abstract schema of his function does not dictate his concrete choices on the field. This abstract schema is merely the *chosen* context of praxis, just as nationality is a context *given* by birth.

The example of an airplane pilot shows how praxis is not the mere actualization of the functions given by tools and techniques. In times of emergency, the pilot has the final decision about the precise use of the plane. But this is to stress the negative aspect of tools and instruments. In the concrete, tools and techniques give the context for the temporality of praxis. The speed of thought as well as action, the temporality of the world, arise from the airplane. In general, tools and techniques establish in matter a *hexis*, a habituation from which there arises the distinctive temporality of praxis. Obviously, the pilot of a passenger plane works within a distinctive temporalization of the world.

Both of these examples help us to understand the difference between the way the individual is related to the group and the way he is related to the practico-inert. In the field of practico-inert, matter produces its own idea and the individual goal is overcome by the antipraxis of this idea. In relation to group praxis, on the contrary, the idea is itself a human endeavor to develop a world. Whether this idea be a world of sports or a world brought together through travel, we encounter, at this level where class alienation is not yet considered, nothing but individual participation in a group's transformation of matter into a world. We will see that praxis fulfills itself here in a way exactly opposite to the way it does when the individual confronts class being. We have already noted that in trying to surpass class being, the individual fulfills it: the worker who attempts to develop uniqueness and personality away from the work place establishes thereby an alienated, isolated life as a worker. But, in the group, on the contrary, the very attempt to be distinctive is the attempt to fulfill one's function: to be a good football player or pilot is to transcend the schema that specifies these functions in order better to transform the world into a common result. "Here," Sartre notes, "we encounter the organic individual as an isolated agent in the first moment of his concrete truth" (E, 453; F, 466; NF, 505). "Truth," for Sartre, is neither correspondence nor a system but, in this context, the way an individual fulfills his possibilities.

These observations, however, do not properly define the meaning and intelligibility of the common individual's statute, that is, the way the individual acts within an organized group to accomplish a common result. The answer is that in group praxis, every individual result, no matter how distinctive, *is a means* for the common result. The unique playing of the good halfback is absorbed by the team in its own aim of winning the game, and the brilliance of the pilot is directed toward the safe landing of the passengers. In the viable, organized group (*le groupe organisé*) distinctiveness and originality are not for their own sake but for that of the common goal. In this respect, the individual organism stands both below and beyond the common individual, that is, the individual as common. Through the pledge, the individual organism gives rise to the individual as common. Reciprocally, the common individual is fulfilled only insofar as the schema of his function is transcended by him as an individual. Of course, in the visible group, this moment of surpassing is not for itself; it is aimed at the common result. Sartre notes that it is rare to find a lack of team spirit in sports but such a lack is the rule in the theater. The actor lives for the moment of his personal interpretation, and he uses everyone else to help him achieve his own distinctiveness.

Organization thus does not of itself lead to alienating praxes. Alienation results not from the constraints of a situation but from the presence of an antipraxis that redirects praxis. Through the group, however, the individual incorporates organizational structure with the concrete situation. Organization, like tools and techniques, allows freedom to be efficacious.

## (2. RECIPROCITY AND ACTIVE PASSIVITY)

We have noted that Sartre distinguishes his procedure from that of Marx by claiming that here, in the *Critique*, he is concerned with the question of *being*. We have seen also that this question is twofold: it concerns both the unique materiality of the human reality and the permanent structures of matter. That is, the question of being concerns the relation between freedom and inertia. At this stage of the *Critique*, the question is one of determining how our freedom is restructured by organized praxis. Function is thus not a fleeting or accidental modification of our existence but rather an aspect of our historical being.

As a further development of the group-in-fusion and the pledged group, the distinctive praxis of the organized group is that it directly acts on the members of the group. *This organized praxis is itself a new form of the same mediated reciprocity that initiated the group-in-fusion, and fostered the pledged group.* We must now attempt, with Sartre, to examine this new mediation and reciprocity.

In the group-in-fusion, mediation and reciprocity are an aspect of the lived praxis by which each individual interiorizes multiplicity. "I see," Sartre says, "the advent of myself in the other (the same) insofar as the other sees the advent of himself in me, and, through this very movement of regroupment, everyone becomes in turn a constituent and a constituted third party" (E, 470; F, 479; NF, 566). That is, in the moment of fusion, there arises a new modification of the "I." The "I," at this level, is no longer our intimate awareness of our own behavior and our existence in the world as an object for ourselves and others. Rather, the "I" is the same for each member of the group, and, through this reciprocal mediation, each one constitutes the other and is constituted by the other as the same third. Alterity and seriality disappear in the heat of action.

But such tension cannot be sustained, and it is the pledge that gives the new group a more permanent statute. Through the pledge, each one gives to the other the right to life, and through this fraternity-terror a new mediated reciprocity occurs. In the group-in-fusion, mediation is spontaneous; it is, in the language of *Being and Nothingness,* a radical modification of the prereflective cogito. Only freedom can limit freedom, and, in the group-in-fusion, this limitation is a mutual limitation of each member by each other, insofar as it occurs in the heat of action. The pledge now preserves this modification on a reflective level. Freedom works on freedom so that it becomes a type of worked matter carrying inertia in the absence of its object. In the group-in-fusion, the actual presence of the enemy as well as the movement of my comrades makes every *elsewhere* to be *here;* in the heat of battle, the physical separateness and alterity of each individual are effectively eliminated, although implicitly present. As the heat of action dies down, both physical separateness and the need for a diversity of tasks become explicit. Through the pledge, I affirm that I will not allow the absence of my companion or the diversity of tasks to break the group.

Organization is thus a new development of the mediated reciprocity of the group. Organized praxis is the praxis of the group on itself, in which what A does for the common goal depends on what B does, and vice versa. This distribution of tasks creates both reciprocal inertia and a new type of alterity. Through the bonds of the pledge, reciprocity becomes "centrifugal" (*cen-*

*trifuge*); that is, despite the physical separateness of the members of the group and despite the fact that the group's praxis is directed toward a common goal, each person is nevertheless related to every other through the diversity of their functions. Group praxis thus produces a "cultured" alterity in place of a "natural" alterity such as might result from differences of birth or environment.

This new alterity is based on the fraternity-terror relation that gives rise to the sameness of each as a common individual. Each person submerges natural differences in order to accomplish the common goal and then accepts new differences required by the task to be done. Furthermore, this alterity is completely intelligible; it is only because the other is different from me that we can both work equally toward the common goal.

This cultured alterity is further specified by the unique mediated reciprocity of organized praxis. All group praxis is characterized by mediated reciprocity. But both in the group-in-fusion and the early stages of the pledged group, this mediated reciprocity of one to all and of all to one is more easily understood. Each is related to all others as a common individual who is the same as they are. In the organized group, however, the mediation is a complexity of diverse reciprocal relations. Sartre notes that a positivistic logic would regard this as paradoxical. The relations of a doctor to a patient or of a doctor to a lawyer are not reciprocal. In an organized group, such as a football team, however, the diverse functions are reciprocal because they take place within a totalization already effected by the pledge.

This mediated reciprocity is also a totalization of subsets of reciprocities: The X's are mutually related to the Y's only insofar as both are mutually related to the M's and the N's, and both are mutually related only insofar as they are related to the common praxis. Sartre notes that a calculus of the subsets of reciprocities would be revealing and that cybernetics adumbrates such a theory. Nevertheless, a calculus would leave out the synthetic unity of these relations, abstracting from the crucial fact that these relations take place only within a given bond to accomplish a given goal.

Organized praxis thus works within the synthetic bond of the pledge, and it causes every relation within the group to be a relation of reciprocity. Relations that outside the group are normally relations of exteriority, such as that between the children and the old in a nation, become involuntary reciprocities within a group, through organized praxis.[1] These involuntary reciprocities are real, and they further alter the praxis of the group.[2]

The mediated reciprocity of organized praxis occurs on many levels, some related to the common praxis directly, others indirectly. The organized group

1. Sartre notes that sociologists and others can treat exterior relations within a nation as if these were relations of interiority within a group, as long as they realize that this is a heuristic device.

2. In the text, Sartre illustrates this by showing how an entire group may have to live the conflicts of a minority.

is, in Sartre's term, "pluridimensional." These relations—some voluntary, some involuntary—are sustained *because freedom freely limits itself by structuring reciprocal inertias that function as a sort of "inorganic materiality of freedom."* This freely created inertia will be examined later; now we must determine whether organization can truly be a praxis, continually restructuring itself to fit new circumstances, or whether freedom has here become static and inert.

### (3. STRUCTURES: THE WORK OF LÉVI-STRAUSS)

The seemingly paradoxical feature of organized praxis is that, as organized, it has definite structures that can be put in mathematical relation and studied by the exact sciences, and yet it is free. Indeed, it seems paradoxical that structure makes freedom more efficacious. We can begin to see how this is possible by realizing that the distinctive intelligibility of organized praxis comes from its structure. Structure is the objectified forms of function and, for Sartre, the works of Lévi-Strauss help us to understand the reciprocal relations among these forms.

Lévi-Strauss, Sartre notes, has shown that structure within a group remains invariant even though different individuals substitute for the terms of the relations. In the text, Sartre quotes Lévi-Strauss's example of two patrilineal and patrilocal family groups, A and B, united by the marriage of a *b* woman to an *a* man. Within the group, the acquisition of a wife represents a debt owed to the group that lost a female member. Thus the family of the husband in group A acquired a negative sign $(-)$ and the wife's family a positive sign $(+)$. In the succeeding generations, invariable laws can affix to cousins any one of the double signs $(+ -)$ $(- +)$ or $(+ +)$ $(- -)$. Marriage is forbidden between the $(+ +)$ or $(- -)$ groups and allowed only between those who have the sign $(+ -)$ or $(- +)$. Thus, regardless of individual differences, two precise mathematical sets are constituted, delineating exactly the coeligibility of its members.

The significant point is that these mathematical relations follow from a praxis that aims at the common goal of combating the scarcity of individuals available to each group. These mathematical relations must be seen as aspects of lived relations. Within the concrete group, fact and right, while not deducible from each other in the abstract, are aspects of lived, reciprocal relations. These mathematical relations must now be examined in their proper context.

### i. (Structure and Function)[3]

Mathematical necessity can enter human relations only if necessity first exists there as praxis. This necessity arises from the common aim.

---

3. These subdivisions are given in the French text, but their titles are provided by the editor of the English translation, and the last two are somewhat misleading.

It is nothing other than the praxis as a pledge by which each practical organism becomes the common individual, that is, the third who is the necessary means by which the common goal is achieved. Organization introduces a more definite structure to this necessity originating from the pledge. This structure can be examined on three levels. First, there is praxis itself; second, this implicitly includes *power* (freedom-terror) and *function* (right-duty); and third, these include a schema, or skeleton. That is, organization is first a praxis of the group on itself; second, a relation among the functions; and third, the objectified system of these functions. The important point is that the last layer, the skeletal one, while the most abstract and mathematically exact, is *not foundational* in the sense that it gives rise to the other two. Rather, it is itself a product of organized praxis, as praxis divided into functional relations. Thus, praxis cannot be reduced to the mathematical relations of its inert skeleton, nor can its meaning be deduced from the objectified forms of function.

Structure thus draws our attention through function to the skeletal formation of praxis. In the example cited above, the eligibility of a child for marriage was specified before birth. This would appear to introduce alienation and alterity into the group: each child is already the other who can or cannot marry. On the contrary, this is neither alienation nor alterity but an aspect of praxis as it concretely determines itself to fight the passive activity of the practico-inert. This important point needs to be examined more closely.

Through organization, the group affects itself with inertia in order to combat the inertia of the practico-inert. These two inertias are qualitatively different: the first, that within the group, Sartre terms "active passivity;" the second, that of the practico-inert, "passive activity." The active passivity of the group is completely the result of a directly intended praxis, or at least this is the case at the present abstract level of our study, where we are not considering the alienation resulting from class antagonisms. In the example given by Lévi-Strauss, the determination of the child's eligibility for marriage is an aspect of the group's self-determination of how to live viably with another group. By being born into the community, the child, by what Sartre calls a "second pledge," participates in the original pledge of the community.

Sartre will later examine this second, more common, pledge; here, the important point is that every initiation is reciprocal. On the one hand, the child is determined by the group; on the other hand, this determination is the child's means for its effective freedom. Again we note that, for Sartre, all freedom is situational. Freedom is the way we transcend and realize a situation. There is *always* some situation, even when there appears not to be any. In an important footnote (E, 485–86 n. 45; F, 491–92 n. 1; NF, 581), Sartre says that a free-thinking family whose personal and national traditions are Catholic correctly baptizes a child, educating it so that it can decide for itself how to interiorize this structure of Catholicism. Atheism or agnosticism would simply be another structure rather than the lack of one, and, in the child's Catholic environ-ment, the skeletal formation of Catholicism provides the more viable means of self-improvement.[4]

Freedom is the act by which we interiorize exterior structure, actualizing and transcending it to accomplish our purpose. The organized group, in its abstract, nonalienating form, protects the individual from the unconscious structure of the practico-inert and provides consciously chosen structures. Needless to say, we are dealing here with a group formed in freedom and for freedom. The group is formed for the purpose of combating scarcity, that is, for eliminating inhumanity. The individual must thus always be free to tran-scend the skeletal structure within a function: a halfback cannot be free to be a quarterback, but he must be free to determine how to be a halfback. The group as a whole must also realize that its organization is always in question. The organization is not for itself, but for the common goal. The group can thus change its division of function and its exact skeletal relations.

## ii. (Structure and System)

Structure points in two directions: to the abstract skeletal form of the group and to the more concrete interrelation of functions as they oper-ate in their synthetic powers. In this section, "structure" refers to the way the individual praxes of the members of a subgroup totalize their environment in relation to the aims of a larger group. In a more technical sense, structure will later be shown to be a distinctive moment within the mediated reciprocity that characterizes organized praxis. That is, we will see that the reciprocity of each as a third is altered by the mediation of each praxis through structure.

The point, once again, is to see structure as a metamorphosis of individual praxis, so as to avoid the mystification of viewing the group as a transcendent reality with a life of its own. It is of course true that, in its concrete state, the group encounters ossified structures of larger groups and that these structures have an inert unity of their own in the practico-inert field. Nevertheless, we must not let this fact obscure the important realization that, of itself, group praxis produces its own *inertia* to combat that of the practico-inert. Here the point is to see how a subgroup, or an individual member of a group, is both defined by the structure of the group and transcends this structure in a praxis of the *common individual.*

Structure can be seen as introducing a new moment of reflexivity in the praxis of each individual, making the individual praxis a praxis common to all in the group. This reflexivity can be compared to the pure reflection of action,

---

4. In this footnote, Sartre says that he had first thought that total indeterminacy was the true basis of freedom. But, to repeat, Sartre always maintained that freedom is situational. No doubt he means here that he did not previously view *chosen structures*, such as baptism, as proper situa-tions within which to begin a free life. In general, Sartre was always his own severest critic.

insofar as structure is used but not taken as an explicit object of praxis. This comparison, however, must be understood correctly. In general, the characteristic of organized praxis is that it operates on its object only by first relating itself to the differentiated group. At this level, we are still concerned with elucidating the type of mediated reciprocity characteristic of organized praxis and with showing how those permanent relations discussed by Lévi-Strauss are both produced and used by praxis. We can obtain a first glimpse into the intelligibility of this distinctive mediated reciprocity by seeing how a separated member of a group attempts to carry out the group's goals.

Sartre uses the example of an activist in the USSR attempting to reorganize a local farm group in accordance with new Soviet policy. *Abstracting from all authoritarianism and bureaucracy,* the praxis of the activist reinteriorizes the structure of the Soviet system. (Of course, this system is itself an exteriorization of earlier interiorities.) The activist's interiorization of exteriorities allows him to be both an autonomous power and an expression of Soviet policy. The power of the individual activist occurs only insofar as his individual praxis is also a common praxis that makes a larger structure to exist *here*, for *this* time.

Sartre quotes Jean Pouillon to show that only structure can account for both autonomy and dependence on a synthetic whole. The synthetic whole on which the activist depends is the system of inertia brought about by each person's freely limiting himself to a function in order to accomplish a common goal. At this level, the activist does not confront organization as one who is a part of a transcendent whole. Rather, there exists only the same autonomous power of each, pledging to do whatever is needed to accomplish the common goal. Discipline is also not a blind actualization of rules but the concrete means of being autonomous. The activist's autonomy is also an expression of something larger than himself, in this case the Soviet system. This simple example, however, does not reveal the distinctive mediation that takes place between praxis and structure, and it is this that we must now examine.

### iii. (Structure and the Group's Idea of Itself)

The preceding example of the activist is meant to illustrate the type of comprehension characteristic of organizational praxis. In particular, structure is each common individual's knowledge of the group. This knowledge, both theoretical and practical, is the reflexive moment that characterizes this concrete stage of the dialectic. For the dialectic must be a comprehension of itself as dialectical. In the group-in-fusion and the pledged group, this knowledge is implicit in the exigency of the transcendent object. The accomplishment of the common goal requires a differentiation of tasks; even in the undifferentiated state of the group-in-fusion and the pledged group, this need for diversity is implicitly realized as the individual's knowledge of the group.

This knowledge is the concrete form of the fraternity-terror relation. It is the basis of the group's specific idea of humanity, its truth and its ethic, its idea of the world.

In organized praxis, this knowledge is made explicit in the moment of reflexivity that structures the group. This knowledge is not necessarily thematized; rather, it is the praxis of each common individual as he is aware of both the equal autonomy of each member of the group and the need for diversity of functions. Furthermore, this knowledge can be both practical and theoretical. In this context, theoretical knowledge is not merely thematized practical knowledge; neither is it a projection of practical knowledge or the analytic skeleton of synthetic knowledge. Theoretical knowledge is one aspect of the reflexivity and the reciprocal mediation that is structure.[5]

We have seen that structure has two faces: it is the skeletal interrelation, or ossature, and it is the relations of functions as duty and power. Both of these are aspects of the organized praxis. The group thus forms its own practical and theoretical idea of itself, or, better, this idea, which is structure itself, has both a practical and a theoretical aspect. The practical aspect here presents no problem, for it is praxis as performing its function as duty and power. The theoretical idea of the group is the expression of its structure as ossature. This skeletal structure is indeed thematized by the activist and professional organizer, but this thematization of structure is not an analytic knowledge. It is an aspect of the synthetic moment by which the activist works as an extension of the group, to accomplish a common goal by explaining it to those outside the group.

Nevertheless, this skeletal structure is the basis for analytic knowledge, such as that provided by Lévi-Strauss. Analytic knowledge is indeed a product of synthetic, dialectical knowledge as structure. This is very obvious in primitive societies where analytic knowledge is an artifact, something produced by hand. Sartre quotes A. Deacon's example of a primitive tribesman explaining the tribe's complex marriage relations by drawing lines of different sizes and positions on the ground. Sartre rejects Deacon's interpretation that this proves primitive tribes to be capable of abstract knowledge, as if the capacity for abstraction were a universal human trait. This, Sartre says, is putting the cart before the horse. Abstract knowledge exists to the extent that lived relations are abstract. Theoretical knowledge is the tribe's lived awareness of itself. The analytic construction is presented for the benefit of out-

---

5. In general, the English terms "knowledge" and "to know" have two meanings in Sartre's philosophy. The first meaning, usually expressed by *le savoir* or *savoir*, is that of knowledge as a thematic content, for example, the science of biology. The second meaning, usually expressed by *la connaissance* or *connaître*, is that of knowledge as a specific type of being, that is, praxis as knowledge. For example, biology, as the praxis of biologists, is a distinct series of observations and experiments operating through specific instruments and rules.

siders, and it is an aspect of the tribe's desire to open itself to strangers for its own purposes. Needless to say, this construction is understood to be "analytic" only by those whose praxis has constructed concepts as objects.

In a primitive society, the "analytic knowledge" does not exist separately from the group's totalizing praxis. Such separation would require a second order of knowing, that is, an order that is present in our history and in which praxis itself can exist on an analytic level. Sartre is indirectly referring to a notion of "ideology." There are practitioners of knowledge who accept analytic reason to be natural reason. This acceptance implies the whole complex referred to earlier in this work, namely, a correspondence theory of truth that is supposed to justify a neutral, pluralistic view of the world. On this level, analytic reason is an alienating praxis that does not provide its own intelligibility.

# (4     The Constituted Dialectic)

We have thus far examined what, in analytic terms, can be called the conditions for the possibility of common praxis. True, we have distinguished abstractly a constituent from a constituted dialectic, but everything that has been said up to now has concerned individual and common praxis as a constituent dialectic. In this way, we have considered the radical modification that occurs to (nonhistorical) action as it becomes (historical) praxis. This transformation has involved a change in the very being of the organic individual, altering the very quality of all relations of interiority. (As already noted, the term "organic" emphasizes that our dialectic develops within a materialism that recognizes two states of matter, that of the human body and that of other things in the world.) In its most abstract aspect, we have seen that praxis is serial action working in the milieu of scarcity. This leads to a fundamental alterity, or otherness, of human behavior: each person in his otherness confronts all other persons in their otherness. Furthermore, insofar as social behavior is part of a collective, each is the other, as a third through whom mediated relations of reciprocity occur. This alterity is eliminated in the group-in-fusion, and a new mediated reciprocity is achieved. This, in turn, is sustained by the pledge, and the common individual created by the pledge is given further permanence through the inertia introduced by organizational praxis. But all of this, Sartre remarks, is to emphasize the radical modification of the individual as interiorizing multiplicity. We have been considering the conditions of common action rather than the distinctive existence and being of common praxis. Sartre says, with perhaps the only bit of humor in the book, that the dialectic thus far has been simple and has not really attempted anything new.

The problem is to see how the common result can be a distinctive reality, for individuals are the only ontological entities. Here again, we must note Sartre's radical nominalism and recall that it affirms the existence of only the concrete material and the meanings embedded in matter through individual praxis. The group has no ontological status as an entity; it is not a suprareality, capable of being explicated by an exterior dialectic, already referred to in the first part of Sartre's introduction (6). Indeed the existence of such a dialectic would confront us with the paradoxes mentioned earlier concerning the exterior dialectic. Nevertheless, the group effects a common result, one beyond what any individual could produce.

Although it is composed of a multiplicity of organic individuals, the group can produce a common result. The explanation for this seeming paradox is that the individual can comprehend the common result, though unable to produce it. Here we must recall that comprehension is an aspect of praxis itself and not an operation of an intellectual faculty. This comprehension is adumbrated in the organic individual's use of tools. The unity of a tool is that of its differentiated parts, the handle and head of a hammer, for example. In the ability to handle a tool, we see the basis for the possibility of using a differentiated unity as a means to an end. Of course, we must note again that we are not stating an ahistorical judgment about the deducibility of group praxis from the organic individual's ability to use tools. Rather, *given* group praxis, its intelligibility can be seen to be connected with the use of tools.

On the level of *being* rather than process, the tool is a common product. Whether it is produced by one individual through many operations or many individuals each performing one operation, the tool is an organized structure meant to be used as a means to an end. Of course, this end is not necessarily a common end, and the comprehension and use of tools is not, of itself, group praxis. What has been said about tools can also be said about the individual's understanding of history and the many ways we use language, such as when we speak about "*the* storming of the Bastille."

Just as the individual can comprehend a common result, so the individual can organize a group as if it were a tool to accomplish goals. Historically, such groups formed around single individuals may be the least interesting, but they indicate that the intelligibility of the group does not exceed that of the individual's comprehension. Furthermore, a sovereign individual can use the freedom of others as organized inertias to accomplish a goal beyond his own powers; this shows that common praxis is not the activity of a hyperconsciousness.

In the previous discussion of function, we incidentally touched upon the distinctive character of common praxis. The organic individual, we noted, was both below and beyond function. The power of function comes from the organic individual, and, in operating through function, the individual achieves a new level of sociality. But this observation brings us back to our present problem of the distinctiveness of common praxis. We seemed to have avoided organicism only to fall into a nominalism and realism that evaporates the reality of common praxis and its result.

Sartre's example of the manhunt illustrates the distinctiveness of common praxis and its common result. The hunted person is well aware of the ambiguous unity of the group seeking him. They are neither a hyperorganism nor an aggregate of isolated individuals. Unlike isolated individuals who may by chance be searching for the same person, these members of the manhunt are *everywhere the same*. They produce a new temporality of simultaneity that makes every elsewhere to be *here at the same time*. Those waiting for the hunted man behind the rocks and in the trees, those encircling him, are all the same eyes and hands. No animal could hunt him in this way.

The group perfects and transcends organic unity rather than imitating it. Everything within the organism—the blood, bones, and organs—have the same level of temporality as the organism itself. A group, however, incorporates lived temporality with the passive temporality of the practico-inert, so as to accomplish, through actions that are multiple and the same, a common result. The hunted man is aware that the time needed to run past the trees is given by the distance in inert matter. He also knows that the group is placing itself so as to make this passive, inert temporality its own. If the hunted man runs into one of the group, he may, for a time, struggle with him as one individual against another. But this member of the group can summon many others at once, and even if he is defeated, the many others are still there.

The common praxis is then a multiplicity of praxes, each of which is a mediation for attaining a common result. There is no embodiment of a Platonic form but a discrete number of practices brought together by the exigency of the times and united by the pledge. The distinctiveness of each one in the group is aimed at capturing the hunted man. But again, we seem to be emphasizing a modality of individual praxis, and the uniqueness of common praxis appears to have eluded us again.

## (2. SPONTANEITY AND COMMAND)

Group praxis is not reducible to individual praxis, and yet both are on the same level of being. That is, group praxis results from the individual's interiorization of multiplicity, and yet it is more than the sum total of discrete individual actions. This paradox cannot be resolved by an a priori analysis that attempts to relate the individual to the common praxis; we must rather turn our attention to the way the group is structured and restructured through the praxis of individuals and other groups.

We have seen earlier that each person in the group-in-fusion acts as a regulatory third whose spontaneous commands are fulfilled by the group. As a group moves toward greater stability, the general character of the regulatory third becomes more specified. In a revolutionary group, an agitator-organizer will emerge. He is not a leader, nor one who commands or is in charge. But he acts as a director, a medium, and a channel for popular opinion. More importantly for our present purposes, the organizer designates the common praxis as an individual, and the common praxis is understood by every individual. Whatever differentiation may occur because of specialization, the common result is not beyond the comprehension of the individual. Each person does not produce the common result as one who is incapable of understanding its nature. "The individual," Sartre says, "integrates himself into the group and the group has its practical limits in the individual" (E, 524; F, 522; NF, 617).

This point leads Sartre to make an important observation. The fundamental relation of the individual to the group is not determined by whether the authority flows downward from the top, in an authoritarian manner, or upward, from popular support. Politically, the situations will be different; different relations of reciprocity will exist. Coerciveness and terror will also change in character as they are removed from its source, which is the pledge of each to all as an equal third. But in *every* existence of organized praxis as organized, each common individual can comprehend the common goal and can realize that it cannot be accomplished by his own power. The common individual also implicitly recognizes that this common result must be achieved by a differentiation of powers. Moreover, he comprehends that he produces this organization through every other as a common third. Here we are beginning to reach the distinctive feature of the common praxis: it is something constituted; that is, the common individual and the common praxis are both a result and a means.

### (3. DISAGREEMENTS IN
### ORGANIZATIONAL SUBGROUPS)

An idealist philosophy would incline us to have a simplistic notion of a group as something formed by an agreement of minds. Sartre states that we must reject not only the dualism implied by such notions as "mind" and "soul" but also the notion of agreement as an innate capacity. We tend to speak of agreement among individuals as if it were self-evident that the capacity for such agreement is a philosophically neutral position from which to begin discussion. Actually, such a view implies a completely idealistic philosophy of history. It implies that, apart from concrete social conditions, truth can exist in every other as something *objectively* other to each. The implicit paradigm is from science. For example, we know the laws of physics as something "other," something objectively neutral to our own subjective beliefs, and this "objective other" is the truth.

Agreement, as in science, is of course possible, but the possibility of agreement is itself a social product of groups. The possibility for agreement is won from conflicts within a group. Given this agreement, a new heterogeneity of freedom can arise, one that is based on *common praxis* as something constituted by the *conflicting praxes* of individuals and subgroups. (Isolation is itself a mode of behavior that an individual adopts within a group.)

It is becoming obvious that the group is both a product and a means. *Common praxis is produced by individual praxis, through the internal medium of organization, so that the individual can produce a result beyond his own power.* Sartre illustrates this through two examples, that of a group attempting to resolve the traffic problems of Paris, and that of the more general group already alluded to, namely, the scientific community in its acts of discovery and exposition.

For the most part, groups are formed to resolve conflicts in the practico-inert field. The tension resulting from the number of car owners, the number of parking lots, the need for roads to be built and maintained, and so on, is an objective state. But we must not consider this objectivity idealistically, apart from the people who live it. The owners of cars may be tangentially aware that the building of more parking lots and roads must be resolved in the milieu of scarcity of the city's budget. But, as car owners, they live this tension as a partial, contradictory solution to the traffic problem. When a group of experts is formed to solve the traffic problem, this contradictory, lived tension is not left behind. Each expert both reflects and lives, on a reflective level, each synthetic partial part (owner-car) of the solution, assuming there is a solution. Aside from the fact that he represents the car owners, the expert's reputation within his group is at issue, and this reputation is an aspect of his life in the concrete. Each individual and subgroup trying to resolve the traffic problem thus relives the tensions within the practico-inert. A solution (*l'invention*) is reached not by a mere agreement of minds, but when individuals or subgroups see a way of resituating or restructuring themselves so as to attain a viable solution. They act as regulatory thirds but not without a price to themselves and to the other members of the group. By transcending itself and offering to the other members of the group a transcendence of difference toward a goal, the individual or subgroup, when effective, establishes *thought*. That is, each individual or subgroup within the group now restructures himself (or itself) so that the solution presented is the solution of the group. Thought takes place in each as something everywhere the same, because, through the regulatory third, a new group has emerged.

Universality is consequently not an innate quality of a human nature but something constituted by the social process. Within this milieu of won agreement, discussion can now take place, difference of opinion can now be weighed. "Finding a solution is the synthetic, individual relation between structures brought together in living synthesis and the structural relations rearranged in response to this synthesis, in a practical field rent by contradictory exigencies" (E, 531; F, 526–27; NF, 623).

For Sartre, scientific agreement has no more privileged status than that of any solution found by a group. Here we may note that, in general, science tends to give priority to the mode of exposition. It is accepted that discovery may be due to personal idiosyncrasy, but exposition must be universally communicable to all members of the scientific community. This is presented as if it were a socially unconditional truth: there are isolated individuals who may discover a scientific truth, but scientific truths can only be verified when they can be subjected to objective tests. Actually, once this position has been explicated, we recognize its philosophic presuppositions as well as its social context. Indeed, only in something resembling a Cartesian philosophy could an "individual mind" discover a truth and then formulate it for others to acknowledge. When science is placed within its concrete, historical context, we recognize that scientific discovery is itself something that takes place only within a given community in which universality and agreement have become the accepted mode of truth. Whatever accidents or bizzare psychological insights, such as dreams, may occasion a scientific discovery, they already imply the universality and truth they seemingly oppose. In the very act of seeking a solution or discovery, the scientist already acts within a reason that has been constituted by group praxis, a reason in which universality is something historically won. The scientist then uses the common praxis precisely in order to surpass it. The surpassing becomes a "discovery," which then acts as a regulatory third, by means of which everyone sees the same truth *here* as *there*. But alterity is eliminated and universality achieved only because the scientist works within a pledged group, that is, a group that already "lives the world" scientifically.

On one level, the scientific attitude does not seem to challenge the existence of a scientist. No matter what his class or society, he can agree with a fellow scientist about a scientific truth. But, on a deeper level, his life reflects a conflict that is in the society itself. The same medicine can cure the rich and the poor, friends and enemies; the same bombs kill all indiscriminately. Thus, the scientist as a *concrete* individual uses the common praxis of science to formulate scientific truths. But this common praxis is only one moment in the dialectic of his life as a scientist. The common praxis of science aims at being something independent of and superior to individual praxis, in a very special way: it aims at being the activity of an independent, scientific hyperconsciousness. The scientist's goal is that science should produce science. But this goal is itself something humanly produced through the organization of group praxis. Group praxis produces an inertial system, such as science, within which any individual can produce a common praxis that exceeds the power of individual praxis. But this moment is an aspect of the individual's fully concrete praxis. We must now study more closely this inertial system produced by group praxis.

## (4. Praxis as Process)

The distinct intelligibility of common praxis follows from its degree of translucence, which, as we have seen, is less than that of individual praxis. We have already seen that common praxis is imbued with inertia, arising from the pledge, function, and organization. Freedom freely limits itself, and these limitations are then accepted as something given. Thus, once the group has specified its functions, the individual then experiences the organization, with its rights and duties, as having an inertia of its own.

One of the characteristics of the organizational group, however, is that it is hierarchical; its members encounter inertia on different levels. In the concrete, a group interacts with the seriality in a society on many levels. A football team is not free to direct its energies merely to winning a game. Aside from the antagonism that may result because the teams are owned by managers, the simple necessity of transporting its members brings the team into contact with the inertia of the practico-inert field. The team must depend on the system of public or private transportation, and even if it has transportation of its own it must depend on drivers and mechanical parts.

The group's viability thus depends on its links with the practico-inert field. On one level, the task of the group is merely to cope with these links, such as its relation to transportation. Here again, Sartre notes, we can see how a group is different from an organism. In an organism, relations of distance are themselves organic. It is only when something goes wrong that the organic individual experiences distance as something inert: I swallow a painfully hot liquid and feel it going down my throat. Group praxis, however, always works across a field in which distance remains an aspect of the inert environment. One practical consequence of this is that the group's unity is always an on-going effort. The group originated as an interiorization of multiplicity, in order to accomplish a common goal in a milieu of scarcity. On this level, the group meets the exteriorization of its interiorized multiplicity: an accident may cause one member to be isolated, another late.

Group praxis thus always encounters the inertia of its own links with the practico-inert. These links are contingent, but they are not a surprise, in the sense that, from the beginning, the group recognized that it needed them if it was to operate in the world.

On another level, these links occasion a new interiorization of inertia. The football team does not merely make arrangements for transportation; these arrangements themselves become a function. The group's interiorization of multiplicity includes not merely the players on the field, but also the managers, coaches, drivers, mechanics, and so on, all of whom make the game possible.

These links to the practico-inert reveal common praxis as *praxis-process.*

Praxis and process are both activities directed toward a goal. But, of itself, praxis is a unified, intentional structure aimed at attaining a goal, such as a football team's praxis of winning a game. Process, however, is the concrete steps taken toward this goal in the practico-inert field. These steps are, as a totality, aimed at the common goal, but they are also more or less independent. If a football team arrives late after a long, delayed hazardous trip, this step that is normally passed over in the team's process of trying to play and win becomes a factor in the game itself.

From another perspective, process can be comprehended not only as an intentional activity but also as an object within the larger practico-inert field. Both praxis and process are free activities insofar as the group determines its own rules to accomplish a freely chosen end. As seen within the larger, historical field of the practico-inert, process may appear to be carried along passively: the combat team won its battle, the nation its war, but in a larger context the victory was defeat, and, given the historical forces, it could not have been otherwise.

If the general movement of the *Critique* is valid, there will always be an even wider perspective from which the members of the group could have comprehended the intelligibility of their praxis and process and changed it in light of this new knowledge. But the important point at present is that, in a general way, this counterpraxis of the practico-inert is indeed taken into account in the very formation of the group. The group is instituted to counteract the passive activities of the practico-inert. Here the group can be comprehended as interiorizing the passive structures of the practico-inert precisely as these are seen to be a counterpraxis against its own praxis.

All these new relations are *constituted* by the individuals within the group. Thus, the relations within the organized group are not only mediated but also *worked* relations. The group also creates its own multileveled system of inertia to combat the complex, inertial system of the practico-inert field. This stratified system is produced by individual praxis as it works through function to achieve a common goal.

Thus, *common praxis has no separate ontological status.* Common praxis is constituted by the individual as mediating between the emerging common individual and the unfolding common goal. The concrete individual enters the group from a complex, serial structure that includes, for example, his family, and he works from his entire concrete existence to achieve the statute of a common individual.

### (5. TAYLORISM)

The distinctive intelligibility of group praxis thus lies in the fact that it is something produced: individuals organize themselves in a way that is analogous to the way they organize matter into tools. As an object, organization is a hierarchical complexity of organic individuals and inert objects, all of which forms an inertial system through which common praxis aims at a common result. This objective system, however, is never a totality. It both aims at and negates the unity of individual organic praxis. It attempts to integrate all parts into a unity to achieve the final goal, and it simultaneously negates this unity in favor of a multiplicity of individual surpassings whose totality and power far exceed organic praxis.

As a multiplicity of surpassings, group praxis is more significant in relation to the entire synthetic dialectic as it moves from constituent to constituted reason. That is, the mechanical aspect of an organizational system is comprehensible only as a movement of dialectical reason. Objectively, the product of a machine is resolvable into its composed parts, and as such, these parts can be put into a one-to-one relation with the movement of the machine. The entire production process can then be understood by analytic reason. Nevertheless, the process is only comprehensible as something produced by humans for humans.

The important point at present is that common praxis is not the activity of some mysterious superorganism, but rather a completely comprehensible network of actions. This is particularly evident in the way specialization, at the end of the nineteenth century, ushered in the second industrial revolution. Sartre refers to Frederick W. Taylor as the first of the organization men, the first to divide complex praxis into many simple parts, each capable of being performed by an individual with little training. This division does away with the praxis of the skilled laborer. Specialization works on the distinctive temporalization of a praxis, treating it not as an activity but as a passive object that can be subdivided. Each subpart has a passive temporality, one that can be measured and fixed to each individual part. On the other hand, the skilled laborer's product was effected as a unity; temporality was an aspect of the entire process. For example, to work faster was to produce a work of inferior quality. But, once the process is divided, temporality becomes the context and not the mere aspect of a process. The work is divided so that six people working together can produce more than one person working six times as long. The next step in Taylorism is the substitution of machines for unskilled labor. The entire praxis has now been resolved into a process; the common result is nothing more than the totality of the steps needed to accomplish it.

The example of Taylorism makes two things very evident. First, the common praxis is something produced by a multiplicity of individual praxes to accomplish what no individual can do alone. Second, this process is not only comprehensible, it is reducible, *as an object,* to the sum total of its analytic parts. But this objective unity is negated by the synthetic movement of group praxis. Neither individuals nor machines can function independently of human praxis. Machines may be able to operate on their own, exclusively for their own purpose, but this could never be a human intention. Such a world would be a hell of the practico-inert.

Group praxis thus aims at constantly negating the unity of the practico-inert as well as its own unity, insofar as this tends to become ossature. We must thus now examine the unique kind of existence groups have, an existence that seeks unity while negating it. *For neither the common individual nor the common praxis is ever achieved as a totality;* both remain rather the organic individual's constant effort to achieve unity with other human beings through the pledge and through function.

# (5      The Unity of the Group as Other: The Militant)

*The group derives its unity from outside through others, and in this initial form its unity exists as other.*[1]

The task of elucidating the *being* of a group requires that we examine the group in a more concrete social setting. The term "being," in this sense, refers to the unity of a group, and an idealism might attempt to determine this unity independently of its fluid, complex, material environment. But, from his early monograph, *The Transcendence of the Ego,* Sartre has consistently held to the view that unity and being are synthetic, the result of freedom working matter and being reworked by it. Thus far, we have been examining both group praxis and seriality separately as if they could occur independently of each other. *It is now evident that seriality and alterity come into existence through groups and are characteristics of the nongrouped.*[2] Reciprocally, it is precisely in relation to the nongrouped that the group receives its initial unity.

Depending on circumstances, the nongroup is either a mere logical designa-

1. As already noted, this description and the one in chapter 6 are given by Sartre, but their placement is ambiguous in both the original and revised French editions. The original edition treats them as major part titles, with the result that there are four parts to book II. The so-called critical French edition treats them as dangling subheads within part 1, giving us only two parts in book II. With some reservations, I am following the revised French edition. In either case, these pivotal sections are obscured by the English chapter titles.

2. In this present context, "unity," "being," or "essence" is revealed only when it is surpassed. In *The Transcendence of the Ego* and in *Being and Nothingness,* objectification (as opposed to alienation) was shown to result either because the other tries to limit us to our past or because the other, in bad faith, gives a foreign meaning in our action. Both meanings come together in Sartre's study of Genet, where Genet is fixed by the townspeople as a thief. In the *Critique,* however, fundamental alienation or alterity is described, rather than mere objectification, because all group action exists in a milieu of sustained scarcity that occasions class antagonisms. Douglas Collins, in *Sartre as Biographer* (Cambridge, Mass.: Harvard University Press, 1980), 80–110, provides an interesting study of Sartre's *Genet* in relation to the notions of alienation and collective responsibility in *Critique I.* Collins, however, accepts too close a relation of the thought of Sartre to that of Hegel. "Sartre often seems to operate on the basis of a coherence rather than a correspondence theory of truth" (107). But Sartre's nominalism implies a rejection of both the correspondence and coherence theories of truth.

tion or a practical relation, realizing a distinctive seriality within the group. (It is obvious that groups may occasion the formation of other groups, but this is not at issue here.) Where the relations of the nongrouped to the group are real, the group realizes its unity, its *being*, through these relations. For example, when we mail a letter, we treat the post office both as an inert extension of our arm and as an inertial system of pledged individuals. In this respect, Sartre says that the post office gives power to the consumer rather than to the group of post office personnel. It is a power, of course, that may fail. For someone who mails a letter, the post office is a completed totality with a distinctive interiority. This interiority absorbs the individuality of those who work within the post office; they are each *inessential* in relation to the essential common product of delivering mail. Relations of reciprocity may exist between a particular individual posting a letter and a clerk, but these are incidental to the main activity of receiving and delivering mail. Thus, from this respect, those who post letters serve as a mediation between the agents and the common result of delivering of the mail. On their part, those working in the post office make themselves the inessential means required by the consumers and the common result. Their power is their service to the common good, in this instance the nongroup of those who use the post office.

For the consumers, the post office is thus not a totalized praxis, altering and re-altering the world into a postal system, but rather a totality, a *being* with its own given norms. This is not a mere psychological projection onto the group by the nongroup. Those who are in the group interiorize this unity as their being-for-others, and the group is always in danger of becoming nothing other than its ossified being-for-others.

In this way, Sartre says, the dilemma between being and norms is resolved. Norms appear to be both a priori and humanly created. Both appearances are true. A group is a free product of free individuals. But given the group with its common purpose, functions and norms are established that are then accepted as a priori by the nongrouped. This acceptance is then interiorized by the grouped. Indeed, in the concrete, the two movements cannot be practically distinguished, for in its practical dealing with the group, the nongroup initially encounters norms already interiorized by the group as the norms that the nongroup expect the group to have. A post office will require packages to be tied and sealed in a certain way, not to make the delivery easy for the mail carriers, but because they interiorize the expectations of those posting letters for mail to be delivered intact.

What has been said about a somewhat passive group, such as the post office, can also be said about a militant group representing a certain political view. The nongrouped do not particularly heed the individual characteristics of the political representative. They hear the personal qualities of his discourse, in terms of an abstract, a priori schema determined by party doctrine. Nevertheless, the political representative's discourse is not the result of mere memory, but of learning how to think as others think. But, at this point, the issue of the being and unity of a group leads us to consider how groups become institutions.

(6 The Institution)

*In the interiority of the group, the movement of mediated reciprocity constitutes the unity of the practical community as a perpetual de-totalization engendered by the totalizing movement.*

(1. MEDIATED RECIPROCITY IN THE GROUP)

This section more properly completes the description of organized praxis as such; the transformation of organized praxis into institutionalized praxis properly begins in the following section ("Purges and Terror").

Our dialectical comprehension of the group has revealed that its unity first comes to it from its being-for-others. This unity is said to be "first" because it is abstract. But we must constantly keep in mind that the abstract is real and that, in this case, the group's being-for-others and its unity return to qualify it on many different levels. Of course, the group clearly has its own interior unity emerging from the pledge of each as an equal third. An idealistic philosophy would attempt to see the group's interior unity as its essential organic unity, and its external unity coming both from its object and its relations to the nongrouped and to other groups as accidental. But, for Sartre, we can comprehend group praxis only by delineating the contradictory movement between its external and internal unities.

Viewed from the outside, the group functions as an organized totality structured to accomplish a common end. From this respect, the regulatory thirds are inessential movements whose uniqueness is absorbed in the common result. Viewed from within the group, however, the concrete praxis of each as a regulatory third is complex and differs according to the historical reality of the group. Indeed, the specific way each functions as a regulatory third defines the *truth* of all the relations of reciprocity within the group. In these sections, Sartre examines the two extreme cases: the one where the individual attempts to become inessential in a way that practically destroys individual freedom and the other where individual freedom returns to its state of individuality prior to the pledge.

These two cases will be more easily understood if, following Sartre's lead, we first examine in more detail the way each person in a group is a regulatory third. Let us consider the case where A performs a regulatory action and B's action is regulated in relation to A. Both actions must be understood in reference to a common end, such as a football team's scoring a goal in the process of trying to win a game. The regulatory and regulated actions are reciprocal; that is, A can regulate only because B submits to being regulated. For example, A intercepts a pass and becomes the regulatory third rearranging the entire team around his interception. From this perspective, A's action is essential; it has become here and now the concrete means of scoring a goal. Of course, A's action is still a mediated reciprocity; his function arose through the functions of all his teammates. But the point here is that A's action is one of *limited sovereignty,* limited by B and every other teammate. Sovereignty means one's ability to organize the environment to accomplish one's end, and this is precisely what A has been able to do by intercepting the pass. But this sovereignty is limited because, although B's action is now regulated by A, B is not passively carried along by A's action. On the contrary, B's action is regulated only to reveal that he also is a regulatory third with limited sovereignty; B may have to throw a crucial block or be ready himself to catch a pass. Thus, each person on the team is sovereign in a way that is limited by the reciprocal sovereignty of everyone else.

This sovereignty does not make each person transcendent to the group, regulating it from the outside as a spectator; rather, it is an aspect of the transcendent-immanent relation of each as a regulatory third. Each regulatory act attempts to totalize the group, but the act detotalizes it, revealing each as a quasi sovereign: A intercepts the pass, but this act does not, of itself, arrange his team into a substancelike entity that absorbs the other players as if they were A's mere instruments. Every regulatory act of totalization is also a detotalization, revealing every other as a limited sovereign.

Thus the internal unity of the group is not that of a totality, but that of a fractured, contradictory unity of a detotalized totality. The unity, resulting from the pledge, does not give the group ontological unity; rather, it is the source of differentiation and limited sovereignty. Moreover, the group's being-for-the-other, its external unity that arises from its object—here the winning of the game—"haunts" this internal unity. The external unity is also continually being interiorized by the regulatory thirds, altering their concrete behavior.

Frequently, external unity can be crucial, for two reasons. First, the coerciveness resulting from the fraternity-terror relation is based on the myth of *rebirth.* This myth both defines and produces the traitors as the absolute evil responsible for the original fractured unity of the group, a fractured unity that is capable of appearing again to destroy it. This mystification results because the group aims at a common praxis that increases the freedom of all yet also tries to absorb each freedom as an inessential unit needed to fight the anti-praxis of the practico-inert. The group thus both masks the violence of its origins insofar as it emphasizes freedom and keeps its violent origin alive in the Manichaean myth of an absolute evil that can justify repression. Needless to say, we have yet to see how this myth of rebirth concretely functions in the group.

Second, the group's unity, its being-for-others, returns so that the group interiorizes it as its concrete context, its *being-from-behind* (*être-de-derrière*). The group does not have, as it were, a pure, innocent interiority that subsequently is altered by the way others see it. Rather, the group's spontaneous reciprocities are all *initially* affected by the way the group interiorizes its being-for-others. That is, the unity of each within the group is complex. Each person tries to attain an impossible unity that would result in an ideal fraternity yet also realizes the impossibility of being merely an inessential element in a smoothly running machine. The tension between the limited sovereignty of each as a regulatory third and the group's common praxis leads to the two extreme forms of reciprocity referred to earlier, which are now to be examined. It is within the context of these extremes that Sartre's descriptive title must be understood. We shall see that the practical unity of the group is less than that of a superorganism: the only ontological entities are individuals. At the same time, the practical unity of the group is more than each member's subjective awareness of this unity as it is projected onto the aggregate of group members. As we shall see, each individual in the group is radically altered by a distinctive mediation, and this alteration exists in each, even when he is not reflecting on it. This mediation, through each as a third, alters the human organism so that its primary intentionality is now a common good as a totality that is never achieved. The totalizing movement is thus a detotalization, in which each member is both a regulatory third and a sovereign. Even in the extremes to be studied, this tension is not completely eliminated.

### (2. PURGES AND TERROR)

Although our aim here is to comprehend how institutions arise from organized groups, we must recall that this procedure does not imply a temporal process. Depending on circumstances, institutions may arise prior to any organized praxis. *Given the existence of institutions,* it is now regressively clear that they arise as a further attempt of the group to achieve the impossible ideal of a praxis that is ontologically one. Implicit throughout the *Critique* is the idea that there is no a priori necessity for the thematization of this impossible ideal. But a different situation would have given rise to different "institutions" and a different history for us.

The organized group institutionalizes its pledged inertia so that its praxis will be more unified. But organized praxis can never have the unity of organic praxis and, from this impossibility, the fraternity-terror relation arises as constantly attempting to keep individual praxis in line with common praxis.

We mentioned earlier that this fraternity-terror relation can degenerate into two extremes: the one in which common praxis is absorbed into individual praxis, that is, in which the common individual as the regulatory third returns to the primacy of freedom prior to the pledge and asserts a complete sovereignty; and the other in which the individual attempts to absorb himself in the common object so that the moment of individual praxis has almost no weight in the outcome. Both extremes follow from the precariousness of the quasi sovereignty of the regulatory third. On the one hand, the regulatory third, for example, the halfback on a football team, is indispensable, not in the sense that he cannot be replaced but in the sense that only an individual praxis can complete the assigned function. A well-organized team may, at its own discretion, perform in machinelike manner, but it is a team only insofar as it is not a machine. That is, the player's success is also his possibility of failure. On the other hand, on a team where the players are overly conscious of their success, the common praxis suffers as individuals attempt to achieve personal records. At the other extreme, a player can also lose team spirit by lacking initiative and seeing himself as a mere passive object in the team.

In Sartre's terms, the "conflict between the essential and inessential is not at all theoretical" (E, 583; F, 568; NF, 671). This conflict is practical, because, although the individual is, in the abstract, inessential to the function, he is de facto the one on whom its fulfillment depends. And, Sartre notes, it is precisely at this level that conflict arises. Individual praxis produces the division of labor that makes both conflict and cooperation possible. It is idealistic to imagine that by removing the division of labor one will find a whole human being freely willing to cooperate toward a common good. Praxis constitutes the possibility of cooperation, which exists only together with the possibility of conflict.

Returning to our two extreme cases, we see that each constitutes different possibilities for cooperation and conflict. Both tend to reintroduce seriality within the group, but in different ways. In the first case, each player competes as the sovereign other; in the second, each allows himself to be the passive other moved blindly by some planned play. Within this perspective, institutions initially arise to prevent the organized group from relapsing into either one of these two alienating serialities. Formally, however, the structures of an institution are more easily revealed, on this abstract level, as an attempt to avoid the extreme of sovereignty at the price of falling into the extreme of passivized freedom.

Regressively, institutions are seen to arise because my quasi sovereignty makes my being-in-the-group ambiguous. If I attend a formal meeting in a hall, I am *in* the group as one who is also an exile. To paraphrase Kierkegaard, one grand act of commitment can never wed me to a group so completely that I am carried along by it as a passive object. The very freedom that gave rise to the pledge and gave to each the right of life over every other is still mine. I can revoke my pledge; I can leave the hall. Thus, in the very moment when I am most in agreement with the assembly, I am also a potential exile, capable of being a rebellious regulatory third forming a splinter subgroup. My regulatory actions always have the contradictoriness of "intercession-secession." That is, through me, everyone organizes himself toward the common praxis and everyone can become an exile. To prevent this splintering, the organized group alters its practices from an organized praxis into an institutionalized one. *The formation of institutions are thus seen to be at the level of praxis. Constituent praxis works on itself to constitute organized praxis; organized praxis further works on itself to produce institutions, or better, institutionalized praxis.* Of course, both restructurings of the group occur only because of and through external pressures.

We have seen that the first unity of praxis comes from its object. The group also produces its own organized unity to combat the counterpraxis of the practico-inert. In the institution, organized praxis produces a deeper degree of unity. Functions become more like organs, and individuals intensify their identity with the common praxis. This deepening identification arises from a double mediation. Each person freely allows himself to be regulated by every other as a tool for the common purposes. Everyone's action becomes the common freedom through a terror-imperative imposed by every other. In itself, this terror-imperative is both a use of terror and a protection against it. To protect oneself against quasi sovereignty's becoming full sovereignty, everyone gives a degree of freedom to inorganic things. An institutionalized praxis is an ambiguous combination of things imbued with freedom and freely constituted praxis imbued with things. Thus, the praxis of the postal clerk is more imbued with the inorganic than is that of the halfback. (On the other hand, a letter is more likely to be delivered than a particular play is to be successfully completed.)

The fear of being fired from the post office may appear to be a mild form of terror, but this only reminds us that there is no Aristotelian essence of terror. The meaning of each terror will be revealed only by studying the concrete historical circumstance. In the text, Sartre uses the example of the Convention in France from its first meeting in 1793 until the purges that followed. This extreme case reveals political heterogeneity to have been replaced by a forced homogeneity that masks violent individual differences. Fraternity-terror, which is each individual's equal yielding of control over himself and every other, degenerates into a reign of terror in which a few attempt to define the terror relation. *This* degeneration is *different* from what Sartre calls a "normal degeneration" that occurs in every institution as it introduces its own alterity to combat the alterity of the practico-inert. But in the Reign of Terror, Sartre says that our dialectical investigation brings us back to the practico-inert. But this should not surprise us; groups are formed to combat the practico-inert, and that they may, in their degenerate institutionalized forms, become the very thing they combat is an ever-present danger that cannot be removed.

## (3. INSTITUTIONALIZATION AND INERTIA)

Institutions are a natural development of the organized group; they develop from external and internal pressures exerted on the organized group in its fight against the counterpraxis of the practico-inert. Yet in their completely degraded form, institutions become part of the very practico-inert field that they were formed to combat. In this respect, as we will see, they have intentional structures, such as those of our industrial society, that must be decoded if we are to comprehend and direct our history. The emphases in the following remarks are on the degraded form of institutionalized praxes, because, on a large scale, these types of institutions de facto characterize our social environment.

In vital groups everyone works within a milieu of freedom. Through the freely given pledge, powers and functions are constituted so that the organic individual becomes the common individual working for the common goal. Nevertheless, individual praxis is not thereby absorbed as something inessential; each individual praxis is recognized and remains essential, not only fulfilling old functions but also restructuring new ones. But, in its degraded, institutionalized form, function perpetuates itself for itself and produces the type of individuals needed to sustain the institution. The institution, in this sense, becomes actively its own goal; the initial goals of the organized group are retained, although the vital intentionalities are lost and become frozen as destiny. This alteration of the organized group is something both passively suffered and actively brought about. Sartre here considers the passive aspect of this aberrant transformation.

On one level, the degeneration of organized groups into alienating institutions has its origin outside the group. For any number of external reasons, such as physical separation of its members or the introduction of spies, seriality enters the group. The new terror relation that responds to this threat leads to the institution, in the degenerate sense of the term. Terror, in this new sense, could not exist if the individual relations within the group had not been weakened. De facto, for the most part, institutions arise because each individual group member is no longer able to act as a regulatory third whose limited sovereignty makes every *elsewhere* to be *here*. To be more precise, each individual praxis is no longer also a common praxis balancing individual initiative with function. Rather, separation and circular alterity enter the group, so that each individual sees himself as the impotent other at the service of function. Of course, the degenerate institution will use power and terror to enforce obedience, but, as Sartre indicates, these could not succeed if the original bond of mediated reciprocity had not become one of impotence.

In the vital group, function gives one the right to do one's duty, but in the degenerate institution, one must first earn, by subservience, the right to fulfill one's function. For example, in the army one meets first "the duty to do one's best in order to get one's right to do one's duty recognized" (E, 604–5; F, 584; NF, 691). The pledge that had united each to all collapses, and the institution defines relations in mistrust and suspicion.

Recalling that we are focusing on degenerate institutions, which unfortunately have become the norm, Sartre notes that, out of viable, organized praxis, "institutional man" (*l'homme d'institution*) emerges, with two simultaneous but contradictory praxes. First, institutional man attempts to remove any uniqueness and initiative within himself so as to justify its removal in others. He is, for example, an officer, but like the enlisted man he too merely takes orders. Second, his uniform, office space, and other signs of rank make institutional man the "absolute other," the one who must be obeyed blindly and the one in whom all reason and justification exist. In general, even where the institution retains a vital praxis, ritual also introduces mystification. The power of the group no longer exists in the pledge and constituted freedom, but in a "power-man" who surrounds himself with quasi-mystical trappings. If this power-man is successful in his ritual dance, he induces in those about him the belief that the inorganic is the fundamental human reality: orders and decisions appear as commandments written in stone.

The being of the institution thus tends to become the inorganic bond supporting the relations of impotence within the degraded group. These bonds define a circular alterity in which everyone, through every other, makes himself also to be an *institutional man*, fated to fulfill the needs of the institution rather than the common good.

We are all born into institutions. We never stand on some pristine, free territory from which we can choose to play or not to play at being institutional. Institutions define the very context of our free praxis. Nevertheless, although we can never be above institutionalized praxis, we can fight this degenerate praxis insofar as we are either within vital groups or, as we shall see, connected to them by our class being. We can indeed critique an institution, such as the army, from a relatively external position, but our critique will still be laden with alienating aspects arising from our own institutionalized being.

## (4. Institutionalization and Sovereignty)

From another perspective, the ossification of organized groups is seen to occur internally through the institutionalization of power. The original sovereignty of each mediating third becomes a function of a "sovereign person." The sovereign person, or subgroup, both unifies the dispersing group and intensifies the degenerate condition from which sovereignty emanates. *Sovereignty as a function exists only in and through the weakness of organized groups.*

Numerous external conditions can disrupt communication within the organized group. Functions and individuals keep a tenuous relation to each other, and as they begin to operate more on their own, suspicion enters into the group. Even without a collapse into complete seriality, each person suspects every other of violating the pledge. Each is also aware of the group's inability to discover and to punish a particular traitor. At this level, the fraternity-terror relation that unites each to all and all to each becomes itself institutionalized, and functional sovereignty emerges.

The sovereign appears as the original unifier of the group. Indeed, the possibility for the existence of sovereignty exists only within a group that has already degenerated into an institutionalized structure. The sovereign appears as the interiorization and unification of functions that are becoming disparate. But the institutionalization of sovereignty also increases and maintains the very disparateness that it appears to remedy.

The sovereign's power arises from impotence and alterity rather than from a higher source of power, such as the mutual consent of those who obey or from God. This becomes apparent if we reflect that, in the abstract, sovereignty itself, as opposed to sovereignty as a function, needs no foundation: it is praxis as it reorganizes our practical field according to our needs and projects. This relation is an original given: "Man," Sartre says, "is *sovereign*" (E, 610; F, 588; NF, 696). In the pledged and organized group, sovereignty is freely limited in relation to the common praxis. The organic, sovereign individual freely agrees to become a common regulatory third who may also have to be regulated through the equal sovereignty of others. Indeed, a temporary leader may emerge who effectively organizes all functions as a means to an end. But this functioning of power through an individual is due to circumstances. The temporary leader does not have a hierarchical function; rather, he is merely another regulatory third, equal to every other. Temporarily, by mutual consent, the person made sovereign by the pledge uses the power of every other to accomplish the common goal. Strictly speaking, those regulated retain their power and do not obey the regulatory third. In following him, they follow themselves, aware that he happens to be here and now the best channel of their power.

*All power, Sartre says, emerges from noninstitutionalized sovereignty or in the contexts of the pledged and organized groups, from organized sovereignty. The task is thus not to see how the sovereign obtains power, but how this power becomes constituted in him as a distinct function, a sovereign will that others obey because they are impotent.* However, before examining this question, we should note that the power of an institutionalized sovereign is nothing compared with the power of limited sovereignties within a vital group.

Sovereignty is not superimposed onto institutions, but is given within the institutional structure itself. The original bond of fraternity-terror, which gives to each the equal right of life over each other, becomes dissipated. The mediated reciprocities that united the functions in an organized praxis are weakened, and the resulting impotence and alterity establish an *absence* of power that must be filled if the group is not to degenerate completely. Sovereignty as an institutional function has an abstract but real priority over the existence of a *sovereign will*. And, as Sartre explains in a long footnote (E, 616–17, n. 80; F, 594 n. 1; NF, 702–703 n. 1), a complex relation of obedience to a sovereign is present with the institutionalized group. Obedience is not derived from anything higher than itself, and it makes little difference for the institutional man whether he agrees or disagrees with an order. His disagreement never challenges the system. His obedience is his own complex acceptance of himself within the institutionalized group.

The sovereign thus reinteriorizes within himself the institutionalized inertias fragmenting the group. Lest their impotence become complete and their alterity degenerate into the seriality of a collective, everyone silently agrees to obey the sovereign will. Thus, the sovereign appears as the only one capable of understanding the common praxis and the only one with the power to enforce it. Actually, the original praxis no longer exists, and the sovereign suffers from the same fragmentation as other members. Nevertheless, insofar as the others remain passive, he is able to enforce his will. Indeed, through his de facto power, he establishes his de jure power and authority. There is no a priori means, Sartre says, of determining whether the sovereign will attempt to use others to accomplish a common goal or merely to impose his own will. In either case, a new statute of *order* and *obedience* emerges at the level of the institutionalized group.

Within institutionalization, mediated reciprocity is broken. The sovereign emerges as an *untranscendable third* through whom all mediation must take place. This means not that every order must pass through him, but that every institutionalized function is mediated by him, as he is the foundation of the institution. Each one experiences directives as something given by an untranscendable third. This is a "contradictory" movement: everyone is still produced through mediation as a common individual, but mediation is no longer through each individual as a separate regulatory third for every other. Rather, the mediation is through one person as that person is an untranscendable other. The sovereign will is initially given as that which I cannot transcend. In this way, a new statute of *obedience* arises: I must divest myself of my freedom and force myself to use my will as a means to accomplish the sovereign will. The end is never questioned or even known. Through obedience, I become a mere means to an end that I believe another knows.

Thus mystification enters into the group: the sovereign appears as the unifier of group praxis establishing everyone's freedom but emerges only with fragmentation and *justifies in the institution of sovereignty the fragmentation he supposedly remedies.* Each individual's personal freedom also becomes mystified. Abandoning all my original free *praxis,* I now see my freedom to consist merely in the obedience or disobedience of orders. The institution now appears to give me rights, but these rights preserve my institutionalized impotence. The sovereign cannot permit the attempt to reestablish the original bonds of mediated reciprocity with its limited sovereignty for all.

Sartre now returns to take another look at those collectives we discussed earlier, such as the radio and the newspaper. These were correctly seen as collectives in which all read or listen in their otherness. But these collectives are also groups, more or less organized or institutionalized. As organized groups, they impose themselves on collectives. We will see that institutions can more or less manipulate the serial structure of collectives. Nevertheless, social structures, such as newspapers and radio, cannot completely control mass collectives; the very alterity of a collective, each individual's flight from self, makes such control impossible.

## (5. States and Societies)

The most significant form of sovereignty is that which takes place within societies. The entire early part of the *Critique* implied that "a society is not a group, nor a grouping of groups, nor even a struggling grouping of groups" (E, 635; F, 608; NF, 719). The peoples of a society are collectives. Nevertheless, a society must have some unity to distinguish it from another society. Externally, this unity is a territory that functions as a container for the ensemble of peoples. Analytically, the territory can be said to be a necessary but not sufficient condition for a society. The sufficient condition can be said to be the internal bond of groups to series induced by historical developments, such as means of production or defense against a common enemy. The most obvious aspect of the bond of groups to a series is that of the state. The state is itself an institutionalized group operating both on other groups within the collective and on the seriality of the collective.[1] Many institutionalized groups operate on other groups, but what distinguishes the state is its pervasive sovereignty.

1. Sartre gives three formal, abstract ways institutionalized groups can relate to collectives: The institutionalized groups can work on a common, inorganic object, on other groups, or on seriality. The state belongs to the second class, and within this class it is specified by its unique sovereignty. Of course, on a more concrete level all three aspects can be involved with different priorities.

The sovereignty of the state is ambiguous. It involves both mystification and true contradictory praxis. In general, mystification is praxis that appears to be one thing but is really another. Mystification occurs in the state, because, regardless of its historical evolution, the state frequently appears to embody the diffuse sovereignty of the members of its society. But, as we have seen, this sovereignty is an institutionalized function that arises from and sustains the impotence of those within the society. The members of the government are indeed united to the sovereign as to an untranscendable third. These members do share in the sovereign's power, even if not as equals. But those outside the institutionalized group of the state have no real share in this power.[2]

The state's mystification, however, succeeds; that is, this mystification is a praxis because it is a cloaking based on a reality. The people believe that the state embodies their own diffuse sovereignty, and something like this is negatively true. The people of the collective have no single organized power of their own, and their passive acceptance of the state's sovereignty is negatively an approval of this power. Furthermore, insofar as the state has its own sovereignty, it appears to justify itself to the collective of its people. The sovereignty is, as it were, reflected onto the society, and it appears as the ideal unity of the collective people. But the collective cannot be a group, for if it were, it could not have another group as sovereign over it. And here we touch upon the state's real "contradictory" praxis, as opposed to mystification.

The state both aims at uniting the ensemble of people into a unified society and keeps them sufficiently disparate so that they cannot form a group. Thus, granting that our future study will reveal the reality of classes, we can say here, conditionally, that the state emerges and represents the dominant class within a society. The state's praxis in this regard is again "contradictory." The powerful states de facto emerge from the dominant class to protect the interests of this class. But the state is also the institutionalized group that perpetuates itself as *the* sovereign organ of the society. The state thus acts to keep the dominant class as merely *one* of the classes. In this respect, the state may ally itself with the proletariat, insofar as the proletariat, for the present, may be the more politically united group.

The state thus aims at keeping the dominating class dominant, within a balance of powers that allows the state itself to be the sovereign governing organ. Thus, Sartre says, Marx is only partly correct in claiming that the state is held together by civil life and not civil life by the state, for, in order to keep from losing its own viability, the state does act on civil life. Indeed, we approach here the deepest contradictory praxis of the state. The state does ameliorate class conflicts and, seemingly, put its powers at the service of the common

2. This is consistent with what Sartre has said about the vote. See book I, chapter 4, note 11.

good. The state appears to act on society to form a nation that is the union of the peoples of the society. But the state always aims at manipulating groups to keep the sovereign power for itself as an end in itself. The state both acts for the common good and for itself as an absolute end. The state thus emerges as the union of the peoples of a society, insofar as this union is their *absolute other being*, their *nation*.

### (6. OTHER-DIRECTION: THE TOP TEN, RACISM, AND ANTI-SEMITISM)

Sartre's examples are here aimed at showing how small institutionalized groups manipulate large collectives. Although these groups are degenerate, they impose a more or less unified praxis on the loose seriality of collectives. The aim of this new praxis is to control and predict the behavior of the collective. From this perspective, modern means of education and communication are not merely epiphenomena, that is, incidental features of the individual's historical experience. Rather, they are some of the means the sovereign group uses to alter the spontaneous behavior of society's members.

This new serial behavior, constituted by the praxis of the sovereign, creates a situation in which everyone in the collective *freely* and *spontaneously* chooses to be other than himself. Through education and mass media, particularly advertising, we are taught to be "other-directed."[3] This new alienation differs from the more abstract statute of seriality that characterized the *constituting* dialectic discussed in the first part of this *Critique*. There, we indeed saw that serial behavior means that each one acts as the other, who is other than himself. For example, we buy a newspaper on the way to work not as a member of a group. True, we each buy our own paper, but our private purpose is already alienated from us by mediation: we are the uneducated other who *needs* to be enticed to reading by big headlines and gory pictures, or we are the sophisticated other whose intelligence requires everything to be understated, whether it be world poverty or the possibility of nuclear destruction. Thus, the newspaper does not bring us together for united action. It does not, by its general institutionalized structure, invite us to forget our differences and be freely the same as every other in order to accomplish a common purpose. For example, in order to save publishing costs, we are not asked to share our paper with others as might be done with a pamphlet or paper circulated through a political group. The newspaper, with its modern promoting techniques, addresses each one in the false privacy of an isolation, created and sustained by larger institutionalized structures to which the newspaper be-

3. Sartre credits American sociologists for this apt term, and the editors of the English translation refer to David Reisman's *The Lonely Crowd* (New Haven, Conn.: Yale University Press, 1950) (E, 643).

longs. A typical newspaper can no more invite critical reflection on itself than it can ask to be eliminated.[4]

At this new, more concrete stage of the *constituted* dialectic, however, we see that we are not merely blindly led to be other than ourselves. Rather, a situation is created in which it is natural for us spontaneously *to choose* to be a self alienated from true bonds of reciprocity with others. To be other-directed is to be freely united to everyone, precisely insofar as we are all private individuals who do not relinquish our isolation from every other.

Reciprocally, to speak analytically, the conditions for the possibility of this free "choice" exist because the sovereign of a nation, as well as of other institutionalized groups, creates and sustains the *real illusion of a serial totality*. The sovereign's praxis creates the illusion that we are united to every other in our isolation, that is, that we are a group of isolated individuals, each uniquely different and yet united, just as the numbers first, second, and third are each unique and yet are all members of the set of ordinal numbers. But a true group breaks out of seriality. The sovereign sustains the illusion of a false totality, in order to prevent society from forming real groups that could threaten his power.

In the text, Sartre illustrates our other-directed behavior by his experience, during one of his trips to the United States, concerning a publicity campaign for the top ten records. On the one hand, the resulting choice was supposed to represent public opinion, the convergence of the independent thinking of a free populace. On the other hand, the announcement of one week's choices substantially increased the sales of these records in the subsequent weeks. This "guaranteed music" was something that one wanted in one's collection and wished to give as a present to others. Furthermore, listening to the music that others had chosen as the best created a situation in which one chose precisely the music that he thought the other would like. And this choice was a "free" choice of each one casting a vote. This does not mean that a different type of music may not gain public attention, but it can do so only by means of the same alienating techniques. For, in reality, pressure groups and groups of so-called experts channel choices based on buying and selling of *new* records, regardless of their value as music. Sartre notes that this buying and selling gives one the music-collection of the other as other, that is, the collection of no one.

Advertising and other media devices reflect serial listeners, viewers, and

4. It is indeed true that, from another perspective, a free press is one of the strongest means of fighting institutionalized evils. Nevertheless, from our perspective, even the most "liberal" newspapers are institutionalized groups that control collectives through alienating their members. Only bad faith, however, would cause someone to use this as an excuse for eliminating or controlling the "free press."

readers back on to themselves, creating the illusion that they are part of a totality. In manipulating seriality, this illusion of totality was created precisely in
order to obtain the appearance of a synthetic result where no synthesis existed.
Nevertheless, some result is achieved—for example, as many records as possible are bought. This result was achieved because the small pressure groups
have reflexive awareness; they are able to reflect onto collectives the illusion
of the collective's own unity in order to control them.

Sartre also indicates the difference between racism, in regard to the persecution of the Jews, and anti-Semitism as a movement. Racism is a form of
manipulated seriality. It is a specific form of the other-directed behavior of a
collective. Anti-Semitism as a movement, however, is the result of a degenerate group action, but, as such, its autonomous praxis is never condoned by a
sovereign of a nation. The greatest evil for any institutionalized government is
the independent union of its people for any purposes whatsoever. The sovereign thus always maintains a situation of manipulated seriality; and, precisely
insofar as we are members of a society, we can never escape other-directed
behavior.

### (7. BUREAUCRACY AND THE CULT OF PERSONALITY)

Collectives also influence sovereign, institutionalized power.
Bureaucracy and the cult of personality are two specific forms of this influence. We have seen that the sovereign increases the inertia of the collectives
by forcing seriality to the limit of other-directed behavior; reciprocally, the
collective becomes an inorganic weight prohibiting the sovereign from using it
as an instrument for common praxis. Bureaucracy and the cult of personality
both block effective sovereign praxis and sustain sovereign power in existence.

In general, bureaucracy is a complex of three relations. First, within the
bureaucratic hierarchy, the relationship downward maintains and indeed increases the other-directed behavior of lower officials. Second, among peers,
mistrust and serialized terror give rise to a bastardized pledge aimed at preventing one's own dismissal rather than at furthering a common praxis. Third,
all subordinates are mere instruments for the sovereign; he is the only organism capable of true praxis. The sovereign thus attempts to become the only
source of viable action. This is done by pushing the inertia of his subordinates
to the limit, to make them the pure, inorganic means to his own end. But this
praxis of the sovereign individual, or subgroup, annihilates each one as a regulatory third and destroys every instrumentality for working toward a common
end. Sovereignty institutionalizes every relation of interiority, prohibiting in-
feriors from being true channels for the needs of the masses. Those out of line
with other-directed behavior are considered "troublemakers," a concept,

Sartre observes, that has meaning only for those already within a sovereign group.

Bureaucracy and the cult of personality are, for Sartre, more extreme in socialist countries. This does not imply, for him, the superiority of bourgeois democracies; it does imply that, from the perspective, of sovereignty, the class antagonisms within a democracy, with their conflicting pressure groups, do allow for some breakthrough into the bureaucratic structure. In bourgeois democracies, the sovereign is forced to heed some of the needs of the dominated class and to adopt a more viable praxis in regard to pressure groups. What bourgeois democracies reveal is that socialist countries must head in the direction of "debureaucratization, decentralization, and democratization." Specifically, Sartre notes that the "dictatorship of the proletariat" is an absurd notion; the proletariat is a serial structure incapable of grouping itself to rule. The USSR, he continues, eliminated the bourgeoisie but established a "*monopoly of the group.*" "From the point of view of the masses the sovereignty of this group was neither legitimate nor illegitimate; its practical legitimation was due to the fact that the sovereign constructed his own legitimacy by his mistakes and crimes: this is the judgement of history" (E, 661; F, 629–30; NF, 745).

The constituent dialectic has shown us that sovereignty as a function, with its reciprocal impotence of other-directed behavior and bureaucratic structure, arises from degenerate group praxis. In this respect, it is the antipraxis of the constituted dialectic. This counterpraxis can only be combated by a viable group action that aims at withering away the state. For, in our present historical situation, the sovereign state has turned praxis into process; that is, it has turned viable human goals into inhuman destinies.

PART TWO *Dialectical investigation as totalization: The level of the concrete, the place of history*

# (7    The Place of History)

Finally, Sartre says, we arrive at the concrete. However, this concrete, he notes, is not historical praxis as it transcends past, historical being toward a new goal. If the program of the *Critique* is valid, such a dialectical comprehension is possible, although it would require both the completion of the second volume of the *Critique* and many other efforts to interpret the meaning of our contemporary situation. The concrete that we approach here is rather the formal structure of past, historical being. This past was constituted by former constituent praxes of collectives and groups. It is received as constituted by others. We now realize that even the constituent praxis, studied in the book 1 of the *Critique,* was initially affected by a constituted inertia that had to be transcended, even as the inertia itself was a past transcendence of earlier praxes. That is, the historical past is never a mere fact; it is always something that has succeeded or failed. It is itself a "transcended being," as, for example, the formation of the American Constitution is *an achievement* for Americans. Thus, historical praxis, if it is to be vital, must transcend this transcended being rather than repeat it. (I believe that this simple observation is a clue to appreciating the goal of the *Critique.*)

Since our present level of investigation assumes, but does not establish, history as a totalization of totalizing groups, it is impossible to see how new constituent praxis can completely transcend the formal constraints of past, constituted being. Nevertheless, we do know that *a* history, if it exists, is *not* a totality, but an open-ended process established by human praxis. There is, to repeat, no a priori reason why praxis should have constituted *a* history. If it did, however, then formal constraints have been established for all humanity. We must thus transcend *a* past, as well as regional pasts. If history is not one, then the "transcended being" here referred to is regional—for example, that of Europe, or Western civilization. Whether "the set of formal contexts, curves, structures and conditionings which constitute the formal milieu"

(E, 671, F, 637; NF, 673) of history is regional or universal, the emphasis here is on revealing these constraints, rather than on showing how they can be controlled and altered to establish the possibility of a new humanity.

It is now apparent that collectives and groups did not form independently of each other. This was already known uncritically at the beginning of this study, but here our investigation shows that groups and collectives mutually structure each other. Everyone in society is structured by the multiplicities of group praxis. On the level of the historical concrete, our humanity has a particular, historical structure created by the multidimensional praxes of synchronic and diachronic groups. This study attempts to reveal the structure of this humanity. But here we should note again that, no matter how we isolate ourselves, we never discover a pure human nature that has later been corrupted by history. Indeed, the isolation of the critical investigator is itself a form of the alienation critiqued. The praxis of the *Critique* is thus not, to repeat, an attempt to provide a suprahistorical study of history. Our approach is circular and conditional; it is within history itself. If we can recognize alienation, it is not because this critical study is free of alienation; it is rather because this study is circular, revealing *certain extremes of alienation* that allow us to see the road on which we all travel. These extremes can be seen by examining more closely the object of group praxis, for it is from the object that the truth of the group is revealed. This relation of group praxis to its object is complex, and Sartre describes three of its principal characteristics.

1. The group brings about totalizing structures within collectives, other groups and worked matter, such as machines. Thus we have seen how groups cause other-directed behavior. Reciprocally, these and other totalized structures retotalize the internal structures of the group, and there is always the possibility that the originally planned praxis will be radically altered.

2. No matter how successful the *result* of group praxis, it will always be alienated from the originally intended praxis. Here we can distinguish the effects of diachronic and synchronic groups. Synchronic groups act at the same time for a more or less common goal. If almost all the groups in a society work for a common goal, such as happens during a national war, it is possible to escape alienation from the effect of other synchronic groups. Nevertheless, it is impossible to escape the effects of diachronic groups. A diachronic group is a group whose praxis explicitly involves an appropriation of a common past, such as happens when refugees are united in a foreign land. More generally, the different generations within a society constitute diachronic groups, more or less united. One generation can never truly know what the meaning of its praxis will be for the next. This does not mean that a new, younger generation can do whatever it wishes, but rather that the direction of its transcendence is not given in the historical milieu of its past being. Sartre gives the example of the "costly French victory of 1918." This victory

had two interesting features: it encouraged the French to control their population, and it inclined the children, for whom the victory appeared as a costly, hideous affair, toward pacifism. On the other hand, the Germans reacted to defeat by increasing their numbers, and their children saw the defeat as a humiliation to be revenged through nazism.

Historically, the cumulative effect of diachronic groups is brought together into the constituted unity of a nation, and, in a more complex way, this unity is appropriated as the reflected image of human evolution and progress. Later, we will discuss in more detail the distinctive praxis of diachronic groups, a transcending praxis that explicitly involves an interpretation of the past. Sartre simply notes here that these different temporalizations are unified by what he calls "retro-anterogressive" movement; that is, each generation establishes its temporality by receiving the unified praxis of earlier generations, and, reciprocally, each generation constitutes this received unity by its new transcending praxis. In this respect, the past being of the transcending praxis of a new generation is itself constituted with the constituting praxis itself. Thus nazism constituted the fact of the German defeat of 1918 *as a disgrace to be revenged*. The defeat was given by an earlier generation, but not its quality as a disgrace to be revenged. From a broader, historical perspective this same process is the basis for our perception of a continually evolving humanity. But, as we have seen, there are several temporalizations, and temporal unity is itself a complex, synthetic result constituted for a purpose. Nevertheless, *within the given structure of a complex, constituted temporalization*, progress or the lack of it truly exists.

3. Apart from any counterpraxis of other groups, the activity of a group is alienating, insofar as it always occurs in a milieu of sustained scarcity; that is, a group can never free itself completely from alienation, *insofar as alienation exists on a historical level*. The significant group does not arise out of a benign situation in which contented individuals get together for a common goal. Scarcity, alienation, and impotence give rise to a terror-fraternity pledge. The context of group praxis is the attempt to alleviate scarcity, flee from alienation, and dissolve impotence. But a group could escape completely from alienation only if it were the entire society. Nevertheless, group praxis, as an attempt to flee from alienation, does indeed alter the statute of seriality in the collectives from which it arose. This last observation brings us to the question of the *truth* of group praxis.

In extremely ossified groups, the relation of truth to objective praxis and internal structures is clearly revealed. Sartre credits studies in the United States for showing that certain groups do not merely induce other-directed behavior in collectives but become themselves other-directed in their being, that is, in their materiality. The goal of these groups is not merely to manipulate those outside the group but also to manipulate those within the group. As a member of these groups, one does not merely study other-directed behavior in order to control those outside the group; rather, the hierarchical structure of the group, with its various techniques, is the apprenticeship through which one becomes other-directed. In order to make the other buy a product that he would reject as a private individual, it is not sufficient to *pretend* to be the other insatiable consumer who needs it. One must *become*, in one's own being, this same other who needs this or other similar products. The "advertising man" is a good example of what Sartre has in mind. People who work in advertising frequently do not see themselves as manipulating others, for they themselves have become the manipulated other. A knowledge of advertising does not reveal the "tricks" of the trade so that one can avoid them in one's private life. Rather, tricks are knowledge, and the true "advertising man" is the perfect consumer needing and buying what is most advertised. Here alienation is not merely in the object; it is the being and praxis of the group. That is, exterior other-directed behavior arises here from the group's interior other-directed practices. This extreme case also shows that a group's degeneration is not a matter of time. Degeneration can be the initial structure of a group. Regardless of temporal priority, Sartre observes that in our advanced technological societies, other-directed behavior is a subtle, objective structure, conditioning us on almost an infinite number of levels.

### (2. THE CIRCULARITY OF DIALECTICAL INVESTIGATION)

There is a complex, circular, dialectical relation between collectives and groups. This dialectic is more than a reciprocity between the constituting dialectic, as the free praxis of organic individuals, and the constituted dialectic, as the practico-inert field of past frozen freedoms. As we move from the abstract to the concrete, collectives and groups are seen to influence each other, not only in their given structures but in the ways they affect each other's capacities for new possibilities. In this respect, it is again important to note that the collective as an aggregate of isolated, free individuals is not an abstraction, but a fiction. Another fiction is the concept of the group as a bond uniting free individuals, who find their common object either from within the depths of their personal freedoms or from an untutored comprehension of a felicitous, transcendent object. "There are revolutionary pastorals on the group which are the exact counterpart of Robinsonades" (E, 678; F, 643; NF, 760).

Nevertheless, there *is* free, organic praxis; and there *is* the field of the practico-inert, as the frozen freedoms of past praxes, with their given inertias and projected human destiny. But, from the beginning of our dialectical investigation, free, organic praxis, in its most abstract form, was always accepted as something initially altered by the praxis of a constituted dialectic that was present but not yet critically examined. Thus, initially, the collective was not a mere aggregate of individuals but a serial connection of alterity and impotence arising within a milieu of scarcity. And it was hypothetically claimed, but not yet critically established, that the condition for the possibility of alterity and impotence, as well as the milieu of scarcity itself, was worked matter. Now it is becoming clear that a type of free praxis sustains and activates these alienating characteristics as they are the condition for the possibility of our history, even as group praxis tries to escape them. Antipraxis is thus revealed to have two meanings: it is an aspect of every praxis, and it is the special form of degenerate group praxis, as it becomes ossified. To the extent that we are all affected by other-directed behavior, we act as antipraxis. But, in a more complete sense, antipraxis is exemplified by the extreme case just referred to: a group that interiorizes other-directed behavior as its praxis. *Antipraxis is thus an institutionalized praxis; it is praxis become process, praxis lived as destiny.*

Thus, the second book of the *Critique* began by examining group praxis precisely as it was an escape from the practico-inert with its antipraxis. This movement, as we have said, brings us to the concrete. It involves, Sartre says, a double circularity on the part of group praxis. However, before moving to this twofold characteristic, we should again note briefly the significance of calling the movement between collectives and groups "circular": neither collectives nor groups exist apart from each other, and it makes no sense to ask which came first historically.

Sartre calls the first circular movement "static." The group interiorizes the characteristics of the collective from which it arose, even as it transcends them toward its common goal. It cannot be repeated too often that the historically significant group is a flight from impotence, alterity, and scarcity, and not a benign union of content individuals. True, as already stated, the group can neither be reduced to the collective nor deduced from it. But once the group is given, it sustains itself as a transcending praxis of *this* collective and not of some homogeneous one. This is again very evident in the extreme case where the group interiorizes the other-directed behavior of the collective; the only difference between such a group and the collective is that the group's other-directed behavior is the result of a hierarchical, institutional structure. But, even in the absence of this extreme of inertia, the group is modified by the transcended being of the collective, particularly as sustained by other diachronic groups. Reciprocally, however, the group does produce a "common field" that transcends *this practico-inert*. This "common field" modifies the collective, both insofar as it is praxis that attempts to escape the collective and insofar as it is a future collapse into the practico-inert. Here we can make a subdivision: the group influences the collective positively by creating the illusion of a totality and synthesis in the nongrouped. This illusion, however, is not a fiction, for it arises from the freedom of the group, which manifests itself as defining its own purpose to the nongrouped, who lack a common goal. *Negatively*, group praxis structures the collective into a nongroup. A nongroup is not another group, or a so-called countergroup, but a new alteration of the collective into those who have, to a greater or lesser extent, chosen not to be grouped. Clearly, this statute is more or less important depending on the significance of the group.

The second circular movement is *dynamic*. Here we have seen that the praxis of a group involves an active movement from the pledge to organization and finally to institutionalization. The successful praxis of a group demands that it mimic the alienating structures of the practico-inert, until, given our present historical condition, it becomes one of these structures itself. Every group, Sartre notes, does not have to pass through all the stages, and it can emerge, for historical reasons, immediately ossified. But it will then have simultaneously all the structures indicated above. Reciprocally, however, this dynamic group praxis does alter the collective. Thus, the collective that appears when group praxis has failed is not, for better or worse, the same collective that existed prior to the formation of the group.

### (3. THE WORKING CLASS AS INSTITUTION, GROUP-IN-FUSION, AND SERIES)

There is no logical priority to the formation of groups or collectives; nevertheless, on the level of being, there is only the collective. That is, there are only individuals and the constituted relations established among them by praxis. No group—including groups-in-fusion and pledged, organized, and institutional groups—exists apart from the collective from which it has arisen and to which it relates. True, the group-in-fusion and the pledged group negate the alterity and the impotence of the collective, but this negation is lived by each individual of the collective insofar as each one negates this impotence and alterity as his transcended past. Furthermore, no individual can escape seriality on every level. The member of an active political group, for example, experiences alterity and impotence in other aspects, or, better, in other dimensions, of life—as a family member, for example, or as a consumer. A group that could raise itself above all serial connections that tie each of us in impotence and alterity to every other would unite people of a different humanity from ours.

Nevertheless, if organicism, the claim that individuals of a community participate in a higher being than their own existence, is to be rejected on all levels, so also must we reject all forms of an analytic empiricism affirming the existence only of atomistic individuals united by extrinsic relations. The human reality, for Sartre, has no a priori nature; thus, both community and isolated existence are constituted by praxis itself. Furthermore, this praxis constitutes internal, necessary relations that delineate the material structure of human life, that is, its being. A group does not have a distinct being. But each member of a group has a different statute than those outside the group. Ontologically, there exist only individuals and their totalizing praxis. Nevertheless, it is one of the major points of this dialectic that it would be wrong to conceive of individuals as living historically on a homogeneous, analytic, two-dimensional plane. In the abstract, that is, from a local perspective, praxis collapses into mere action, as when one fills a glass of water to quench one's thirst. But, as soon as wider—that is, historical—dimensions are introduced, dimensions that exist to a greater or lesser degree in every praxis, then intentionalities of a more than linear structure are revealed. Filling a glass of water from a faucet of an apartment, for which one pays rent by going daily to a job that one hates, is serial behavior revealing alterity and impotence. This behavior is not an epiphenomenon, that is to say, it is not an alteration added to the individual's existence. It is the existence itself as lived on this dimension. Thus, as our historical perspective has now become wider and thus more concrete, the complex structures of class praxis are finally revealed as an alteration of our organic existence.

We have only begun the sketch of class being. This effort will continue until the end of the *Critique*. The thrust will be both to show class being as a complex social structure maintained by a distinctive praxis and to reveal its dialectical intelligibility. If dogmatism and relativism are to be avoided, we must see that praxis establishes and maintains different socialities with their necessary structures. We can never describe these necessary structures as if we were an outside observer. We thus comprehend the multidimensional class praxis by situating ourselves within it or, better, by realizing that we are situated within it. Furthermore, our dialectical comprehension of our multidimensional situation is not a logical feat, for we are multidimensional. Thus, when we pay rent, we perform a multidimensional activity that is complex but nevertheless intelligible if we take care to situate ourselves, with proper knowledge, within the various levels of our own historical complexity.

Sartre remarks that this comprehension of class praxis by those who situate themselves within it is "*both sufficient and inadequate*" (E, 708 n. 102; F, 667 n. 1; NF, 789 n. 2). That is, comprehension can reveal the immediate context of transcendent being, with its present future projections, but not new praxis as it will de facto unfold. Nevertheless, we can be in a position to comprehend the intelligibility of this new praxis *as it unfolds*. This does not mean that we can predict the new praxis. Prediction is possible only when the situation has so degenerated that the involved groups have become institutionalized. In that case, the only effective praxis will be the counterpraxis of the practico-inert. It is this limiting case, Sartre notes, that gives the basis for the analytic approach to group praxis.

For the purposes of our study, the main features of class praxis are the distinctive ways it functions on the three levels of the collective, the active group, and the institution. Precisely insofar as an action is a class praxis, it exhibits at least these three dimensions. Here it may be useful to elaborate, from a different perspective, one of Sartre's earlier examples: A working woman who has an abortion carries out the sentence of the dominating class. If she gave birth to the child and raised it in poverty, she would be carrying out a similar sentence. Ontologically, her action is a class action, whether she is aware of it or not. She may believe herself to be completely isolated and impotent, but her praxis is, in fact, modified by the praxes of the active groups and institutions that are dedicated to her class. But more importantly, the aim of both the active groups and the institutions is to make class members understand their status within their class. Thus, it is likely that this woman knows of her plight of being an underprivileged member of society. At the very least, the condition for the possibility of this knowledge exists. If this woman is indeed aware of her position in society, then, when she has an abortion, she does so not as one who is serially impotent, but as one who is demanding redress and some degree of satisfaction for her situation. Her behavior is now thoroughly a class behavior. It redounds both to other members of her class, lessening their serial impotence, and to the groups and institutions that have aided her, revealing to them that they have in some way touched her. This praxis, although numerically one, exists differently on several levels. The praxis of a class member who is not a member of an active group or institution affects the class differently than one who belongs to these groups. The members of the active group, whether a group-in-fusion or a pledged group, dissolve seriality for all *here*. Although a class, Sartre notes, is never a group, even in revolutionary times, the active groups within the class establish the possibility of greater fusion. Reciprocally, this possibility of greater unity is lived as an aspect of class praxis. Thus the class consciousness of the woman in Sartre's example establishes the possibility of greater militancy, not as an abstract possibility but as a structure of her organic being.

Indeed, from another perspective, the institutions within her class, the organized union with its permanent officials and their more or less frozen structures, reflect onto class seriality a "schema of totalization." The institutions, with their permanent officials, become the possible means through which a sovereign power can be used to organize the class for militancy. Of course, active groups, institutions, and seriality all influence each other. For example, an active group, such as one leading a nonauthorized strike, not only recalls institutions, such as a labor union, to their original goals of fighting the dominant class, but it also establishes the possibility of altering these institutions or forming subgroups within them.

Here it might be helpful to clarify what it means to call praxis "totalizing." Loosely speaking, every intentional act is totalizing. Primitive farmers cultivating land totalize their environment insofar they produce a transcendent, unified object—"cultivated land"—that embodies their numerous, separate acts. Strictly speaking, however, totalization is an aspect of praxis and not of (nonhistorical) action. The action of the primitive farmer, like Robinson Crusoe, is linear, that is, on a two-dimensional plane of organic action transcending inorganic matter. Praxis is multidimensional; it brings together facets of different social levels, individuals, groups, and institutions. It does this not by an added reflection or effort but by being praxis itself. And this praxis is simultaneously a comprehension, although this comprehension may exist more or less explicitly on the part of the member of the collective. To return to our earlier example, the praxis of renting an apartment involves both a comprehension and an activity that operate simultaneously on many levels. Privately, the apartment chosen may reflect personal preferences. But this same choice may also express class distinction and participate in large-scale economic situations, such as an inflationary period that raises rents in most large cities throughout the world. Moreover, the individual renter may be implicitly or explicitly aware of these levels of praxis, but what is important for our purposes is that the condition for the possibility of explicit comprehension exists in the situation itself. Newspapers, radio, television—all these media—create a milieu in which the phenomenon of renting can be known to share in large-scale economic and social forces.

But here we have to recall an earlier reservation. We are assuming that there is one totalization for all of our history. Although the *Critique I* does not critically validate the perspective of *a* history, we nevertheless are aware of such uncritically. It seems obvious to us that our history is inextricably bound up with a technological world. Every means of decrying the technological world must use technology. The Eastern mystic can effectively denounce technology only through modern means of technology. Furthermore, the fact that the cheap production of consumable goods are moved from one foreign market to another indicates a human environment that has been practically totalized to be *one*. If the above could be critically established, the conditions for the possibility of a praxis existing on this historical level would also be given.

Our present perspective thus uncritically accepts that there is *a* history for our present situation; critically, however, it establishes the *Critique* only regionally: Sartre expressly refers to the French working class, particularly until 1936. From this regional perspective, the class praxis of the working class is characterized as a "praxis-process" that is also a "bet." First, to describe class praxis as a "process" is to call attention to the fact that it is historical, insofar as it is constituted. Every praxis, as an intentional act, transcends or surpasses the given in its situation, and from this perspective it is *constituting*. But, as historical, this transcending is reciprocally something that is itself constituted. To understand the distinctiveness of calling praxis "constituted," we must first recognize that every intentional act is reciprocally affected by its object. The cultivated land is the truth of the primitive worker as a "farmer." And the rescue of a drowning person is the truth of the act of bravery committed by the one who risks his life. In both cases, these truths can express a transcendence that establishes a new truth for the individual in his relation to his situation. The primitive farmer may have been a former nomad, the present-day brave rescuer a former coward. But class being, on the other hand, presents an untranscendable limit. The praxis-process that surpasses it establishes it. Thus, an action is a constituted praxis precisely insofar as its truth has already been given to it in the same act by which it transcends it. The working woman who insists on her right to have a safe abortion in a professional hospital *fulfills her class being even as she transcends it.* Her praxis is part of a *process* of establishing woman's rights within her class. Insofar as this process is the manifestation of institutions, it is intentional but authorless. Second, the woman's praxis exists as a "bet," insofar as those within her class commit themselves to the class struggle without adequate knowledge or guarantees of success. It is a continuing but ambiguous struggle to free oneself from dominance. Thus, insofar as the dialectic remains only regionally established, there will always remain an aspect of our praxis that appears stolen from us by unknown forces.

For Sartre, the concrete features of class being are only determined by historical circumstances, of which the changing means of production are only one. In the text, Sartre describes very carefully the differences between the class being that existed in the early days of skilled labor and the class being that existed in the more recent times of interchangeable workers. During the anarcho-syndicalist movement, the skilled workers considered unskilled workers as not truly workers. Rights for workers meant rights for an elite. In this respect, there was more than one dominating class. The universal machine, however, had the effect of making all the workers see themselves in their common humanity, the same insofar as they all received wages. Permanent union officials could now represent all the workers, even though these officials did not do any specialized work. These officials existed both as the possibility of becoming regulatory thirds and as the permanent sovereignty of the workers, when these workers were passive.

### (4. ECONOMISM, MATERIALISM, AND DIALECTICS)

We may still wonder how we can comprehend class praxis, particularly since on one level it operates as the authorless antidialectic. Sartre reminds us that Engels tried to make history comprehensible by reducing class struggle to the inert complex of the means of production. Thus, assuming, for simplicity, only two classes, the means of production *of themselves* produced an opposition between the dominated and the dominant class. Those within the class merely actualized an aggressive tendency in the material social order. Engels had objected that Dühring referred too easily and too quickly to oppression as the cause of class conflicts, but, in so doing, Engels went to the other extreme, adopting an economism that eliminated the reality of class struggle. Engels thus tried to make history comprehensible by reducing the opposition between the dialectic and the antidialectic to an opposition of the forces of nature. But he thereby eliminated both the dialectic and analytic reason as means for comprehending history, for unless we see the dialectic as praxis and the antidialectic as this praxis turning on itself, then history, as well as science, becomes a mere unintelligible brute given. We must insist again that we do not first discover intelligibility in nature and then extrapolate it into history. Intentional human praxis is that which is first and foremost intelligible, and nature itself is meaningful only in light of praxis.

The naturalization of history robs it of its intelligibility and is, in fact, contrary to experience. *There is real oppression* in the world, and real class struggle. Human beings provide more than merely the blind energy for actualizing an inert mechanism of opposition. The social order is itself a human product, intelligible in the light of the circularity of human praxis. Praxis is both embedded in matter—giving matter objective meanings and inertia—and an interiorization and transcendence of these embedded meanings. Objectified, antagonistic relations thus refer both to past institutionalized acts of oppression and to present oppressive acts that sustain and surpass institutionalized praxis.

It is not only the means of production that causes alienation, but oppression and repression as well. Below the infrastructure of the means of production is an actively oppressed working class struggling to free itself from the active and daily dominating praxes of a dominating class. It is true that we must not interpret this class struggle in either an idealistic or a voluntaristic sense. We are not referring to a group of atomistic individuals freely united to oppress another group. Class antagonism does not result from the manipulations of a few wicked people. Such individual or even group acts of oppression could never, of themselves, have established a system such as class oppression.

A praxis of oppression is more inhuman than an isolated murder, for such praxis arises from and transcends inertia, reestablishing the possibility of a new praxis of class oppression. Sartre uses the example of the French colonization of Algeria. From the perspective of the conquering French, the Muslims were other-than-human; they were subhumans who were either mindless savages to be controlled or devils that could not be defeated. Once the force of aggression established a colonial system, it was as easy for the French officials to act through it as it was difficult for the Muslims to evade it. Nevertheless, it was sustained only by people who were willing to be the instrument of a capitalist nation or by pressure groups wishing to make profits at any cost. True, this praxis of oppression is originally comprehensible as a move for profit. A stage of totalization had been reached by French capitalists, such that Algeria appeared as a natural object of colonization. Nevertheless, this stage of totalization was itself produced by former alienating praxes. And, more importantly, neither past praxes nor economic conditions produced, of themselves, the distinctive oppression that was the colonization of Algeria. This colonization was neither deducible from nor reducible to economic conditions or past practices; it was a new praxis of oppression.

### (5. RACISM AND COLONIALISM AS PRAXIS AND PROCESS)

The praxis of oppression is at the root not only of economic conditions but of sociological ones as well. "Pauperization"—the rapid appearance of a poor, uneducated, unemployed, atomized populace of natives —is not an unfortunate or necessary result of an advanced society coming into contact with a backward one. Rather, it is the result of the common praxis of oppression and exploitation. True, what might be called, in analytic terms, the condition for the possibility of this violence, as a unified and serial structure, arose out of the practico-inert field of the colonizing country. Thus, whenever colonization is actualized, it is true that it is actualized in a framework that already constitutes a specific act of colonialization as justifiable. But this violence, as an inertial system, was itself established by prior human praxis.

Nevertheless, it is also important to realize that colonialization, as a specific form of class struggle, is not merely a praxis but a *process* as well. We will see later that to reduce class struggle to pure praxis is to make class antagonism an idealistic conflict among supraorganic forces. Sartre's point here is that colonialization arises out of the practico-inert violent background of bourgeois, capitalist society, yet transcends this violence in acts of extreme exploitation. Once established, these acts of superexploitation create a new practico-inert, with conditions of even more intense violence. But these conditions *must be constantly recreated and sustained by the colonialists.* In order to understand more clearly how this superexploitation occurs, Sartre describes two aspects of colonialization as a process-praxis. He continues to use the French occupation of Algeria as an example.

First, colonialization is a clear example of the reality of class struggle, because it merges a distinctive type of oppression with its exploitation. The term "colonialization" attempts to mask the violence of the occupation. This masking is necessary: A liberal democracy can live with, indeed is based upon, exploitation—for example, the illusion of the free contract. Yet it cannot openly condone the excessive inhumanity involved in violently oppressing people for profit. Indeed, initially the colonialization of Algeria was not a clear, common national goal of obtaining a cheap labor force. There were political factors. Nevertheless, violence was present, and it resulted in large-scale killings of Muslims. If the governmental institutions did not, at first, have a clear common goal of colonialization, they had not excluded the possibility either. A structure of inhumanity had already been established within French society. If it were possible for bourgeois French capitalists to treat their fellow citizens, at best, as merely the inhuman others who by law had to be given a decent wage, then the condition for the possibility of treating the Algerian Muslims as alien, subhuman creatures was already given.

Still, this structure of violence as a *hexis*, that is, as a habitual state, did not of itself lead to active oppression. Violent pressure groups, rapacious for profit, had to organize and transcend this *hexis* toward superexploitation. Propaganda attempted to justify the continuing invasion by claiming that it was not really an invasion but merely the industrialization of an under-privileged group. Clearly, however, this was not enough to justify violence. A new *idea* was needed, an idea never spoken but present in the praxis of colonialization itself, namely, racism: violence had to be used because the Muslim was subhuman. And the people of the liberal metropolitan areas were told that no one knew this better than the colonialist. Individual colonialists entered into a self-justifying structure in which they saw themselves as the human others threatened by the wild, inhuman Muslims. Of course, there were degrees of racism, but even tolerance assumed the inhumanity of the Muslim.

Colonialization, however, is violence not only as praxis but as *process*. It is process because it arose from a network of earlier violence and continued into a network of new violence. It is praxis because violent people used habitualized violence to establish a new violent network. This transcending violence of superexploitation is neither deducible from the old nor, when given, is it reducible to it. It is a new praxis recreating itself on every level and continuing itself as a new process: *colonialization*. The Muslim society was thus atomized by violence; the old feudal forms of labor were destroyed to create a cheap labor force. The new industrial centralization did not arise from the old; it was imposed and it created its own poor class, one that was dependent on wages for subsistence. Some of the members of this newly created poor class were then helped, and this help was pointed to as justifying colonialization.

Of course, this type of decentralization was characteristic of capitalism even in France. But in colonialism, it could be carried out as an "economic experiment," isolated from other pressure groups that could moderate its inhumanity. This economic experiment operated within the context of a Manichaeism that could at any moment both justify the annihilation of the Muslim as the purely inhuman, and glorify the colonialist as the savior. (Needless to say, it is the colonialists who have made themselves subhuman.) At times, this "incarnate violence" was actualized against the Muslim, but its main function was to justify as humane every violence short of extermination.

This Manichaeism brings us to another aspect of colonial praxis. Colonialists are conditioned by the violent structure of colonialization even as they try to condition the structure itself. To be a colonialist *is to allow oneself to be molded as an oppressor.* Praxis is here always in the context in which French culture defines the colonialist as the human other and the Muslim as the subhuman other. Of course, an individual colonialist may not beat Muslims and may even attempt to treat them "humanely." The truth of the situation, however, is always present: the Muslim is one who deserves by nature to be beaten. And the Muslims cannot free themselves of this inhumanity imposed on them by the entire colonial apparatus. For colonialization takes from them their own heritage and gives them nothing in return. Superexploitation attempts to transform them into a pure means for profit. A particular Muslim may now, in this context, be treated very well. The situation is not changed, however, except that the colonialist now appears as a savior. (In a similar way, an anti-Semite may indeed have a "best friend" who is a Jew, precisely to justify his anti-Semitism.)

Although a handful of Muslims may be educated, the aim of colonialism is generally to keep those colonized from entering into the society of the occupying country. The goal is cheap labor, and this goal requires the daily practice of keeping the Muslim on a subhuman level. Behind these daily practices is the African Army, justifying the violence of the Muslim to the colonialist. And to be human, the Muslim must be violent. For one aim of colonialization is to prevent the Muslims from forming active groups. This goal, however, structures a situation in which adverse Muslim groups are always potentially present. But colonialization itself also creates, within the seriality of Muslim society, the false illusion of a common praxis. It does this so that any individual opposition can always be repressed violently as a group praxis in revolt.

Furthermore, the ever-present possibility of revolt keeps the colonialists themselves from ever uniting into a true group that could transcend the colonial structure. This structure simultaneously keeps both the colonialist and the oppressed as *other than themselves:* The colonialists, insofar as they at least accept the colonial structure, allows themselves to be situated as the human *others,* the ones in a strange land inhabited by fierce aliens. The Muslims, newly revealed to be subhuman, ashamed of their primitive past, and incapable of attaining *en masse* the humanity of the conquerors, have no human option except individual violence. The inhumanity of the colonialists is their praxis as colonialists. It is, for example, the existence of every colonialist who enjoys a high standard of living, and the reciprocal existence of the average Muslim existing on starvation wages. That the total colonial praxis aims at its own annihilation is part of the economic experiment of seeing how far a starved people can be pushed before it is unable to work. The inhuman experiment must go to an extreme, provoking violence in reaction: "The violence of the rebel was the violence of the colonialist; there was never any other" (E, 733; F, 687; NF, 813).

# (8   Class Struggle and Dialectical Reason)

Sartre here continues to show that our history is the result of real class struggle. To repeat, this struggle has two aspects: On the one hand, Sartre insists that Engels was right in affirming against Dühring that class oppression cannot conceivably result from the violence of individual, cruel capitalists. Such violence would evaporate in its local environments and not lead to oppressing and oppressed classes of society. On the other hand, Engels was wrong in simplistically attributing class struggle to the means of production and the inexorable economic laws that produce the capitalists and the proletariat. For Sartre, on the contrary, class oppression involves both a practico-inert system in which the *idea* of oppression already exists and the interiorization and transcendence of this idea by the praxis of individual human beings. This praxis is both that of serially connected individuals and that of active groups. Further, it is a praxis-process. It arises from violence as a *hexis* and evolves to a new structure, giving the possibility of greater violence. But it is human beings and not things that are actively violent. It is individual, organic praxis that both sustains the *hexis* of violence and carries it to new heights.

Marxists, Sartre maintains, emphasize how the means of production and economic laws produce either the worker in relation to the capitalist or the capitalist in relation to the worker. But they do not show how the praxis of capitalists produces workers or how the workers' own free praxis allows them to be produced as a reserve labor force. Sartre asks us to recall that our experience reveals human relations to be reciprocal. In the abstract, apart from the sociality introduced by our history, every human action is immediately reciprocal. Intentionality merely requires that consciousness is *of* something-other-than-itself. Sartre's point here is that all action, whether contemplative, affective, or more obviously exteriorly directed, is also reciprocal. It constitutes its object while being constituted by it.[1] For example, the farmer who tills the

---

1. But this reciprocity is never, for Sartre, a transcendental constitution that reveals the object's "true" objectivity and reciprocally reveals a transcendental unity of consciousness.

soil is a farmer through the land that he is cultivating. The "intention of cultivating" is primarily the action of cultivating and secondarily the habitual orientation to this praxis that preexists in the land; that is, there is no neutral act of digging into the ground that subsequently becomes an act of cultivating by some exterior, imposed relation, such as might arise from the farmer's mental intention.

Sociality does not eliminate this abstract reciprocity, nor does it merely localize it as an instance within a class. Sociality radically alters this reciprocity so that, as we have seen, it now occurs only as mediated by a third and, even more concretely, by the specific mediation within a group. Indeed, uncritically, we are first and foremost aware of this more complex, historical reciprocity. We must always keep in mind that we are not attempting to reconstruct history from an ahistorical perspective that would claim to know the past as a brute given. *Our* past is the past of our present history; it is the past that we regressively discover from our present perspective and concretely transcend in our present praxis. This does not mean that this past is relative in a skeptical sense. Rather, the living past is the meanings embedded in matter, in institutions, and, more subtly, in the entire cultivated environment into which we are born.

We discover and interpret the "inert past"—that of inscriptions, books, and the behavior of primitive societies—only through the past that we here and now transcend through our present praxis. It is in this sense that we now see scarcity to be the milieu that "gave rise" to violence and oppression. There is no a priori reason why scarcity should lead to oppression rather than cooperation. But scarcity did *not* lead to cooperation, and we have no practical idea what such a humanity would have been like. Regressively, we can conjecture that scarcity provided the condition for the possibility of a humanity in which the few protected themselves against the many by accumulation of goods and thereby acquired the power to establish a system that made our history possible. We know for *certain*, however, that the present praxis of accumulating surplus capital is embedded in the capitalist process itself. Furthermore, Sartre notes, this praxis shows that the process can continue only by constantly increasing reserve capital needed for improvements. This praxis also reveals the necessity of retaining a large reserve populace of unemployed as a source of relatively cheap labor. Violence and oppression are thus inherent in the system itself. True, Sartre is directly referring to the capitalism of the first part of the nineteenth century, but his point is that we must not think that these obvious excesses were due either merely to a worldwide economic advancement that unfortunately demanded suffering or to the praxis of a few cruel and selfish capitalists. Class oppression is due to a continuing praxis-process of oppression in which everyone in the class is serially connected with each oppressor. Each is the other who is oppressing only because the other oppresses.

Bourgeois humanism tends to mask the Manichaean ethic of the capitalist.

This ethic actually portrays the worker as *free to do only evil*. Like the colonialist, the worker is the alien subhuman. But there is a difference. The capitalist first raises the worker *abstractly* to the fully human level of the capitalist. In the moment of the contract, the worker shakes the hand of the capitalist as an equal in a universal humanity; in the next moment, the worker discovers he has freely accepted to become a commodity.

Bourgeois humanism thus has two moments. First, there is the empty pseudoconcept of a humanity in which everyone exists as free, atomistic individuals. But here we must recall what has been said about reciprocity. Humanity comes to each of us only through the humanity of others. We can only be fully human to the extent that the praxis of each makes the other to be human. Second, this pseudoconcept allows for a real mystification to occur: there is indeed a moment during the contract when the worker is raised to the level of a fully free individual. The worker can reject the contract just as the employer can reject the worker. But this equality is constituted by the capitalist for the control of the worker. Constraint is the control of a freedom, and what the capitalist needs besides machines are freedoms that can be controlled. The constraint is apparent in the possibility of being unemployed, with all its consequences. And the violence hidden in this is apparent in the waste of lives so evident in the nineteenth century, a waste that could not be explained economically. The capitalist uses the free contract to reveal the worker as the Manichaean personification of Evil, as the alien subhuman that must live on the brink of extermination for the sake of the truly human.[2]

Bourgeois humanism is thus the other side of racism. Racism begins with postulating the other as subhuman; it then justifies this Manichaean hatred by incidentally treating a particular subhuman as human, as if admitting that he escaped, by chance, from the contamination of his race. Bourgeois humanism, however, begins by postulating the other as human but then blames him for not living up to his humanity by being a capitalist. In the ethic of the capitalist, the workers' subhumanity is revealed by their having to choose between wages and unemployment: if workers possessed true freedom, they would control others and not allow themselves to be controlled.

This humanism is not incidental to capitalism. It is capitalism as it understands itself. The fully human is the one with initiative, and the one with initiative is the one who can manipulate others for profit. If others allow themselves to be manipulated, it must be because their laziness, stupidity, or other traits reveal them to be subhuman. Of course, the individual praxis of the

2. To reflect briefly on a contemporary example: As I am preparing this manuscript for the typist, Mayor Koch of New York has begun a program of employing the homeless of the city to clean the subways in exchange for housing, food, and a pay of sixty cents an hour. Except for those in the unions, most people, *including many of the homeless,* think that the program has value—and indeed it does. But deep layers of mystification must be involved for the homeless to see this solution as fitting.

capitalist is not determined completely by the capitalist system. Indeed, Sartre notes, an individual petit bourgeois, like Flaubert, may discover that he is using others despite his intentions. The inhumanity then exists as the "frozen shouts"within the system. Others, however, may relish the exploitation and increase the inhumanity. Furthermore, the capitalist competes as an individual. Once he enters the system, his goal is no longer a common goal relating goods to needs. Locally, on a superficial lateral level, he may have genuine discussions with workers about production. But he competes, as it were, vertically, in a market where he is the other competing with every other as other.

But the important point at present is that the capitalist's system is not, as Sartre sees Engels to have maintained, a completed totality, but a serial relation, a collective within which active and institutional groups operate. The capitalist thus finds himself within a collective whose totalization is always a flight, always beyond in some transfinite goal. This totalization is hypothesized *as if it were* a completed totality, in order to invert the economic laws: in reality, each individual's serial behavior constitutes economic laws, but, as a totality, the capitalistic system *appears* to have laws that govern individual behavior.

In this context, "liberalism," like humanism, operates as a practical idea for the capitalist. It postulates two contradictory principles: first, that rigid laws, specifically economic laws, cause certain types of social disasters and, second, that these laws are to be made less rigid by treating society as a totality within which wealth is to be better distributed. But this view merely accepts the capitalist mystification that society is really a totality of free, atomistic individuals who merely have to be given a better chance to compete. Such competition, however, would lead back to rigid laws, for it implies the necessary accumulation of wealth for the privileged few. Equality is merely the equality to be ruthless. Furthermore, and on a deeper level, liberalism, like capitalism, aims at preventing the masses from grouping together for their own common goal. Like capitalism, it fears what such a humanity grouped together for its own common goal would mean for the survival of the elite.

### (2. MALTHUSIANISM AS THE PRAXIS-PROCESS OF THE BOURGEOISIE)
### (i. June 1848)

Our goal in this concluding part of the *Critique* is to establish critically the existence of opposing classes and to show that this real conflict constitutes our history. On an abstract level, a class appears to be a complex of serially connected individuals, active pressure groups and institutionalizations. Critically, it is becoming clear how this ambiguous totality, neither group nor hyperorganism, can be an objective structure, and how through this structure there can be a distinct class praxis. Indeed, the existence of opposing classes is being established simultaneously in and through the existence of a class praxis of exploitation and oppression.

The above procedure must be understood dialectically and not as a positivistic cause-effect argument. That is, at each more concrete stage of comprehension, the internal, reciprocal relation of class being to class praxis is examined. The aim is to see if an individual, serial praxis can "participate" in a common statute while not being part of an active group. This participation implies that there is effectively a distinct class praxis or, to be more precise, that class praxis is an aspect of everyone's action as historical. My use of the term "participation" must not be accepted in a Platonic or otherwise idealistic sense. In this last part of the *Critique*, Sartre is particularly careful to show that class being and class praxis are the result of how we have worked the environment and how this worked matter then affects our future. Specifically, Sartre here continues to lay the groundwork for showing how the claim of Malthusianism, that poverty is due to increased population and limited resources, is not an a priori economic law but rather a relation between human beings and goods, established by the praxis of oppressing classes in order to keep a reserve populace of cheap labor.

Sartre's example is that of the French revolution of 1848.[3] The main point of the example is to exhibit, in a more concrete way, *how there can be a class praxis even though a class is not a group.*

The revolution unmasked the class oppression that had always existed. The fact that this oppression was at times ambiguous and complex, involving the upper bourgeoisie, the petite bourgeoisie, and the skilled and unskilled proletariat, did not make it less real. In the final analysis, there were massacres: the dead and those who killed them. True, there was never any assembly uniting itself by a pledge through the mediation of every other as a third. But there was a quasi pledge, a negative willingness of the upper bourgeoisie to go along with the pressure groups and institutionalized forces killing the populace. The bourgeois saw clearly that they were in a struggle to death with the lower classes.[4] This comprehension was practical and reciprocal. The proletariat was revealed through numerous reports as a violent mob capable of a unified action that would tear down the social edifice. And indeed the proletariat does have this abstract, material capacity. If it were ever armed, no force could stand against it. For the bourgeoisie, local massacres were justi-

---

3. The details are easily readable in the original text; the aim of this commentary is to place them in the context of the developing dialectic. Nevertheless, the significance of these details must not be overlooked, for the argument here concerns a historical unveiling.

4. Sartre notes that the violence of this oppression gives the French and the Italian proletariat a distinct statute. In this respect, it should be noted here that there are many bourgeoisies and proletariats, and the degree to which there is a single, worldwide, oppression is an open question.

fied to prevent a possible common action by the proletariat. Of course, the bourgeois saw themselves as the upholders of justice, but they could not deny that they were on the beneficient end of this justice. They justified their position as a reward for their humanity. In their Manichaean ethic, all social evils were due to the workers. In the moment of the contract, the workers admitted to being human, but, by their own voluntary acceptance of wages for labor, they then confessed to their subhumanity. They had to be either forced to be human or treated as subhuman. The upper bourgeoisie accepted that the national workshops, whose purpose was to give work and bread to the poor, had failed because *the workers were lazy.* The riots were thus unjustified, and the killings of the workers were moral. The bourgeoisie justified the killings by making the proletarian a criminal.

The average bourgeois was united to these active killings on three levels. First, he allowed himself to be defined within a rights-duty system instituted and confirmed by a sovereign power that accepted and upheld him as the upper class. Second, he *passively but practically* accepted the killings. He could have escaped this real qualification, or statute of his being, by actively forming with democratic members of the bourgeoisie to oppose the massacres.[5] But he saw and accepted his other-being in the active oppressive praxes of his fellow capitalists; he merged with this other in a common class being. Third, he accepted his instrumental relation with pressure groups that were working to sustain and foster his position in the social structure. He allowed his own praxis to be contaminated with this instrumentality; he accepted the inertia that fostered a long-term oppression of the lower classes. He thus practically accepted himself as the common enemy of the poor. True, he had not gathered in any assembly hall with other bourgeois to denounce the worker. Nevertheless, he daily saw and practically accepted himself as the other bourgeois, doing and approving what was being done to the worker. The average bourgeois thus spontaneously interiorized his common class being as a class antagonist of the worker; his praxis had become a class praxis.

Reciprocally, the average proletarian saw the bourgeoisie as united against him. He had a relative or friend who had been killed, and he was implicitly aware of the bourgeoisie as the class that aimed at his extermination. Each group gave the other its other-being from which it interiorized a statute of unity. In the next generation, the children would receive the statute as their concrete, common past being. This past would not of itself determine the positive content of each individual life, but it would give the context that each must transcend. In the language of *Being and Nothingness,* common past

5. Sartre notes that this statute is not adequately captured by the term "collective responsibility." Within the present context, he seems to be referring to the fact that, although they are serially connected with their fellow capitalists, individual capitalists are still responsible for their efforts or lack of efforts in breaking from this seriality.

being would be an aspect of each child's prereflective, nonthetic awareness of the world. As the child matured and reflected on its relation to its parents and its friends, it would gradually establish a unity between the diachronic and synchronic aspects of its personal history. The child would either rebel against this humanly constituted destiny or fulfill and further it.

Specifically, for the bourgeois son, reflection reveals the Manichaean dimension of the past, the massacres and their justification as a priori givens. Of itself, reflection does not spontaneously establish a critical distance between the one reflecting and the object reflected upon; rather, it spontaneously attempts to integrate the present with the past as given.[6] Critical reflection requires a distinct effort to escape the normal context of reflection. The bourgeois son could see himself as one who is oppressing the poor. But inertia makes it easier to go ahead with new forms of justification. The past is easier seen as a sacred "birth" than as an evil that has to be halted and remedied. Within this Manichaean ethic, the bourgeois father becomes the savior. "The absolute refusal to retreat, as a use-truth revealed by the action of the fathers, was adopted by the sons as a double inert limit, that is to say as an impossibility and as a pledge" (E, 769; F, 716; NF, 847).

The long-term results of the bourgeois class praxis, Sartre notes, are still with us in the revolutionary character of the French proletariat. The immediate results were, however, ambiguous. Class consciousness was raised, but the hope of reform was lost. What was asked for was state regulation, a form of state aid that kept the worker as an inferior being. An enlightened capitalism would have seen this to be in its best interests, but naked hatred was revealed in the insistence on the wage contract as the only public relation with the poor. In this respect, Sartre says that Marx was of course right in his claim that the worker is the secret of the bourgeois society. But "in France in 1848, the bourgeois first constituted himself as the secret of the worker; he appeared to his wage-earners as the necessity that they should live the impossibility of living, or as the impossibility of their struggling against poverty without running the risk of being exterminated on his orders" (E, 766; F, 716; NF, 845).

(ii. Bourgeois "Respectability" in the Late
Nineteenth Century)

We have already seen how, despite seriality and alterity, the bourgeois were able to comprehend their membership in a class, by either ac-

---

6. Although Sartre does not call attention to it, his position here is in keeping with what he said in *Being and Nothingness* concerning those reflecting in bad faith. That is, to one in bad faith, reflection does not reveal "bad faith" as an object. Reflection is itself in bad faith and attempts to justify the bad faith. Nevertheless, one does have fleeting glimpses, on the levels of both reflection and spontaneity, of one's bad faith as a situation that is being maintained. These "glimpses" could be heeded, but usually they are easily "passed through."

tively approving of or passively acquiescing to the bloody repression of workers. Within the complex structure of class being, serially connected individuals, institutions, and active groups, it is the latter two that give the *schema of comprehension* for individual praxis. Each praxis is a transcendence of a practico-inert schema; but the schema gives the material condition for the possibility of this transcendence, even as it sets the limits.

As we have just seen, the active groups give the archetype of bourgeois praxis. These groups reflect an elusive but real unity on the collective, a unity that is always *elsewhere*. Seriality is not dissolved; nevertheless, each individual lives his other-directed being as a transcending of another's praxis. That is, his praxis is his own only insofar as he is also the other bourgeois and, like every other, transcends this common praxis in order continually to approximate *the* bourgeois and sustain the class.

This practical, projected passage to the limit gives the bourgeois the statute of a common individual who is also the other. There is no true common action with its clearly accepted joint responsibility. Rather, each as other does what every other as other must do. But unlike ordinary other-directed behavior, this behavior arises from and is rooted in distinct violent acts of oppression that were done for the benefit of the bourgeoisie. This oppression was carried out not only through pressure groups but also through a distinct serial mode of behavior that was later to become institutionalized, namely, respectability. To understand French nineteenth-century bourgeois respectability as an oppressive praxis is to see it as a form of lay puritanism and as an aspect of the praxis-process of Malthusianism. This bourgeois respectability was both a new form of class oppression and a way of justifying past oppression. Its signification, however, was different for those who originated it and for those who carried it out. For the originators, respectability was a diachronic determination of the original acts of violence against the workers during the 1848 revolution. It also transcended this violence synchronically, by instituting a new behavior of oppression. In this sense, respectability, as we will see shortly, was a "use-truth" (*vérité d'usage*) for the bourgeoisie. For the heirs, respectability became a diachronic determination of respectability as a *hexis*, that is, a reified schema of received and approved actions. The synchronic determination of the heirs' praxis of respectability was their explicit comprehension of it as not only justifying the original acts of murder but also instituting a novel form of oppression.

Respectability was the way the bourgeois justified upper-class status. This could not be done, as with the aristocracy, by birth, nor by merit alone, since this upper-class status had to be passed on. There was also a general recognition that technical skills justified one's social merit. This new justification could only be, in Sartre's terms, "a merit which was a birth and a birth which was a merit" (E, 773; F, 719; NF, 851). Of course, this justification was not a logical exercise. It was occasioned by the growing accumulation of wealth, and, at least for the heirs, a bourgeois utilitarianism that was itself based on the need to reinvest large profits in machines. But what concerns us here is not the social conditions of its origins, which gives the condition for the possibility of its existence. Rather, we are here concerned with respectability as an intelligible praxis that was both an oppressive behavior toward the proletariat and a justification of the bourgeois class.

We have seen that capitalism required that everyone be equal by nature in the moment of the contract. It was not nature that distinguished the employers from the employees; rather, it was something that the employers ascribed to themselves, namely, "culture." This culture was an antinature, a restriction on the wild excesses of nature. The men wore stiff shirts, the women corsets. The women, in particular, ate before they went out to dinner and, Sartre notes, they did not hide their frigidity. For the individual bourgeois, this behavior was not always a sham. But, regardless of any personal synchronic determination and transcendence of this praxis, respectability was primarily a public affair. No bourgeois who wished to remain in the class would have thought of doing the opposite, namely, being ascetic in private and showing normal, natural appetites in public.

Respectability as a public behavior therefore revealed even the body of the bourgeois as cultured and superior to that of the worker. This superiority was not given by nature but was attained through the meritorious efforts of each bourgeois as a member of his class. The worker, through his own fault, had a mere body of nature, and was thus responsible for both the wild brutality of nature and its laziness. The archetypical acts of massacres aimed at eliminating the worker were justified, as was the present need to keep this uncultured animal either in restraint or under benign tutorship. By being hard on themselves, the bourgeois justified their stern behavior toward the worker. That their ascetic behavior was within a context of plenty, a hunger that at any moment could be satisfied, showed for them the superiority of their freedom rather than the sham of their hunger.

For the heirs, the sternness of the parents' behavior justified their inheritance and their class statute. (In this context we can also speak of class status, for, in this context, the term "status" is seen to indicate a distinctive alienation and oppression.) But if in one sense this praxis is received from the previous generation, in another it is a new kind of oppressive behavior by the new generation. If the parents are more responsible for initiating the praxis, the heirs are more responsible for instituting respectability as a new statute of their class behavior. For the heirs, respectability is clearly comprehended as an other-directed class behavior. This comprehension is itself an "other-directed" comprehension within the context of an accepted, practico-inert idea of "respectability." Thus, each bourgeois comprehends that he, as other, is respectable for every other bourgeois, and that every other bourgeois, as other, is respectable for him. He puts on a stiff collar for every other bourgeois, aware that every other dresses in the same way for him. But this is not a common action that springs from interiority and goes out, through reciprocity and mediation, to a common object. Each bourgeois dresses for the other; in this sense, no one dresses. *The* bourgeois is only given in a flight to infinity that is always elsewhere but never here to be examined. This seriality merely imitates the group. In a group, every elsewhere is *here;* in class praxis every "here" is elsewhere. Even bourgeois thoughts, precisely as bourgeois, are flights toward something that is always elsewhere; there are thoughts about popular artists, but each thinker thinks the thoughts of the other. Authors, painters, and other notables pass on and new ones appear without anyone being personally aware of their passing or their appearing. This way of thinking reflects what Sartre calls "objective class spirit."

The term "spirit" is here used merely in the sense of a medium through which signs circulate among class members. It is important to see that respectability and the thoughts, speech, and actions performed within a class spirit are indeed class praxis. Active groups establish archetypical practices that situate the thoughts and practices of each bourgeois. This schema, however, is not the simple past being that provides the context for normal, reciprocal organic praxis. Normal reflection would not allow for appropriating cruel, archetypical practices as mine; that is, reflection, of itself, does not go beyond the spontaneous praxis from which it arose. Other-directed comprehension is a type of "third knowledge." It is about others who did something for me as the other. That is, I am always the other, the bourgeois *over there*, for whom those massacres were done. And I see *my* new oppression, the putting on of *my* stiff collar, to be also acts done *there* by the other bourgeois who must restrain the worker for me. I may, indeed, personally transcend this "other-directed" class comprehension by my gentle behavior toward the workers I employ. But my respectability shows to them and myself the ever-present possibility of actual violence. Even when I am kind, I am kind as the other whose justice may, at any moment, require the punishment of the worker. I see my own violence as a sacred task that may be demanded of me, even though I may be personally against violence. By my daily praxis I keep myself from myself, lest I face the naked truth of my violence and oppression. But this "self-deception" is not a logical feat. It is the class praxis itself, insofar as each one's praxis is spontaneously the praxis of every other in the class. It is as the public other and for the public other that the bourgeois is respectable.

(iii. Class Struggle in the Twentieth Century)

Capitalism merely requires the exploitation of the employee, that is, the controlled use of the worker as a commodity whose value is labor power. True, this exploitation is a form of oppression, but, in the abstract, oppression in a capitalist system should always be for the sake of higher profits. The bourgeoisie should not fear a content proletariat, happily swapping its human energy, initiative, and creativity for money. Also, insofar as capitalism is a means for moving the industrial process forward to new markets, the standard of living for more and more workers should become better. There is no logical a priori need for workers to compete among themselves for better and better living conditions. To postulate that innate "greed" moves human beings to compete among themselves is to make the free, organic individual into a mechanical device. Where something like "greed" exists, it is produced by human beings as part of a social fabric that then is accepted, stabilized, and heightened by the free, appropriating praxis of other human beings actualizing a "condition for the possibility of greed" as it exists within the practico-inert. Greed, as a mere interpersonal relation, could never account for the accumulation of wealth that characterizes our history.

The point for the present discussion is that, of itself, capitalism as an economic process does not require oppression as an end. Indeed, although a passive oppression is always present in the exploiting relation of the employer as controller to employee as controlled, oppression is also the contradictory of exploitation. For naked oppression leads to the death of the employee, the elimination of labor power.

Thus, Sartre notes, there is no logical impossibility in imagining a society where multiplicities have formed within class conflicts. Expanding on this notion, it may seem logically possible for an intelligent, paternalistic capitalism to develop, in which every worker would be educated to accept a modest increase in standard of living so that every other worker's standard of living might likewise be raised.[7] Under such enlightened oppression, for oppression it would still be, industrialization would gradually raise the standard of living for all the people in the world. This is very clearly seen in farming. Of themselves, the technological advances in farming could enable a world in which all were nourished. But the world in which we practically live, the world of *our* history, is one in which we pay farmers *not* to grow wheat, while large portions of humanity starve.[8] This situation could not be an epiphenomenon, that is, an accidental or incidental feature of an economy gone slightly astray.

---

7. It is within this context, I believe, that John Rawls's notion of justice might be incorporated within a Sartrean framework. The "veil of ignorance" that Rawls alludes to could, for Sartre, be only a cultural phenomenon. See John Rawls, *A Theory of Justice* (Cambridge, Massachusetts: Harvard University Press, 1971), pp. 136–42. Nevertheless, in a local context in which the historical constraints are already accepted, the veil of ignorance would seem to eliminate specific injustices. I believe that William L. McBride hints at this approach to Sartre and Rawls in his excellent study *Social Theory at a Crossroads* (Pittsburgh: Duquesne University Press, 1980).

8. Granting all the technological difficulties, the world could still be fed if the will to do so

It exists because, in the concrete, exploitation is also an oppression that contradictorily seeks the death of the oppressed.

Regressively, we can comprehend the existence of the condition for the possibility of class violence to have arisen from scarcity. As we have remarked, we may *conjecture* that the origin of scarcity arose from a primitive, prehistorical fact that there was not enough food for all. But regressive comprehension does not depend on such an ahistorical perspective. The important point is that our present praxis maintains and furthers an intentional structured milieu of scarcity that no longer depends on its earlier origins. This *structured scarcity* gives the condition for the possibility of a history that has developed through class conflicts. This conflict is not the inert movement of an antidialectic clashing with a dialectic; it is the conflict of praxis against praxis or, to be more accurate, praxis-process against praxis-process. True, history cannot be understood as resulting from the clashes among important individuals, although history is often presented in this extremely elitist context. Nor can history be understood as resulting from the praxes of organized groups, for these are usually small and sporadic. *If there is true class conflict, it can only be understood as the opposing praxes of collectives whose amorphous but real unities compose active groups, institutions, and individuals connected by seriality.*

For pedagogical reasons, the above remarks have been presented somewhat foundationally and idealistically. They must be understood, however, as coming at the end of our study, where I hope a degree of universality has been earned. Still, it is important to observe that, although Sartre proceeds from the abstract to the concrete, he has not developed this *Critique* from abstract formulations to concrete reality. Rather, he always begins with concrete examples considered from an abstract perspective. Here, as we are approaching the end of this study, the perspective has become more concrete. Still, Sartre parenthetically notes, we have not reached historical fact, "except as a simple temporalisation, solidified in the past and transcended" (E, 788; F, 731; NF, 865). That is, we will not in this volume of the *Critique* critically justify that, on the most concrete level, we are living within *a* history, a history that alters every aspect of our situation and life and is reciprocally altered by our life and situation. This non-Hegelian comprehension can only be achieved by seeing history as a happening. Through a collective, free praxis that has no a priori reason for being the way it is, history developed necessary structures that are now maintained and furthered by new free praxes. Thus Sartre's procedure, even in these concluding remarks, is to see the universal only as constituted by praxis. We do not begin with a notion of *the* proletariat, and it is dubious, that

---

were present. The condition for this possibility exists, just as it existed for space travel prior to the actual development of the technology.

there is one viable concept of the proletariat. Sartre here critically examines the French proletariat during the nineteenth and early twentieth century. Nevertheless, he does imply that the study can be extended analogously to other nations and other times.

In the early part of the twentieth century, despite worldwide industrial expansion, the French proletariat was radicalized through the extreme behavior of the bourgeoisie. As we have seen, the behavior of the bourgeoisie maintained itself through a constituted a priori, serial vow of each bourgeois as other to every other as other. The substance of this vow was that each would retain his class by remaining the same. The third generation of French bourgeois saw and accepted that the two massacres of workers gave birth to its diachronic and past unity. That is, these two distinct massacres, together with the present serial quasi pledge not to change, structured the practical history of each French bourgeois. To be more precise, each bourgeois saw, through the vow of the other not to change, his own transcendence, and, through this objective spirit, the massacres were constructed *anew* as the past of their history.[9] In the abstract, these massacres could have been viewed as something for which the bourgeoisie should atone. To accept such a perspective, however, might have entailed the willingness to eliminate their class status. The third generation of French bourgeois thus accepted the bourgeois class structure, with its need to both further and justify oppression. This new justification took the form of Malthusianism, and it is now possible to see how this Malthusianism was not an economic law but a collective praxis.

Sartre considers Malthusianism as a praxis from two perspectives. First, this praxis was constituted by two previous generations of praxes as received in matter, that is, in machines and institutions insofar as they related employer to employee. Second, this praxis was reconstituted by the need for a new violence to fit the times. The acceptance of the massacre entailed the continuing need to see the proletariat as a mob capable of subhuman violence aimed at destroying civilization. Clearly, *this* proletariat could not be allowed to increase and become stronger through an industrialization that sought expanding markets and greater profits. More important than profits and more important than the entire capitalistic economic process was the need for the French bourgeoisie to keep its status. A new oppression was needed, even at the price of exploitation. The workers had to be kept weak and divided. "A bloodletting" was required in Sartre's terms, rather than open violence.

This second aspect of Malthusian praxis had three further aspects. First, it

9. The reciprocal determination is obvious, that is, that the past, as reconstituted, affected them. It is now clearer why Sartre's a priori notions, such as scarcity, are not historical a prioris in the usual sense of the term. First, these a prioris are comprehended regressively, and not from an implicit ahistorical perspective. Second, and more important, the a priori structures of the practico-inert are maintained and furthered by new praxes. Reciprocally, our present praxes reveal the historical past we have chosen to retain.

gave the dominant class control over the birth rate. Despite the possibility of expansion, the French bourgeois acted in a milieu in which expansion was not possible because there were not enough raw materials. It was necessary for them to accept as true that there could not be enough jobs for all and enough to feed all. Each bourgeois saw in the other the need to limit production. For the worker, this specification of the milieu of scarcity became a decision of life or death. For the women, in particular, it became the question of whether to have *this* additional child. Here, Sartre refers to his earlier comments about every generation's choosing its dead and specifically to the fact that, when a poor working woman has an abortion, she carries out the sentence passed on her by society.[10] It is now possible to see that *it is a sentence,* because the scarcity of jobs and food was managed by the upper class to control the birth rate. Second, this practice was inseparable from the refusal to expand markets. Third, as we have noted, it lead to competition for jobs. Indeed, unions helped encourage a few workers to attain a high standard of living at the expense of other workers. From this perspective, the bourgeoisie used the proletariat to exterminate and control itself. This created the condition for the possibility of the many to compete among themselves, thereby forming subclasses.

We have now to explain how this Malthusianism was possible, that is, how the bourgeoisie could keep its status by keeping its profits at a given level. It is here that the earlier discussion of Malthusianism as a device becomes relevant.[11] In the abstract, mass production should lower the cost of an item, each item yielding only a small profit. But by externally fixing the price higher than the minimum needed to attain a satisfactory profit, the large manufacturers could sell fewer items for the same profit. Of course, this also implied a strange willingness to forgo additional profits by expanding markets. This device of the larger manufacturers oppressed the smaller ones for two reasons. First, the smaller manufacturer had additional production costs, and was forced to sell his products at a price that barely allowed him any profits. Second, by refusing to expand, the larger manufacturer could increasingly consolidate his operations, producing his product even cheaper to net greater profits.

Malthusianism was thus a class praxis, polarized by pressure groups but serially propagated throughout the bourgeois collective. Each bourgeois was responsible as a member of the collective, and he comprehended his praxis as part of a collective praxis of oppression. This does not mean that there was an open conspiracy, a group decision, or collective meetings. But each, as other, saw himself in the other as the one who was controlling the market because every other was controlling it. Furthermore, each saw the unity of his class reflected to him from the proletariat. The proletariat appeared to be a poten-

10. See book II, chapter 7, p. 236.
11. See section 2 in this chapter.

tially unified mob that could avenge itself for the earlier massacres and for its present oppression.

Reciprocally, in the new strikes the workers saw their unity in the fact that the bourgeoisie was yielding to their demands. Regardless of the circumstances that led them to yield to the newly propagating strikes, especially during 1936, French workers were able to see their own unity in the yielding of the bourgeoisie to their class demands. As with all strikes, these new strikes appeared as a first violence, but they were really a response to the bourgeoisie's original violence. The strikes spread serially. Their cumulative effect revealed to the proletariat its existence as a class that had been and was continuing to be oppressed by the praxis of dominating classes. This comprehension opened new possibilities of a common freedom. Sartre notes that the proletariat saw its common freedom not as a thing to be achieved once and for all but as an infinite task.

The French situation reveals this class conflict to be a fight to the death. Normally, even for the French, machines intervene, masking the violence, keeping it passive so that everything can continue. But when the work is stopped, the dominating class's naked hatred and fear of the dominated is revealed. This hatred is a praxis; it is also a process. If class conflict were only praxis, there would be simply a complex of historical, reciprocal relations of love or hate, with no significant inertia to continue into the future; if it were only process, there would exist only a practico-inert field whose naked mechanism could not even be named. We would have to imagine an impossible deism in which a universal, transcendent mind contemplated a world moving by itself. That is, process itself would disappear. Class conflict thus implies both *praxis* and *process*. It is praxis as arising from historical inertia but as transcending this inertia through new praxis. The priority is always to praxis as that which initiates, sustains, and transcends the original inertia. Furthermore, unity comes to classes through praxis. Reversing the entire philosophic tradition, Sartre comments about this praxis: "*Praxis,* as the action of multiplicity, is far from being an opacity in dialectical rationality. On the contrary, dialectical rationality implies the basic priority of constituted *praxis* over Being and even over *hexis* simply because in itself this rationality is nothing but the *praxis* of the multiplicity insofar as it is maintained and produced by free organic *praxis*" (E, 789; F, 731; NF, 866).

### (3. CLASS STRUGGLE AS A CONFLICT OF RATIONALITIES)

Each class, as we have noted, both comprehends and receives its unity through the unity of the other class. Since the relation of the oppressor class to the oppressed is antagonistic, this unity has a double contradictory aspect. The oppressed see themselves as being molded into a thing by the oppressing class, and they comprehend the need not to be this inert unity. They also see themselves as serially impotent, powerless to resist the oppressing action. But, in their victorious strikes against the employers, they also discover their own common freedom. Groups-in-fusion attain individual concessions here and there, and the comprehension of these victories spreads serially throughout the working class. Unions as sovereign groups of the class are formed, even though, unfortunately, they frequently ally themselves with the sovereign power of the government. Each element of the class structure— the sovereign groups, the combat groups-in-fusion, and the mass of serially connected individuals—is affected by the comprehension of victorious action against bourgeois class action. Moreover, each of these three aspects of class being has a circular influence on the others, an influence that is itself in each case mediated by the antagonistic relation to the other class. For example, the awareness that others are actively fighting and resisting over *there* affects the passivity of those serially united *here*. What this effectively means is that even the serial behavior of the members of the class is intentional. Class praxis is not blind. The class praxis of the workers aims at freeing them from a dominance that they comprehend. This comprehension may vary in degree, but it is a comprehension in any case. Sartre illustrates the intentionality of class praxis, negatively, by the example of a small combat group in enemy territory, completely separated from its main unity and unable to receive any communication. Such a unit loses comprehension of the movement of its army against the enemy. But if it receives the slightest communication, it is aware of its position insofar as it is part of a total army.

Class praxis is thus neither the praxis of the individual as such nor the common praxis of the common individual in the group. *Class praxis is praxis functioning on its widest historical level, and its distinct unity is seen in the practical connection among serially connected individuals, active groups, and institutions.* Indeed, the comprehension of this unified class praxis is nothing but the behavior of twentieth-century workers in their jobs. Sartre notes that when a worker limits his productivity—to avoid establishing a norm whereby other workers will be expected to work more than they are able and also to discourage others from establishing a norm beyond his own capabilities— then he is already, on a practical level, the master of the dialectic. On the other hand, the employer's behavior appears to be, and indeed is, formulated *as if* it were based on analytic knowledge. Everyone is a free, atomistic individual, capable of choosing to work or not to work. Everyone is also free to work as hard as he wishes and to earn as much as he can. If he works hard enough, he may even become an employer. Finally, everyone receives the wage suited to his efforts. Aside from any deeper exploitation, what is obvious here is that this analytic approach masks a reciprocal, dialectical comprehension of the situation on the part of the employer. For, as is clear even in socialist countries, where one worker works more than the others, that is taken not as justifying additional recompense but as becoming the norm for all, on the basis that if one can do the work, all can do it. Indeed, the employer comprehends dialectically that if one works harder than the others, everyone will see himself as the other competing for the same job.

The degree of our dialectical comprehension of class praxis is related to the degree of our alliance to active groups. For each of us, our class unity is not fixed or homogeneous but, rather, synthetic and fluid. It occurs within a shifting complexity of institutional groups, groups-in-fusion, and serialities, and it is mediated by the relation of conflict at every stage. Furthermore, this synthetic circular mediation has a distinct temporality that is its dialectical truth: *I* do this *here* because another has done that *there,* in the hope that still another will do something similar in the future. Of course, in the concrete, this temporality is also mediated by groups-in-fusion and institutional groups. The real meaning of my behavior is my praxis insofar as it is also a process, influenced by active and frozen groups and participating in the complex of material symbols, such as the dress and behavior of my class.

Sartre's point is that even when we utter such statements as "You can't fight city hall," these statements in fact hide a practical knowledge of the means to fight city hall. Indeed, if it were totally impossible to fight city hall, the question of fighting it would never arise. (Can we really imagine the average Egyptian of 2,000 B.C. saying, "You can't fight the Pharaoh"?) Thus Sartre reflects, following Marx on this point, that only social praxis gives the concrete possibility of social consciousness arising within the masses. This possibility does not arise everywhere in the same way. In America, where capitalism has been allowed to run more freely without an initially imposed Malthusian practice, a clear radicalization of dominating and dominated classes has not arisen. Oppression and the violent reaction of the proletariat does not result merely from the means of production and the worker's social structures but also from a concrete, national past. Furthermore, this neopaternalism, characteristic of advanced capitalistic countries like America and England, demands a certain industrial advancement that was not present in the early nineteenth century. Capitalism developed policies of concession in certain countries where the proletariat was less radicalized. In this context, Sartre admits that in England, for example, colonial expansion never endangered the homeland and was never coupled with a calculated limitation of new sources of export. Sartre would clearly agree that class oppression exists in both America and Britain but that the classes are more complex and the mystification more subtle. The type and degree of oppression would have to be examined in each concrete context.[12]

12. Surely the ability to buy a second television set hides for many the oppression of migratory farm workers, the low wages of illegal aliens, and the sweatshops still in eastern New York garment factories, not to mention the exploitation of many parts of the Third World.

The bourgeois intellectual class frequently uses analytic reason to justify their oppressive role. Still, to repeat, this does not mean that analytic reason can comprehend the bourgeois practice. On the contrary, the comprehension of both praxis and antipraxis is through the dialectic. Analytic reason could not mystify itself. Rather, it is a tool used by the bourgeois class to justify oppression to itself and to mystify the proletariat into believing that it is not being oppressed but instead is suffering the consequences of its own laziness or lack of natural talent. Again, this does not mean that the intelligibility of bourgeois praxis is analytic. Bourgeois praxis is also dialectical, although in a different way and with a different priority than the dialectical praxis of the proletariat. The dialectic gives the bourgeoisie the perspective from which to use analytic reason: equality is affirmed in the moment of offering the proletariat a contract and denied because the contract is to accept wages *from* the bourgeoisie, thus making the wage earner not equal to the employer.[13] Such slogans as "good pay for an honest day's work" create an intellectual Manichaean milieu that a priori justifies those on top as virtuous.[14]

Sartre notes that the radicalization of the French proletariat was not brought about by ordinary exploitation and the bourgeoisie used analytic reason in a uniquely oppressive way. In the early nineteenth century, the proletariat was respectful of the bourgeoisie and its property, and of God. They accused the bourgeoisie of being atheistic. But the bourgeoisie used the very ethics that justified property in a way that made the proletariat condemn itself. No matter how bad the working conditions were, or how low the wages, the free contract guaranteed, at any moment, the abstract humanity of the worker. Further-

13. A phrase often heard in America, "Those who cannot *do*, teach," reflects the ambiguous position of the bourgeois intellectual vis-à-vis the upper classes, whose salaries are much higher. The liberal milieu in America fosters general education, but there is still a silent fear of educating the populace too far. To a great extent, the unspoken belief is that education is for the sake of making money and that educators are tools enabling others to achieve a humanity that the educators themselves cannot attain.

14. One has merely to point out how easy it is for a criminal to make money to see the contradiction in this view. It is interesting to note how in America we alternate between glorifying criminals and condemning them. Indeed, the use of dialectic is evident in the different ways analytic reason is used to justify the "criminal practices" of those rising to the top in business. Slogans such as "That's the way it is in business" are used to justify initiative that is abstractly recognized as immoral but nevertheless concretely accepted because it follows public practices. Thus, for example, to put addictive elements into children's food in order to increase sales is acceptable because it follows the norms of competition. (A business ethics may condemn such practices, but it can never question the morality that made them possible, namely that the purpose of business is to make a profit.) No manufacturer wants to hurt children, but each does so because he knows that his competitors will. In contrast, the lower-class criminal who makes a fortune selling drugs to children is condemned, not so much for his crime as for his lack of *true initiative*. More importantly, it is assumed that, unlike the businessman, the criminal intends the evil. Analytic reason excuses the behavior of the upper class because it is serial—everyone does it—while simultaneously affirming that those in this class have justifiably achieved their status because of their individual initiative. The recognition of the contradiction, however, is through dialectical reason.

more, if the laws were unjust, the proletariat had the abstract, legal means of changing its situation by electing its own representatives. The proletarians were made to see themselves as deserving their condition. It was this extreme intransigence of the bourgeoisie, an intransigence that existed in varying degrees throughout the nineteenth century, that eventually enabled the proletariat to see its oppression clearly. Thus, theoretically, the bourgeoisie implicitly affirms analytic reason and denies dialectical reason. Practically, however, it uses the dialectic to construct an analytic reason that defines a humanity suited to its own class. "The bourgeoisie claims to be human by virtue of intelligence, culture, scientific knowledge, technical abilities, etc.; and while these powers must belong to everyone, the workers partly lack them" (E, 800; F, 741; NF, 877).

Bourgeois intellectuals, according to Sartre, know the contradiction in the humanism of their elite class. They are capable of knowing the true universality of the human condition, a universality that exists at least potentially in the proletariat. Traditional Marxists, Sartre comments, have not understood the proletariat's attraction for the bourgeois intellectual. The bourgeois intellectual has the ability to formulate a universal humanism and to elucidate the materialistic dialectic that has become the proletariat's own concrete praxis.

Regressively, we see that the condition for the possibility of the proletariat's praxis is that our de facto history has developed in a milieu of a cultured scarcity. Scarcity has become the necessary condition for our history because we have made it to be so. The practical realization of this by large segments of the lower classes means that we have arrived at a position in history where the universality of human oppression can be practically comprehended and transcended.

(4. THE INTELLIGIBILITY OF HISTORY:
TOTALIZATION WITHOUT A TOTALIZER)

In these concluding remarks, Sartre reviews the reasons for the intelligibility of class praxis. He further proposes the question of whether our history as a struggle among classes is intelligible and comprehensible to us in its totality. We have seen that, in a restricted, local context, we can comprehend *action* as the immediate, positive reciprocity among individuals, such as, for example, in a family discussing how to satisfy its needs or planning how to celebrate someone's birthday. In its abstract, nonhistorical context, action can also be comprehended as our local attempts to modify the environment to suit our needs. In this respect, Sartre calls attention to "the coefficient of adversity of matter," mentioned in *Being and Nothingness*. These coefficients are not a surprise or a detriment to freedom. Rather, they are an integral aspect of freedom, for freedom is always the action of a situated organism. The human organism may not *succeed* in conquering its environment, but the intelligibility of the free organic action is given in the attempt itself.[15] The intelligibility of a successful climb to the top of a mountain is no greater than another's failure to reach the top. Despite accidents, miscalculations, fear, or laziness, the attempt reveals the human organism's practical power over its environment. Indeed, to be more precise, free, organic action is that through which the material inert becomes an environment, with both its practical malleability and its resistance.[16]

In a footnote (E, 811 n. 131; F, 749 n. 1; NF, 888 n. 1), Sartre remarks that our practical power over things is revealed by a woman who jumped from a train, and in her pain kept repeating, "I shouldn't have jumped." But our direct practical power over things, as well as our direct, positive reciprocity with others, is abstract. We have seen that "abstract," in this context, does not mean theoretical. Action, as distinct from praxis, is abstract because it practically prescinds from the question of historical significance and historical influences. In this respect, action is praxis stripped of its historical relations and limited to a very local context. On its own level, this abstract freedom is real and it may be positive. A family may truly enjoy a birthday celebration devoid of conflict. On this level, it is not necessary to see action as developing within a milieu of scarcity. In this respect, it also seems consistent with Sartre's philosophy to suggest that a bourgeois liberalism is relevant to eliminating local injustices. Within local parameters, one must condone a government that gives a poor child a chance at a general education, regardless of the wider historical alienations that are involved.

But, in our historical milieu, abstract action is altered by wider forces, although the degree of the influence can only be determined by a study of the concrete situation. In an extreme case, such as a national war, the alteration is obvious and frequently tragic. A family celebrating a birthday party in Hiroshima during 1945 had its happiness evaporated when the atomic bomb exploded.[17] Of course, a personal tragedy such as the mother's falling down the stairs would also have altered the birthday celebration. But every life, precisely as organic, lives with the threat of accidents. The destruction of war, however, is suffered as the consequence of one freedom's being controlled by another freedom. War reveals that we live within a fixed material context in which a part of humanity is defined as subhuman. The ultimate purpose of dropping bombs is not the immediate killing but the subsequent domination

15. In this abstract context of action, Sartre can be viewed as maintaining a position midway between those who see the value of an act in the intention and those who see it in the result. For Sartre, the value of an act resides in the act as it goes *toward* its result. This view is illustrated, for example, in his short story "The Wall" (Jean-Paul Sartre, *The Wall and Other Stories*, trans. Lloyd Alexander [New York: New Directions, 1948]).

16. Of course, terms such as "organic action" or "organic praxis" are redundant and are used only because of the pervading Cartesian context of our philosophic vocabulary.

17. Following Sartre, I think it is appropriate to critique one's own society first before critiquing other societies.

and control of nations. The meaning of praxis is that it is the comprehension of our intelligible struggle against the Manichaeism of the other who would define the law of humanity for us. For Sartre, of course, this struggle is not, at its heart, the simplistic fight of national wars as such, but the continuing struggle of the lower classes against the higher classes, precisely insofar as the higher classes have power groups directing and being directed by the sovereign government.

Our study began with the uncritical acceptance of our complex historical situation as a contingency that gives rise to necessary relations. *Beginning from the present,* our regressive study sought to elucidate the intelligible structures of praxis. The aim was not to reveal how history may have arisen from prehistorical actions. This latter enterprise is important, but the investigator must realize that this objective past is not easily separated from the past of *our* history. The *Critique* has established that to claim to know the past as past is to adopt a nonhistorical perspective on history that uncritically puts us at the end of our own history. The end of history is signaled neither by the apocalyptic pronouncement of its demise nor by the cultured isolation of philosophers or mystics intuiting or listening for poetic gleamings of a new reality. A history ends only when old praxes cease. "The Middle Ages" have ended, but *our* history, that of the last century and a half, is still with us. The *being* of our history is greater than our individual lives, but this "greater than" itself both has been made by and is sustained through our praxes. History can be altered only if we unite to form and direct a new "greater-than-human," which can then become the condition for the possibility of new praxes. There was no original fall from grace or a state of nature, except that fall which we collectively have brought on ourselves, and there is no salvation except that which we collectively can provide for ourselves.

Still, if we have not come to the end of our history, we have reached a stage where our struggle against our own inhumanity can be comprehended in each of our attempts to attain greater freedom. This struggle is meaningful not as a conflict between an *isolated* individual and the forces of history, but rather as the collective struggle of individuals within a class fighting against oppressing classes. The struggle is meaningful and therefore comprehensible, although the degree of understanding will depend on the individual's involvement in the struggle. This involvement will reveal the bonds among pressure groups, institutions, and serially connected individuals. Today, we can see that we are being manipulated at a distance. The struggles in Poland and Vietnam show how clearly the average person comprehends the historical significance of their fight for freedom. Peasants there were both aware of and opposed to all forces that would keep them oppressed, whether Communist or American. Of course, it is possible that an enemy's power will be so great that a person's freedom is engulfed and turned into a pure thing. But such absolute defeat is based on ignorance, such as the failure to comprehend and control new weapons. This ignorance in itself reveals that where struggle continues as effective, it is comprehensible. Nevertheless, this intelligibility does not imply that the struggle is only among organized groups. This praxis is a class praxis. The situation is totalized without a totalizer. But can such totalization indeed be intelligible?

Implicitly, we have already answered this question in our elucidation of group praxis and the praxis of class being. We have seen that neither group praxis nor the praxis of class being is the praxis of super–quasi organism. There is no superunity, there is no complete synthesis. On the level of *being*, that is, on the level of concrete materiality, there is only individual praxis as this takes place within a material complex, such as factories, machines, dress codes, and other material symbols of communication. But neither group praxis nor the praxis of class being can be reduced to the praxis of isolated individuals united by mere external relations. Neither group praxis nor class being are epiphenomena.

We have seen first that group praxis is constituted praxis; that is, it is the free praxis of an organic individual insofar as it arises from a mediated reciprocity with some other as a third. This mediation allows individual praxis to be also a common praxis. Furthermore, this mediation is not added to organic praxis; it is praxis precisely insofar as it is historical. Also, this mediation takes place through an environment molded by past freedom and still carrying the inertia of these freedoms. But, at every level on which constituted praxis is examined, a free constituent praxis can be seen to have been its origin. Thus, ultimately, constituent praxis is the origin of constituted praxis, but not in a foundationalist sense. Constituted praxis can neither be reduced to nor deduced from constituent praxis. Constituted praxis appears as a *new* reality. Once given, its intelligible origins can then be seen to reside in constituent praxes. In this sense, from the perspective of a society in which groups-in-fusion and pledged and institutional groups are given, we can *regressively* comprehend constituent praxes as giving the conditions for the possibility of constituted praxis.

We can further elucidate the necessary, intelligible structures of constituted praxis as it arises from constituent praxis. To claim that praxis is constituted is effectively to maintain that freedom radically controls itself, through mediation and the pledge, so that it reacts to the active passivity of the practico-inert with a cultured passive activity. In this way, each individual praxis is internally modified so that its primary intentionality is a common result. That is, through the mediation of a third and within the context of an inertial system, constituent praxis alters itself into constituted praxis; it becomes a quasi system so that it can fight the antipraxes of the practico-inert. On the other hand, insofar as constituent praxis itself arises from matter, it is also initially altered by previous constituted praxes. In this respect, constituent praxis transcends its constituted past being.

Thus, the general intelligibility of constituted praxis is that it is both inertia and transcendence. That is, it is the received residue of freedoms, with their given intentionalities and momentums, and it is free praxis appropriating this counterpraxis for new purposes. The individual is important, for individuals produce common freedom as an aspect of their individual freedom. This new type of freedom, both individual and common, exists primarily in the individual and secondarily in the environment.

Again, from our historical perspective, we see *scarcity* to have always been a praxis. That is, constituted praxis always carries within it a struggle arising from a sustained scarcity. We have no way of knowing what a historical, positive group praxis, working outside the context of scarcity as praxis, would be like. It is idealism to extend to our historical relations either the positive relations we conjecture to have existed in very early times or the relations that exist today on local levels. Our dialectic is both situated and materialistic; each level must be approached openly, so as to reveal its unique intelligible structure. In this way, we see conflict not as an epiphenomenon to a history gone astray. Instead, conflict is the concrete intelligibility of our praxis; that is, it is the intelligibility of action as historical.

Our study has also revealed that groups appear as concrete only in relation to the class to which they belong. Although groups-in-fusion and pledged groups do not endure, they do raise the awareness of both their class institutions and their serially connected individuals. On this truly historical level, individual freedom is neither an abstract common freedom nor a general serial relation. The nature of one's freedom depends on whether one is in the oppressor or oppressed class. The praxis of the oppressor reveals itself to the oppressed as constituting "the necessity for living the impossibility of life," and it further reveals the need of the oppressed to transcend this destiny. On an abstract level, a modern woman working in an office may enjoy a dinner with friends while simultaneously comprehending, on an historical level, the absurdity of a situation that requires her to work for low wages in a job that she hates in a society whose scarcity is to a great extent caused by male dominating praxes of those in the upper classes. That is, she can see that her situation is due to a class praxis.

But how is this comprehension possible when it involves a struggle of freedoms trying to outwit other freedoms? Sartre uses the example of a chess game as a clue to understanding the intelligibility of class praxis. A chess game reveals that each one actively comprehends the freedom of the other. The subject-object relation is here not a mode of subjectivity; it is, rather, a self-elucidating praxis that projects, through the materiality of the situation, the other's freedom as also self-elucidating. In this interplay of freedoms, one attempts to transcend a projected reciprocity. I attempt to comprehend how the other could outwit me if I move there, and so instead I move here. Praxis is thus revealed to be the negation of a negation: my move here is both a negation of where I think the other would expect me to move and a negation of the other's response. The conflict of freedoms is precisely what makes the contest intelligible. As soon as the outcome is determined, so that only one move is possible, the game ceases to be a contest, and the other's freedom becomes an object. But the important point is that the game is comprehensible to those engaged in it and to those watching, precisely insofar as it is an open-ended activity, that is, a praxis. Comprehension is the self-elucidating praxis of both the players, and intelligibility exists in the game itself. A grand master, for example, might see where the game is heading better than those involved. There is no transcendent third totalizing the conflict. The totalization comes about through the conflicts of freedoms as they are objectified in this situation. This conflict is not a mutual hatred exchanged by Cartesian minds, nor is it the mere Hegelian existence of the other as a scandal and threat to my freedom. Conflict, from this perspective, exists in the situation of the players in practical relation to the chess board. A programmed contest merely imitates the original human praxis.[18]

In every struggle, we have an urgent relation to our objectified being. An army, Sartre notes, that does not comprehend its *being,* that is, its numbers, equipment, configuration, is headed for defeat. But this objectified being is also a being-for-others. In an urgent relation, this being-for-others is not merely a fixed objectivity. It is our projection of the other as already attempting to defeat us and as now being defeated by us instead. An army is a threat to another only if it already comprehends the other's power and has already attempted to transcend that power.

We thus comprehend our class struggle both because we are taking part in it and because it is intelligible as a struggle. But is there *one* struggle—*one* totalization, *one* history, *one* truth? *Critically,* our investigation has not justified this assumption. What we have shown is that historical totalizations, such as in France, reveal struggle to arise from a milieu of scarcity. *Uncritically,* the meshing of national interests, economies, and the speed of communication seem to indicate one totalization. But the task of establishing this is complex.[19]

Thus far, our investigation has been regressive from only a synchronic perspective.[20] That is, at each stage, we have taken into consideration only forces

18. The fact that there can be only one winner would not, of itself, create a milieu of scarcity. Children often play games in which there can be only one winner, without competing for financial rewards or a sense of superiority.

19. To repeat, this task was to have been accomplished in the second volume of the *Critique.* See above, Introduction, chap. 2, note 8.

20. In this respect, there has been some ambiguity in the temporality of the progressive-

simultaneous in time and then compared this complex of forces with a complex of future simultaneous forces. For example, we saw that a later humanism revealed that of the anarcho-syndicalist as a limited humanism. The relation between these humanisms was based on the differences in their materialities, namely, the practico-inert and the materiality of a new transcending praxis. For example, we examined the substitution of universal machines, such as the lathe, by machines adapted to a division of labor. We noted that the consequent praxis of an unskilled labor force saw its common humanity through the new machines.

But what Sartre calls the "diachronic depth of practical temporalization" has not been attempted. If it were, we would have a different perspective on the way the present sustains and surpasses the past and the way this past of our present reciprocally alters our present. The task would be to see this temporalization as an unfolding. This unfolding would not be from an atemporal past to the present. Nevertheless, it would attempt to comprehend the past of our history. That is, if there is *a* history, the regressive study would have to reveal *a* past, not in the sense of a prehistorical beginning capable of being comprehended from a transhistorical perspective, but in the sense that one past *now* exists for us. Furthermore, the movement would have to *then* become progressive. This new synthetic, progressive movement would not aim at predicting the future. Rather, it would attempt to reveal how we have developed a single history by sustaining in existence only those aspects of our past that are useful for our present technological society. The purpose of the completed study will be to show how our past praxes gave us the limits of our humanity, and how we now sustain these limits in existence. That is, its goal will be to reveal the present, constituted, a priori conditions for our history in the hope that these can be altered and directed toward a better humanity than we now possess.[21]

---

regressive movement. This movement begins from the present and works backward. But what is this "present"? It seems clear that our historical present extends back to the end of the nineteenth century, to this last epoch thematized by Marx; in the *Method*, Sartre referred to three recent stages of praxes and thematizations, namely, those of Descartes, Kant, and Marx (see "Background" chapter, p. 31), and he noted that we are still within the last stage. But Marx has to be rethought, because of the alienation of Stalinism, the existence of novel events such as international corporations, and, most importantly, because his comprehension was not, for Sartre, on the level of being. From this perspective, the "present" is the last fifty years. Thus, the earlier oppressive praxes of the bourgeoisie appear the way they do in the analysis of respectability because different and new manifestations of this oppression still exist; for example, one must stand when a judge enters a courtroom, even though the jury has the responsibility for deciding the innocence or guilt of the accused. Once again, this does not imply that the earlier forms of oppression were not real and objective, but only that their present intelligibility exists because they are the diachronic depths of a *present praxis*.

21. This entire paragraph is an interpretation; Sartre is very cryptic here.

# Bibliography

Sartrean scholars are unanimous in praising the comprehensiveness of the existing bibliographies of Sartre's extensive writings and the writings of his critics. After mentioning a few of the standard bibliographies, I will limit my own list to those works actually cited in the text. English translations are given for Sartre's writings, with the original versions included only if they were cited.

### BIBLIOGRAPHIES

Belkind, Allen J. *Jean-Paul Sartre and Existentialism in English: A Bibliographical Guide.* Kent, Ohio: Kent State University Press, 1970.

Contat, Michel, and Michel Rybalka. *The Writings of Jean-Paul Sartre.* Translated by Richard C. McCleary. 2 vols. Evanston, Ill.: Northwestern University Press, 1974.

Lapointe, François, and Claire Lapointe. *Jean-Paul Sartre and His Critics: An International Bibliography (1938–1980).* Rev. ed. Bowling Green, Ky.: Philosophy Documentation Center, 1981.

Rybalka, Michel. Bibliography in *The Philosophy of Jean-Paul Sartre,* edited by Paul A. Schilpp. La Salle, Ill.: Open Court Publishing Co., 1981. (This listing is more select but also more usable than the others cited here.)

Wilcocks, Robert. *Jean-Paul Sartre: A Bibliography of International Criticism.* Edmonton: University of Alberta Press, 1975.

### WRITINGS OF SARTRE

*Anti-Semite and Jew.* Translated by George J. Becker. New York: Schocken Books, 1948. Published in England as *Portrait of the Anti-Semite.* Translated by Eric de Mauny. London: Secker & Warburg, 1948.

*Being and Nothingness.* Translated by Hazel E. Barnes. New York: Philosophical Library, 1956.

*Between Existentialism and Marxism.* Translated by John Mathews. New York: Pantheon Books, 1974.

*The Communists and Peace with a Reply to Claude Lefort.* Translated by Martha H. Fletcher and Philip R. Berk. New York: George Braziller, 1968.

*Critique de la raison dialectique.* See *Critique of Dialectical Reason.*

*Critique of Dialectical Reason.* Vol. I. *Theory of Practical Ensembles.* Translated by Alan Sheridan-Smith. London: New Left Books, 1976; Verso, 1982. Originally published in *Critique de la raison dialectique (précédé de Question de méthode).* *Tome I. Théorie des ensembles pratiques.* Paris: Librairie Gallimard, 1960; rev. ed., 1985.

*Critique de la raison dialectique (inachevé). Tome II. L'intelligibilité de l'Histoire.* Paris: Librairie Gallimard, 1985.

*The Flies and No Exit.* Translated by Stuart Gilbert. New York: Alfred A. Knopf, 1947.

*The Ghost of Stalin.* Translated by Martha H. Fletcher. New York: George Braziller, 1968. Published in England as *The Spectre of Stalin.* Translated by Irene Clephane. London: Hamish Hamilton, 1969.

*Life/Situations.* Translated by Paul Auster and Lydia David. New York: Pantheon Books, 1977.

*Literary and Philosophical Essays.* Translated by Annette Michelson. New York: Collier Books, 1962.

"Materialism and Revolution." In *Literary and Philosophical Essays. Nausea.* Translated by Lloyd Alexander. New York: New Directions, 1959.

*Portrait of the Anti-Semite.* See *Anti-Semite and Jew.*

*Problem of Method.* See *Search for a Method.*

*The Psychology of the Imagination.* Translated by Bernard Frechtman. Secaucus, N.J.: Citadel Press, 1966.

"The Purposes of Writing." In *Between Existentialism and Marxism.*

*Question de méthode.* See *Search for a Method; Critique of Dialectical Reasoning.*

*Saint Genet: Actor and Martyr.* Translated by Bernard Frechtman. New York: George Braziller, 1963.

*Sartre by Himself.* Translated by Richard Seaver. New York: Urizen Books, 1978.

*Search for a Method.* Translated by Hazel E. Barnes. New York: Alfred A. Knopf, 1963. Same translation published in England under the title *Problem of Method.* London: Methuen & Co., 1964. Published in French in the *Critique de la raison dialectique (précédé de Question de méthode).* (See *Critique of Dialectical Reason.*) First published in the Polish periodical *Twórczość,* 1957, no. 4:33–79.

*Situations.* Translated by Benita Eisler. New York: George Braziller, 1965.

*Sketch for a Theory of the Emotions.* Translated by Philip Mairret. London: Methuen & Co., 1962.

*The Spectre of Stalin.* See *The Ghost of Stalin.*

*The Transcendence of the Ego.* Translated by Forrest Williams and Robert Kirkpatrick. New York: Noonday Press, 1957.

*The Wall and Other Stories.* Translated by Lloyd Alexander. New York: New Directions, 1948.

*The War Diaries: November 1939–March 1940.* Translated by Quintin Hoare. New York: Pantheon Books, 1984.

*The Words.* Translated by Bernard Frechtman. New York: George Braziller, 1964.

OTHER WORKS

Anderson, Perry. *Considerations in Western Marxism.* London: Verso, 1979.

———. *In the Tracts of Historical Materialism.* Chicago: University of Chicago Press, 1984.

Aron, Raymond. *History and the Dialectic of Violence.* Translated by Barry Cooper. Oxford: Basil Blackwood Publishing, 1975.

————. *Marxism and the Existentialists.* Translated by Helen Weaver, Robert Addis, and John Weightman. New York: Harper & Row, 1969; New York: Simon & Schuster Publishers, Clarion Books, 1970.

Aronson, Ronald. *Jean-Paul Sartre.* London: New Left Books, 1980.

Barnes, Hazel E. *Sartre.* New York: J. B. Lippincott, 1973.

————. *Sartre and Flaubert.* Chicago: University of Chicago Press, 1981.

Beauvoir, Simone de. *The Ethics of Ambiguity.* Translated by Bernard Frechtman. New York: Philosophical Library, 1948.

————. *Force of Circumstance.* Translated by Richard Howard. Harmondsworth, England: Penguin Books, 1968.

Catalano, Joseph S. *Commentary on Jean-Paul Sartre's "Being and Nothingness."* New York: Harper & Row, 1974; repr. Chicago: University of Chicago Press, 1980.

————. "Good and Bad Faith: Weak and Strong Notions." *Review of Existential Psychology and Psychiatry* 17 (1984) 79–90.

————. "On the Possibility of Good Faith." *Man and World* 13 (1980): 207–28.

Caws, Peter. *Sartre.* London: Routledge & Kegan Paul, 1979.

Chiodi, Pietro. *Sartre and Marxism.* Translated by Kate Soper. Atlantic Highlands, N.J.: Humanities Press, 1976.

Collins, Douglas. *Sartre as Biographer.* Cambridge, Mass.: Harvard University Press, 1980.

Cumming, Robert Denoon. *Starting Point: An Introduction to the Dialectic of Existence.* Chicago: University of Chicago Press, 1979.

Danto, Arthur C. *Jean-Paul Sartre.* New York: Viking Press, 1975.

Desan, Wilfred. *The Marxism of Jean-Paul Sartre.* Garden City, N.Y.: Doubleday & Co., Anchor Books, 1965.

————. *The Tragic Finale.* New York: Harper Torchbooks, 1944.

Fell, Joseph P. *Heidegger and Sartre: An Essay on Being and Place.* New York: Columbia University Press, 1979.

Flynn, Thomas R. *Sartre and Marxist Existentialism.* Chicago: University of Chicago Press, 1984.

Foucault, Michel. *The Archaeology of Knowledge.* Translated by A. M. Sheridan-Smith. New York: Harper & Row, 1976.

Gorz, André. "Sartre and Marx." *New Left Review* 37 (1966) 29–35.

Grene, Marjorie. *Sartre.* New York: New Viewpoints, 1973.

Hartmann, Klaus. *Sartre's Ontology.* Evanston, Ill.: Northwestern University Press, 1966.

————. "Sartre's Theory of *Ensembles.*" In *The Philosophy of Jean-Paul Sartre.* See Schilpp.

Hayim, Gila J. *The Existential Sociology of Jean-Paul Sartre.* Amherst: University of Massachusetts Press, 1980.

Heidegger, Martin. *Being and Time.* Translated by John McQuarrie and Edward Robinson. New York: Harper & Row, 1962.

————. *On Time and Being.* Translated by Joan Stambaugh. New York: Harper & Row, 1972.

Hirsh, Arthur. *The French New Left: An Intellectual History from Sartre to Gorz.* Boston: South End Press, 1981.

Husserl, Edmund. *Cartesian Meditations.* Translated by Dorian Cairns. The Hague: Martinus Nijhoff Publishers, 1969.

Jameson, Fredric. *Marxism and Form.* Princeton, N.J.: Princeton University Press, 1971.

———. *The Origins of Style.* New Haven, Conn.: Yale University Press, 1961; New York: Columbia University Press, 1961.

Kierkegaard, Søren. *Concluding Unscientific Postscript.* Translated by David F. Swenson. Princeton, N.J.: Princeton University Press, 1941.

Kline, George L. "The Existentialist Rediscovery of Hegel and Marx." In *Phenomenology and Existentialism,* edited by Edward N. Lee and Maurice Mandelbaum. Baltimore, Johns Hopkins University Press, 1967.

Laing, R. D., and D. G. Cooper. *Reason and Violence.* London: Travistock, 1964; New York: Pantheon Books, 1971.

Levenas, Emmanuel. *La theorie de l'intuition dans la phenomenologie de Husserl.* Paris: Alcan, 1930.

Lévi-Strauss, Claude. *The Savage Mind.* Chicago: University of Chicago Press, 1966.

Lichtheim, George. *Marxism in Modern France.* New York: Columbia University Press, 1966.

Lukács, Georg. *History and Class Consciousness.* Translated by Rodney Livingston. Cambridge: MIT Press, 1971.

McBride, William L. *Fundamental Change in Law and Society: Hart and Sartre on Revolution.* The Hague: Mouton Publishers, 1970.

———. *The Philosophy of Marx.* New York: St. Martin's Press, 1977.

———. *Social Theory at a Crossroads.* Pittsburgh: Duquesne University Press, 1980.

McMahon, Joseph H. *Human Beings.* Chicago: University of Chicago Press, 1971.

Madsen, Axel. *Hearts and Minds.* New York: William Morrow & Co., 1977.

Morris, Phyllis Sutton. *Sartre's Concept of a Person.* Amherst: University of Massachusetts Press, 1976.

Murdoch, Iris. *Sartre, Romantic Realist.* New York: Barnes & Noble; Sussex, England: Harvester Press, 1980. Originally published as *Sartre, Romantic Rationalist.* New Haven, Conn.: Yale University Press, 1953.

Poster, Mark. *Existential Marxism in Postwar France: From Sartre to Althusser.* Princeton, N.J.: Princeton University Press, 1975.

———. *Sartre's Marxism.* Cambridge: Cambridge University Press, 1982.

Rawls, John. *A Theory of Justice.* Cambridge: Harvard University Press, 1971.

Richardson, William J. *Heidegger: Through Phenomenology to Thought.* The Hague: Martinus Nijhoff Publishers, 1967.

Rorty, Richard. *Consequences of Pragmatism.* Minneapolis: University of Minnesota Press, 1982.

———. *Philosophy and the Mirror of Nature.* Princeton, N.J.: Princeton University Press, 1979.

Schilpp, Paul A., ed. *The Philosophy of Jean-Paul Sartre.* La Salle, Ill.: Open Court Publishing Co., 1981.

Schrag, Calvin. *Radical Reflection*. West Lafayette, Ind.: Purdue University Press, 1980.

Sheridan, James F. *Sartre: The Radical Conversion*. Athens, Ohio: Ohio University Press, 1973.

Stone, Robert V. "Sartre on Bad Faith and Authenticity." In *The Philosophy of Jean-Paul Sartre*. See Schilpp.

Theunissen, Michael. *The Other: Studies in the Social Ontology of Husserl, Heidegger, Sartre, and Buber*. Translated by Christopher Macann. Cambridge: MIT Press, 1984.

Thompson, Kenneth A. *Sartre: Life and Work*. New York: Facts on File, 1984.

Warnock, Mary. *The Philosophy of Jean-Paul Sartre*. London: Hutchinson Publishing Group, 1965.

# Index

Printed and bound by CPI Group (UK) Ltd, Croydon, CR0 4YY

13/04/2025

14656512-0003